MW00560598

THE ARCHAEOLOGY OF PREHISTORIC ARABIA

Encompassing a land mass greater than the rest of the Near East and eastern Mediterranean combined, the Arabian Peninsula remains one of the last great unexplored regions of the ancient world. This book provides the first extensive coverage of the archaeology of this region from c. 9000 to 800 BC.

Peter Magee argues that a unique social system, which relied on social cohesion and actively resisted the hierarchical structures of adjacent states, emerged during the Neolithic and continued to contour society for millennia. He also shows how the historical context in which Near Eastern archaeology was codified has led to a skewed understanding of the multiplicity of lifeways pursued by ancient peoples throughout the Middle East.

Peter Magee is Professor of Near Eastern Archaeology at Bryn Mawr College. He has excavated widely in the Middle East and South Asia, most notably in the United Arab Emirates at the sites of Muweilah and Tell Abraq, since 1994. He also co-directed the excavations at Akra in northwestern Pakistan from 1997 to 2001. He has published extensively on the archaeology of Arabia, Iran and South Asia. He is the author of *Excavations at Tepe Yahya, Iran, 1967–1975: The Iron Age Settlement* (2004).

CAMBRIDGE WORLD ARCHAEOLOGY

SERIES EDITOR
NORMAN YOFFEE, *University of Michigan*

EDITORIAL BOARD
SUSAN ALCOCK, *Brown University*
TOM DILLEHAY, *Vanderbilt University*
TIM PAUKETAT, *University of Illinois*
STEPHEN SHENNAN, *University College London*
CARLA SINOPOLI, *University of Michigan*
DAVID WENGROW, *University College London*

The Cambridge World Archaeology series is addressed to students and professional archaeologists, and to academics in related disciplines. Most volumes present a survey of the archaeology of a region of the world, providing an up-to-date account of research and integrating recent findings with new concerns of interpretation. While the focus is on a specific region, broader cultural trends are discussed and the implications of regional findings for cross-cultural interpretations considered. The authors also bring anthropological and historical expertise to bear on archaeological problems and show how both new data and changing intellectual trends in archaeology shape inferences about the past. More recently, the series has expanded to include thematic volumes.

RECENT BOOKS IN THE SERIES
FRANCES F. BERDAN, *Aztec Archaeology and Ethnohistory*
KOJI MIZOGUCHI, *The Archaeology of Japan*
MIKE SMITH, *The Archaeology of Australia's Deserts*
A. BERNARD KNAPP, *The Archaeology of Cyprus*
LI LIU AND XINGCAN CHEN, *The Archaeology of China*
STEPHEN D. HOUSTON AND TAKESHI INOMATA, *The Classic Maya*
PHILIP L. KOHL, *The Making of Bronze Age Eurasia*
LAWRENCE BARHAM AND PETER MITCHELL, *The First Africans*
ROBIN DENNELL, *The Palaeolithic Settlement of Asia*
CHRISTOPHER POOL, *Olmec Archaeology and Early Mesoamerica*
SAMUEL M. WILSON, *The Archaeology of the Caribbean*
RICHARD BRADLEY, *The Prehistory of Britain*
LUDMILA KORYAKOVA AND ANDREJ EPIMAKHOV, *The Urals and Western Siberia in the Bronze and Iron Ages*
DAVID WENGROW, *The Archaeology of Early Egypt*
PAUL RAINBIRD, *The Archaeology of Micronesia*
PETER M. M. G. AKKERMANS AND GLENN M. SCHWARTZ, *The Archaeology of Syria*
TIMOTHY INSOLL, *The Archaeology of Islam in Sub-Saharan Africa*

CAMBRIDGE WORLD ARCHAEOLOGY

THE ARCHAEOLOGY OF PREHISTORIC ARABIA

Adaptation and Social Formation from the Neolithic to the Iron Age

PETER MAGEE

Bryn Mawr College

CAMBRIDGE
UNIVERSITY PRESS

CAMBRIDGE
UNIVERSITY PRESS

32 Avenue of the Americas, New York, NY 10013-2473, USA

Cambridge University Press is part of the University of Cambridge.

It furthers the University's mission by disseminating knowledge in the pursuit of education, learning and research at the highest international levels of excellence.

www.cambridge.org
Information on this title: www.cambridge.org/9780521862318

© Peter Magee 2014

This publication is in copyright. Subject to statutory exception and to the provisions of relevant collective licensing agreements, no reproduction of any part may take place without the written permission of Cambridge University Press.

First published 2014

Printed in the United States of America

A catalog record for this publication is available from the British Library.

Library of Congress Cataloging in Publication data
Magee, Peter, 1968–
The archaeology of prehistoric Arabia : adaptation and social formation from the neolithic to the iron age / Peter Magee.
    pages   cm. – (Cambridge world archaeology)
Includes bibliographical references and index.
ISBN 978-0-521-86231-8 (hardback)
1. Prehistoric peoples – Arabian Peninsula.   2. Excavations (Archaeology) – Arabian Peninsula.   3. Social archaeology – Arabian Peninsula.
4. Arabian Peninsula – Antiquities.   I. Title.
GN855.A72M25   2014
939.4'9–dc23   2013027340

ISBN 978-0-521-86231-8 Hardback

Cambridge University Press has no responsibility for the persistence or accuracy of URLs for external or third-party Internet Web sites referred to in this publication and does not guarantee that any content on such Web sites is, or will remain, accurate or appropriate.

CONTENTS

List of Illustrations.. *page* viii

Acknowledgements.. xiii

A Note on Dating... xv

1   Arabia and the Study of the Ancient Near East 1

2   Ecological and Environmental Diversity in Arabia 14

3   The Formation of Arabian Society: 7000–3000 BC 46

4   Eastern Arabia from 3000 to 2000 BC.. 87

5   The Bronze Age in Western Arabia 126

6   Eastern Arabia from 2000 to 1300 BC.. 152

7   Humans, Dromedaries and the Transformation of Ancient Arabia ... 197

8   Intensification and Consolidation: Arabia from 1300 to 800 BC...... 214

9   Expansion and Engagement: Arabia and the Ancient Near East 259

10 Adaptation and Social Formation in Ancient Arabia...................... 275

References 279

Index 305

ILLUSTRATIONS

1.1.	Carsten Niebuhr	*page* 5
2.1.	The main geographical features of Arabia	15
2.2.	Southeastern Arabia	16
2.3.	al-Hajjar mountains, United Arab Emirates	17
2.4.	Musandam peninsula, Sultanate of Oman	17
2.5.	Ras al-Hadd peninsula, Sultanate of Oman	18
2.6.	al-Madam plain, Sharjah, United Arab Emirates	19
2.7.	View towards the village of al-Hamra, Dakhiliya, Sultanate of Oman	19
2.8.	Date palm grove, al-Hamra, Sultanate of Oman	20
2.9.	Rub al-Khali desert, Sharjah, United Arab Emirates	20
2.10.	Gazelle (*Gazella gazella*) in the al-Areen Nature Reserve, Bahrain	21
2.11.	Dromedary camel (*Camelus dromedarius*)	22
2.12.	Wahiba sands, Sultanate of Oman	23
2.13.	South and southwestern Arabia	26
2.14.	Dhofar, Sultanate of Oman	27
2.15.	The Asir region, Saudi Arabia	30
2.16.	Central and northern Arabia	31
2.17.	Hasa oasis, Saudi Arabia	33
2.18.	Mangrove (*Avicennia marina*), Kalba, United Arab Emirates	35
2.19.	Arabian oryx (*Oryx leucoryx*)	36
2.20.	Terraced agriculture, Ras al-Khaimah, United Arab Emirates	37
2.21.	Arabia and the Indian Ocean world	40
3.1.	Main excavated early Neolithic sites in southern Arabia	53
3.2.	Main Neolithic sites dating from the sixth and fifth millennia BC in southern Arabia	55
3.3.	Neolithic sites and rock art locations in central and northern Arabia	59
3.4.	Rock art at Shuwaymas, Saudi Arabia	60
3.5.	View of Jebel Buhais excavations, Sharjah, United Arab Emirates	63

3.6.   Primary Neolithic burials, Jebel Buhais 18, Sharjah, United Arab Emirates   63
3.7.   Secondary Neolithic burials, Jebel Buhais 18, Sharjah, United Arab Emirates   64
3.8.   Neolithic burial decorated with pearl and softstone beads   65
3.9.   Location of main coastal sites containing Ubaid pottery in eastern Arabia   68
3.10. View of Neolithic site of as-Sabiyah, Kuwait   70
3.11. Model of a boat made in local red ware, as-Sabiyah, Kuwait   70
3.12. Bitumen with barnacles from as-Sabiyah, Kuwait   71
3.13. Location of main sites of the late fifth and early fourth millennia BC   75
3.14. Platform of cattle skulls, fourth millennium BC, Shi'b Kheshiya, Yemen   80
3.15. Detail of cattle skulls, Shi'b Kheshiya, Yemen   80
3.16. View of Akab, Umm al-Quwain, United Arab Emirates   81
3.17. Mound of dugong bones, Akab, Umm al-Quwain, United Arab Emirates   82
3.18. Detail of dugong bones, Akab, Umm al-Quwain, United Arab Emirates   82
4.1.   Hafit tombs, Ras al-Khaimah, United Arab Emirates   92
4.2.   Plan of Hili 8, al-Ain oasis, United Arab Emirates   95
4.3.   Location of main Umm an-Nar settlements and tombs   99
4.4.   Umm an-Nar tomb, al-Ain oasis, United Arab Emirates   100
4.5.   Plan of Bronze Age settlement of RJ-2, Ras al-Jinz 2, Sultanate of Oman   102
4.6.   Umm an-Nar Black on Red Ware vessels, Ajman, United Arab Emirates   108
4.7.   Umm an-Nar tomb, Tell Abraq, Sharjah, United Arab Emirates   110
4.8.   Black on Grey Ware vessel from Tell Abraq, Sharjah Archaeological Museum   110
4.9.   Softstone incense burner from Tell Abraq   111
4.10. Softstone vessels, Bronze Age settlement of RJ-2, Ras al-Jinz 2, Sultanate of Oman   112
4.11. Copper objects, Bronze Age settlement of RJ-2, Ras al-Jinz 2, Sultanate of Oman   113
5.1.   Location of main Bronze Age sites in southwestern Arabia   127
5.2.   Bronze Age Hammat al-Qa, Dhamar, Yemen   129
5.3.   Town wall remnants, Hammat al-Qa, Dhamar, Yemen   129
5.4.   Residential architecture, Hammat al-Qa, Dhamar, Yemen   130
5.5.   View of Hammat al-Qa, Dhamar, Yemen   130
5.6.   Residential architecture, Bronze Age Kharyab, Dhamar, Yemen   133
5.7.   Residential architecture, Kharayb, Dhamar, Yemen   134
5.8.   Excavation of a stone-constructed building, Kharayb, Dhamar, Yemen   135
5.9.   Plan of Bronze Age settlement of Sabir   139
5.10. Bronze Age Sabir culture ceramics, Ma'layba, Yemen   140

5.11. Tayma, Saudi Arabia, surface of the sabkha north of the oasis
(from southeast)   145

5.12. Tayma, Saudi Arabia, outer city wall, Square W18 (from west);
sandstone foundation and mudbrick construction; preserved
height c. 6 meters   146

5.13. Location of Tayma and 'kite' sites in western Arabia. The dots
indicate the presence of large kite systems after Kennedy and
Saeed 2009   148

6.1. Location of main early second millennium BC sites in the central
and northern Arabian Gulf   153

6.2. Main residential area, early second millennium BC settlement of
Saar, Bahrain   155

6.3. View of temple, early second millennium BC settlement of Saar,
Bahrain   155

6.4. Bronze needle with bone handle, early second millennium BC
settlement of Saar, Bahrain   156

6.5. Wadi Suq softstone vessel lid from southeastern Arabia, early
second millennium BC settlement of Saar, Bahrain   157

6.6. Local pottery, early second millennium BC settlement of Saar,
Bahrain   158

6.7. Main altars in the Barbar Temple Phase II, looking southwest,
1956   159

6.8. Bull's head from the Barbar Temple   160

6.9. Barbar Temple, the pool of Phase IIb, looking southwest, 1960   161

6.10. Barbar Temple, staircase of Phase IIa, looking west, 1959   162

6.11. Late-type burial mounds at Aali with the Royal Mounds in the
background, looking north, c. 1960   163

6.12. Royal Mounds at Aali, 1956   165

6.13. Dilmun stamp seal in Style IA from Tell F6 on Failaka, Kuwait-
Danish excavations in 2011   170

6.14. Tell F6 on Failaka, Kuwait, with the 'palace' excavated by a
Danish mission c. 1960, the temple excavated by a French mission
in the 1980s and the new trenches by the Kuwait-Danish mission,
2008–2009   171

6.15. Location of main Wadi Suq period sites in southeastern Arabia   183

6.16. Wadi Suq bronze weapons, Jebel Buhais burials, early second
millennium BC   184

6.17. Wadi Suq softstone vessels, Jebel Buhais, Sharjah, United Arab
Emirates   185

6.18. Wadi Suq painted beakers, Jebel Buhais, Sharjah, United Arab
Emirates   185

6.19. Wadi Suq spouted and storage jars, Jebel Buhais, Sharjah, United
Arab Emirates   186

6.20. Various types of Wadi Suq tombs, Jebel Buhais, Sharjah, United
Arab Emirates   188

6.21. Location of main Late Bronze Age sites in southeastern Arabia   190

6.22. Late Bronze Age pottery, Tell Abraq, Sharjah, United Arab Emirates   191

6.23. Late Bronze Age pottery, Tell Abraq, Sharjah, United Arab Emirates: (a) imported Mesopotamian vessel fragment; (b, c) local goblets with string-cut base; (d) local pottery with bitumen   191

6.24. Iron Age I pottery, Tell Abraq, Sharjah, United Arab Emirates   192

6.25. Late Bronze Age arrowheads, Jebel Buhais, Sharjah, United Arab Emirates   193

6.26. Late Bronze Age floor with postholes, Tell Abraq, Sharjah, United Arab Emirates   194

7.1. Location of main sites mentioned in this chapter   198

7.2. Relief showing dromedary and rider from Tell Halaf, Syria   209

7.3. Ceramic figurine of dromedary, Muweilah, c. 1000–700 BC, Sharjah, United Arab Emirates, with detail showing painted decoration and saddle   211

7.4. Painted dromedary terracotta figurine from a multiple burial (early to middle first millennium BC) from Tayma, Area S/Tal'a   212

8.1. Location of main southeast Arabian sites mentioned in the text   215

8.2. Cross section of a falaj system tapping a mountain aquifer   216

8.3. Shallow wells at Muweilah, Sharjah, United Arab Emirates, c. 1000–800 BC   218

8.4. Plan of Iron Age II settlement, Rumeilah, al-Ain oasis, United Arab Emirates   220

8.5. View of the Iron Age settlement of Salut, Wadi Bahla, Sultanate of Oman   221

8.6. Iron Age II storage jar, Muweilah, Sharjah, United Arab Emirates   222

8.7. Iron Age II bowl, Muweilah, Sharjah, United Arab Emirates   223

8.8. Iron Age II bridge-spouted vessel, Muweilah, Sharjah, United Arab Emirates   223

8.9. Iron Age II softstone vessels, Rumeilah, al-Ain oasis, United Arab Emirates   224

8.10. Plan of Iron Age II settlement at Muweilah, Sharjah, United Arab Emirates   228

8.11. Columned building, Iron Age II settlement at Muweilah, Sharjah, United Arab Emirates   230

8.12. Bronze production refuse, Iron Age II settlement at Muweilah, Sharjah, United Arab Emirates   230

8.13. Incense burner, Iron Age II settlement at Muweilah, Sharjah, United Arab Emirates   232

8.14. Detail of incense burner, Iron Age II settlement at Muweilah, Sharjah, United Arab Emirates   233

8.15. Incense burner with figurine of camel, Iron Age II settlement at Muweilah, Sharjah, United Arab Emirates   233

8.16. Location of main southwest Arabian sites mentioned in the text   241

8.17. View of late second millennium BC settlement of ad-Durayb Yala, Yemen   246

8.18. View of the town wall of ad-Durayb Yala, Yemen   247

8.19. House A, ad-Durayb Yala, Yemen   247

8.20. Early South Arabian inscriptions from ad-Durayb Yala, Yemen   248

8.21. Location of main late second/early first millennium BC sites in
       northern Arabia   252

8.22. Tayma, Area O, painted pottery bowl (diam. c. 28 cm) with
       representations of birds (late second to early first millennium
       BC), Qurayyah Ware   253

8.23. Tayma, Area S/Tal'a, painted pottery beaker and small bowl
       ('San'aiye' pottery) from a child's grave (early to middle first
       millennium BC)   254

9.1. Location of main sites mentioned in the text   260

ACKNOWLEDGEMENTS

This volume would not have been possible without the assistance and support of numerous people. I would like to thank the many scholars of ancient Arabia and adjacent regions who have made available to me their unpublished or difficult-to-find papers, have been quick to send their recently published papers in the knowledge that I was working on this manuscript or have taken the time to share their thoughts on Arabian archaeology. These include Anne Benoist, Joaquin Córdoba, Ricardo Eichmann, Emily Hammer, Marc Handel, Peter Hellyer, Nasser al-Jahwari, Sabah Abboud Jasim, Derek Kennet, Lamya Khalidi, Michael Macdonald, Joy McCorriston, Dan Potts, Abdullah bin Suhail al-Sharqi, Hans-Peter Uerpmann, Margarethe Uerpmann, Christian Velde, Lloyd Weeks, Tony Wilkinson and Michele Ziolkowski. Many of these scholars have answered questions about their work and recent discoveries, and for this I am also appreciative. I would particularly like to thank Hans-Peter and Margarethe Uerpmann, who read parts of the manuscript and made many useful suggestions. On the occasions when our trips to the United Arab Emirates and elsewhere coincided, they were also very generous in their responses to my incessant questions about the earlier stages of Arabian prehistory. Marc Handel made numerous suggestions for improvement – his knowledge and good humour have provided the perfect accompaniment for our years of working together in the UAE. Diane Barker, Robert Carter, Sabina de Maigret, Ricardo Eichmann, Arnulf Hausleiter, Flemming Højlund, Robert Killick, Adelina Kutterer, Steffen Laursen, Joy McCorriston, Sophie Méry, Lynne Newton, Dan Potts, Hans-Peter Uerpmann, Lloyd Weeks and Tony Wilkinson generously supplied photographs for reproduction in this book, and Emily Hammer completed the excellent maps that accompany the text. I would especially like to thank Dan Potts, who introduced me to the subject of Arabian archaeology as an incoming graduate student at Sydney in 1992 and who agreed to advise my PhD on that subject. His support has taken myriad forms, including advice on and encouragement for my first fieldwork project in the UAE, as well as access to his library and, more important, his thoughts about ancient Arabia. The energy and meticulousness with which he pursues his research continue to inspire me and all those who have been fortunate enough to study with him.

To my many colleagues and friends in the UAE, I am thankful for the advice and help that you have provided since I began work there twenty years ago. I am especially grateful to Dr. Sabah Abboud Jasim, Director of the Sharjah Directorate of Archaeology (Sharjah, UAE), whose friendly assistance and generous support have been critical to our excavations at Muweilah and Tell Abraq. It was our discoveries at this site that first turned my attention towards the larger picture of Arabian archaeology and in no small way provided the inspiration for this volume. Eisa Yousif, also of the Sharjah Directorate of Archaeology, first brought me to Muweilah twenty years ago and has remained a trusted friend and colleague since. He sat with me in the scorching heat of Mleiha in the summer of 2012 and helped me with the translation of many difficult-to-find Arabic publications. Two anonymous reviewers and Professor Norman Yoffee made numerous corrections and offered suggestions for the text. Their wise counsel improved this book considerably; any errors that remain are solely my responsibility. I am also indebted to Beatrice Rehl, Regina Paleski and Mary Becker for their excellent editorial work on the initial manuscript.

Lastly, I would like to thank Susie, Joe, Tom, Rory and Claire. I have been absent too many times writing this book, and even when I was present it must have seemed as though I was locked into a different world. Without their patience, love and understanding over the past six years this book would simply not have been completed.

The book is dedicated to my mother, Margaret Terese Magee, and to the memory of my father, Patrick Joseph Magee, who brought us from their homeland to a land of new opportunities where we could smell the boronia, watch the snakes and lizards and listen to the locusts in spring.

A NOTE ON DATING

Throughout the text, I have used BC to indicate 'before Christ' in calendric terms, and all calibrated ^{14}C dates have been converted to BC using the latest agreed-upon international calibration curve and CALIB 6.1. It is accepted that this calendric system and system of notation may not be the most appropriate for discussing pre-Islamic Arabia, where the threshold of BC to AD (or BCE to CE) has so little relevance, but its use facilitates comparison with similarly dated cultures throughout the Middle East.

CHAPTER 1

ARABIA AND THE STUDY
OF THE ANCIENT NEAR EAST

INTRODUCTION

> If there is any country which is seen to lie completely outside the stream
> of ancient history, it is Arabia. In spite of its vast extent; in spite, too, of its
> position in the very center of the civilized empires of the ancient East,
> midway between Egypt and Babylon, Palestine and India, – its history has
> seemed almost a blank. For a brief moment, indeed, it played a conspicu-
> ous part in human affairs, inspiring the Koran of Mohammed, and forging
> the swords of his followers; then the veil was drawn over it again, which
> had previously covered it for untold centuries. We think of Arabia only as
> a country of dreary deserts and uncultured nomads, whose momentary
> influence on the history of the world was a strange and exceptional phe-
> nomenon. (Sayce 1889: 406)

Thus wrote Archibald Henry Sayce, the great Welsh professor of Assyriology
at the University of Oxford in 1889. Sayce countered his own introduction by
then expounding upon how the study of ancient inscriptions during the previous decades had begun to cast light on the rich history of pre-Islamic Arabia.
The possibility that Arabia had a prehistoric past, that is, human occupation
before the era when inscriptions became common in the eighth century BC,
and that these prehistoric cultures were in some way worthy of study did not
occur to Sayce, whose views not only were typical of his day but continued to
be symptomatic of the position of Arabian studies for most of the twentieth
century. To be fair, Sayce was a nineteenth-century Assyriologist par excellence, and for him inscriptions and languages defined ancient cultures. He
could write prose in twenty ancient and modern languages, and, according to
his obituary in the *Journal of the Royal Asiatic Society of Great Britain and Ireland*,
his last words included 'When will more Ras Shamra texts be published?'.

In the past few decades, scholars have focused greater attention on Arabia's
'dreary deserts' and discovered a rich archaeological record. These discoveries are presented at annual published conferences like *The Seminar for Arabian
Studies* and in journals such as *Arabian Archaeology and Epigraphy*, which is now

entering its third decade of publication, and *Atlal*, the official journal of the Saudi Arabian Antiquities Department. Most recently, an enormous and successful exhibition of archaeological remains from Saudi Arabia entitled *Roads of Arabia* toured France, Germany and the United States to much public acclaim. A *New York Times* (23 July 2010) review announced, 'A new frontier has been opened in the history of Arabia and its connections with the outside world. The Arabs have traditionally been characterized as latecomers on the Middle Eastern scene. For a people whose beginnings are now known to go back 6,000 years, this is not really the word.'

This growing awareness of Arabia's ancient past can be contrasted, however, with the position it continues to occupy within the discipline of Near Eastern archaeology. Consider the fact that between 30 April and 4 May 2012, hundreds of Near Eastern archaeologists descended upon the city of Warsaw for the Eighth International Congress of the Archaeology of the Ancient Near East (ICCANE). Widely acknowledged as the most important meeting of its sort, the conference brings together scholars whose research focuses on the prehistoric to Islamic cultures of the modern countries of the Middle East. In Warsaw, participants listened to more than 250 papers on a wide variety of topics. Of these papers, only 8 (3%) reported on research conducted in the modern countries of the Arabian Peninsula. This is despite the fact that the Arabian Peninsula occupies a land mass greater than Iraq, Syria, Jordan, Lebanon, Egypt, Palestine, Israel and Turkey combined.[1] When Arabia does enter the realm of Near Eastern archaeology, it is usually limited to the brief periods when incense was traded from the southern part of Arabia to Mesopotamia or the Levant and then onwards to the Mediterranean. It is this interaction with the powerful and well-studied centres of the Old World that largely defines Arabia's entry into scholarship and was responsible for Sayce's and his successors' interest in the epigraphy of southern and northern Arabia. Scholarship that positions the study of ancient Arabia in a broader Near Eastern context (e.g., Tosi 1986b; Wilkinson 2003) or detailed studies that have focused on one part of Arabia (e.g., Potts 1991a) are very rare.

I don't pretend that this book will rectify the situation. However, I do hope that the following chapters not only will provide an overview of the archaeology of prehistoric Arabia, but will illustrate the unique material culture and adaptive processes that characterize Arabian society from c. 9000 BC to 800 BC. I hope that in the process it will become clear that ancient Arabia was an important part of the ancient Near East, yet was unlike it in many ways. It

---

[1] According to the CIA's *World Factbook* the combined land mass of Saudi Arabia, Yemen, Kuwait, Oman, UAE, Bahrain and Qatar is 3,100,922 km². The combined land mass of Iraq, Syria, Jordan, Lebanon, Egypt, Palestine (Gaza and the West Bank), Israel and Turkey is 2,535,241 km². Even if one were to add the well-studied countries of Greece, Italy and Cyprus to the former countries, their land mass would still be less than that of the Arabian Peninsula.

is an appreciation of this diversity of ancient lifeways that makes Arabia worthy of study in itself and in the context of the region as a whole. However, before I begin this task, it is necessary to explore further the biases and assumptions that contour Near Eastern archaeology and continue to marginalize the study of ancient Arabia.

NEAR EASTERN ARCHAEOLOGY AND THE STUDY OF ARABIA

The relationship between the codification of Near Eastern archaeology as a Western academic discipline and the actions of colonial powers in the nineteenth and twentieth centuries is well established (Bahrani 1998; Liverani 2005). A desire to excavate did not drive Western colonial powers to control the Levant, Egypt and Iraq – economic and political reasons were far more important – but these regions figured prominently in the Western mind because of their critical position in the Judeo-Christian tradition. The Western medieval and later notion of *translatio imperii* is important in understanding why these regions were so prominent (Goez 1958). In the Middle Ages, the likes of Richard de Bury and Chretien de Troyes could trace the origins of their own civilizations back to Greece and Rome. European colonialism's opening of the Near East to archaeological and historical exploration provided an opportunity to go one step farther, because, as Liverani has noted, '[a] Euro-centered world view assumed that high culture originated in the Middle East (Egypt and Mesopotamia) then passed to Greece and Rome, the Christian Middle Ages and up to the western European world of the Industrial Revolution' (Liverani 2005: 224).

It was this mindset that prompted Botta, Layard, Sarzec and their nineteenth-century contemporaries to remove so enthusiastically the monumental art and artefacts from the capitals of Assyria and Sumer and transport them to London and Paris, centres of political authority at the time (Caubet 2009). Close political and economic ties between the Ottoman Empire and Germany facilitated the work of German archaeologists, whose explorations at Ashur, Babylon, Tell Halaf, Bogazköy and Uruk continued from the late nineteenth into the early twentieth century. As Bahrani has noted, these early European expeditions were 'unambiguous in defining the purposes of their mission. Since human civilization was thought to originate in Mesopotamia, and this civilization was transferred from the East to the West, the two justifications for the archaeological expeditions were repeatedly stated as being the search for the "roots" of Western culture and to locate the places referred to in the Old Testament' Bahrani (1998: 166).

By the 1920s, these epistemological frameworks were formally established in the praxis of Near Eastern archaeology as an academic discipline. The single biggest contributing factor had little to do with archaeology or the study of the ancient world. It was, in fact, a meeting of delegates from the United Kingdom,

France, Italy and Turkey that took place in a porcelain factory in Sèvres in 1920. The concluding Treaty of Sèvres, and earlier the Treaty of San Remo, laid the groundwork for the League of Nations mandate system, which gave Britain control over Iraq and Palestine, and France control over Syria and Lebanon. Colonial administrators like Gertrude Bell, appointed director of archaeology in Iraq in 1922, rapidly took control of the granting of excavation permits and ensured that Western archaeologists had free rein to explore their own 'origins'. She was responsible for the drafting of generous antiquity laws, which, while undoubtedly an improvement on previous Ottoman rules, permitted Western archaeologists to export half of the antiquities they found (Magee 2012). The same situation occurred in Palestine, Syria and Lebanon. Spectacular discoveries like those made by Sir Leonard Woolley at Ur and their subsequent display in museums further ignited Western interest in Mesopotamia. Larger projects fuelled by the private wealth of pre-Depression America resulted in even greater discoveries, such as those of the University of Chicago's Oriental Institute in the late 1920s in the Diyala region. Mesopotamian archaeology was born and was to remain the focus of much of Near Eastern archaeology for the next century.

For the most part, Arabia lay outside the confluence of these historical, ideological and political currents. Excluding the area of the Hijaz and areas of western Yemen, much of Arabia also lay outside direct Ottoman control and thus in the aftermath of World War I did not fall under European control in the same manner as Syria, Jordan, Palestine, Egypt and Iraq. The British had forced a truce on the southern states of the Arabian Gulf in the early nineteenth century and continued to attempt to influence politics in that region up until the formation of the United Arab Emirates (UAE) in 1971. Similarly, the British attempted to influence local political systems in what was to become Saudi Arabia, Yemen, Bahrain, Qatar and Oman. However, this influence was unlike the wholesale establishment of political control that the French exercised in Syria and Lebanon or the British exercised in Palestine, Iraq and Egypt.

Arabia was not, however, entirely excluded from the nexus of connectivity between the Judeo-Christian tradition and the colonial practice of archaeology. Consider, for example, Fritz Hommel, the German Orientalist who became professor of Semitic languages at Munich in 1885. In addition to writing works such as *Geschichte Babyloniens und Assyriens* (1885) and *Geschichte des alten Morgenlandes* (1904), Hommel considered Arabia an important topic of study. When the German-American Assyriologist Hermann Hilprecht was approached to write a volume that would 'convey to the intelligent English reading public a clear conception of the gradual resurrection of the principal ancient nations of Western Asia and Egypt' (Hilprecht 1903: iii), he called upon Hommel to write the section on the exploration of ancient Arabia. Arabia was of interest to these early researchers and to travellers such as Niebuhr (see Text Box 1) and Palgrave because it was considered to represent the most ancient

TEXT BOX 1. EARLY EXPLORERS OF ARABIA: CARSTEN NIEBUHR

Figure 1.1. Carsten Niebuhr. Print Collection, Miriam and Ira D. Wallach Division of Art, Prints and Photographs, New York Public Library, Astor, Lenox and Tilden Foundations.

(continued)

TEXT BOX 1 *(continued)*

The travels of Carsten Niebuhr (Figure 1.1) in Arabia, Egypt, Iran and India occasioned one of the earliest European accounts of Arabian society. Born in what is now Germany in 1733, Niebuhr was asked in 1760 to join an expedition organized by King Frederick V of Denmark at the prompting of Johann David Michaelis at the University of Göttingen in Germany. The focus of this expedition was the people, cultures and ecology of Arabia and adjacent parts of the Near East.

The organization and focus of the project were typical of those emanating from European universities, especially Göttingen. Organized 'scientific' travel was conceived of as a rigorous academic discipline that contributed to an understanding of the world and, perhaps equally important, the place of Europe within the ever-expanding borders of world knowledge. Courses in 'apodemics' (the science of travel) were offered at Göttingen. Given this intellectual background, it is perhaps no surprise that the expedition represented a wide range of disciplines. An outstanding philologist, Frederik Christian von Haven, a contemporary of Niebuhr's in Copenhagen, joined the project. Other than Niebuhr, however, the most well-known member of the project was the young Swedish botanist Peter Forskål, who had studied under Linnaeus, the father of modern botanical taxonomy, at Uppsala. Forskål was one of Linnaeus's 'apostles' whose job it was to travel throughout the world and bring back botanical specimens that could be configured into Linnaeus's taxonomy.

Alongside this scientific component were the academic and racial interests of the project's proponent, Johann David Michaelis, who was a professor at Göttingen from 1746 until his death in 1791. One of the preeminent biblical scholars of the eighteenth century, Michaelis believed that the study of contemporary Middle Eastern languages, culture and nature would shed light on the Old Testament. In a manner that resonates with some of those factors that marginalized the study of Arabian archaeology, Michaelis believed that eighteenth-century Arabia was an immutable case study that could illuminate the ancient biblical world. He writes in his *Mosaiches Recht* (*Moses Law*): 'If we did not have these customs of the Arabs, we would very rarely be able to elucidate the laws of Moses in reference to an older customary law. The ancient customs have been preserved in this people, who have been cut off from the world and who have seldom been brought under a foreign yoke. Indeed, when reading a description of the nomadic Arabs, one believes oneself to be in Abraham's hut. Travel descriptions of Arabia, and of neighboring Syria, will be of much greater help for us than one might dare to think given the great distance of time at stake here' (1: 12–13; quoted in Hess 2000: 68).

Michaelis presented to Carsten Niebuhr no fewer than 235 printed pages of questions that were to direct the project's research. Among these were questions about the tides in the Red Sea (so as to better understand the parting of it by Moses) and many linguistic questions the answers to which Michaelis believed would lead to a greater understanding of the Old Testament.

In 1761 the expedition set sail for Arabia manned by Niebuhr, Forskål, von Haven, a doctor called Cramer, an engraver by the name of Bauernfeind and a servant called Berggren. Shortly after arriving in Arabia in October 1762, von Haven and Forskål died of malaria. The remaining members of the team spent the next months in Yemen recording cultural and botanical details and linguistics as per Michaelis's instructions. After leaving Yemen, they journeyed to Bombay, and en route all other members of the expedition, except for Niebuhr, died, probably also from malaria. Niebuhr eventually travelled overland back to Europe and on the way made important copies of cuneiform inscriptions at the Achaemenid capital of Persepolis and Naqsh-i Rustam. He finally arrived back in Copenhagen in November 1768. He accepted a position in Danish public service but didn't travel again. He died in 1815.

Despite the disastrous personal costs, the mission was from a scientific perspective hugely successful. In 1772 Niebuhr published *Beschreibung von Arabien*, and this was followed in 1774 and 1778 by his two-volume detailed account of the journey, *Reisebeschreibung von Arabien und anderen umliegenden Ländern*. These texts were widely translated in the decades following and became essential reference works for Oriental research. The latter two volumes contained his engravings of the inscriptions from Persepolis and Naqsh-i Rustam, which were to prove critical to the decipherment of cuneiform (Nyberg 1960).

Such was Niebuhr's influence that Palgrave dedicated his 1865 publication, *Personal Narrative of a Year's Journey through Central and Eastern Arabia, 1862–1863*, to Niebuhr, whom he called 'the intelligence and courage that first opened Arabia to Europe'. Although Peter Forskål, the young botanist who joined the expedition, died at the age of 32 he is also remembered for his pioneering contribution to the study of Middle Eastern botany. In 1775 Niebuhr published Forskål's notes as *Descriptiones Animalium – Avium, amphiborum, insectorum, vermium quæ in itinere orientali observavit Petrus Forskål*. Perhaps the greatest testament to Forskål was the decision of Linnaeus to name one of the plant specimens he collected in Arabia *Forsskaolea tenacissima* because the plant's hardy and stubborn character reminded Linnaeus of his young student. Several plants that are native to Arabia and adjacent regions bear his name, including the samh seed, *Mesembryanthemum forsskalei*, that grows in the Nafud desert (as mentioned in the main text).

and timeless aspects of 'Semitic' life. As Hommel notes: 'In no other country have old manners and customs been so firmly retained as among the Semites in Western Asia, and here again most of all in Arabia; so that a more exact knowledge of those customs often furnishes an instructive commentary upon the life of the past ages, as we see it in the Bible and in other ancient records' (Hommel 1903: 698). This belief in the timelessness of the inhabitants and landscape of Arabia was to remain a key feature of research through most of the twentieth century (as discussed later).

Arabia also featured in one important part of the Judeo-Christian tradition: the story of the Queen of Sheba, who travelled to the court of King Solomon as recounted in the book of Kings. This story remained prominent in Western perceptions of Arabia and the Orient, and it is hardly surprising that it was with the express purpose of investigating its veracity that the first large-scale archaeological project of the modern era commenced in the Arabian Peninsula. In the 1950s, Wendell Phillips and the American Foundation for the Study of Man excavated a number of sites in southern Yemen in search of the home of the Queen of Sheba and the source of incense, the abundance of which led Pliny to label southern Arabia 'Arabia Felix', or 'Arabia the Blest'.

Phillips (1955) made important discoveries at a number of sites, including the capital of the Sabaean Federation, Marib.

Nevertheless, in the post–World War I period, the study of Arabia, especially ancient Arabia, become increasingly marginalized. The term 'Middle East', coined in 1902 by Captain Alfred Mahan of the US Navy (Culcasi 2000: 585), was increasingly used to refer to those areas that had fallen under the influence of British and European colonial powers. The first institutionalization of the term came in 1921 when Winston Churchill established the Middle East Department of the British Colonial Office. This office had jurisdiction over Palestine, Transjordan, Iraq and Egypt – Arabia was excluded.

In the decades following World War II, the ability of European powers to influence domestic affairs in the Middle East waned. Local archaeology authorities in Egypt, Iraq, Syria, Jordan, Palestine and Israel developed with their own sets of laws that sought to protect their cultural heritage and affirm their own national projects through the curatorship of antiquities and archaeology (Magee 2012). Today, very few archaeologists conducting fieldwork in the Middle East would see themselves as operating under a colonial umbrella, nor would they so readily identify the remains they were excavating as a part of their own cultural heritage (for the case of Israel, however, see Abu el-Haj 2001). Given these developments, one might think that the geographical scope of Near Eastern archaeology would have expanded to include Arabia. Indeed, European archaeologists, particularly the Danish, did take an increasing interest in the Arabian Gulf from the mid-1950s onwards, and this has continued with a rich tradition of archaeological fieldwork in Kuwait, Bahrain, Qatar, the UAE and Oman. This work is of such scope that substantial syntheses were available by the 1990s (Potts 1991a). In addition, a government-directed 'comprehensive survey' was conducted throughout Saudi Arabia in the 1970s. This endeavour, which represented an unparalleled attempt to obtain total coverage of a nation's visible archaeological remains, revealed a rich and extensive archaeological heritage. Nevertheless, the archaeology of Arabia still rests on the margins of the current practice of Near Eastern archaeology. Why is this the case?

ARABIA, ENVIRONMENT AND THE ANCIENT STATE

On one level, the answer to this question is obvious: since the middle of the nineteenth century the study of Egypt, Mesopotamia and the Levant has provided artefacts and texts that have fuelled scholarly endeavour and created the impetus for further research and analysis. In other words, a 'scholarly feedback mechanism' has calcified the practice and definition of Near Eastern archaeology. On a deeper level, however, the anthropological conceptualization of the past that has taken hold of archaeology since the 1950s has contoured research towards identifying familiar modes of social existence. In short, the search for 'complex societies' drives contemporary archaeological research throughout the Middle East. These societies 'differ from simple [societies] (or "complicated societies" in the sense of Hallpike (1986: 278)) essentially in the degree and nature of social differentiation in them. Complex societies have institutional-ized subsystems that perform diverse functions for their individual members and are organized as relatively specific and semi-autonomous entities' (Yoffee 2005: 16). In other words, they have much in common with the contempo-rary Western or Western-like states within which are located the educational institutions that fund, teach and research Near Eastern archaeology.

The ultimate manifestation of complexity in the ancient Near East was the 'state'. Although Yoffee (2005) has critiqued and deconstructed this concept, a neo-evolutionary perspective that seeks to gauge how far societies progressed towards 'statehood' still dominates research. The state is seen as 'successful' because it is viewed as having resolved the vexed relationship between pop-ulation growth and food production. This is most explicit in descriptions of the emergence of the first state, that of Uruk, in the fourth millennium BC. Current scholarship argues that the presence of continual rivers on which transport occurred combined with rich alluvial soils and changing climate regimes permitted evolutionary success in southern Mesopotamia by c. 3800 BC (Algaze 2001). Thus, new politico-managerial strategies allowed Uruk to 'surpass their immediate neighbors and potential competitors across the Near East in terms of scale, degree of internal differentiation, and in the degree of hierarchy present in surrounding settlement grids' (Algaze 2005). In short, the ancient state and its ever-present but problematic (Pauketat 2007) younger sibling, the chiefdom, were the winners (in both ancient and epistemological terms), as they had resolved the dynamic relationship between environment and population. This relationship is dynamic because both variables are sub-ject to positive change: population growth can be maintained because fertile landscapes offer opportunities for cereal agriculture, if controlled through management and intervention, that is, irrigation.

In contrast, the environment of Arabia has been generally perceived as homogenous and static (Culcasi 2000: 591; for the Middle East more broadly see Said 1978: 54–55). The concept of 'timelessness' is critical in this regard. This timelessness was a strong rationale for early European exploration such as that undertaken by Niebuhr and continued to motivate travellers well into the twentieth century. In *Arabian Sands*, the renowned British explorer Wilfred Thesiger comments that he travelled to Arabia because he 'craved for the past, resented the present, and dreaded the future' (Thesiger 2008: 34). Of course, it wasn't only the landscape that was considered unchanging – its inhabitants were as well. The Bedouin, in particular, were considered to main-tain the same lifestyle as they had for millennia. Indeed, Eliahu Elath, then the Israeli ambassador to Britain, informed the Royal Asiatic Society in 1957 that Bedouin society was 'a stagnant society – economically, socially and culturally'

(Elath 1958: 125). This lack of change and directionality in social conditions rendered Arabia unworthy of study within the parameters of Near Eastern archaeology and its obsession with recognizable complexity.

Within this conceptualization, not only are the inhabitants of Arabia's deserts seen to be static in their behaviour, but they are actually portrayed as opposing progression and advancement. The Israeli ambassador to Britain, already quoted, was explicit on this matter in his account of the Bedouin of the Negev: 'It is no accident that one who knew him – and his destructive qualities – well has called him not only "the son" but also "the father" of the desert. Like a sea, the desert seemed to have flood and ebb tides of its own, sometimes overflowing it shores and destroying fields and dams, leaving only a barren expanse where later Bedouin might come to graze their flocks for a season then pass on' (Elath 1958: 125).

Of course, this conception of the Arabian desert fits more broadly into a paradigm of alterity that defined European, and particularly British, views of other cultures. As Perkins (1998) has demonstrated, it was part of the dominant colonial enterprise of the nineteenth century and is equally represented in British views of Australian indigenous society, for example. In Arabia, however, it had a particular resonance because it appropriated what was considered by some to be the indigenous Arabic paradigm of the Desert and the Sown, also known as the Bedu and the Hadhar. With its transfer into Western scholarship, initially through Montesquieu, Chardin and others (Gates 1967) and then through the eyes of nineteenth-century explorers who travelled in the Middle East, this complicated paradigm soon became a reductionist climate-based typology that presented two opposing states of existence: one agrarian-based, rich and active (e.g., the Fertile Crescent, Mesopotamia and Egypt), the other one poor, nomadic and violent (Arabia).

When the study of Arabia did enter mainstream Western scholarship, it did so only because the dynamic states of the ancient Near East traded or extracted economic resources. Thus, the importation of incense into the southern Levant has remained a popular topic of scholarly research since at least Sayce's comments noted earlier. The importation of copper from south-eastern Arabia into Mesopotamia has also been the focus of recent scholarship. In each case, it has been argued that this economic engagement brought about rapid social and economic change in Arabia which otherwise would not have been possible on a purely autochthonous level.

ADVANCING THE ARCHAEOLOGY OF ANCIENT ARABIA

A key theme of this book is that Arabia's unique environment meant that its inhabitants *were* as likely as those of the other regions of the Near East to experience economic and social change. In Chapter 2, I examine the environment of Arabia. In doing so, I show that far from being a static, homogenous desert, the Arabian Peninsula is in fact a region of great ecological and environmental diversity, both spatially and chronologically. Throughout the region, there are mountains, wadi systems, alluvial plains, deserts and marine environments, each of which contains unique biota that encourage distinctive forms of human occupation. Alluvial plains surround the mineral-rich mountain chains of the southeast and west; permanent water sources often flowed through most of the Holocene, just as they do today in Oman; there were regions in which at various times enough rainfall fell to grow crops; and the Peninsula sat at a strategic position between Africa, the Near East and Asia. Without doubt, however, the dominant landscape of Arabia was and still is desert. At various times, and with various degrees of intensity, these deserts reinforced a highly delineated and demarcated environment.

The idea that Arabia was as open to the vicissitudes of environmental change and variation as the rest of the Near East does not mean, however, that it provided the necessary backdrop for the emergence of societies similar to those in Mesopotamia, the Levant and Egypt. A secondary theme that I develop in this book is that Arabia's unique environment fostered and reinforced social formations that were fundamentally different from those in the Fertile Crescent. This theme is borrowed and adapted from the fourteenth-century Arab theorist Ibn Khaldun's (1377/1967) notion of *assabiya* and has been developed by this author (Magee 2002, 2007) and others, particularly Serge Cleuziou and Maurizio Tosi, over the past decade in reference to discrete periods within southeast Arabian prehistory (Cleuziou 2002, 2009; Cleuziou and Tosi 2007). Assabiya is most commonly translated as 'group feeling' or 'social cohesion'. It is a social mechanism which derives from shared experiences of desert life and which, according to Ibn Khaldun, is antithetical to an urban existence based on royalty, wealth and luxury. Its emphasis on kin relations permits groups to overcome difficulties or confront problems and achieve what is referred to in modern anthropological literature as 'cultural reproduction'. Although it is best defined as an ideological framework and has been recently focused upon as such by other scholars studying ancient southern Arabia (McCorriston 2011), I argue that it has an explicitly materialist manifestation during several periods of Arabian prehistory. Throughout the book, therefore, it is deployed to explain cultural reproduction in prehistoric Arabia and thus provides a counter-narrative to the emphasis on hierarchical complexity that dominates Near Eastern archaeology. I am not suggesting, however, that Arabia was characterized by simple, acephalous or egalitarian societies. Assabiya is not synonymous with equality. Indeed, as Rosenthal, the most important translator of Ibn Khaldun has noted, assabiya refers to 'man's innate psychological need to belong and give political support to a group dominated by one or more leading personalities' (Ibn Khaldun 1377; trans.

Rosenthal 1967: 566). In his *History of the Arab Peoples*, Hourani goes further and defines assabiya as 'a corporate spirit oriented towards obtaining and
keeping power' which was 'held together by the sense of common ancestry,
whether real or fictitious, or by ties of dependence, and reinforced by common acceptance of a religion' (Hourani 1992: 2).

Assabiya, then, provides an alternative framework for understanding the
maintenance of societies and their ability to overcome the fundamental environmental challenges faced by all societies in the Middle East. Structure and
authority are necessary to confront these challenges, but in Arabia they differ significantly from what is represented in the dominant neo-evolutionary
models commonly employed in Near Eastern archaeological research.
According to Rosen (2005) it is the key concept of the institution that is critical to understanding Ibn Khaldun's idea: 'But it is precisely the intermediate
idea of an institution – in the sense used by Western social scientists to refer
to the performance of role that is not a function of personal attributes – that
forms no part of [Ibn Khaldun's] theory' (Rosen 2005: 598). It is this absence
of institutional power, rendered archaeologically as an absence of monumentality, which defines much, if not all, of Arabia's prehistory and which,
paradoxically, rendered Arabia an unattractive hunting ground for nineteenth-
century researchers intent on filling Western museums.

The traditions, social mechanisms and identity that define assabiya in prehistoric Arabia are not immutable, nor were they locked into a 'primitive' and
static social framework. Ibn Khaldun thought assabiya existed in a cyclical
form and was lost when desert groups become sedentary and urban and then
re-emerged when urban life collapsed. In this book, our focus is on how the
concept of social cohesion provides a framework for understanding millennia
of prehistoric Arabia and how, once formed in the Neolithic period, it was
reinforced in subsequent millennia by the construction of tombs, as well as by
everyday actions and practice (see Bourdieu 1977). I document how the pres-
sure brought about by delineated resource availability, changing climate and
foreign contact and trade continually gives rise to new methods of fostering
social cohesion. At these times, societies changed, settlements expanded and
economies grew. That does not mean, however, that the archaeology supports
in toto Ibn Khaldun's vision of history. As Pauketat has noted: 'Investigating
the relationship between the appearance of towns and domestic life is about
understanding how different people caused, accommodated, or resisted
change. It is about understanding how collective memories were negotiated,
remembered and forgotten, how traditions were invented and reinvented
continuously and how politics and daily practice intersected' (Pauketat 2007:
107). Indeed, in several cases, the tensions created by increased societal stress
as a result of foreign trade and contact were too great and society began to
fundamentally change. Some societies transitioned to a political structure and

processes of legitimization that emulated other Near Eastern states; but others rejected 'the genealogy of enslavement and alienation' and 'the advent of public repression' (Bernbeck 2009: 57) that defined the existence of their neighbours in the urban states of the Fertile Crescent and maintained social cohesion.

The time frame in which I investigate these issues begins with the Neolithic occupation of Arabia in the early Holocene period and ends around 800 BC. This time frame is justified for several reasons. The upper limit marks the beginning of the widespread human occupation of Arabia that coincides with the Holocene Moist Phase. Human exploitation of Arabia at this time set in train a series of social and economic characteristics that were to persist and be transmuted through subsequent millennia. Substantial and important syntheses of the archaeology of Arabia from c. 800 BC onwards already exist (Breton 2000; Hoyland 2001), and there is no need to duplicate these, nor would space allow for the detailed examination that they deserve. Rather than impose an absolute and arbitrary chronological limit on the book's scope, however, I extend the book's coverage to some events, such as the rise of the Sabaean Federation and Nabonidus's occupation of Tayma, inasmuch as they represent the culmination of cultural processes that began centuries and millennia earlier.

Finally, it is my hope that this examination of the archaeology of these millennia of human occupation in Arabia has both an explanatory function (i.e., helping us to understand the past) and an emancipatory function (i.e., 'fostering critical self-consciousness about the present'; Saitta 2005: 386). In this way, the archaeology of prehistoric Arabia has the potential to promote a broader understanding of the multiplicity of lifeways pursued by the inhabitants of the Middle East. Achieving this goal will have made this book worth the effort.

CHAPTER 2

ECOLOGICAL AND ENVIRONMENTAL DIVERSITY IN ARABIA

INTRODUCTION

The Western image of Arabia conjures vistas of sandy deserts and parched nomads leading their dromedary caravans, scenes that might be found in tourism brochures or on the covers of *National Geographic*. Even Wilfred Thesiger in his still popular *Arabian Sands* and Charles Doughty, whose *Arabia Deserta* was a best-seller in its time, emphasized the desert as a defining feature of Arabia. David Lean's canonical movie, *Lawrence of Arabia* (1962), cemented an image of a hot, dry and inhospitable desert occupied by forever-disorganized Bedouin and the occasional flamboyant and erratic Englishman. Despite its characterization as inhospitable, Europeans have been continually drawn to this image, or as Alec Guinness, playing Prince Faisal bin Hussein bin Ali al-Hashemi, quips: 'The English have a great hunger for desolate places.'

As I noted in the introduction, this image has done much to marginalize the study of ancient Arabia. The depiction of Arabia as a uniformly inhospitable environment and its inhabitants as 'timeless' has discouraged detailed archaeological research. By way of contrast, in this chapter I will detail the great ecological and environmental diversity that defines Arabia through space and time (Figure 2.1). The easiest way to approach this is to divide Arabia into southeastern Arabia, western Arabia and northeastern Arabia. None of these areas is self-contained and all, at different times, provide conduits for interaction within Arabia and with the Indian Ocean and Middle East. In each area, jagged mountain ranges rise up from alluvial plains and serve to delimit deserts. Not only are resources scattered across these environments, but the position of Arabia between the Mediterranean climatic regime and the Indian Ocean monsoon, both of which have vacillated over the past 12,000 years, means that zones that are now arid were once relatively well watered. Understanding the varied potential for human settlement throughout these regions and across time is, by necessity, the first step in conceptualizing the archaeology of prehistoric Arabia.

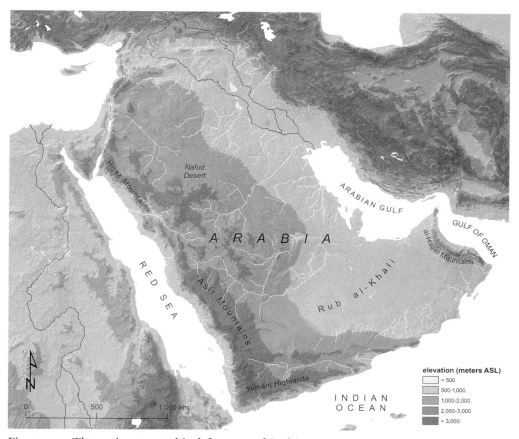

Figure 2.1. The main geographical features of Arabia.

In local Arabic, the mountain range that rises up from the alluvial plains and deserts of southeastern Arabia is called 'al-Hajjar', or 'the rock' (Figures 2.2 and 2.3). There can be no more apt name for these mountains that dominate the local landscape and peak at Jebel Shams (Mountain of the Sun), 3,000 meters above sea level. To the north in the Musandam peninsula, the al-Hajjar plunge into the blue waters of the Straits of Hormuz, creating a dramatic landscape often referred to as the 'fjords of Arabia' (Figure 2.4). A few islands re-emerge from the Straits, including Quoin island, which marks the accepted entrance to the Gulf and on which still stands the lighthouse built by the British in 1914. The al-Hajjar run southeast from the Musandam, rising at Jebel Shams in the Dakhiliya of Oman and then petering out towards Ras al-Hadd peninsula (Figure 2.5).

These mountains and their adjacent environments define southeastern Arabia. As explained by Glennie (1995), they represent a complex sequence of geological events beginning with a basal Hawasina series that includes segments of ocean floor thrust upwards during an episode of subduction. The al-Hajjar supergroup is superimposed on the Hawasina as a result of obduction

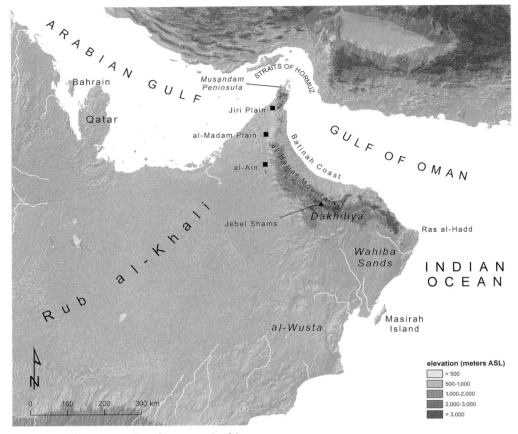

Figure 2.2. Southeastern Arabia.

of the ocean floor onto the Arabian continental margin. Today, as one drives across the UAE from west to east, the banded layers of ocean floor rise up on either side of the modern freeways. At various places, the effects of weathering and erosion create a contrasting landscape of rolling mountains and jagged ophiolites.

Their complex geological history means that the al-Hajjar mountains contain a wide range of resources that could be exploited by humans once appropriate technologies were available. Two of the most commonly exploited materials were copper, for which this area was famous in antiquity (Weeks 1999, 2003; Weisgerber 1980, 1981), and softstone (soapstone, steatite or chlorite), which was carved into vessels and amulets with simple tools. Limestone is also commonly available at points where oceanic sediments are exposed. Basalt – the result of volcanic eruptions on what were once ocean floors – is also commonly available and perfect for use in grinding stones or platforms. Through weathering and erosion the al-Hajjar also supply clay that could be used for ceramic vessels and figurines.

Figure 2.3. al-Hajjar mountains, United Arab Emirates. Photo: the author.

Figure 2.4. Musandam peninsula, Sultanate of Oman. Photo: Tor Eigeland/
Saudi Aramco World/SAWDIA.

Figure 2.5. Ras al-Hadd peninsula, Sultanate of Oman. Photo: the author.

Over millennia, seasonal water courses (wadis) have cut deep gorges through the al-Hajjar. Not only do these provide transport routes across the mountains, but the alluvial sediment discharged through the Pleistocene and early Holocene has formed wide, splaying gravel plains on both the eastern and western sides of the mountains. These alluvial concentrations are known by a wide variety of local names, including al-Jiri, al-Madam and al-Ain in the UAE (Figure 2.6). In the Sultanate of Oman, where the mountains are higher and rainfall more significant, this alluvial plain is massive and is simply referred to as the Dakhiliya, or the 'Inland' (Figure 2.7). Nizwa, the most important city of inland Oman, is located in this area. These alluvial plains and the wadis from which they originate contain soils that support agriculture (Stevens 1978), but as in all of Arabia, the availability of groundwater provides the basis for the cultivation of date palms and other plants (Figure 2.8).

The alluvial plains are bounded to the south and west by the Rub al-Khali (the Empty Quarter) and its northern extension, which runs up to Ras al-Khaimah in the UAE (Figure 2.9). In the Western imagination, the Rub al-Khali is the Arabian desert par excellence. Indeed, throughout the nineteenth century the term 'Rub al-Khali' was synonymous with the 'desolate places' so admired by the English, according to Guinness's Prince Faisal. The crossing of it by Bertram Thomas in 1928 and Thesiger in the 1950s has become a trope for European exploration in Arabia. The term 'Rub al-Khali' is, however, deeply problematic and, as I will discuss in regard to other toponyms in later

Figure 2.6. al–Madam plain, Sharjah, United Arab Emirates. Photo: the author.

Figure 2.7. View towards the village of al-Hamra, Dakhiliya, Sultanate of Oman. Photo: the author.

chapters, is an example of a geographical term that has been appropriated and (re)constructed to reaffirm an entirely external and ultimately simplistic characterization of Arabia. Although written in Arabic, there is nothing to suggest that the term was ever used by the people who dwelt in the deserts or fringes thereof. For these people the desert was, of course, never 'empty'. In a rarely cited paper, Nabih Amin Faris (1957) suggested that Doughty introduced the term in the early nineteenth century, and since then it has been considered,

Figure 2.8. Date palm grove, al-Hamra, Sultanate of Oman. Photo: the author.

Figure 2.9. Rub al-Khali desert, Sharjah, United Arab Emirates. Photo: the author.

Figure 2.10. Gazelle (*Gazella gazella*) in the al-Areen Nature Reserve, Bahrain.
Photo: Burnett H. Moody/Saudi Aramco World/SAWDIA.

erroneously, to be indigenous. Ultimately, the term carried 'an echo of the belief, shared by practically all early Arab geographers, that the earth is divided into two halves, northern and southern, and that each half is in turn divided into quarters, eastern and western. According to these geographers, one half of the earth lies concealed under the water, and the other half is exposed above it. Half of the exposed half is empty, from the equator southward' (Faris 1957: 29). Western geographers and explorers quickly discarded these cosmological inferences and emphasized the barrenness of the landscape, and consequently their achievements in conquering it.

As we shall see, the great sandy deserts of the Rub al-Khali were rarely 'empty' of human and animal life in the periods with which this book is concerned. Even in the recent past, flocks of gazelles (Figure 2.10), oryx, hares, foxes and, of course, dromedaries (see Text Box 2; Figure 2.11) (wild and domesticated) inhabited the margins and, depending on the climate, the interior of the desert. Traversing the deserts is very difficult without the use of dromedaries or more modern forms of transport, and the width of the Rub al-Khali and its northern extension in the UAE varies considerably. In the very north before it interfaces with the alluvial plain near al-Khatt, it is only a few kilometers in width. Farther south in al-Ain, the desert belt stretches for 80 kilometers before reaching the Arabian Gulf. This distance increases to nearly 300 kilometers in the Dakhiliya of Oman.

TEXT BOX 2. THE DROMEDARY CAMEL

Camelus dromedarius (Figure 2.11) is the animal most associated with the Arabian desert. As discussed in the text (Chapter 7), its domestication fundamentally changed human–environmental dynamics, but even before it was domesticated its biology ensured its existence in even the most arid of conditions throughout Arabia.

Dromedaries can experience adaptability of body temperature, quite unlike any another mammal, from 34°C to 41°C and in doing so avoid perspiration and moisture loss. Even with this ability, they can still tolerate water loss to an extent unparalleled by humans or most other mammals. When they have access to water, they consume up to 100 liters in ten minutes and store it effectively in their bodies. Contrary to popular belief this water is not stored in the hump, which actually contains fat that is converted to energy when food is scarce. Key to much of this adaptive success is the oval shape of a dromedary's cells. This permits blood to keep moving during severe dehydration and assists in the storage of water when it is available.

Today domesticated dromedaries have a life span of about forty years, although this is obviously the result of selective breeding over several millennia. A female dromedary will start to mate at around 4 or 5 years of age, and after a gestational period of about fifteen months a single calf is born. During this time, the female dromedary can produce large amounts of milk, which is a favoured drink of many the inhabitants of Arabia today. Unlike dairy milk or sheep and goat milk, camel milk cannot be naturally made into yogurt or butter and must be consumed quickly. Today, a large domesticated male dromedary will weigh about 400 kilos, supplying significant amounts of meat, which, as noted in the text, made it a valuable hunted animal throughout Arabian prehistory and an important component of the domesticated meat supply for the past 3,000 years.

The biological name for the dromedary, *Camelus dromedarius*, applies only to domesticated species. There is no agreed-upon term for the wild ancestor of dromedaries: *Camelus arabs* has been proposed but is not yet widely accepted (Uerpmann and Uerpmann, in press). Some scholars have suggested that the domesticated dromedaries of the Arabian Peninsula derive from the wild North African *Camelus thomasi* which existed during the Pleistocene. This might be the case but cannot be assumed given the difference in the regions inhabited by each animal. It is agreed by all scholars, however, that no wild dromedaries still exist anywhere in the world. The dromedaries that live

Figure 2.11. Dromedary camel (*Camelus dromedarius*). Photo: the author.

in the central Australian desert (the largest concentration of feral dromedaries in the world) are often referred to as 'wild', but these are a feral population that derive from dromedaries from India, Pakistan and Afghanistan imported in the nineteenth century to facilitate exploration and transport across the deserts of central Australia. Such is their success in adapting to this environment that they currently number an estimated 1 million and will double in population every nine years.

Figure 2.12. Wahiba sands, Sultanate of Oman. Photo: the author.

The Dakhiliya is bounded to the south by another desert, the Wahiba sands, which is separated from the main processes of desert formation in the Rub al-Khali and which contains distinctive flora and fauna (Dutton and Bray 1988) (Figure 2.12). Farther to the south the flat deserts of the al-Wusta region and the Rub al-Khali form an effective division between these regions and that of Dhofar, and in doing so they provide a convenient boundary for southeastern Arabia.

On the eastern side of the al-Hajjar a narrow alluvial plain runs down to the Gulf of Oman. Known locally as al-Batinah (the Belly) it begins in the area around Dibba in the north of the UAE and stretches in a crescent shape all the way down to Muscat, the capital of Oman. The plain widens south around Sohar, resulting in greater horizontal sorting of alluvial deposits. Today, this segment of the Batinah is the agricultural heartland of Oman, and all manner of fruits, cereals and, of course, dates grow here (see Text Box 3). The Batinah terminates south of Muscat.

Text Box 3. The Date Palm

In the West, dates are a luxury food and are never viewed as more than an occasional treat. In contrast, dates have been a staple part of the diet in Arabia and other parts of the Middle East for millennia. The tree from which dates come (*Phoenix dactylifera*) also provides a myriad of resources that are critical to everyday life.

Although the exact place and chronology of initial date palm cultivation are unclear (see Chapter 3), it is likely that the date palm was first deliberately grown by humans somewhere in the area of the Arabian Gulf or Indo-Iranian borderlands. The date palm is dioecious, that is, there are both female and male plants. Before cultivation by humans, wind pollination would have been the only method by which the female trees provided fruit. Manual cultivation would have required knowledge of the male and female plants and how to pollinate the female. Once pollination is achieved, the female plants bear large amounts of fruit. The first crop occurs when the tree is 5–7 years old and may be limited to about 10 kilos. The tree will continue to produce fruit for about another five years with an increasing yield every year. Mature date palms can produce between 60 and 80 kilos per year. Before the introduction of sugar-based products, the fruit was an important source of calories for energy, vitamins (especially A and C) and moisture.

Typically the date palm fruit is harvested in mid-summer. It can be eaten at this stage, at which time it is referred to as *khalal*. Over the coming months the date is transformed into the soft (*rutab*) and then dried (*tamr*) forms in which it is most commonly eaten. Throughout the Arabian Peninsula, dates are also made into a form of syrup called *dibs*. This involves putting large amounts of dates sealed into baskets made from date palm fronds onto a crenulated surface with a jar at one end. Due to the force of gravity, the dates slowly exude syrup, which is collected in the jar. These installations, called *madbhasa*, were a common feature of large houses and forts throughout eastern Arabia. They have also been discovered in archaeological contexts on Qala'at al-Bahrain dating to the middle of the second millennium BC and at the first millennium BC settlement of Muweilah in the United Arab Emirates. The dibs kept for several months and was an important source of calories and sugar until the next summer's harvest.

The fruit of the date palm was only one benefit of its cultivation. Rows of date palms created small micro-environments that were shaded from the harsh sun and nourished by leaf and other detritus. All manner of plants could be grown in this interstitial zone, including fruits, melons, grasses and cereals. The date palm tree also provided a wide array of materials for construction and handicrafts. The frond of the date palm was the main building material in the construction of *barasti* huts that were common along the coastal edges of eastern and southern Arabia. The fronds were also used for making baskets and ropes, while the midrib of the frond was used to make furniture. The frond was also a fuel source in the firing of ceramics. Once the tree no longer fruited, the main trunk was a critical part of house construction. In fact, the width of rooms within traditional building in eastern Arabia (2–3 meters) was dictated largely by the maximum load-bearing span of the trunk of the date palm. In many ways, therefore, the cultivation of the date palm by the inhabitants of ancient Arabia transformed their existence.

Although a great diversity characterizes the physical geography of south-eastern Arabia, the unifying feature of this entire landscape today is the climate. Long dry summers in which temperatures can reach 55°C characterize the current climate. Anyone who has spent any time in the UAE or Oman in August will know that such temperatures are indeed hot enough to fry an egg, at least on the bonnet of a Land Cruiser. The winters are milder, with an average temperature of about 25°C during the daytime. The extreme heat of the desert is not only a factor in our understanding of ancient occupation in southeastern Arabia but also a limiting factor in archaeological exploration. Most North American and European archaeologists carry out fieldwork in the Middle East during the Northern Hemisphere summer, at which time southeastern Arabia is prohibitively hot. Only during the winter is the weather conducive to fieldwork, but the academic calendar hardly suits extended field seasons during these months.

As southeastern Arabia lies north of the Inter-Tropical Convergence Zone (ITCZ) and thus out of reach of the influence of the Indian Ocean monsoon, there are only two sources of winter rainfall. The first derives from the cold and dry masses of air that move across the Zagros in Iran and meet the more humid and warmer air of the Arabian Gulf. The second, and more common, source derives from the westerlies that move from North Africa and the Mediterranean southwards into Arabia. The rainfall from both these sources exhibits a high degree of inter-year variation. In Sharjah, for example, 8 millimeters of rainfall fell in 2001, while 168 millimeters fell in 2006 (Murad 2010). Over many years rainfall averages out to less than 100 millimeters per year for the UAE and slightly more for the areas of Oman to the east of Salalah.

Although rainfall is limited, a large aquifer formed during the Pleistocene and early Holocene and recharged today by periodic rainfall provides most of the water exploited in the recent past. This massive aquifer extends from the Dakhiliya westwards, running north through the Oman peninsula. Today, because of overexploitation, it is largely inaccessible without the use of diesel-driven pumps. In antiquity, however, it is likely that the water table was much more accessible. Hydrological studies conducted in al-Ain in the UAE indicate that water was accessible at 6 meters below the surface at c. 2500 BC (Jorgensen and al-Tikriti 2002). By the seventeenth century AD, water was 14 meters below the surface. Today, the water table has dropped to nearly 70 meters below that evident in the Bronze Age. The relative ease of accessing the water table in Bronze Age al-Ain should not, however, be considered relevant to southeastern Arabia as a whole. al-Ain is very near the al-Hajjar mountains, and as one moves farther away from the piedmont, the water table becomes deeper and more inaccessible. Towards the coast, however, the freshwater aquifer interacts with denser salt water that permeates large areas of the low-lying sandy shoreline. This interaction, known as the Ghyben-Herzberg interface, results in accessible freshwater lenses along the coast (Murad 2010). The relative

ease with which these can be tapped is offset by the fact that the freshwater
lenses are easily overexploited, and this results in saltwater intrusion, rendering
it of little use to humans (Sherif et al. 2012).

WESTERN ARABIA

Driving southwest today from the Dakhiliya in Oman, one notices that the
number of date palms and acacia slowly declines, culminating in the flat, stony
desert plateaux of the al-Wusta region. Emerging from this desert area are the
tablelands and mountains that announce the region of Dhofar and the transition to southwestern Arabia (Figure 2.13). A series of mountains that rise up
from the surrounding plains and run parallel to the Indian Ocean coast dominate Dhofar. The most prominent of these are Jebel al-Qamar, Jebel al-Qara
and Jebel Samhan, but the mountain chain continues into Yemen. On the
seaward side of these mountains in the Dhofar region, lush vegetation transitions to a 12- to 15-kilometer-wide coastal strip dominated by the remains

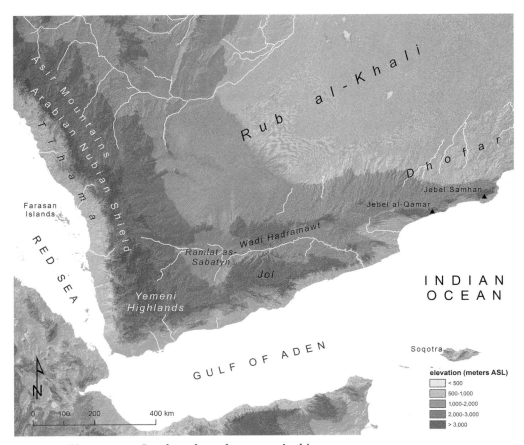

Figure 2.13. South and southwestern Arabia.

Figure 2.14. Dhofar, Sultanate of Oman. Photo: Dr Lynne Newtown.

of ancient and still active recent lagoons. The coastal strip thins farther south, and near Hoff the mountains descend to the sea. Green rolling hills contain forests of *Ficus sycamorus*, *Cadaba* and *Woodfordia*, while grasslands dominate the northern zone of the mountains. These stretch inland for about 150 kilometers, becoming progressively drier until they meet the southern edge of the Rub al-Khali.

If there is one region in Arabia that stands in contrast to the dominant Western image of a dry inhospitable land, it is the tablelands and mountains of Dhofar (Figure 2.14). Western explorers have always been struck by its verdant, lush nature. Captain Bettesworth Haines of the Royal Indian Navy wrote in 1845, '[T]he soil is good, [with] wild clover growing in abundance and affording pasture for cows and immense flocks of sheep and goats, while in many places the trees as so thick that they offer a welcome shade impervious to the scorching rays of the sun' (Haines 1845: 117). The reason that the grasslands and forests are fertile and lush is that the northern edge of the Indian Ocean monsoon finds landfall in this area of Arabia (see Text Box 4). It brings summer rainfall in the form of slow drizzle, known locally as *khareef*. In the mountains the annual rainfall averages between 200 and 300 millimeters and is supplemented by fog precipitation. The heavy mountain rainfall recharges sub-surface water transported by karst systems. The transportation and subterranean storage of water result in several zones of permanent standing water along the mountain flanks of Dhofar – for example, in the Wadi Darbut and Wadi Andur, each of which drains and

TEXT BOX 4. THE MONSOON AND MARITIME TRADE

Today the Indian Ocean monsoon is of critical importance to South Asia. Like all monsoons, it is caused by the differential heating of the land and oceans from early summer and then again in early winter. Around May the South Asian land mass begins to heat up faster than the air above the Indian Ocean and Arabian Sea. The creation of a low-pressure system over land causes moisture-laden air to blow onto the land mass, and monsoon rains eventuate. Today, the monsoon bursts over the west coast of India around Thiruvananthapuram at the beginning of June.

This summer cycle of the Indian Ocean monsoon, also known as the southwest monsoon, brings much-needed rains to South Asia, and the economic viability of agriculture relies upon it. The creation of winds moving towards the Indian subcontinent in a northeasterly direction was critically important for seafaring from Arabia, Africa and Iran to South Asia. From May to September, boats leaving the southern edges of Arabia and ports in northeastern Africa could use the monsoon winds to travel to South Asia and sometimes beyond into Southeast Asia. In the winter cycle, or northeast monsoon, the wind patterns reverse as air above the cooling land mass moves back towards the Indian Ocean. This causes winds to blow towards Arabia and East Africa. In the past, this facilitated trade in the opposite direction and was used for the return trip of those boats that had made the summer trip to South Asia. How early such trade started is still a matter of debate. There can be little doubt, however, that contact between Arabia, Mesopotamia and South Asia as evidenced at many sites in the late third millennium and early second millennium BC was facilitated by these trade winds.

The predictability of the monsoon was important for this early seafaring in the Indian Ocean, but the monsoon winds themselves were not enough to ensure safe and regular traffic. Navigation by celestial observation, avoidance of the violent storms caused by the monsoon and knowledge of the ports in which one could find fresh water and supplies were critical. These all developed over time, probably from the Neolithic period onwards. Today the dhows that sail from Oman and the UAE to Iran and South Asia are equipped with the latest GPS navigation systems and radar. It is telling, however, that many are still constructed along traditional lines in towns such as Sur on the Oman coast, an acknowledgement of the long history of seafaring in this part of Arabia.

cuts through Jebel Samhan. Another outstanding feature of the climate of Dhofar is the temperature: in contrast to summer temperatures in southeastern Arabia, those in Dhofar average around 35°C, and in winter they drop to around 18°C.

To the north and continuing to the west, low calcareous plateaux, referred to as the Jol in Yemen, dominate the landscape. Numerous wadis, the most important of which is the Wadi Hadramawt, effectively cut the Jol into a northern and southern section. This long wadi system stretches from the eastern edge of the Ramlat as-Sabatyn and runs southeast to the coastal plain. Today the whole region receives limited rainfall, no more than 100 millimeters per year. As noted by Edens and Wilkinson (1998), however, drainage systems in the Wadi Hadramawt provide the potential for soil accumulation.

The Ramlat as–Sabatyn, a sand sea that is effectively a southern extension of the Rub al-Khali, bounds the Jol and the wadis that dissect it. A number of rocky outcrops like Jebel Ruwaiq and Jebel Alam al-Aswad punctuate the rolling dunes of the Ramlat. Rainfall here is limited to the vestiges of the summer monsoon, which provides much less than 200 millimeters per year. Because it falls in the hottest months of the year, evaporation is very high and standing water is rare. Wadi Dhanna to the west discharges into this desert, creating rich alluvial fans and the potential for flood irrigation, while Wadi Hadramawt runs west to east and links the Ramlat with the coast and Wadi Masila.

To the west, the Jol is bounded by the series of rocky outcrops located near the modern town of Habban, which also sits at the transition zone to the Yemeni Highlands. Driving northwards along the road that separates these two regions today, one is struck by the steep escarpment of the Jol and the low, jagged foothills of the highland piedmont. The Highlands generally reach 2,000–3,000 meters above sea level, with the highest point 3,760 meters above sea level and located near the modern capital of Sanaa. They continue as a spine along the Indian Ocean coast and then run north, parallel to the Red Sea, before they descend into the Asir region of Saudi Arabia (Figure 2.15).

The rainfall regime of the Highlands stands in stark contrast to that of the surrounding regions. In gradients running approximately north to south, the rainfall increases steadily from the interface with the Jol to more than 1,000 millimeters per year at the centre of the Highlands. This is largely monsoonal rain that falls in the summer months but is supplemented by some winter rainfall. However, in contrast to the rain-deprived regions to the west, east and north, the Highlands experience very little soil accumulation. High-energy runoff ensures that sediments are quickly discharged into wadi systems and transported towards gravel fans and the deserts.

A coastal strip locally referred to as the Tihama runs on the western and southwestern edge of the Highlands. Wadi accumulations flowing from the Highlands punctuate the flat coastal plain, which is otherwise a hot and very dry region. Rainfall is generally less than 100 millimeters per year on the coast. It increases rapidly as one enters the Highlands: thus, rainfall at Ibb in the central Highlands can average 1,000 millimeters per year, whereas a village in the Tihama, less than 100 kilometers due west, will receive less than 100 millimeters.

The Tihama extends northwards as far as the modern city of al-Wajh in Saudi Arabia, but as one moves northwards the mountains of the Arabian Nubian Shield (ANS) increasingly encroach upon the coastal plain (Figure 2.16). This mountain range begins in southwestern Yemen and extends all the way to the southern Levant. By the Tabuk province in northwestern Saudi Arabia, the mountains of the ANS reach the coast. In the Asir province of Saudi Arabia, these mountains receive significant rainfall (500 millimeters per year) in late winter and spring, supporting agriculture today. The timing of this rainfall

Figure 2.15. The Asir region in Saudi Arabia. Photo: Tor Eigeland/Saudi
Aramco World/SAWDIA.

reflects the weakened influence of the summer monsoon. Rainfall declines
precipitously farther north, so that by Jeddah rainfall is less than 100 millimeters per year. Even where there is slightly higher rainfall, such as in Medina,
there is still not enough for rain-fed agriculture to be practised.

The ANS transitions to the Nejd (Uplands) and central deserts of Saudi
Arabia. Several plateaux representing steppic zones between the mountains and
the Nafud desert are centres of modern and ancient settlement. Modern-day
Buraydah represents one such settlement, but others such as Hail and Tayma in
the Hijaz were important in the past. Although rainfall is very limited today in
this region, Pleistocene and early Holocene rainfall ensured the development
of massive, deep fossilized water aquifers such as the Saq Formation and the
Wajid and Tabuk aquifers. Access to the water table varies greatly depending on
location. Today at Tayma, for example, fresh water can be obtained at a depth of

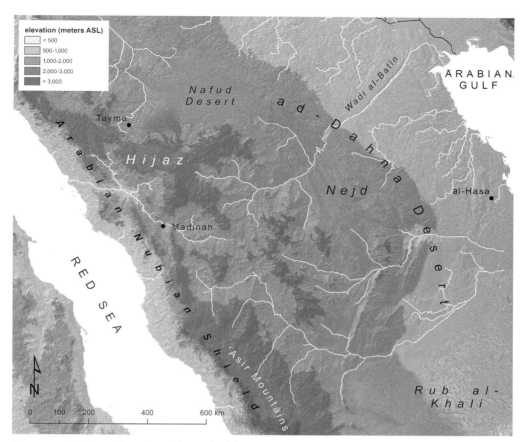

Figure 2.16. Central and northern Arabia.

only 4 meters (Eichmann et al. 2006a: 165), and irrigation systems water fields throughout the oasis (al-Najam 2000). In contrast, at Madain Salih (Hegra) water is currently found at a depth of 17 meters, although it was much more accessible at the beginning of the twentieth century (Nehmé et al. 2006: 67).

To the north and east of Tayma lies the Nafud desert, one of the defining geographical features of northern Arabia. At nearly 300 kilometers long and 250 kilometers wide and with massive red-sand dunes and strong winds, it is in the Western mind second only to the Rub al-Khali as the definitive Arabian desert. Late-nineteenth- and early-twentieth-century European explorers considered the crossing of the Nafud a feat comparable to the crossing of the Rub al-Khali. In David Lean's *Lawrence of Arabia* it serves as a metaphor for the uninhabitability of the Arabian environment. To take the Turkish garrison at Aqaba, Lawrence proposes an overland route and an attack from the north. 'You are mad!' Ali bin Hussein responds. 'To come by Aqaba by land we should cross the Nafud desert.... The Nafud cannot be crossed; [it is] the worst place God created!'

To the eccentric and arguably arrogant Englishman, nothing is impossible. In some of the most memorable scenes in the film, Lawrence leads a band of tribesmen across the unbearable Nafud and ultimately on to victory at Aqaba. Setting aside the fact that Lawrence probably never actually crossed the Nafud (Vincent 2008: 15), the desert is in any case not without resources that, if not encourage, at least permit human occupation. Many early Western explorers commented upon the spring vegetation that grows there (e.g., Rutter 1930: 513, who writes of the 'meadow-grass' of the Nafud). After the winter rains, a variety of plants, mostly of the *Calligonum-Artemisia* group, come to life (Chaudhary 1983; al-Turki and al-Olayan 2003), and many are excellent fodder for dromedaries (Carruthers 1910: 8). One of the most important of these is *samh*, the Arabic term for the seeds and leaves of several annual herbs (*Mesembryanthemum forsskalei*, *Mesembryanthemum nodiflorum* and *Aizoon canariense*) (Mandaville 2011: 116–119). In the recent past, the seed of this plant was ground to make a type of flour from which bread is made, and nutritional studies have indicated that it provides twice as much protein as corn, rice or wheat (al-Jassir et al. 1995). Ghada (*Haloxylon persicum*) is also common and was used for grazing and firewood (Mandaville 2011: 102). On the edge of the Nafud, in the transition zone to the Nejd, a wide variety of shrubs and grasses grow, and some of these extend well into the sands themselves (Llewellyn et al. 2011). Until the modern period, all of this vegetation provided grazing for herds of oryx, the hunting of which remained a traditional activity until their numbers dwindled in the twentieth century.

NORTHEASTERN ARABIA

The ad-Dahna desert, a thin band of high sand dunes that runs north to south in a crescent, connects the Nafud to the Rub al-Khali. It borders the sedimentary formations that slowly dip away from the western mountains and Nejd. Rainfall is uniformly limited in this region to below 200 millimeters per year, falling mostly in the winter. Across the ad-Dahna, in northeastern Arabia, several geomorphological features, such as basins and Pleistocene era riverbeds represented, for example, by the Wadi al-Batin, encourage rapid filtration of winter rainfall (Bergstrom and Eten 1965) and the formation of shallow aquifers. These are easily tapped out, however, in coastal environments where overexploitation results in saltwater intrusion.

Deep-water fossilized aquifers also occur across the central areas of this region, particularly in al-Hasa province, where they support large oases (Figure 2.17). The Neogene and Damman aquifers are the most important and stretch under eastern Saudi Arabia, Bahrain and Kuwait. These aquifers lie above a deeper aquifer known as the Umm er-Radhuma (Bakiewicz et al. 1982), and a permeable aquitard between the Umm er-Radhuma and Damman aquifers ensures flow between the two. The aquifers originate in the interior around Nejd and

Figure 2.17. Hasa oasis, Saudi Arabia. Photo: Tor Eigeland/Saudi Aramco World/SAWDIA.

are bounded to the south by the Rub al-Khali and the formations in southeastern Arabia discussed earlier. Currently, the water of the deeper Damman and Um er-Rudham aquifers would not be drinkable according to WHO standards, as it exceeds 1,000 ppm total density of solids (Bakiewicz et al. 1982), but the quality of water largely correlates with increased exploitation in the modern period, and it is likely that it was fresher in pre-modern times.

Regardless of how the quality of water has changed in the past millennia, accessibility to the water is determined largely by the folding sedimentary stratigraphy of eastern Arabia. For example, wells dug 260 kilometers inland in the 1960s regularly reached water at a level of 60 meters or more. For even fresher water the wells were deeper. Closer to the coast, in the city of Qatif, the Neogene aquifer could be tapped at 10–15 meters. Deeper wells, tapping the Damman aquifer, were 100–140 meters deep (Ebert 1965). At Jabrin in the 1940s, fresh water, almost certainly from the Neogene aquifer, could be tapped at only 3 meters under the ground. These aquifers extend under the Arabian Gulf and are the main source of water on the island of Bahrain, where in the past large wells could tap fresh water with relative ease.

In the pre-modern period the productivity of wells and springs that tapped these aquifers was extraordinary. For example, nine main springs and wells were active in Hofuf oasis in the 1940s, providing a total discharge of 350,000 liters per minute, enough to irrigate more than 10,000 hectares of date palm gardens (Twitchell 1944). The output from these wells was such that in the Hofuf oasis it permitted cultivation of a plant that might be the least associated with Arabia. According to Potts (1994a), citing Destrées (1874), rice was the second-most popular cultivar in the Hofuf oasis in the middle of the nineteenth century, and in the 1940s rice was still widely cultivated in this region (Twitchell 1944: 384). This rice, sometimes referred to as Hassawi rice, is considered by some (e.g., al-Bahrany 2002) to be an indigenous variety of *Oryza indica*, raising the possibility that its cultivation is of considerable antiquity.

RESOURCE VARIATION IN ARABIA

Arabia is not, therefore, a land of 'dreary deserts'. By pulling back from the details presented in the preceding sections, it is possible to identify the main characteristics of resource variation within the Peninsula and how this has the potential to influence human settlement.

There are two scales of resource variation operating simultaneously in Arabia: a regional, or micro, scale and a peninsula-wide, or macro, scale. In each case, resources not only are restricted to specific environments, but also occur in close proximity to other resource zones. To begin with the regional, or micro, scale, in the Arabian southeast, a desert-piedmont-mountain sequence bounded on both sides by coasts dominates the landscape. Each of these environmental zones contains specific resources that are largely unavailable in the immediate adjoining environment. Both the Arabian Gulf and Gulf of Oman provide access to bountiful marine resources. One of the most important of these resources is largely intangible – it is simply access to the oceans and the potential for maritime trade with the rest of Arabia, Iraq, Iran and South Asia. More tangible resources include fish, which could be dried and imported inland, as well as shellfish, which could be kept for a day or two, and mangroves, which were a rich source of food and wood (Figure 2.18). In each case, the ability to economically integrate with inland communities was dictated by the speed with which these resources could be moved across the desert to the interior. For the west coast, this meant traversing an extension of the Rub al-Khali that, given the climate and geography that has dominated since the mid-Holocene, was difficult without the use of the domesticated dromedary.

The desert regions themselves had the potential, therefore, to act as gateways between environmental zones. In their own right they were also important. Not only did they contain a wide variety of animals, but seasonal vegetation that could be consumed by humans and used for grazing grew here. The latter had the potential to facilitate sheep, goat and, of course, dromedary pastoralism. The Arabian oryx (*Oryx leucoryx*; Figure 2.19), an excellent source of meat, also prefers the desert and steppic areas, although within these environments tends to prefer hardened sand areas in steppes and inter-dunal troughs. For long-term

Figure 2.18. Mangrove (*Avicennia marina*), Kalba, United Arab Emirates. Photo: the author.

human survival, access to water is, however, most critical. Rainfall is minimal, but an aquifer that is recharged in the mountains runs below the sandy desert belt of southeastern Arabia. As noted previously, it is most accessible near the coast, where it interfaces with salt water and is closer to the surface.

There is slightly higher rainfall in the mountains, and water can be accessed through the deep wadis that cut east to west across the mountains and provide the potential for small-scale terracing (Figure 2.20). Soil accumulation is limited here, and one needs to move some distance into the alluvial plains to access the most fertile soils. Fluvial and alluvial action has ensured that the areas at the very base of the mountains are the most difficult to utilize, since they contain large and mostly immovable boulders from the mountains. Through the process of sorting, the alluvial sediment becomes finer the farther one moves away from the mountains; concomitantly, however, the water table becomes increasingly difficult to access.

In summary, no individual resource zone within southeastern Arabia contains a wide spectrum of resources necessary to ensure a continuous supply of terrestrial and marine food as well as materials such as stone, copper and wood. To gather and exploit all of these resources within one region inevitably requires movement across the landscape and traversing a sand dune desert.

A similar situation occurs in western Arabia, where contrasting summer rainfall patterns brought about by the Indian Ocean monsoon provide an

Figure 2.19. Arabian oryx (*Oryx leucoryx*). Photo: Burnett H. Moody/Saudi
Aramco World/SAWDIA.

even starker picture of divergent resource zones. As in southeastern Arabia,
the coastal zones represented by the Tihama and the coastal edges of the Asir
and Hijaz provide access to the unique marine resources of the Red Sea and
Indian Ocean as well as the potential for maritime trade with Egypt and East
Africa. The scattered resources of the Hijaz and the ability to tap aquifers
along the eastern plateaux and basins provide the necessary conditions for
small-scale oasis agriculture. These oases also provide staging points for travel
to northern Arabia and the Levant. The Nafud desert, like the Rub al-Khali
in southern Arabia, operated as an important transition zone between different environments. There is no question that at various times it presented a
formidable obstacle to movement and regional integration, but this aspect can
be overstated – it also provided seasonal resources that could be exploited by
pastoralists.

Figure 2.20. Terraced agriculture, Ras al-Khaimah, United Arab Emirates.
Photo: the author.

The Highlands of Yemen and the Asir of Saudi Arabia are the most resource-rich environments in this region. As Edens and Wilkinson have noted, 'The structure of Yemen's prehistory can generally be perceived as a long-standing settlement core in the moist Highlands that only occasionally became integrated with major currents of interregional trade' (Edens and Wilkinson 1998: 109). It is indeed the case that the very high rainfall when combined with complex terracing facilitates small-scale agriculture – perhaps even double cropping – in this region. In addition, the Highlands and the ANS mountains of western Arabia contain a wealth of mineral resources. Obsidian, for example, is available at several locations in the Yemeni Highlands (Khalidi 2009; Khalidi et al. 2010). Copper and iron are also available through the stretch of mountains, and the former was heavily exploited during the Bronze Age (Weeks et al. 2009). Softstones, carnelian, agates and gold are also present in exploitable quantities (see Mallory-Greenough et al. 2000).

As well as a blessing, the heavy rainfall in the Highlands is, however, also a drawback. The sharply dissected wadis, such as Wadi Dhanna, collect torrential rainfall and carry it towards the Ramlat as-Sabatyn. Mixed in with the water is sediment that has the potential for soil formation. It is carried and deposited on the western edge of the desert and forms rich alluvial plains in an environment in which there is less than 100 millimeters of rainfall per year. Thus, the high rainfall creates a heavily demarcated environment characterized by mountains with limited arable land – but plentiful rainfall – and alluvial flanks with limited rainfall but significant soil accumulation.

The distinctive rainfall and climate patterns in southwestern Arabia are also responsible for the limited distribution of one of its most well-known resources: the dried sap of the Boswellia tree, more commonly known as frankincense (see Text Box 5). There are nearly twenty species of *Boswellia*, but two were most prized in antiquity for their frankincense: *Boswellia sacra* and *Boswellia frereana*. The former grows in southern Arabia and, because of the unique rainfall regime in this area, grows in only two specific locations: around the Dhofar region in Oman and the plateaux of Mahra and the Wadi Hadramawt in Yemen. Currently, the western limit for *Boswellia* is about 47°E, running in a line from the eastern edge of the Ramlat as-Sabatyn and the entrance to the Wadi Hadramawt.

The Ramlat as-Sabatyn operates as a transition zone between the Wadi Hadramawt, the Jol and the highlands of southwestern Arabia. There is little question that its formidable dunes would have hindered the movement of goods from each of these zones. However, as we will see, there is also very early evidence for the exploitation of this desert, in the form of cairn burials in the rocky outcrops at Jebel Ruwaiq and Jebel Alam al-Aswad.

In summary, Arabia has a wide variety of ecological niches, each of which contains potentially important resources that can sustain human societies. No single region can be considered to control all of these, and the ability to move materials across environments, or share access to them, is critical. The Nafud, Rub al-Khali and Ramlat as-Sabatyn deserts play a key role on several levels. Not only do they operate as transition or gateway zones, but they also contain unique resources that permit human occupation in environments where competition is minimalized. This image can be contrasted to that found in the well-studied areas of the Middle East such as Mesopotamia. According to Algaze, the inhabitants of southern Mesopotamia could 'exploit several complementary ecosystems at the same time including (1) the irrigable alluvial plain, which provided high once a year yields of subsistence crops, principally barley, (2) smaller irrigable areas near the rivers, providing for intensively cultivated gardens and orchards where multiple high-value crops could be produced throughout the year, (3) fallow fields within and outside the irrigated areas that provided extensive pasture lands for millions of sheep and goats and some cattle, and (4) rivers, artificial canals, freshwater marshes, and brackish lagoons and estuaries that provided plentiful protein in the form of fish and fowl, as well as reeds and other useful products' (Algaze 2001: 201). Despite the elaboration of this description, Mesopotamia, like Egypt, was in reality a river system that offered a limited range of resources within a constrained environmental zone. The contrast to Arabia, where an abundance of resources was available across highly divergent and demarcated environments, could not be greater. *How this environment contoured and promoted a society that was fundamentally different from*

TEXT BOX 5. *BOSWELLIA* AND FRANKINCENSE

The *Boswellia* genus contains numerous species, four of which provide sap which when dried and placed upon hot charcoal produces a large amount of fragrant smoke. The frankincense for which Arabia was famous in antiquity is the dried sap of *Boswellia sacra*.

This deciduous tree grows up to 8 meters in height in limited environmental and climatic ranges. It tolerates humid, hot conditions, but with limited seasonal variation, and can be grown on rocky calcareous soils. For this reason, its natural range today incorporates Dhofar in Oman, parts of Yemen and northeastern Africa. The tree starts producing resin when it is about 8–10 years old. Extracting the resin entails peeling back a thin layer of bark and making a shallow incision in the trunk. After two to three weeks this sap is discarded and another cut made to access the pure sap of the tree. Several harvests continue from April to October. As the resin comes into contact with air, it dries and is then harvested. Slower-growing trees in the Dhofar region produce the very best frankincense in Arabia, but even within this region there are recognized variations in the quality of the sap. Frankincense of the best quality is obtained in the relatively dried wadi beds behind Jebel Samhan, whereas the incense which is considered of poorest quality (although still widely sold and used) comes from the coastal plain, where the trees are exposed to the summer monsoon rains.

The production of frankincense is an important part of the economy today in Dhofar, just as it was in the past. In the first few centuries AD, production expanded as demand for frankincense grew in the Roman Empire. Large maritime emporia, such as Khor Rori in Oman and Qana in Yemen, were engaged in maritime export, while dromedary caravans carried frankincense overland to Gaza and other ports in the Mediterranean. Frankincense's primary use was to produce a fragrant smoke; however, it should be noted that today in Arabia, just as in the past, the sap of *Boswellia sacra* is chewed for its medicinal qualities, especially to relieve indigestion. The smoke is also believed to repel mosquitoes, an important consideration given the prevalence of malaria in this region in the past (see the fate of Carsten Niebuhr's expedition to Arabia, described in Chapter 1).

that in Mesopotamia is a key theme of this book. In exploring this, however, we need to understand that Arabia was never a closed ecological system and that its unique position between and within the Middle East, Africa and South Asia provided the potential for interaction and the absorption of cultural influences across a vast portion of the Old World. It is to this issue that I now turn.

ARABIA AND THE INDIAN OCEAN WORLD

Southeastern Arabia and its mineral-rich al-Hajjar mountains are located in close proximity to the Arabian Gulf and Arabian Sea (see Figure 2.21). Contact with Bahrain and southeastern Iran is relatively easy: it is less than 150 kilometers from the major cities in the north of the UAE to the port of Bandar Abbas. The plentiful fresh water available in eastern Arabia and on Bahrain provided numerous opportunities to break up a northern maritime journey to

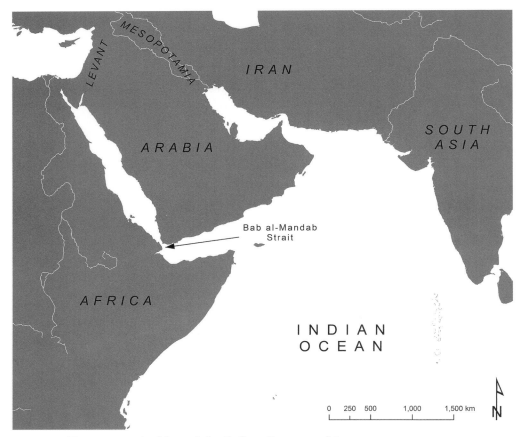

Figure 2.21. **Arabia and the Indian Ocean world.**

southern Mesopotamia, 800 kilometers to the north. Interaction with areas to the east was also possible for settlements on the eastern side of the al-Hajjar. Almost exactly the same distance separates Ras al-Hadd, on the eastern edge of Oman, from the port city of Karachi in Pakistan. Except for the northerly route along the Makran coast, this trip would be in the open water but would be greatly assisted by the Indian Ocean monsoon, which provides the necessary winds to carry sail-powered ships to the northeast of South Asia. With mastery of the sea, eastern Arabia is, therefore, very much open to engagement with Mesopotamia, South Asia and Iran.

Thirty kilometers separate the southwestern tip of Arabia from northeastern Africa across the Bab al-Mandab. Once one is outside the strait, the distance between southern Yemen, particular the aromatic-rich area between the Wadi Hadramawt and Dhofar, and northeastern Africa is rarely more than 300 kilometers. North of the Bab al-Mandab, the distance between western Arabia and Egypt is as little as 200 kilometers, which is comparable to the distance between eastern Arabia and Iran across the Arabian Gulf. Moreover, throughout the southern Red Sea, groups of islands provide a stepping stone between Africa and Arabia. Recent research on the Farasan Islands has, for example, highlighted a long history of Holocene occupation that would have facilitated cross-sea contact (Bailey et al. 2007). Just as in southeastern Arabia, but perhaps even more so given the smaller distances involved, southwestern Arabia lies, therefore, on a natural conduit with eastern Africa and Egypt.

ARABIA AND THE MIDDLE EAST

The interior regions of western Arabia and the Asir are more oriented towards the inland zones of the rest of the Middle East. The significant aquifers in western Arabia and the Hijaz provide the basis for rich and fertile oases that operated as nodal points from which routes branched out in several directions, often following well-established wadi systems. Beginning in the south, the Wadi al-Dawasir provides communication routes between Najran and areas of the Arabian Gulf coast, whereas a northern route from Najran led straight to Medina. At Medina, there was another opportunity to travel northeast via Hail to southern Mesopotamia or go northwards to Tayma; a route went from Medina towards al-Ula that gave access to the Red Sea via Tabuk.

Routes north from Tayma are limited because of the Nafud desert, but skirting the western edges of the desert and heading east brings one to the Jawf. From there, a series of wadis connect to the Euphrates and onwards to Baghdad. The first is the Wadi Arar, which stretches northwest until it meets its major tributary, the Wadi Ubaiyidh, which runs straight to the Euphrates, just south of the Bahar al-Milh, or the Salty Sea. The importance of this trade route is no more clearly indicated than by the early Islamic fortresses and palaces that dominated the entrance to the Wadi Ubaiyidh at Ukhaidir (Finster and Schmidt 2005). There is also a northwestern route from Jawf via the Wadi Sirhan to Azraq and then onwards to the Levant and Syria.

These routes across northern and western Arabia thus form a series of nodes, each of which provides an option to head towards either the Levant or Mesopotamia. Combined with the maritime routes to Mesopotamia, Iran, South Asia and Africa, this means that Arabia is positioned at a central location between the major regions in which early human sedentary settlement developed.

CLIMATIC VARIATION IN ARABIA

As I noted in the introduction, the notion of 'timelessness' is well imbedded in Western popular and scholarly perceptions of Arabia. Environment and human behaviour are inexorably bound in this perspective because a perceived lack of resources causes humans to be constantly on the move, always trying to meet a minimum subsistence level. Obviously, Sayce and his successors did not understand the complex palaeoclimatic history of Arabia, and that this perspective was maintained into the twentieth century is hardly surprising. It is surprising, however, that more contemporary research has not recognized that Arabia, because of its unique geographical situation between two climate zones, has experienced significant climatic changes over the past 12,000 years. Our understanding of these changes owes much to the pioneering work of H. A. McClure (1976), who focused on the appearance of lake sediments in the Rub al-Khali as potential evidence for earlier, moister climates. Since then, numerous studies have shown that the past 12,000 years have witnessed tremendous shifts in climate throughout Arabia. These climate shifts affected numerous aspects of human settlement, not just in terms of water availability but also in terms of the flora and fauna in the Peninsula as whole.

THE HOLOCENE MOIST PHASE

Most of Arabia looked vastly different 10,000 years ago than it does today. This is because the Peninsula lies between the North Atlantic and the Indian Ocean monsoon (IOM) climate systems. As previously noted, currently the monsoon skirts the southern edges of Arabia, bringing summer rain to the region from Dhofar to the Yemeni Highlands. Most scholars argue that this important northern limit of the IOM depends upon a shift in the Inter-Tropical Convergence Zone (ITCZ) (Staubwasser et al. 2002). There is compelling evidence that a series of global processes led to a northward movement of the ITCZ and a concomitant northern movement of the IOM sometime around 9000–8000 BC. This would have led to significantly more summer rainfall throughout most of Arabia during the early to middle Holocene. Throughout this volume I will refer to this climatic period as the 'Holocene Moist Phase', although other names exist. The evidence for its effects can be found in a series of stalagmites, palaeosols and dried lake sequences throughout Arabia. The stalagmites are particularly important, as isotopic shifts within their composition are very sensitive proxies for increased summer rainfall. Two cave stalagmite sequences are critical for dating the onset of this period. The most southerly, at al-Qunf cave in the Oman, indicates that the Holocene Moist Phase began c. 8600 BC (Fleitmann et al. 2003; Fleitmann and Matter 2009). Stalagmites in the slightly more northern Hoota cave, also in Oman, indicate increased rainfall around 8100 BC. To Fleitmann and Matter, the correlation between the distance north and the later onset is significant, for it suggests time-dependent northward movement of the ITCZ. This argument would seem to be confirmed by the recently published lake sequence from Awafi in the northern UAE (Parker et al. 2006). Considerably north of Hoota cave, this sedimentary sequence indicates the onset of the Holocene Moist Phase around 7000 BC. Dried lakebed sequences in the Ramlat as-Sabatyn confirm a similar climatic trajectory for southwestern Arabia, and recent research on the edges of this desert document soil formation beginning around 6800 BC (Pietsch and Kühn, 2012). The northward shift of the ITCZ thus brought time-transgressive climate change to Arabia.

How far north the monsoon brought summer rainfall is not yet determined. Sedimentary records collated by Sanlaville (1992) suggest that a moist phase is evident near Jebel umm Suman in the Nafud and Wadi as-Sulb and Wadi Hanifah. At nearly 28°N, the Jebel umm Suman evidence would indicate that the vast majority of Arabia was receiving significant summer rainfall from the beginning of the Holocene Moist Phase. At the same time, palaeoclimatic research in northwestern Arabia (Schultz and Whitney 1986) and the northern Red Sea region (Arz et al. 2003) indicates that winter rainfall derived from North Atlantic and Mediterranean systems dominated these very northern reaches of Arabia. Regardless of the origin of the rainfall, recent research at Tayma has indicated the existence of an environment that at 8000 BC looked vastly different than it does today. According to Engel et al. (2011) and Wellbrock and Grottker (2010), increased precipitation led to the formation of a lake near Tayma that was approximately 13 meters deep and measured 18.45 kilometers square. After about 6500 BC, the lake began to shrink but then expanded again, eventually becoming only periodically filled by the fifth millennium BC (Ginau et al. 2012). Engel et al. estimate that to sustain the lake at its maximum, precipitation was three times the current regime of around 50 millimeters per year (Almazroui 2011). Whether this precipitation was the result of monsoon activity or derived from North Atlantic and Mediterranean systems is still not certain.

The Holocene Moist Phase was not consistent through time. The Qunf cave record indicates declining rainfall events around 7100 and 6200 BC. More generally, most of the climatic proxies indicate that the intensity of the monsoon declined slowly beginning around 6000 BC. However, there is no absolute agreement about when the ITCZ migrated south again, thus bringing an end to the Holocene Moist Phase. Unlike the time-transgressive evidence for the onset of the Holocene Moist Phase, proxies do not indicate the expected southward migration of the ITCZ. Lake proxies such as that at Awafi and Maqta are susceptible to misinterpretation, since rainfall may decline to below the level at which sediment was transported into the lake but still be considerably above current conditions. The Qunf and Hoota caves are perhaps more sensitive indices in this regard, and both seem to be indicate that the ITCZ migrated to the very south of the Peninsula to approximately its current position by about 4000 BC. At this time, isotopic signatures from the Qunf cave stalagmite indicate a northern origin for rainfall, which was likely occurring in winter.

How did the Holocene Moist Phase compare with the climate today? Modelling actual amounts of rainfall is very difficult, although Drechsler (2008) suggests that summer rainfall might have been between 150 and 200 millimeters per year for the inland plains of southeastern Arabia, or about double what it is today. Geochemical data from palaeosols on the edge of the Ramlat as-Sabatyn have been used to calculate an annual rainfall of between 400 to 600 millimeters (±235 millimeters) (Pietsch and Kühn, 2012), comparable to the 250–500 millimeters reconstructed for southern Oman (Radies et al. 2005). In summary, there is no doubt that freshwater lakes were present in desert regions, and some wadis would have flowed all year round, just as they do today in parts of Yemen and Oman. Arabia, which consistently appears below the limit of dry farming on maps of the ancient Near East and well outside the Fertile Crescent was, in fact, experiencing rainfall that exceeded that of Mesopotamia and the Levant for most of the Holocene.

There is disagreement concerning how the end of the Holocene Moist Phase by c. 4000 BC affected local vegetation patterns and the environment. Whereas some have favoured an interpretation akin to an abrupt drought event, more detailed palynological data from terrestrial cores from Kawr al-Jaramah in western Oman suggest that a more nuanced interpretation is necessary (Lézine 2009: 750–759). Even though most scholars would accept that by 4000 BC the Indian Ocean monsoon's effects on southern Arabia had significantly declined, the Kawr al-Jaramah record indicates that there was still sufficient freshwater input to sustain fern vegetation and the presence of *Rhizophora* mangrove. The latter is no longer common in Oman and has been replaced by *Avicennia* mangrove, which can tolerate more saline conditions. It is not until 2500 BC, however, that *Rhizophora* becomes absent from the Kawr al-Jaramah record. At the same time, xeric plants like *Prosopis cineraria* start to become more common. The combination of this palynological and sedimentary data obtained by marine cores in the Arabian Sea suggests that, even though slow, a decline in summer rainfall began c. 4000 BC and this caused the increased growth of desert vegetation. The pace of the decline was such that it was not until 1,500 years later that the threshold which would no longer permit the growth of tropical plants such as *Rhizophora* was reached in the Kawr al-Jaramah area.

MIDDLE TO LATE HOLOCENE CLIMATE CHANGE

The termination of the Holocene Moist Phase saw the onset of climate conditions similar to those prevailing today. Nevertheless, there were several climatic events in the subsequent millennia that had the potential to significantly affect human settlement. The sedimentary core from Awafi in Ras al-Khaimah suggests a marked but stepped process of aridification with peaks at 3900 and 3200 BC (Parker et al. 2006). The same lake record indicates a return to moist winter conditions for the period from 3200 to 2200 BC. Around 2200 BC, the Awafi record indicates a total desiccation of the environment. As Parker points out, a climatic deterioration is recorded at this time in the North Atlantic,

North Africa, Near East and Arabian Sea. A palaeobotanical and sedimentary record from Suwayh in Oman would also seem to confirm this event's impact in Arabia (Lézine et al. 2002). It has been argued by some that the Akkadian Empire collapsed because of increased environmental and subsistence stress during this time (Weiss et al. 1993), but this is by no means widely accepted (see Kuzucuoğlu and Marro 2007).

The Awafi record indicates that moist conditions returned for most of the second millennium BC to southeastern Arabia. Around 1000 BC the last major climatic change relevant to the time frame of this book occurs (Parker et al. 2006). At this time, dune reactivation consistent with declining rainfall is found. Although whatever rainfall that occurred was likely to be winter rainfall derived from the North Atlantic westerlies, it is interesting to consider that sea cores off the Pakistan coast have also indicated a severe reduction in the intensity of both summer and winter monsoon precipitation (Lückge et al. 2001). Other regions across southern Arabia provide evidence of dune emplacement at this time, suggesting that the deterioration in rainfall was widespread (Bray and Stokes 2003).

CONCLUSIONS

Spatial and chronological variation in the availability of water, vegetation and other resources characterizes Arabia throughout the Holocene. This variation created both temporal and geographical niches that provided abundant resources for human settlement. No niche, however, contained a sufficiently broad spectrum of resources that exploitation of other resources was not desirable, if not necessary. As I argue in the next chapter, the initial Holocene populating of Arabia was driven and contoured by these variations in available resources. However, success in this environment required highly adaptive resource procurement strategies that in turn fuelled unique social and economic lifeways. Once established in the early Holocene, these cultural systems were renegotiated and reconfigured through subsequent millennia as the inhabitants of Arabia further adapted to a changing landscape containing ever-sharply defined resources as well as the potential for interaction with numerous neighbours.

CHAPTER 3

THE FORMATION OF ARABIAN
SOCIETY: 7000–3000 BC

INTRODUCTION

Immense changes in social and economic order characterize many Near
Eastern societies at the beginning of the Holocene. Scholarly attention has
focused on understanding how these communities moved away from a hunter-
gatherer lifestyle and began to cultivate plants and raise animals. Since the
pioneering research of the Australian archaeologist V. G. Childe, the causes
of this 'Neolithic revolution' have been studied in detail (for an overview see
Asouti and Fuller 2011; Barker 2006; Watkins 2010; Zeder 2011). For most
archaeologists working in the Near East today, these events conceptually set in
train a series of changes that led to the emergence of urbanism, writing and
highly structured political, social and economic order. In other words, for most
archaeologists the Neolithic stands at the beginning of the march towards state
complexity, the search for which, as I noted in Chapter 1, largely defines the
current practice of Near Eastern archaeology.

Yet it is rarely emphasized in the literature that the majority of people
inhabiting the Near East, and indeed the world, did not become sedentary
agriculturalists during these millennia. Such people occupied large parts of the
region and altered their subsistence strategy in order to adapt to environmental
and climate changes. This was particularly the case in Arabia, which experienced no agricultural revolution during the early Holocene. Population groups
inhabiting the Peninsula were in contact with agriculturalists, and indeed may
even have derived some of the basis of their subsistence from them. However,
the subsistence strategy they pursued differed radically from that evident
throughout the Fertile Crescent. It was a strategy that was uniquely suited not
only to the highly demarcated environmental zones of Arabia, but also to the
relative climatic optimum that prevailed during the Holocene Moist Phase.
Adaptation to these environments resulted in social formations that differed
from the increasing disharmony and inequality that characterized contemporary societies in the Middle East.

THE HOLOCENE PEOPLING OF ARABIA

The Palaeolithic–Neolithic Transition

By the sixth millennium BC, large numbers of nomadic pastoralists occupied and exploited the coasts, deserts and inland plains of Arabia. The question of where these population groups came from and where they obtained the domesticated animals that formed a critical component of their subsistence strategy is still debated. The possibility that they derived from pre-existing 'Palaeolithic' groups depends upon the existence of an upper Palaeolithic occupation of Arabia, scholarly acceptance of which has see-sawed over the past thirty years. Widespread surface collections characterized as 'Palaeolithic' in the 1960s and 1970s in eastern Arabia were dismissed by a French mission to Qatar in the 1980s, which argued that while formally Palaeolithic in technology, the stone tools found in these areas were probably Holocene in date (Tixier 1986). In the late 1990s and early 2000s, renewed insistence on a Palaeolithic occupation of eastern Arabia resulted from fieldwork in Oman and eastern Arabia, conducted principally by Rose. The so-called Sibakhan industry was tentatively dated to Oxygen Isotope Stage 9-7 (400,000–180,000 years ago) or less likely the Oxygen Isotope Stage 5e pluvial, which dates to 128,000–120,000 years ago (Rose 2004).

Most recently, spectacular evidence for *stratified* Palaeolithic occupation of southeastern Arabia was revealed by the excavations at Jebel Faya in the inland regions of Sharjah in the UAE (Armitage et al. 2011; Uerpmann et al. 2009). A series of three stone tool assemblages recovered in a stratigraphic rock shelter sequence were dated by a series of optically stimulated luminescence (OSL) dates. Assemblage C, the earliest, was dated by three OSL dates to between 127,000 and 95,000 BP. The associated stone tool technology showed strong affinities to northern and eastern Africa, suggesting to the authors that the earliest levels at the site attest to the dispersal of anatomically modern humans from Africa into Arabia. They concluded, 'It is likely that populations expanded and moved through the interior of Arabia, as well as via the coastline, and used adaptive strategies incorporating terrestrial resources. The presence of humans at Jebel Faya early in MIS 5 indicates that a significant range expansion occurred during MIS 5e. The African affinity of assemblage C implies that a wetter southern Arabian climate rather than technological innovation was responsible for this range expansion. With more arid conditions during MIS 5d and 5b, this population probably became disconnected from that in south Arabia, as the corridor across the Nejd Plateau was lost' (Armitage et al. 2011: 455). The finds are thus multitudinous in their importance, both for Arabian archaeology and more broadly for our understanding of the spread of modern humans across Asia.

The Faya excavations also provide evidence for a climatic period that may mark a truncation between the Pleistocene and Holocene. A thick layer of sterile sand separates the Paleolithic occupation from any Neolithic (Holocene) occupation of the site. This layer, which may be tentatively dated to between 38,000 and 10,000 BP, coincides with a major deterioration of the Arabian climate attested as aeolian dune emplacement at several palaeo-climatic proxies throughout the region (Armitage et al. 2011; Uerpmann et al. 2009: 7). The sterile nature of the sand deposit, and the lack of any corresponding assemblage which may be datable to a time frame roughly equivalent to the Epipalaeolithic cultures of the Levant (Kebaran and Natufian), raise the possibility that human occupation of southeastern Arabia was minimal during these millennia. Perplexing from this perspective is the recent publication of mtDNA evidence from several modern population groups in southern Arabia which suggests that significant population movements from the Near East to southern Arabia occurred between 13,000 and 12,000 BP (al-Abri et al. 2012). Balancing these various strands of evidence will hopefully prompt further research in the largely unexplored, but key areas of central Arabia.

Regardless of these issues, early Holocene occupation of southwestern Arabia is now attested at several sites. A number of ^{14}C dates from al-Hawa in the Ramlat as-Sabatyn range from the eighth to the seventh millennium BC – a time frame in which occupation is also attested at nearby sites in the piedmont of the Yemeni Highlands (Lézine et al., 2010) and at Manayzah in the Wadi Hadramawt (McCorriston and Martin 2009). In the southeast Arabian inland, the excavations at Jebel Faya have provided evidence for so-called Fasad points, a simple pointed blade, that were previously found in the Qatar B group and might illustrate influence from Pre-Pottery Neolithic B (PPNB) flints in the Levant. A piece of shell from the same strata was ^{14}C-dated to between 8500 and 7700 BC (Uerpmann et al. 2009).

While the Faya evidence confirms human reoccupation of the inland by the middle of the ninth millennium BC, evidence from sites on the east coast of Oman and the UAE suggests that humans preferentially occupied more favourable zones in which maritime resources were located in close proximity to mountains and alluvial plains. Excavations during the 1980s in the Wadi Wutayya on the coast of Oman revealed a series of fireplaces dated to the late tenth to early ninth millennium BC on the basis of ^{14}C samples (M. Uerpmann 1992). The coastal environment of Oman was more favourable than any of the inland regions during this period and would thus have provided a refuge for human settlement. With the advent of the Holocene Moist Phase, these groups eventually reoccupied the inland zones and by the sixth millennium BC onwards had transitioned towards a nomadic herding mode of existence that became widespread throughout Arabia. While the characteristics of this are generally agreed upon, the question of the origin of the subsistence package employed by these Neolithic communities is still much debated.

EXTERNAL ORIGINS OR LOCAL EMERGENCE?

Many scholars have argued that the most convincing explanation for the appearance of Neolithic pastoralists in Arabia can be found in the so-called Levantine hypothesis, which emphasizes the strong Levantine character of both selected stone tool technologies and the domesticated animals that were critical to subsistence in Arabia. Drechsler's detailed analysis of Neolithic archaeozoological remains from throughout Arabia led him to conclude that '[a] compilation of published archaeozoological assemblages dating roughly to the early and middle Holocene indicates the presence of domesticated sheep (*Ovis*), goat (*Capra*), and cattle (*Bos*) in almost all of the samples.... The location of archaeological sites in southern Arabia falls beyond the natural habitant of the wild ancestors of sheep (*Ovis orientalis*) and goat (*Capra aegagrus*). Consequently, these species had to disperse across Arabia as domesticates in the form of reproductively viable herds' (Drechsler 2007: 93–95). A Levantine origin for these domesticated animals is strongly suggested by the fact that they were already domesticated in the Levant. The so-called Qatar B group of blade arrowheads, which are known from eastern and southeastern Arabia, are also argued to show strong similarities to Levantine PPNB lithics. More recently, the discovery of a dry-stone wall apsidal house on the island of Marawah, off the coast of Abu Dhabi, has also prompted parallels to domestic architecture of the PPNB period in Ain-Ghazal in Jordan (Beech et al. 2005).

Most scholars accept that the Holocene Moist Phase is key to understanding why and how these technologies and adaptations moved from the southern Levant into Arabia. The increased rainfall that defined the Holocene Moist Phase resulted in fertile grasslands for pastoralism, as well as providing a range of wild animals, such as oryx, for hunting. The veracity of this model depends on how far north the Inter-Tropical Convergence Zone (ITCZ) moved during these millennia, an issue which is still unresolved. However, there can be no question that once population groups moved into the central regions of Arabia they would have had access to an environment rich in resources. Geographic information systems (GIS) modelling of the environment and possible pathways for the movement of these groups by Drechsler (2007) has raised the intriguing possibility that the subsequent southward retreat of the ITCZ, and thus the decline of summer rainfall, cut these pastoralists off from areas farther north. They became effectively marooned in an environment that was losing those characteristics that had first attracted them to this region.

While the climatic optimum model explains the existence of pastoralist groups in Arabia, it does not necessarily explain *why* pastoralist groups with domesticated sheep and goat initially moved into Arabia. Part of the answer to this question may be found in the eastern Jordan steppic regions, where a process of increased pastoralism can be found towards the end of the Pre-Pottery Neolithic (PPN) period (c. 6000 BC). These regions had been previously occupied by Epipalaeolithic hunter-gatherer populations that exploited abundant wild resources. Sheep and goat begin to appear in the faunal assemblages at a number of sites towards the end of the seventh millennium BC. Interpretations and explanations of this phenomenon in many ways crystallize scholarly approaches to desert habitation in a way that I will revisit several times in this book. Köhler-Rollefson (1992) suggests that the emergence of pastoralism in these steppic areas was the result of increasing subsistence stress brought about by sheep and goat domestication in the fertile settled areas to the west. She argues that as sheep and goat became increasingly important in these regions, they began to exploit arable land and interfere with crop production. The solution, according to Köhler-Rollefson, 'would have been to capitalize on one of the advantages of animal over plant resources – their mobility – and seasonally remove goats from the vicinity of settlements and cultivated fields. The ideal venue for such undertaking was the steppes and desert to the east that were unsuitable for cultivation but, at least during the crucial growing season, sprouted enough vegetation to nourish large numbers of domestic herbivores' (Köhler-Rollefson 1992: 13–14). In this scenario, nomadic pastoralism replaces the hunting of wild animals, as it is a 'more purposeful and productive manner of exploitation' (Köhler-Rollefson 1992: 14).

A more detailed analysis of the faunal assemblages from these desert sites led Martin (1999) to question Köhler-Rollefson's conclusions. On the basis of detailed archaeozoological data from the east Jordanian sites of Wadi Jilat 25, Wadi Jilat 13, Azraq 31-ELN and Burqu 27-2, she concludes that herding did not dominate the subsistence of these late Neolithic desert pastoralists. Nor was there any evidence for seasonality or management of the herd for milking – as suggested by Köhler-Rollefson. Rather, sheep and goat pastoralism became part of a broader subsistence strategy that maintained a focus upon the abundant wild hunted resources of the desert; in other words keeping domesticated sheep and goat added to the benefits of exploiting existing desert resources. This perspective provides a feasible model for why pastoral groups began to engage with the Arabian desert and goes some way in explaining why groups may have continued to move farther south into areas in which wild resources and grasslands provided the necessary backdrop to maintain a mixed hunter/pastoral economy. The recent discovery of a site containing PPN lithics at Jebel Qatar in the Nafud desert (Crassard et al. 2013) might attest to the movement of such groups into the Arabian Peninsula.

Thus far, we have considered the evidence only inasmuch as it details the external origins of some of the Arabian Neolithic subsistence strategy. An increasingly vocal school of thought has downplayed these influences in favour of a model that sees the development of an Arabian Neolithic economy as mostly autochthonous in character. Serge Cleuziou and Maurizio Tosi have argued in a series of publications (e.g., Cleuziou and Tosi 2007; Cleuziou 2009) that the subsistence strategy and tool kit of the Neolithic inhabitants of Arabia were likely developed from local resources with limited foreign input. While they admit that there is very little evidence for local domestication of sheep and goat, they argue that trade, rather than migration, brought these domesticates to southern Arabia and that 'the beginning of animal husbandry may be considered as a response to the depletion of big game herds after a few millennia of intensive hunting ... it may be that herding came in to supplement a decreasingly rewarding hunting economy before it fully replaced it' (Cleuziou and Tosi 2007: 56).

To complicate matters, Neolithic sites in the Wadi al-Tayyilah and adjacent sites in the Khawlan al-Tiyal of the Yemeni Highlands have revealed Neolithic archaeozoological remains that include cattle which cannot be classified as either wild or domesticated (Fedele 2009). Similarly dated sites in the Wadi Khamar raise the possibility that there were cultural inputs into southwestern Arabia from northeastern Africa. Balancing these with the recognition that other aspects of the material culture had a Levantine origin is difficult. As Fedele has commented, 'How to accord such a scenario – a fundamental independence from the northern Near East – with the apparently indisputable fact that several domestic animals and other cultural elements were of Near Eastern origin, is a problem for future research' (Fedele 2009: 234). The possibility of in situ domestication of cattle has also been signalled by Bökönyi's analysis of archaeozoological material from ash-Shumah in Yemen, although there is some scepticism about these claims based on the deflated nature of the campsites from which this evidence comes (cf. Edens and Wilkinson 1998: 70).

Crassard (2009) provides the most recent and trenchant rejection of the 'Levantine hypothesis' as an explanation of the origins of Neolithic lifeways in Arabia. He argues that specific tool types, especially fluted and trihedral lithics, which are found from Oman to Yemen and are labelled 'the Haburat facies' by Charpentier (2008: 110), are without parallel in the Levant and thus support an indigenous origin for Neolithic lifeways in southern Arabia. To Crassard, the potentially local character of some flint tools more broadly illuminates the methodological differences between those who see external influence as important, and those, like him, who view developments as purely local in origin: He writes: 'These two models both have their credibility, perhaps dependent on the period under examination. The diffusionist model is however not attested to by archaeological vestiges and thus remains a purely theoretical one. It represents a search for external influences in the attempt to explain absent elements in Yemen, and represents the "escape" generated by generalization in archaeological science, which inevitably leads to diffusionist conclusions' (Crassard 2009: 11). Indeed, there seems little doubt now as the result of Crassard's and others' research throughout Yemen that distinctive regional lithic technologies did develop in the early to middle Holocene, especially at sites like Manayzah in the Wadi Hadramawt.

These important arguments have done much to re-emphasize the local cultural substratum that undoubtedly existed from the beginnings of the Holocene onwards. Nevertheless, they do not explain how the domesticated animals that were so critical for adaptive success came to be in southern Arabia. Maritime trade between the Levant and southern Arabia is unlikely to have occurred, and sheep and goat appear before the beginnings of contact with southern Mesopotamia (as discussed later). Furthermore, the sheep could not have travelled by themselves from the southern Levant, and it is unlikely that the pastoralists who brought them would have returned 'home' after exchanging with the local population. Rather, the movement of people from the southern Levant provides a feasible explanation for the appearance of domesticated sheep and goat in Arabia, even if such people may have come into contact and blended with existing populations whose way of life was dominated by hunting. Moreover, by characterizing the debate as one between 'diffusionist' and 'endemic' perspectives, Crassard downplays the importance of selection, and thus of agency, during these dynamic millennia. In short, what makes the Arabian Neolithic package unique is its blend of local and 'foreign' elements. This results in a distinctive subsistence strategy that is uniquely suited to the early to middle Holocene climate of Arabia. That this hybridity was successful is amply illustrated by a review of the longevity of the Neolithic tradition in Arabia.

THE SPREAD OF THE ARABIAN NEOLITHIC

Regardless of where the Neolithic inhabitants of Arabia obtained their herded sheep and goats, it is now abundantly clear that they used these domesticated animals in a manner that ensured successful adaptation to the Arabian environment for several millennia. By the sixth millennium BC, human occupation of southern Arabia is widespread (Figure 3.1). It has long been accepted that Neolithic Arabia was aceramic, unlike the contemporary cultures of the Levant and Mesopotamia (but see Hashim 2007 for claims of Neolithic ceramics at Thumamah and Zubaidah in Saudi Arabia). The existence of a lithic industry, once called the Arabian bifacial tradition, has been emphasized, and there are significant similarities in lithics found from southwestern to eastern Arabia. More recent research in Yemen and southeastern Arabia has begun to unpack this generic grouping and emphasize local lithic technologies within discrete chronological phases. The Haburat facies, distinguished by trihedral – not bifacial – points, is for example widespread across the southern reaches of Arabia, from Manayzah in Yemen to Marawah off the coast of Abu Dhabi (Charpentier 2001, 2004; Crassard 2009). Excavations at Suwayh in Oman provide reliable ^{14}C dates for this assemblage, leading Charpentier to assign a chronology of 6500–4500 BC (Charpentier 2008). While it is hardly surprising that recent research has begun to illuminate discrete chronological

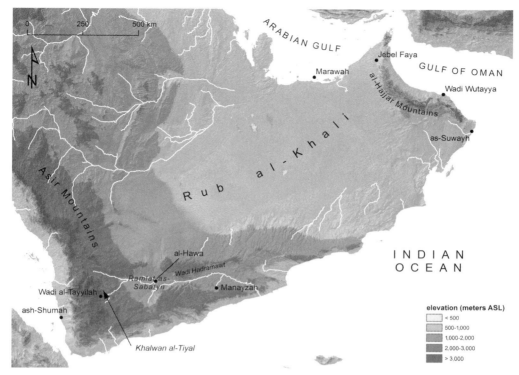

Figure 3.1. Main excavated early Neolithic sites in southern Arabia.

and regional variations within the Arabian Neolithic, it is also true that broad
similarities still characterize human occupation from southwestern Arabia to
the Gulf littoral.

From the Bab al-Mandab to the Straits of Hormuz

Shell middens and encampments in the Tihama attest to intensive occupation of the southwest Arabian coast from the sixth millennium BC until the
Bronze Age. Arabian bifacial tradition lithics are found at these sites but are
complemented by a localized flint technology that includes backed point
and lunates (Edens and Wilkinson 1998: 65). Numerous shell middens imply
intensive exploitation of marine resources. In addition, the site of SRD-1 on
the northern bank of Wadi Surdud has provided evidence for bead production in the form of rock crystal bead waste and chalcedony drills (Edens and
Wilkinson 1998; Tosi 1986a). The site also revealed ostrich eggshells, which
may point to exchange with or seasonal movement to and from the interior
regions. In addition to the exploitation of fish and shellfish, the Neolithic
inhabitants of the Tihama appear to have herded cattle. One ^{14}C date from a pit
at SRD-1 suggested that herding cattle had already begun by the sixth millennium BC (Tosi 1986a). As noted previously, some have argued that cattle were

domesticated in situ, although further evidence is required before this can be argued with certainty.

Moving east from the Tihama one ascends the Yemeni Highlands, where rainfall can exceed 1,000 millimeters per year. Excavations at sites such as GQi and WTHiii revealed extensive round stone constructions, some of which contain benches and hearths (de Maigret 1984a, 1984b; Fedele 1985, 1986). Several Neolithic lithic facies are known from this region. The two most important are the Qutran and the Thayyilan, each of which comprises a distinctive array of foliates, scrapers and points. The latter contains fewer bifacial stemmed points than the former, leading Fedele (1985) to suggest that it is later than the Qutran. Edens and Wilkinson (1998), by contrast, argue that the difference is more ecological in nature and reflects the sharply demarcated environments of the Highlands. This may also explain some of the subsistence differences noted between these sites. Domesticated sheep and goat account for half of the faunal assemblage at GQi and are twice as common as domesticated cattle (Edens and Wilkinson 1998: 69). Wild cattle, an unidentified equid and ibex were also hunted. In contrast, cattle are much more common than sheep and goat at WTHiii, perhaps reflecting differences in available pasture. Evidence for cultivation is non-existent, but it is possible that wild grasses and other plants were processed.

The use of obsidian for the manufacture of stone tools at numerous sites in the Highlands and Tihama is one of the defining features of this period (Khalidi 2009; Khalidi et al. 2010; Tosi 1986a; Zarins 1989a, 1990). Initial research by Francaviglia (1985, 1990) raised the possibility that some of this obsidian was obtained from across the Red Sea in the Horn of Africa. More recent analysis of obsidian sources and artefacts from the Highlands and Tihama suggests a much more complicated picture in which both linked and delineated interaction spheres exploiting local sources connected the Highlands and the Tihama with each other and with northeastern Africa (Khalidi et al. 2010) (Figure 3.2). African obsidian was imported in an already semi-worked fashion into many sites in the Tihama, suggesting regularized contact and exchange (Khalidi 2009; Khalidi et al. 2010). That the inhabitants of the Tihama procured their obsidian from the Horn of Africa should come as no surprise: although obsidian sources in the Yemeni Highlands were closer as the crow flies, travelling up the escarpment and across the Highlands would be more difficult than crossing to the northeast African coast, possibly through the many islands that are found in the southern reaches of the Red Sea.

In contrast, the inhabitants of the Highlands appear to have utilized both local and northeast African sources of obsidian (Barca et al. 2012). The extent to which these divergent procurement patterns were the result of qualitative differences in obsidian remains unknown. At the same time, the most recent research has shown that highland sources, such as that found at Yafa ridge, were

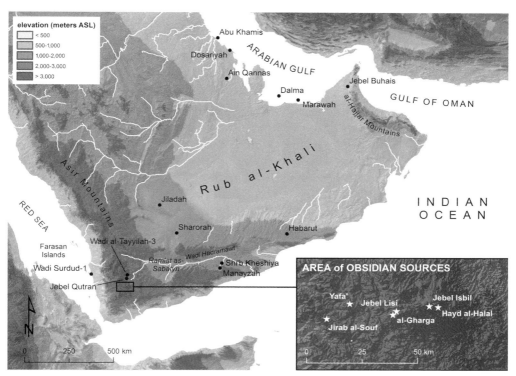

Figure 3.2. Main Neolithic sites dating from the sixth and fifth millennia BC in southern Arabia.

traded as far as Omani Dhofar, more than a 1,000 kilometers to the east (Khalidi et al. 2010). As Khalidi notes, 'The factors that influenced prehistoric populations to exploit certain obsidian sources and not others and to move through diverse territories, sometimes at very large distances, is possibly representative of larger patterns of socio-economic behavior and cultural appropriation' (Khalidi 2009: 87). Regardless of why this interaction occurred, the movement of obsidian within and between these zones can be viewed as an important archaeological proxy for the mobile nature of the Neolithic population of Arabia.

The Jol plateau, which is incised by the deep Wadi Hadramawt and its tributaries, lies to the east of the Highlands. Recent excavations in one such tributary, the Wadi Sana, have detailed evidence for early to middle Holocene occupation of this area of Yemen (Crassard et al. 2006; McCorriston and Martin 2009). The sites of Manayzah and Kheshiya are of particular importance. Well-preserved in situ remains, consisting largely of hearths, were excavated at Manayzah. A ^{14}C date (c. 7400–6700 BC) on one of these hearths produced the earliest securely attested Holocene occupation thus far discovered in southwestern Arabia (McCorriston and Martin 2009). Although this level produced few remains, subsequent layers produced a wide range of faunal and lithic material. Cattle, sheep, goat and gazelle dominated the sixty-nine bones that could be identified to the species level. It is likely that these remains include domesticated animals, but hunting was still clearly important in the subsistence strategy, even more so if some of the goat remains are, in fact, local wild ibex. Local obsidian and flint tools provide further information on the ancient economy at Manayzah. While some show typological parallels to the broader Arabian bifacial tradition, discrete and unique forms of projectiles dominate the assemblage. As previously noted, fluting was particularly important at Manayzah, and according to Crassard (2009) some of the fluting was functionally redundant, suggesting that the creation and use of such tools had a broader social-symbolic meaning or role.

Flint scatters attributable to the Arabian bifacial tradition have also been found farther north, from the Asir (Zarins et al. 1981: 20–21) to the central regions of Saudi Arabia. Increased rainfall during the sixth and fifth millennia transformed the Rub al-Khali into a rich zone for pastoralism. Lakes in various areas would have served as critically important water holes for human and animal consumption. Today, with considerably less than 100 millimeters of rainfall, vegetation still occurs in the Rub al-Khali. In the northern Rub al-Khali, the *ghada* shrub (*Haloxylon persicum*) is common, while in the interior of the deserts, *hadh* (*Cornulaca arabica*) and *abal* (*Calligonum crinitum*) grow. Each of these sustains human life today in one form or another: as a vegetable for consumption, as firewood or even as an ingredient in the tanning of animal skins to make leather, as with abal (Mandaville 2011: 140). During the Holocene Moist Phase, these plants are likely to have existed in greater quantities and were probably accompanied by other plants that provided grazing and subsistence potential.

It is perhaps not surprising, therefore, that archaeological research has indicated that the Rub al-Khali was anything but empty during these millennia. Neolithic occupation was first detailed by Edens (1982) on the basis of four sites at the western and southern edges of the desert. Jiladah, Sharorah, Janub al-Mutabthat and a site near Manfadin are concentrated in inter-dunal troughs and gravel ridges near water-laid sediments. Strong similarities were present in both the tool types and the presence of bifacial working, leading Edens initially to define the 'Arabian bifacial lithic tradition', although noting that there were sub-regional facies within that tradition. Archaeozoological data from these sites suggest the importance of hunting and domesticated sheep and goat at Sharorah and Janub al-Mutabthat. A few years later, Edens (1988) collated earlier survey data obtained by Smith (1976, 1977), Pullar (1985; Pullar and Jäckli 1978) and Field (1958, 1960, 1971) and the material collected by the comprehensive survey of eastern Saudi Arabia (Zarins et al. 1979, 1981), as well as his own material previously collected around Naqdan, to show that sites throughout the Rub al-Khali exhibited strong similarities in stone tool technology and, in many cases, subsistence strategy.

The discovery of Dosariyah in 1968 by Grace Burkholder and the subsequent survey (Bibby 1973: 64–66) and excavations (Drechsler, in press; Masry 1974) revealed extensive evidence not only for contact with Ubaid Mesopotamia (as discussed later) but also for sheep, goat and cattle pastoralism. Farther north on the coast at Abu Khamis, wild animal hunting and fishing/shellfish gathering dominated the subsistence strategy (Masry 1974; Potts 1993a), whereas at Ain Qannas in the Hofuf oasis the domesticates were supplemented by ass (*Equus africanus*). A similarly mixed economy is likely to have been practised farther south at several sites on the edge of the Rub al-Khali in Abu Dhabi (UAE). These include Khor al-Manahil, Kharimat Khor al-Manahil (Cuttler et al. 2007), Yaw Sahhab (Harris 1998; Kallweit 2001) and Bida al-Mutawa (Crombé 2000). A very large Neolithic site near Jebel al-Aluya in the Adam region of central Oman, recently excavated by a French team (Lemée 2013), reinforces our picture of extensive occupation of interior southeastern Arabia until the end of the Holocene Moist Phase.

In addition to the occupation of the Rub al-Khali and its fringes, the coastal plain and the inland alluvial flanks of the al-Hajjar mountains of southeastern Arabia were critical nodes for human settlement during the Neolithic (see discussion of Jebel Buhais later in the chapter). Detailed reconnaissance by the Abu Dhabi Islands Archaeological Project has revealed a wealth of archaeological sites located on the islands and western coastline of the UAE (Beech et al. 2005; Beech and Shepherd 2001; Hellyer 1988, 1992). The sites of Marawah and Dalma are of particular importance (Beech et al. 2005; Beech and Shepherd 2001). Marawah is a low-lying island about 15 kilometers east to west and 6 kilometers north to south. Two sites, MR1 and MR 11, attest to Neolithic occupation. MR1 consisted of a surface scatter with typical bifacial worked arrowheads and points. MR11 is significantly different and contained a four-room building constructed from local beach rock, a find that represents the earliest known example of stone architecture in the UAE. The house was oval and contained a platform at one end. Flint tools and beads from pearl oyster were recovered, as was a complete imported Mesopotamian vessel. The excavators suggested that more houses are present at the site, and future excavations will reveal the full organization and layout of this settlement.

The construction of a stone house at Marawah reinforces how important exploitation of the coastal zone was during the Arabian Neolithic. In addition to fishing and shellfish gathering, the sea provided turtle, dugong and, in select locations, mangrove wood. Contact with areas across the Arabian Gulf was also clearly important and is an issue I will return to later. Moreover, excavations at the nearby island of Dalma suggest that another traditional component of coastal subsistence might have commenced during this period. At the site of DA11, two carbonized date seeds were recovered alongside numerous post-hole structures and hearths containing a typical Neolithic stone tool assemblage (Beech and Shepherd 2001). Impressions of date seeds were also found

in small fragments of burnt mudbricks. The two carbonized date seeds were
^{14}C-dated and suggested that dates were probably consumed as early as the fifth
millennium BC.

For millennia later, the cultivation of the date palm was critical to oasis settlement throughout Arabia. Its bountiful harvest, as well as the secondary use
of its branches and fronds for the construction of barasti buildings, meant that
up until the recent past it was also a mainstay for coastal settlements in which
few other cultivars could grow. In this regard, the recovery of the Dalma date
seeds is of considerable importance for understanding when coastal exploitation became a formal, reliable component of ancient lifeways in Arabia. That
being said, there is no compelling evidence that the Dalma date seeds represent cultivated, or domesticated, dates as opposed to the collection of wild
dates. There are few known criteria for distinguishing between either state,
and many 'wild' examples of date palms today likely represent 'feral' populations. Nevertheless, it is interesting to consider that the Dalma finds correlate
well with other discoveries of dates in archaeological contexts throughout the
Near East. According to Nesbitt (1993: 30), the two earliest other occurrences
of dates are from Tell el-Oueli in southern Mesopotamia (fifth millennium
BC) and Tepe Gaz Tavila near Daulatabad (5400–4800 BC) in southeastern
Iran. The island of Dalma is located between these regions, and communication between Kerman, southeastern Arabia and southern Mesopotamia was
often intense in prehistory, as it was in the recent past. The possibility that
the inhabitants of Dalma and adjoining regions in the Gulf were beginning
to exploit the date palm, either through cultivation or through intensive wild
harvesting, which may have led to cultivation, must be considered likely but
still unproven.

That the coastal zones of southeastern Arabia became a formal and integral
part of the cultural landscape during the Arabian Neolithic is also indicated
by the presence of burials in Umm al-Quwain in the northern UAE, even if
these are badly preserved and poorly published (Phillips 2002). The remains of
at least forty-one individuals were recovered from this cemetery. Although the
information obtained from these burials pales in comparison with that from
Jebel Buhais (as discussed later), we do know that the dead were buried with
shell beads and oyster pearls. The site was reused numerous times over several
centuries at the end of the fifth millennium BC, suggesting a continued seasonal exploitation of specific coastal locales.

NORTHERN ARABIA

In the north of Saudi Arabia extensive Neolithic occupation has been noted
at Masyoon, 190 kilometers west of Tabuk (al-Ansary 2002), while the comprehensive survey revealed Neolithic flint scatters at numerous sites (Gilmore
et al. 1982: Kilwa and site 202-4; Ingraham et al. 1981: 66; Parr et al. 1978: 36–37;

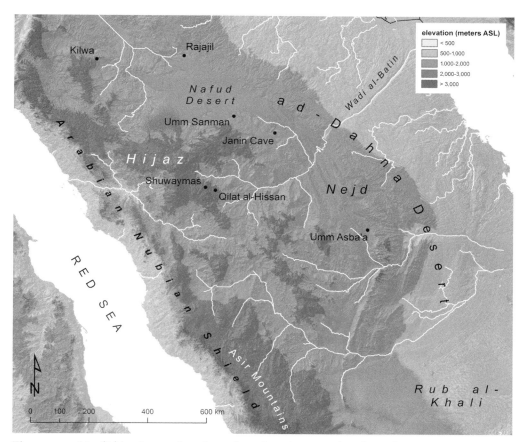

Figure 3.3. Neolithic sites and rock art locations in central and northern Arabia.

Zarins et al. 1980: sites 204, 116, 119, 129, 205, 108). Some of these occur in wadi systems and around rocky outcrops, such as those noted by Ingraham around the Wadi Azlam and Jebel Arrayig al-Yusri and at Wadi Akhdar (Ingraham et al. 1981: 66). Parr (Parr et al. 1978: 36) has also noted that some of these artefact scatters occur within the Nafud desert itself, an observation echoed by Zarins's recovery of Neolithic artefacts in the Banban sands around Riyadh (Zarins et al. 1982: 31–33). The extensive surveys that have identified these surface scatters have also noted the presence of rock art at numerous sites where the sandstone edges of the Arabian shelf provides a suitable canvas for engravings (Figure 3.3). Such rock art had been long noted at Kilwa (e.g., Horsfield et al. 1933), and on the basis of crude stylistic analysis those that show bovids and equids might date to the Neolithic (Gilmore et al. 1982: 21), but few have been subject to the level of analysis undertaken by Anati (1968a, 1968b, 1972, 1974) for the central area of Arabia (see later discussion). Nevertheless, the discovery of comparable rock art in a well-dated settlement at Dhuweilah in

Figure 3.4. Rock art at Shuwaymas, Saudi Arabia. Photo: Lars Bjurstom/Saudi Aramco World/SAWDIA.

eastern Jordan (Betts 1987) confirms a Neolithic date for at least some of these engravings.

More recently, spectacular rock art has been investigated at the sites of Umm Sanman, near the town of Jubbah, and Shuwaymas (Figure 3.4), on the eastern and southern edges of the Nafud respectively, as well as a number of other sites. The rock art at Jubbah is located on the base of an escarpment adjacent to the remains of a lakebed that was likely filled during the Holocene Moist Phase (Bednarik and Khan 2005: 52; Garrard and Harvey 1981; al-Suad et al. 2005). Scatters of Neolithic tools confirm occupation during the sixth millennium BC. According to Bednarik and Khan (2005: 54), cattle, gazelle, oryx, ibex, lion, dog, horse or donkey, ostrich and dromedary are represented. The oldest, possibly Neolithic, rock art consists of 'human and animal figurines, depicted at prominent places, mostly facing east. The typical anthropomorphs with thin linear arms holding "bows and arrows" often occur with large bovid figures with tapering faces and long-horns' (Bednarik and Khan 2005: 54). Whether or not these figures and associated representations of throwing sticks or 'boomerangs' indicate that hunting was widespread is simply unknown because of the inherent chronological uncertainties of rock art. GIS analysis of the rock art at Jebel Katefeh indicates that those images which contain representations of cattle and ibex are oriented towards the position of the palaeolake (Jennings et al. 2013), thus supporting an early date for the rock art. At Shuwaymas on the southern edges of the Nafud an even more extensive rock art site has been discovered, and the final publication of this site is awaited. In the interim, ongoing survey of northern Arabia (Kabawi et al. 1989, 1990) has continued to reveal widespread rock art sites. There is no question that this rock art is of fundamental importance for understanding the Neolithic lifeways of the inhabitants of the Nafud and northern Arabia. In extent, size and intricate nature, it is comparable to Saharan rock art found in Libya, Egypt, Algeria and Morocco, much of which is associated with a climatic optimum throughout North Africa (Kuper and Kröpelin 2006) that is in many ways comparable to that found in Arabia at this time. Further systematic research on this rock art, combined with new technologies of dating, have the potential to contribute to our understanding of the Neolithic in northwestern Arabia in a profound fashion.

That the interior of Saudi Arabia continues to provide new and important discoveries on the Arabian Neolithic is no more clearly indicated than by the reported discoveries at al-Magar, which have been covered in numerous press releases. The accidental discovery by a local farmer of stone tools, carved stone objects and, most extraordinarily, stone statuettes of some form of equid along with organic material ^{14}C-dated to the Neolithic period has raised the possibility that the site is of unique importance for understanding adaptation to the interior of the Arabian desert. Claims that the site represents a location for the initial domestication of horses have served to increase the site's fame. Formal excavations at the site have now begun, and it is to be hoped that the expeditious publication will permit a full assessment of its importance.

THE FORMATION OF A NEOLITHIC ARABIAN SOCIETY

A new and distinctive culture thus flourished in the centuries following the introduction of domesticated animals to Arabia. Firmer chronological data are needed for the millennia prior to this, but it is very likely that this new Neolithic lifeway incorporated aspects of an existing hunter–gatherer subsistence strategy. Mobility was key to these developments. The increased summer rainfall brought about by the Indian Ocean monsoon created a tapestry of rich ecological niches that, when exploited by pastoralism and hunting, provided the basis for a successful subsistence strategy. The resources of no single environment dominated subsistence, nor were they controlled and restricted by any single group. Rather, the mobile component of their lifestyle ensured that population groups had access to divergent environments, almost certainly on a seasonal basis.

As Edens (1988: 36–38) noted many years ago, the distribution of softstone, obsidian, worked stone and marine shell some distance from their original sources suggests intensive interaction between these population groups during the Arabian Neolithic. A recent study has indicated that at least some of the obsidian found in Kuwait at this time actually comes from Yemen (Khalidi 2011), thus indicating a truly peninsula-wide interaction sphere. This interaction had the potential to result in conflict over grazing rights, access to water and so on, and the evidence for Jebel Buhais (see later discussion) suggests that some conflict did indeed occur. However, regularized interaction between groups would also have provided an opportunity for the alignment of ideological and social systems across the entire peninsula. As Frachetti has demonstrated for the nomadic Eurasian steppe, such interaction can be characterized as a form of 'nonuniform complexity' in which 'organizational structures – such as shared trade parameters, building conventions, ideological symbolism, or even the value or signification of particular technological innovations – demonstrate periodic institutional alignments among participant communities without demanding they be subsumed under a coherent political structure or social identity' (Frachetti 2012: 19). Shared principles between and within groups shaped access to resources and, in doing so, restricted control by one group or one segment of a society. It is perhaps at this time, then, that a system of social cohesion, or assabiya, arose and was cemented as an ideological system across the peninsula. The extent to which this system resulted in subsistence strategies that permitted successful human adaptation to the Arabian environment is no more clearly indicated than by recent bioarchaeological research at Jebel Buhais in the UAE.

Excavated by a joint team from the University of Tübingen and the Sharjah Directorate of Archaeology between 1996 and 2005, Jebel Buhais lies in the interior al-Madam plain of Sharjah about 70 kilometers from the modern-day UAE coast (Uerpmann et al. 2006, 2008) (Figures 3.2 and 3.5). Numerous Iron Age and Bronze Age burials are known from around Jebel Buhais, but our comments will focus on the Neolithic site of Buhais 18. Although classed as one site, Buhais 18 consists of at least 500 burials that are effectively part of a single grave used over several centuries during the fifth millennium BC. Both primary and secondary burials are known from the site: primary burials consist of single articulated inhumations, while secondary burials were the result of several stages of treatment, including exposure of the corpse and collecting the bones for interment (Figures 3.6 and 3.7). Because the cemetery was used over several centuries, differentiating between secondary burials and disturbed primary burials was not always possible. Eleven burials were partly burnt in situ, but no other evidence of cremation was found.

Kutterer's (2010) analysis suggests that the secondary burials represent those who died some distance from Buhais, probably on their annual seasonal pastoral routes between the coast and the mountains. This was particularly evident in one burial in which bones had been reinterred to replicate a primary burial. Kutterer notes that '[t]he long bones of arms and legs are also put more or less in the places where they would be found in a primary burial, but also often in reverse position. Obviously the corpse was in a state of partial decomposition

Figure 3.5. View of Jebel Buhais excavations, Sharjah, United Arab Emirates.
Photo: Jebel Buhais Excavations.

Figure 3.6. Primary Neolithic burials, Jebel Buhais 18, Sharjah, United Arab
Emirates. Photo: Jebel Buhais Excavations.

when it was excavated from its primary interment. Therefore some skeletal
parts were still connected by soft tissues while others were already disconnected' (Kutterer 2010: 6). Geological sediments found with this burial were
allochthonous to the Buhais region; among these were pebbles that are found
only in the al-Hajjar mountains, more than 25 kilometers away.

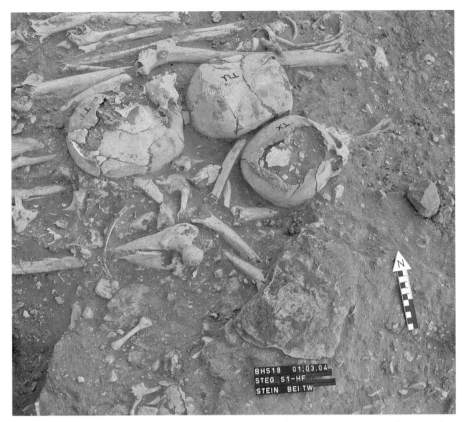

Figure 3.7. Secondary Neolithic burials, Jebel Buhais 18, Sharjah, United Arab Emirates. Photo: Jebel Buhais Excavations.

The dead of Jebel Buhais were buried with a wide variety of personal adornments that reflect the multiple environments in which they lived. Necklaces, pendants or bracelets made from a variety of minerals, such as serpentine, agate, chert or carnelian from the mountains, or shell and coral from the coast, were found on most articulated burials (Kiesewetter 2006: 115). A small number of pierced pearls were also found, and mother of pearl was used to make a number of leaf-shaped pendants (de Beauclair et al. 2006) (Figure 3.8). No other grave offerings, such as flints or animal bones, were found in the burials. The distribution and frequency of ornamentation within the burials were, however, not random. There is clear evidence that children were buried with more beads than adults and that, furthermore, children were typically adorned with more labour-intensive beads, such as stone tubular beads, whereas adults and the 'elderly' were typically adorned with shells. De Beauclair suggests that these adornments, which were likely positioned at the time of burial, either indicate a specific burial rite related to the age of the deceased or mark the greater social loss at the death of a child than at the death of an adult (de Beauclair 2010).

Figure 3.8. Neolithic burial decorated with pearl and softstone beads. Photo: Jebel Buhais Excavations.

A number of firepits and hearths, some older, others contemporary with the burials, provide evidence on the subsistence strategy practised at Jebel Buhais 18. Domesticated sheep, goat, and to a lesser extent cattle formed the mainstay of the faunal component of the diet. Hunted animals (dromedary, oryx, wild ass [*Equus africanus*], gazelle) were rare, representing only 11.4% of the meat in the diet (Uerpmann and Uerpmann 2008a). There are no indications, in the form of either archaeobotanical remains or grinding platforms, of agriculture of any kind. The inhabitants of Buhais were thus pastoral nomads like those Neolithic populations discussed earlier with whom they shared flintworking technology. The excavators suggest that the population spent the spring at Buhais, the summer in the nearby al-Hajjar mountains and the winter on the coast. Each of these environments provided important inputs into the diet, and while the exploitation of each may not be reflected in the archaeozoological material, the beads and pendants discussed earlier come from each of these regions, including both the Arabian Gulf and Gulf of Oman coasts. Jebel Buhais, as a central and visible point between all these environments, would have played, therefore, a key role in their seasonal pattern of migration. The Buhais 18 community thus 'consisted most likely of extended families roaming in widely dispersed groups, and we assume that, for many generations they used the site at Jebel Buhais as a meeting place. The location … lies on a flat ground in the lee of a hillside; there is access to grazing land, firewood, and to a spring, which holds a supply of water. Moreover, the excavation has revealed that BHA 18 was not only used as a campsite but also as a burial ground where the nomads interred their deceased and probably celebrated funeral rites' (Kiesewetter 2006: 115).

The excavation of so many skeletons provides an unparalleled window into the health, diet and lifestyle of the nomadic pastoralists of the Arabian Neolithic. Life expectancy for males and females differed significantly: more females than males died in their teens and 20s, the average age was 33, while male mortality peaked around 40, with an average life expectancy of 36 (Kiesewetter 2006). The causes of death also varied: peri-mortem (near or before death) trauma was more marked in males; the higher mortality at a younger age for females was likely related to childbirth. In her report on the skeletons excavated until 2000, Kiesewetter (2006) argued that males and females were treated similarly during burial. Excavations from 2000 to 2005 confirmed this in respect to spatial divisions within the burial, although the number of males interred as secondary burials increased significantly (Kutterer 2010).

Dietary analysis was based on several aspects of the skeletal record, with 2,499 teeth providing particularly important information. Tooth wear, particularly heavy molar wear brought about by repetitive chewing, indicates a diet rich in meat. A complete absence of caries stands in contrast to the condition of teeth in later populations of the UAE who consumed dates and cereals. These patterns were consistent across the population: no differences were observed between males and females. Some elderly members of the community suffered from gout, but plentiful meat, supplemented with milk and, presumably, some local vegetation, ensured a healthy diet. No cases of vitamin D, vitamin C or calcium deficiency and only rare indications of severe nutritional stress were observed. Most of the latter were observed in younger children and were likely related to weaning stress. Remarkably, the inhabitants of Neolithic Buhais exhibited less nutritional stress than their Bronze Age and Iron Age descendants. They were also taller. In fact, the males were taller than the modern inhabitants of the region (Kiesewetter 2006: 234–235).

In spite of their relatively good health and diet, the inhabitants of Buhais 18 were much more susceptible to trauma than subsequent populations of southeastern Arabia. Almost 14% of juvenile and adult skeletons (i.e., more than 15 years of age) exhibited some form of trauma. Trauma to the skull was most common, but injuries to the arms and hands were also noted. Accidental fractures and trauma were relatively rare. Most wounds did not heal and were fatal, suggesting that the violence was severe and probably the result of clashes between the Buhais 18 community and other nomadic groups. Kiesewetter (2006) makes the compelling argument that this violence was a result of pastoral groups competing over grazing lands.

In the absence of any other comparable published Neolithic burials, it is difficult to gauge the extent to which the inhabitants of al-Buhais should be considered representative of the broader Arabian Neolithic population. It is certainly the case that the defining aspects of their subsistence strategy – mixed sheep and goat herding, and seasonal access to coastal and mountain environments – were common to many parts of Arabia from the southwest to the east. If we can accept, therefore, the Buhais inhabitants as exemplars of the Arabian Neolithic, it can be concluded that by the sixth millennium BC the inhabitants of Arabia had crafted a subsistence strategy that combined the security of pastoralism with the varied subsistence opportunities provided by a seasonal lifestyle. The health and diet of those interred at al-Buhais 18 ensured that people were relatively free from dietary stress and nutritional deficiencies. This subsistence strategy also differentiated the population buried at Jebel Buhais from contemporaries in the Fertile Crescent in two fundamental ways.

Firstly, although there are no similarly studied data from elsewhere in the Middle East that date to this time, generic data on life expectancy are available: According to Rathbun's (1982: 54) analysis of Chalcolithic sedentary agriculturalists from numerous sites in Iraq, Iran and the Levant, males typically died at 30 and females at 28. In other words, the population buried at Jebel Buhais lived on average 15% longer than their contemporaries in and around the Fertile Crescent. Larsen's (1995) extensive review of biological changes in early agriculture communities supports the assertion that those living in the early agricultural communities of Mesopotamia and the Levant suffered higher degrees of infection, caries, disease and nutritional stress than contemporary or earlier populations of mobile non-agriculturalists, like those of Jebel Buhais (but see Gage and DeWitte 2009 for some of the problems associated with palaeodemographics of early agriculturalists).

Secondly, the absence of differential access to foodstuffs on the basis of gender, age and rank at Jebel Buhais stands in stark contrast to the situation of contemporary populations in the Fertile Crescent. Consistent evidence for the emergence of hierarchies based on these social variables is pronounced at agricultural settlements from the PPN period onwards in Mesopotamia, Syria and the Levant. This is reflected in osteological evidence (Molleson 1994) as well as burial rites, settlement architecture and figurative art (Peterson 2010).

In summary, the extraordinary evidence from Jebel Buhais when combined with the archaeological data from an increasing number of sites across the Peninsula indicates that Neolithic Arabia was environmentally and socially different from the rest of the Middle East. The environmental challenges and potentials of a diverse and variegated landscape that was quite unlike that which existed in the Fertile Crescent resulted in the formation of a society constructed upon cohesion and equilibrium. This society did not, however, exist in a vacuum, and intensive interaction with its neighbours marked a further stage in reinforcing and modifying the character of Arabian Neolithic society. It is to the analysis of the first of these interactions that I now turn.

FIRST CONTACT: MESOPOTAMIA, THE UBAID AND THE
ARABIAN NEOLITHIC

Beginning in the late sixth millennium BC, the nomadic pastoralists of eastern Arabia come into contact with sedentary agriculturalists who had within
the *longue durée* of prehistory only recently occupied the southern reaches of
the Mesopotamian alluvium. This is the first of many contacts between groups
whose social, economic and, increasingly, political configurations were vastly
different from each other.

The most obvious evidence for contact is the Ubaid pottery found at more
than sixty sites in eastern Arabia (Carter 2006: 58) (Figure 3.9). It is unevenly
distributed on the east Arabian littoral, with several larger sites, mostly in eastern
Saudi Arabia (e.g., Dosariyah, Abu Khamis, Ain Qannas; see Masry 1974) and
Kuwait (as-Sabiyah), containing significant quantities of Ubaid 3/4 material.
The most important of these is, without doubt, Dosariyah, which currently lies

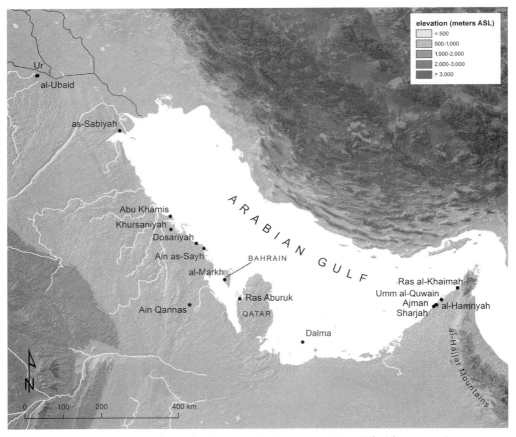

Figure 3.9. Location of main coastal sites containing Ubaid pottery in eastern
Arabia.

less than a kilometer from the coast and consists of a widespread surface scatter with several meters of intact stratigraphy (Drechsler, in press). Thousands of Ubaid and possibly locally produced sherds along with shells and stone tools are reported from this site (Drechsler, in press). Less sizeable quantities are found in smaller sites at Ras Aburuk and al-Markh on Bahrain and on the Abu Dhabi islands north to Ras al-Khaimah in the UAE. That these ceramics are imported from southern Mesopotamia, rather than being local copies, is indicated by geochemical analysis, which shows they are consistent with a southern Mesopotamian source (Oates et al. 1977). The possibility that the ceramics were specifically produced in Ur was raised several years ago by Oates, but subsequent analysis has indicated only a generic south Mesopotamian origin (Roaf and Galbraith 1994). Other than the presence of Mesopotamian pottery, the material culture of these sites fits perfectly within the range of the local Arabian Neolithic: the flints are largely consistent with those found at inland sites which also share a mixed hunting/nomadic pastoralism subsistence strategy. Other materials might also have been transported to eastern Arabia during this time. It has long been thought that the obsidian stone tools found at sites of this period were coming from eastern Anatolia/Armenia and were carried by the same sailors bringing the Ubaid pottery. As previously noted, however, recent evidence (Khalidi 2011) for a Yemeni source of some obsidian might overturn this hypothesis. Only further research and scientific testing will provide firmer data on this issue.

Recent excavations at as-Sabiyah in Kuwait have provided a more detailed picture of the maritime technology that lay behind the distribution of Ubaid pottery (Carter 2006; Carter and Crawford 2010) (Figure 3.10). In addition to large quantities of Ubaid pottery, clay models of boats made in a local red ware (Figure 3.11), paintings of boats on ceramics and more than fifty fragments of bitumen were found. The bitumen contains barnacles (Figure 3.12) and reed impressions that reflect their original use as caulking, or waterproofing, for the craft that must have sailed south from the Shaṭṭ al-Arab in southern Mesopotamia down the Arabian Gulf.

The presence of imported Ubaid pottery has often been assumed to represent a single economic phenomenon that had a defined social effect on the local Arabian population (Masry 1974; Oates et al. 1977). To some extent, this approach reflects the way scholars understand Ubaid expansion elsewhere, particularly in northern Mesopotamia. In that case, contact was characterized by the wholesale importation or production of Ubaid or Ubaid-like materials in northern Iraq and southeastern Turkey during the Ubaid 3/4 period. While there is considerable disagreement about the effects of this expansion (e.g., Stein et al. 2006) and recent excavations may have cast doubt on its directionality and chronology, few scholars would not accept that it represents a sustained cultural and economic phenomenon.

Figure 3.10. View of Neolithic site of as-Sabiyah, Kuwait. Photo: Robert Carter, as-Sabiyah Excavations.

Figure 3.11. Model of a boat made in local red ware, as-Sabiyah, Kuwait. Photo: Robert Carter, as-Sabiyah Excavations.

It is not entirely clear that this is the case with the Ubaid material found in eastern Arabia. Firstly, there is still a considerable lack of clarity concerning the chronology of this interaction. In her detailed analysis of Masry's initial publication of Ain Qannas, Abu Khamis and Dosariyah, Joan Oates brought attention to the fact that while most of the Ubaid ceramics from these and related sites date to the Ubaid 2 (late) to Ubaid 3 period, '[m]uch of the painted

Figure 3.12. Bitumen with barnacles from as-Sabiyah, Kuwait. Photo: Robert Carter, as-Sabiyah Excavations.

'Ubaid pottery from Abu Khamis is undoubtedly later than that published from Dosariyah, but the two sites are certainly partially contemporary' (Oates 1976: 26). Carter (2006: 58) notes that both these sites contain appreciable quantities of Ubaid 4 ceramics, as do the recently excavated sites of DA11 on the island of Dalma. In contrast, as-Sabiyah on Kuwait contains only Ubaid 2/3 ceramics. On the other chronological extreme are the ceramics from al-Markh and Ras Aburuk on Bahrain, which, according to Oates (1976), post-date the Ubaid period completely and may be labelled 'Terminal Ubaid'.

When we consider the absolute chronology of these ceramics, it is clear that they span nearly the entirety of the Ubaid 2 to 4 period, that is, c. 5000–3800 BC. Through this time frame, there is also considerably variation in the spatial distribution of Ubaid ceramics. Abu Khamis, Dosariyah and Ain Qannas clearly account for the majority of Ubaid sherds found in the entire region, while Khursaniyah also contained 'a fairly large quantity' (Carter 2006: 59). At Dosariyah, there is stratigraphic evidence for multiple phases of occupation – all of which contain Ubaid sherds (Drechsler, in press). The precise number of sherds found at these sites remains unknown, but in measuring the impact of Ubaid contact it is clear that we should focus on the immediate area of these three sites and the Eastern Province of Saudi Arabia.

What economic benefit did sailors derive from bringing Ubaid ceramics to this area of Arabia? Copper, which becomes the most important export of eastern Arabia in the third millennium BC, can be ruled out, as there is no evidence for its mining during this period. One possibility that has been raised by several scholars (Oates et al. 1977: 233; Phillips 2002) is that Ubaid pottery and other materials were exchanged for pearls. The pearling industry in the Arabian Gulf is, of course, well known in pre-modern times, but it is clear that this industry is of considerable antiquity (Carter 2005a). More than 100 pearls have been found at fourteen sites dating between the sixth and fourth millennia

BC in southeastern Arabia (Charpentier et al. 2012: 2). They occur from the Arabian Gulf coast of the UAE to Ras al-Hadd facing the Indian Ocean, and many are found in burials, where they were clearly used to adorn the dead. In addition, pearl shells (*Pinctada margaritifera* and *Pinctada radiata*) have been found at numerous Neolithic sites such as Akab and Dalma on the Gulf coast (Beech and Elders 1999: 19; Méry et al. 2009) and Khor al-Milkh on the Gulf of Oman coast (Uerpmann 1992). These were used for making fishing hooks at each site and, of course, the flesh could also be consumed. Preliminary reports from the most recent excavations at Dosariyah indicate that the pearl shell is so common (Drechsler, in press) that it is unlikely it was used only for the production of fishing hooks, leaving open the possibility that intensive pearling took place there.

Whether or not pearls and pearl shells were prized commodities that were exported to Ubaid Mesopotamia remains, however, conjecture. Carter has suggested that the Tigris and Euphrates contain their own pearl shells (Carter et al. 1999: 57); however, the long history of pearling in the Gulf and the export of pearl products suggests that these Mesopotamian examples – if ever exploited – were of very poor quality. More research is certainly needed, and the use of pearls in Ubaid Mesopotamia must be confirmed. At this stage, only the subsequent Uruk period has revealed evidence of pearls (Donkin 1998), but it should be remembered that without the use of sieves and modern recovery methods it is extremely unlikely that pearls will come to the attention of the excavator.

The impact that contact with Ubaid Mesopotamia had on the inhabitants of eastern Arabia has been similarly debated. Carter has noted that the Ubaid pottery found in Arabian Neolithic contexts was oriented 'towards serving and display, both of the ceramics themselves and of the food served. It is proposed that Ubaid pottery was not only used to present food, but was also redistributed in acts of ceremonial gift-giving or exchange at communal events, perhaps in feasting contexts' (Carter 2006: 60). Ubaid ceramics thus had the potential to significantly alter economic and social strategies in the Neolithic populations inhabiting eastern Saudi Arabia. The clearest evidence that this did, in fact, take place is the appearance of a local ceramic industry at several sites in eastern Saudi Arabia and Kuwait. A coarse, chaff-tempered handmade red ware is found at the initial points of contact with the Ubaid world – as-Sabiyah, Abu Khamis and Dosariyah – but not at the inland site of Ain Qannas. According to Oates, this pottery makes up some 60–70% of the assemblage at the larger sites in the central Arabian Gulf (Oates et al. 1977: 222). Judging by preliminary results of the ongoing excavations at Dosariyah, it is found in a variety of shapes – including storage jars and serving vessels. It is difficult to accept, therefore, that this red ware 'represents the ad hoc manufacture of pottery by ceramically untrained Ubaid fishermen or traders, which nevertheless may have been exchanged by them in order to obtain goods from the local population', as suggested by Potts (1993: 176). Rather, its production should be seen as a local economic choice that was embedded in broader decisions concerning labour division and economic roles in a society that was clearly absorbing elite goods into a changing social structure.

In measuring the impact of such contact, we need also to consider how the inhabitants of sites such as Dosariyah, Ain-Qannas and Abu Khamis absorbed knowledge of how Ubaid society functioned. As Frangipane (2007) has convincingly shown, Ubaid society was at this time experiencing rapid social, political and economic change. According to her, it was quickly moving from a 'horizontal egalitarian structure' to a 'vertically egalitarian structure' and experiencing 'a widening gap between the population and a leadership, which was initially only ideological and kinship-based, and which subsequently acquired more social and political roles, leading to an increased capacity to centralize wealth.... New privileged households probably emerged through delegations of power and the attribution of tasks to families with a closer kinship to the chief. In other words, the potential of social stratification inherent in a conical kinship system was able to take on the increasing internal economic competition in fully agriculture-based communities living in a highly productive but unstable environment' (Frangipane 2007: 169). In other words, Ubaid sailors (or Arabian sailors going to Mesopotamia – we still don't know who actually conducted this trade) would have brought knowledge and experiences of a social order that was vastly different from Arabian Neolithic society (or vice versa).

These differences in social order would have been communicated by knowledge, stories and accounts of the economy of Ubaid Mesopotamia. Irrigation agriculture was the key component of the Ubaid economy (Stein 1994) and was tied to the emergence of large permanent settlements and monumental public and ritual spaces, as at Eridu (Safar et al. 1981: 86–114) and Tell Uqair (Lloyd and Safar 1943). Although there were no rivers in eastern Arabia, wells that tap the massive aquifers underlying the east Arabian coast could have easily sustained a similar agricultural regime, just as they did millennia later. Yet there is no evidence that the inhabitants of eastern Arabia shifted towards an agricultural or sedentary existence. As Dietler has argued in his study of consumption and interaction between Greece, Rome and Iron Age France, such 'negative consumption' is an important part of contact and exchange: 'It is necessary to understand what goods and practices were available for appropriation but were ignored or refused, and why this particular pattern of selective consumption emerged from a range of possibilities. In brief, we must find a way to discern and explain the choices that were made' (Dietler 2010: 57). This is of particular importance in reference to Ubaid trade and contact, since it has been suggested that societies elsewhere in the Middle East were structurally influenced by elements of complexity within Ubaid society (e.g., Gibson 2010; cf. Karsgaard 2010). In contrast, the inhabitants of Neolithic eastern Arabia rejected agriculture and the trappings associated with the emergence of complex society in southern Mesopotamia. As a result, the economic basis and social cohesion of Neolithic Arabia were reaffirmed. That is not to say, however, that contact with Ubaid Mesopotamia did not change parts of eastern Arabia. In later chapters, I explore the extent to which the subsequent divergent trajectories in social and political order experienced by different regions within Arabia may be attributed to this first period of contact.

COPING WITH UNCERTAINTY: THE LATE FIFTH AND FOURTH MILLENNIA BC

By the late fifth millennium BC, evidence for the distinctive subsistence strategy and tool kit of the Arabian Neolithic and interaction with southern Mesopotamia declines precipitously. The title 'Dark Millennium' (Uerpmann 2003) has been used to characterize the period between 4000 and 3000 BC, but even those who have used this term have argued that human occupation of southern Arabia experiences massive shifts in subsistence strategy rather than depopulation. That these events are linked to climate change seems certain: the al-Qunf and Hoota cave proxies indicate the southward migration of the Indian Ocean monsoon system to its current position by about 4000 BC, and therefore much of Arabia no longer received any summer rainfall. The palynological data from Kawr al-Jaramah in western Oman (Lézine 2009: 750–759) indicate that this process was gradual and small areas of southern Arabia continued to receive summer monsoon rainfall, just as they do today.

Coinciding with a deteriorating climate is a near absence of occupation of the Eastern Province of Saudi Arabia and south along the shores and interiors of the UAE (Figure 3.13). One of the few sites for which we have detailed evidence for this period is Akab on the shore of a lagoon in Umm al-Quwain, the occupation of which stretches from the fifth into the fourth millennium BC on the basis of numerous ^{14}C dates (Méry et al. 2009). Small soundings at the earlier sites of RA 2 and 3 on the same lagoon suggest close parallels to contemporary inland material culture found, for example, at al-Buhais 18 in the UAE interior (Méry et al. 2009). Conversely, the beads and other stone objects from the late fifth and early fourth millennia BC differ significantly from those that had been made in the earlier Arabian Neolithic, suggesting that the beginning of the fourth millennium BC witnessed a fundamental break in the coastal to inland pastoral exchange that characterized the Arabian Neolithic in this part of southeastern Arabia.

Sites facing the Gulf of Oman provide an exception to this rather limited picture. Excavations at Suwayh 1 revealed a cemetery dating to the end of the fifth millennium BC with tantalizing, but limited evidence of shifting funerary practices during this period (Charpentier et al. 2003). In this part of Oman, Uerpmann (1992) distinguished three lithic facies that date to the subsequent

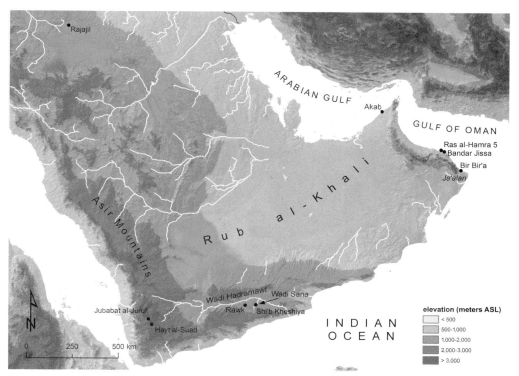

Figure 3.13. Location of main sites of the late fifth and early fourth millennia BC.

fourth millennium BC: the Ras al-Hamra facies defined at RH5, the Bir Bir'a facies named after a site between Quriyat and Ras al-Hadd and the Bandar Jissa facies (Uerpmann 1992). The first two are roughly contemporary, whereas the last dates to the late fourth millennium BC and might properly be considered an aceramic 'Chalcolithic' Age, since the use of copper is associated with it. More recently, Charpentier (2008: 108) has reported more than fifty sites datable to between 3700 and 3000 BC in the Ja'alan, most of them in the coastal zone. According to him (Charpenter 2008: 109), excavations at Ras al-Hadd, Ras al-Jinz, Suwayh and Ras al-Khabbah reveal a pronounced regionalization of stone tool technologies. This likely reflects a decline in interaction between the various population groups inhabiting the different ecologies of the region.

The location of these sites and the large shell middens that accompany site formation attest to the importance of the marine environment for subsistence. In addition, many of the stone tools diagnostic of the Ras al-Hamra facies appear to have specific uses related to shellfish processing, and M. Uerpmann (1992) has argued that the net sinkers are heavy enough to have been used in offshore fishing. Shellfish hooks are common and copper examples are found in the Bandar Jissa facies. Shell- and stoneworking is also common, and the specialized production of stone tools, beads and jewellery made from locally available metamorphic stones occurs at Ras al-Hamra 5 (Cleuziou and Tosi 2007). That site has also revealed evidence for interaction with Iran in the form of a single burnished grey ware pot.

Uerpmann (2003) attributes the intensification of settlement along the Omani coast to the deteriorating climate coupled with the massive environmental and geomorphological differences between the Arabian Gulf coast and the Gulf of Oman coast. The former is a relatively flat desert interface that is rarely fed by waters coming from the al-Hajjar mountains to the east. The situation is different on the Omani coast, where large wadis with significant catchment areas carry fresh water, which increases biodiversity along the coast. As previously noted, freshwater input into the coastal areas did not completely cease in the fourth millennium and was still capable of supporting populations of *Rhizophora*, which in itself would have propagated a rich biotope (Lézine 2009). Archaeozoological evidence confirms a mixed subsistence strategy at known settlements. Domesticated sheep, goat and cattle are found in burials at Ras al-Hamra 5, and as Uerpmann has concluded, '[i]f these bones are the remains of funeral meals, as assumed by the excavators (Salvatori 1996), substantial herds of sheep, goats and cattle must have been kept because in most graves there are remains of more than one and sometimes up to six animals. Such slaughtering events require stable animal populations. In comparison to Jebel Buhais, where the same domestic species are represented, the animals on the Omani coast did not generally suffer from the climatic deterioration of the fourth millennium because the sizes of sheep and goats were equal or even above that of their earlier relatives. Cattle, however, were smaller and fewer than at Jebel Buhais, which might be due to the assumed desiccation. It remains an open question whether the herds could be kept at the coast all year round' (Uerpmann 2003: 79). The coastal zones facing the Gulf of Oman thus appear to have provided a refuge in which populations could exploit marine environments and continue to practise herding during a period of climatic deterioration that adversely affected the inland and Arabian Gulf littoral.

The excavation of 215 graves at Ras al-Hamra 5 (Coppa et al. 1985; Macchiarelli 1989; Salvatori 2007) indicates that even though these coastal regions provided a 'refuge' for habitation, the retreat of the Indian Ocean monsoon and decline in summer rainfall resulted in unparalleled hardships for the inhabitants of southeastern Arabia. The skeletal evidence from these graves indicates that the inhabitants of the coast suffered dietary stress and high mortality. On average, they died at a lower age than those at Jebel Buhais a millennium earlier: more than a quarter of the population died between 20 and 25, and only half of those who survived this age reached 30 (Macchiarelli 1989: 587). There is also compelling evidence for inbreeding within the population, highlighting the inhabitants' isolation. While some studies of prehistoric populations have emphasized the optimal nature of coastal subsistence (e.g., Yesner 1980) and there can be little doubt that the waters of the Gulf of Oman provided much food, it was also the case that the consumption of predominantly marine resources contributed to poor health. Analysis of teeth showed abnormally high attrition, wear and caries attributed to the consumption of grit in dried fish and molluscs. Macchiarelli has argued that it was 'interaction between chronic diarrhoea, exposure to fish-borne parasites, prolonged breast feeding, and protein-caloric malnutrition that could have been largely responsible for stresses resulting in pathological skeletal changes. Moreover, the role of mangrove swamp pathogenic agents on the fishermen's health still has to be fully evaluated, but it is possible to speculate that it was seasonally intense' (Macchiarelli 1989: 587). It is likely that this poor health and the high mortality explain one of the most curious observations at the cemetery at Ras al-Hamra 5. On more than one occasion, women who died in childbirth were accompanied by the baby and, on one occasion, another child (Cleuziou and Tosi 2007: 79). The inability of the society to look after these infants is the most likely cause of their interment.

Grave goods were commonly placed in burials at Ras al-Hamra, with shells and remains of the green turtle (*Chelonia mydas*) often buried alongside the dead. In some cases the placement of a turtle skull and rearrangement of human bones suggest a specific burial ritual involving the metaphysical transformation of the recently deceased into a turtle (Salvatori 2007). The turtle, as an animal which lives in the sea yet produces offspring on the land, would have had a powerful resonance for the inhabitants of Ras al-Hamra, whose lives were locked into a similar duality. Indeed, both marine and freshwater turtles are attested as symbolically powerful animals in traditional coastal societies in South Africa (Hall 2000) and Indonesia (Barraud 1990). For Torres Strait Islanders in Australia, the turtle was a key component of ritual and magic ceremonies that cemented and reinforced their cultural 'seascape' (McNiven 2003). For the inhabitants of Ras al-Hamra, it is possible to speculate that the metaphysical transformation of the dead into a turtle marked a symbolic embrace of, or perhaps return to, the sea, and death thus marked a welcome reversal of the hardships that this coastal community suffered.

There is disagreement, however, about the extent to which the Ras al-Hamra community was a fully 'sedentary coastal community', as argued by Macchiarelli, or a population that continued the coastal (winter) inland (summer) pattern attested during earlier, more climatically optimal periods. According to Cleuziou and Tosi (2007: 80), the inhabitants of Ras al-Hamra spent half of the year in the inland mountain ranges pasturing their animals and hunting. Yet evidence in support of such an hypothesis is minimal. To argue that it is simply an artefact of discovery that has yet to reveal an inland site comparable to Jebel Buhais 18 is to downplay the compelling evidence for climatic deterioration that disproportionately affected the viability of intensive human settlement in the inland regions. Similarly, Lézine (Lézine et al., 2010), drawing upon the discovery of numerous inland sites in the Wadis Hadramawt and Sana and in the Yemeni Highlands, has argued that there remained an important interior occupation in southeastern Arabia. She counters the lack of evidence for such a scenario by claiming that the undated nature of interior sites that lack diagnostic tools means that many may date to this period (Lézine et al., in press). While this might be the case, the massive geomorphological and climatic differences between southeastern and southwestern Arabia render comparison and parallels between the two regions perilous. The present state of evidence favours the conclusion that although there was occasional pastoralism during episodic precipitation events, the intensive and seasonal occupation of the inland that had characterized earlier millennia is not present during the fourth millennium BC in southeastern Arabia and that societies like those at Ras al-Hamra were true 'coastal communities'.

Lézine is, however, correct in noting that the greater diversity of exploitable environmental niches in interior southwestern Arabia provides the potential for human occupation during this climatic deterioration. Tentative indications of crop irrigation have emerged for the fourth millennium BC in Yemen (Edens 2005; Edens and Wilkinson 1998; Harrower 2008), and Ekstrom and Edens (2003) have suggested that wheat, barley, chickpeas and possibly millet appear in late fourth millennium BC levels at Hayt al-Suad and Jubabat al-Juruf (as discussed later). As noted by Harrower (2008), tentative evidence for runoff irrigation appears at the same time in the Wadi Sana, a tributary of the Wadi Hadramawt in Yemen, and while this type of irrigation might have some superficial similarities to systems in the Levant or Iran, it is unlikely that it is anything but indigenous in origin.

If indeed these irrigation systems do date to as early as the fourth millennium BC, we can see in their design a response to decreasing precipitation, as argued by Harrower (2008). As the climate deteriorated, the precipitation pattern in the Wadi Sana shifted from low-energy long-term runoff to short, high-energy episodes. The inhabitants of the Wadi Sana responded to these climatic shifts by implementing two forms of runoff irrigation: diversion channels captured water from hill slopes, and check dams slowed runoff to allow for the accumulation of sediments and nutrients. GIS modelling of watersheds and the position of these features indicate that people strategically used diversion channels and dams in a highly efficient fashion: diversion channels were used in low-flow areas, while dams were used in high-flow areas to maximize the potential for agriculture.

Both Harrower (2008) and McCorriston (McCorriston and Martin 2009) characterize the inhabitants of the Wadi Sana at this time as 'Pastoralist Irrigators'. It is not known what they grew but, on the basis of compelling ethnographic parallels to agropastoralists in Dhofar (Oman) and Mahra (Yemen), they suggest that the inhabitants of the Wadi Sana were engaged in seasonal transhumance which would cycle between agriculture and cattle pastoralism.

The broader implications of research in the Wadi Sana for the themes of this volume are multitudinous. It is generally agreed that the advent of irrigation agriculture in the rest of the Near East was concomitant with increased social, political and economic complexity. It is clear from later developments in the Hadramawt and the wadi systems bordering the Ramlat as-Sabatyn of Yemen that permanent sedentary-agriculture-based settlement was possible in these areas. Faced with the challenge of declining rainfall and the benefits of irrigation agriculture, the fourth millennium BC inhabitants of the Wadi Sana chose, however, to continue to exploit the multiple adjacent resource zones of southwestern Arabia rather than focus their subsistence strategies on agriculture alone. The continued exploitation of multiple environments, even on an occasional basis, as with those buried at Ras al-Hadd, was facilitated by the alignment of ideologies and social beliefs that had begun during the Holocene Moist Phase. In the deteriorating climate of the fourth millennium BC, community and cross-community ties were of even more importance in limiting conflict as resources became scarcer. Recent excavations in both southeastern and southwestern Arabia suggest that commensality was increasingly deployed as a mechanism to ensure continuity in these ties. Two sites, Shi'b Kheshiya in Yemen and Akab in the UAE, highlight this trend in a spectacular fashion.

SHI'B KHESHIYA, AKAB AND THE POLITICS OF COMMENSALITY

In the later stages of the fifth millennium BC a stone circle, approximately 1 meter in diameter, along with numerous hearths, was constructed at Shi'b Kheshiya in the Wadi Sana (McCorriston and Martin 2009). The stone circle was filled and capped with stone to produce a teardrop-shaped platform. Immediately to the side, forty cattle skulls were pushed into the sediment to form an oval that paralleled the orientation of the platform (Figure 3.14). The skulls belong to domesticated cattle, and age determination via tooth eruption and sedimentary analysis suggests that the skulls belonged to adults that were slaughtered at the same time and then had their skulls removed for placement in the ground (Figure 3.15). As the excavators concluded: 'Available evidence for sacrifice and monument construction seems to point to a collective event that drew large numbers of people not normally resident in the Middle Wadi Sana with its restricted winter grazing. The feasters, normally disbursed, clearly herded domesticated cattle and possibly also mixed herds with caprines.… The stone monument and cattle ring commemorated the convergence of a social group or several social groups whose practice of ritual sacrifice emphasized their community ties' (McCorriston and Martin 2009: 246).

A strikingly similar pattern of community consumption can be found at Akab on the distant southeast Arabian coast. Located on an island in the bay of Umm al-Quwain in the northern UAE (Figure 3.16), the site is discussed earlier in reference to its late Neolithic occupation but is most well known as

Figure 3.14. Platform of cattle skulls, fourth millennium BC, Shi'b Kheshiya, Yemen. Photo: Joy McCorriston.

Figure 3.15. Detail of cattle skulls, Shi'b Kheshiya, Yemen. Photo: Joy McCorriston.

a dugong (*Dugong dugon*) slaughtering site (Méry et al. 2009). The killing of dugong for flesh, hide, tusks and oil was an important part of the Neolithic coastal economy along the Arabian Gulf coast. The most recent excavations indicate that the dugong bones are arranged in a careful, predetermined fashion to form a mound structure (Figure 3.17). The base of the structure consists

Figure 3.16. View of Akab, Umm al-Quwain, United Arab Emirates. Photo: T. Sagory, French Archaeological Expedition to the United Arab Emirates.

of mandibles into which are wedged rib bones oriented towards the east or northeast (Figure 3.18). Rows of skulls, in groups of eight, delineate the front and the rear of the structure, in a manner that is not dissimilar to what is found in Shi'b Kheshiya. The lower levels of the structure were impregnated with red ochre, and evidence of postholes indicated that the structure was either roofed or protected by poles. Softstone beads as well as the remains of domesticated sheep and goat were incorporated into the structure.

For Méry (Méry et al. 2009) Akab had a totemic significance: propitiatory rites were conducted to ensure successful fishing and hunting events. While this might be the case, the fundamental role that mass slaughter and consumption played at Akab, just as at Shi'b Kheshiya in Yemen is also marked. In each case, large numbers of animals were killed and the resultant meat exceeded that which could be consumed by local inhabitants, especially in a hot climate. It is tempting, therefore, to interpret both these sites as the remains of ritualized acts of consumption that incorporated multiple social groups. Such activities would have reaffirmed social and tribal networks, ensured ideological alignment and arrested proprietary control at a time of increasing subsistence stress.

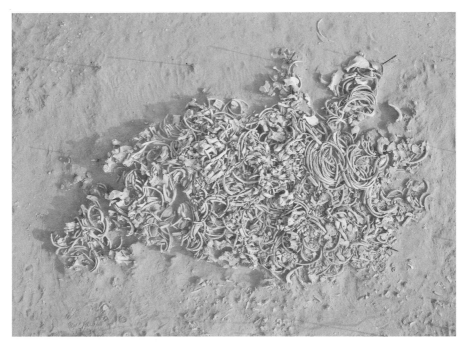

Figure 3.17. Mound of dugong bones, Akab, Umm al-Quwain, United Arab Emirates. Photo: T. Sagory, French Archaeological Expedition to the United Arab Emirates.

Figure 3.18. Detail of dugong bones, Akab, Umm al-Quwain, United Arab Emirates. Photo: V. Charpentier, French Archaeological Expedition to the United Arab Emirates.

CAIRNS, STELAE AND TERRITORIALITY

Although the activities evidenced at Akab and Shi'b Kheshiya served to ensure intra-regional access to resources, overt potential markers of territoriality also emerge as the fourth millennium BC progresses. Towards the end of the fourth millennium BC, cairn tombs are constructed in prominent areas throughout the Wadi Sana in Yemen. If they are, as Harrower (2008) suggests, markers of territoriality, then they represent an attempt at a spatially defined system of landownership, similar to the thousands of slightly later examples found in southeastern Arabia (Chapter 4). As we shall see with the southeast Arabian examples, such tombs need not, however, be an indicator of the emergence of sedentary agricultural communities. Indeed, if the inhabitants of the Wadi Sana had begun to settle in one location all year round, it would have been unnecessary to construct such tombs, since the presence of their settlements would have indicated ownership. Instead, the tombs should be viewed as a compromise between protecting land use and reaping the benefits of a seasonal lifestyle that ensured continued exploitation of the variegated resource zones scattered through southwestern Arabia.

Other evidence for a potential change in the conceptualization of landownership can be found in the unique stone sculptures and decorated stelae that start to appear throughout Arabia in the fourth millennium BC. Sometimes referred to as *menhir* – a word that might be assumed to have an Arabic origin but is in fact of Cornish/Breton etymology – these stone sculptures and stelae take various forms and sizes and are found from Yemen to the north Arabian desert. Two basic categories of menhir can be discerned, the first of which is demonstrably relevant to discussions of the fourth millennium BC. These consist of statuettes carved in the shape of human figures. In Yemen, they have been found in the Khawlan region of the Highlands, in the Jawf and at Rawk in the Jol. When combined with four unprovenanced examples almost certainly from Yemen (Newton and Zarins 2000), this brings the total known from Yemen to sixteen. All these examples have common features: they are carved in stone and consist of detailed modelling of the head with carved features of the torso and legs. A characteristic feature is the representation of the arms, which are brought together in front of the torso. Single or multiple belts and a diagonal sash are the only forms of adornment. Weapons are absent. They are relatively uniform in size: the five examples from Rawk range from 17.5 to 31.5 centimeters, whereas the examples from the Jawf and adjoining regions are from 24 to 40.5 centimeters (Steimer-Herbet 2007, 2010).

Excavations at Rawk in Yemen provide important contextual information on the function of these statuettes (Steimer-Herbet 2007, 2010). At this site, five upright stone slabs were placed into a compacted soil surface in which numerous traces of ash were evident. An adult skull and the almost complete skull of a child and associated fragments of ceramics, a bone pendant and a complete statuette were found against one of the slabs. Adjacent to the stone slabs was a stone bench and ash pits and the fragmentary skeletal remains of a newborn baby. Carbon-14 analysis of the collagen from the associated skeletal material provided a date of 3499–3198 BC.

Strikingly similar statues have been found in Saudi Arabia and Jordan. From the area around al-Ula in the Hijaz, a single sandstone example measuring nearly 1 meter in height was recovered. It displays a stylized human form that is similar to the examples from Yemen. In addition, like some of the examples from al-Jawf in Yemen, a diagonal sash is represented, but unlike all the examples from Yemen the al-Ula statue has a double-edged dagger. As noted by Steimer-Herbet (2010) this dagger is well paralleled in otherwise undated rock art in the Wadi Damm near Tabuk. The three known examples from Hail, on the edge of the Nafud, are also larger than the Yemeni examples. Two of the examples from Hail also exhibit a potentially significant difference in the representation of the arms: whereas all the Yemeni examples show the arms meeting in the front of the torso, these two examples show the arms slightly crossed. Similar iconography is found on the very large statues from Riqseh in eastern Jordan, but further evidence is needed to substantiate the suggestion that this pose is characteristic of the northern tribal regions of Arabia (Steimer-Herbet 2010).

The current patchy state of evidence inhibits our ability to interpret the extent to which the stone statuettes from Yemen, Saudi Arabia and Jordan reflect similarities in burial rituals across the entire region. Nevertheless, such markers represent a new relationship between funerary rites and the conceptualization of the landscape. Although our evidence is also fragmentary for Neolithic burials dating to before 4000 BC, those that we do know about, such as at Jebel Buhais 18, are subterranean and left no obvious physical marker on the landscape. In contrast, the stelae from Rawk and from northern Arabia were visible emplacements upon the terrain. Whether or not such developments reflect a sense of ownership or control over the landscape as might be the case for the cairn tombs discussed earlier remains to be tested. In any case, prefacing these developments, or perhaps even parallel to them, is the evidence from Akab and Shi'b Kheshiya which suggests that cross-community feasting formed a critical part of regional ideology. It is perhaps into this sociocultural context that the enigmatic site of Rajajil should be placed, although until further excavations are conducted at the site much remains unknown about its chronology and function (see Text Box 6).

TEXT BOX 6. RAJAJIL: AN ARABIAN STONEHENGE?

Rajajil is located near the town of Saqaqa in northern Arabia. Given the size and visibility of its remains, there can be no doubt that the occupants of northern Arabia knew of its existence for millennia. It did not come to the attention of Western scholars until 1970 when the epigraphers Fred Winnett and William Reed 'discovered' it during the recording of north Arabian inscriptions. It consists of a more than fifty groups of cut sandstone columns that on first sight appear to be randomly distributed through the landscape. Some of the columns rise to nearly 3.5 meters and are 75 centimeters thick. Investigation of the site by Zarins (1979) in the late 1970s confirmed that the pillars of stones are arranged in a specific pattern.

The site remains one of the most enigmatic yet discovered in Arabia and its exact function a matter of scholarly debate. Zarins has noted that the pillars are oriented generally towards the rising sun. Excavations in one cluster of pillars ruled out any possible domestic function, thus suggesting the existence of a ritual space. The discovery of a few sherds in and around the stone clusters has raised the possibility of a fourth millennium BC date, and certainly the inscriptions found on the columns date to a period after they were erected. Several undated but apparently quite ancient wells have also been discovered nearby. It is possible that the site represents a collective space where pastoral nomads came to meet on a regular basis, perhaps at a time of deteriorating climate, serving a similar collective function as seen at Akab in southeastern Arabia or Shi'b Kheshiya in Yemen. Until further excavations are carried out, however, any interpretation of the site remains in the realm of conjecture.

CONCLUSIONS

From at least the eighth millennium BC, pastoralists and hunters exploited Arabia's relatively fertile environment. Although the domesticated component of their subsistence derived from the Levant, they quickly adapted their food procurement strategies to Arabia's varied landscape. Seasonal mobility ensured that they not only were able to subsist but, on the basis of bioarchaeological data from Jebel Buhais 18, were rewarded with considerable dietary stability. Furthermore, in Arabia, unlike the rest of the Near East during these millennia, there is no evidence of differential access to foodstuffs or other resources that could provide the basis for enduring institutions of authority and power. It is tempting, therefore, to see in the Arabian Neolithic the genesis of tribal structures in which a sense of belonging and social cohesion fostered maintenance and cultural reproduction through subsequent millennia. By the fourth millennium BC, the end of the Holocene Moist Phase brought severe environmental and social challenges. Regardless of whether the subsistence response to these challenges took the form of increased marine exploitation, as at Ras al-Hamra, or experimentation with irrigation and agriculture, as in Yemen, it relied upon intensification of existing niched resources. As the climate deteriorated in the fourth millennium BC, the biggest challenge faced by the Neolithic inhabitants of Arabia was to ensure that access to varied regional niches was maintained. Two very recently excavated but very distant sites, Shi'b Kheshiya in the Wadi Sana of the Jol in Yemen and Akab on the Arabian Gulf coast, suggest that by the fourth millennium BC the emergence of rituals, focused on a central place and associated with the consumption and display of food, played a key role in meeting this challenge and arresting intra- or inter-group competition.

A changing climate was, however, not the only factor that presented challenges to the inhabitants of Arabia. Developments in the economy and social structure of southern Mesopotamia ensured increasing interaction with Arabia. This period of 'first contact' foreshadowed millennia of exchange, interaction and engagement. Arabian society absorbed and responded to this and was sometimes fundamentally altered as a result.

CHAPTER 4

EASTERN ARABIA FROM 3000 TO 2000 BC

THE DISCOVERY OF AN ARABIAN GULF BRONZE AGE

As early as 1880 it was argued that the toponym 'Dilmun', which occurs in Late Uruk (Uruk IV: 3400–3100 BC) texts from Mesopotamia, was synonymous with the island of Bahrain. This discovery we owe to the French-German scholar Julius Oppert, who noted the resemblance between the Greek 'Tylos' and Akkadian 'Tilmun' employed by the Neo-Assyrian King Sargon II (Oppert 1880). Although this identification is now widely accepted, subsequent research has modified our understanding of this term such that it may, at various times, incorporate areas of eastern and northeastern Arabia. In the year before Oppert's publication, the first excavations undertaken in the Arabian Gulf, those of Captain Durand on Bahrain, had confirmed that the occupation of Bahrain was of considerable antiquity. Durand was particularly struck by the thousands of tomb mounds around Aali, which 'forced upon even the most superficial observer that he is standing upon no common soil, but on that of a land which, although now desolate enough, has probably teemed with life, and under whose dust may, possibly, lie the history of countless generations' (Durand 1880: 192).

Durand's recovery of an Akkadian-inscribed stone mentioning the god 'Inzak' or 'Anzak', the patron god of Dilmun (Dalley 2013), piqued the interest of the Assyriologist Sir Henry Rawlinson. In his detailed study of the stone, published as an addendum to Durand's report (Rawlinson 1880), he confirmed Oppert's identification of Dilmun as the island of Bahrain, even though the latter's contribution had already been published three months earlier. To the father of Assyriology, the discovery of antiquities, especially Akkadian inscriptions, on the 'desolate' island of Bahrain and the apparent place Dilmun had in Mesopotamian cosmology was surprising. Rawlinson conjectured that the inhabitants of Dilmun and the Gulf 'owed their early refinement to their position on the great line of traffic between the east and west. Commerce, indeed, has always sharpened the intelligence, and pioneered the way to civilization; and the same influences, which in a later age placed the Phoenicians at the head of European progress, may thus be supposed, at the first dawn of history, to have been in operation in the Persian Gulf' (Rawlinson 1880: 203). This reference to the maritime importance of the Phoenicians was meant to highlight the 'civilizing benefits' of engaging in long-distance trade. Rawlinson was neither convinced nor unconvinced of an ethnic connection between the ancient inhabitants of Dilmun and the Phoenicians, as had been argued by numerous scholars on the basis of statements by Herodotus, Strabo and Pliny.

A decade after Durand's research, Theodore Bent (1890) opened more tombs at Aali. The artefacts he recovered left little doubt for him that the history of Bahrain could be written from the perspective of those great powers, now including the English, that had left or conquered the island: 'In conclusion, I may add that our researches in every way confirmed the statements of Herodotus, Strabo, and Pliny, that the original home of the Puni was the group of the Bahrein, and on quitting these islands we felt what a wonderful commercial pedigree these low lying, unhealthy specks of earth had had. From Phoenicians we pass on to Portuguese, and from Portuguese to Englishmen, who now, as virtual lords of the Persian Gulf, are beginning to recognise their importance' (Bent 1890: 17). In the subsequent decades occasional excavations occurred on Bahrain, including those of Jouannin and Prideaux in the first decade of the twentieth century (Potts 1991a: 209). By the 1920s the myth that connected Phoenician origins with Bahrain had begun to wane (MacAdam 1990: 75). For many scholars the thousands of tombs that dotted the landscape of the island could not, however, be the result of an indigenous process, and thus began what might be considered the second great mythology of Dilmun archaeology. From Jouannin and Mackay in the 1920s to the modern period (e.g., Lamberg-Karlovsky 1982) scholars raised the possibility that Bahrain was, essentially, a huge floating cemetery that was used to bury the inhabitants of adjoining regions, especially Mesopotamia. It was argued that the population of the island could never have been large enough to warrant such a great number of tombs and that its desolate nature was exploited by the inhabitants of Mesopotamia, who did not want to utilize their own rich agricultural fields for the burial of the dead.

It was with the commencement of serious archaeological fieldwork by a Danish team led by P. V. Glob in 1958 that the archaeological record of Bahrain and the Arabian Gulf began to be understood in terms of local cultural processes, leading eventually to Larsen's (1983) magisterial perspective on the ancient and contemporary human ecology of Bahrain. The importance of the Danish excavations are noted in the many references to their work in this chapter. The Danes did not, however, limit their work to Bahrain. Their reconnaissance in Kuwait and Qatar also led to important discoveries. It was the receipt of a telegram in 1953 by Geoffrey Bibby from Temple (Tim) Hillyard working with British Petroleum in Abu Dhabi that led to the opening of a new frontier in Arabian Gulf archaeology. The telegram read simply, 'Twelve tumuli of Bahrain type discovered on island off Abu Dhabi can you and PV come – Tim' (Bibby 1969: 229). A quick weekend flight down from Bahrain and an inspection of the tombs of Umm an-Nar island and the interior oasis of Buraimi confirmed the presence of prehistoric remains, the excavation of which in the coming years was to reveal the Umm an-Nar Bronze Age culture. It seems extraordinary that barely fifty years ago nothing was known about these prehistoric cultures. The transformation of our knowledge in subsequent decades is exceeded only by the transformation of the landscape of southeastern Arabia. When Bibby visited Abu Dhabi, he noted that '[u]ntil very recently the Oman peninsula had been perhaps the most isolated and least explored area of the whole world, and Abu Dhabi was the least known part of the Oman peninsula' (Bibby 1969: 233). Bibby could never have known what a transformation oil was to bring, nor could he have known that the meal he ate that first night in Abu Dhabi, which 'appeared to be a most excellent joint of beef' but turned out to be in fact dugong, spoke of a subsistence strategy with a pedigree stretching back 7,000 years.

Since the late 1950s, dozens of excavations and surveys have clarified the archaeological record of Kuwait, Qatar, Bahrain, eastern Saudi Arabia, the UAE and the Sultanate of Oman. It is hardly surprising that most research has focused on the Bronze Age, since it was this previously unknown culture that the initial Danish excavations revealed. A belief that environmental adaptation was key to understanding settlement intensification throughout the region has emerged as a strong theme in this research. At the same time, geochemical investigation of bronzes, ceramics and other materials has emphasized that eastern Arabia was enmeshed in an extensive network of exchange with Mesopotamia, Iran and South Asia. In this chapter, I approach the archaeology of this time frame with a view to balancing these sometimes competing perspectives. A focus on the archaeology of Arabian society is key to this approach, as it highlights the manner in which the community bonds that were forged during the Neolithic responded to the challenges and benefits brought about by a shifting environmental regime and engagement with societies that were organized in a fundamentally different fashion.

EASTERN ARABIA AND MESOPOTAMIA

Evidence for intensive contact between Mesopotamia and eastern Arabia during the fifth millennium BC was presented in Chapter 3. How late this interaction continued into the fourth millennium BC and what came after is still unclear. Uruk period clay bulla and a stray Uruk sherd near Dhahran hint at a form of contact (Potts 1993a; Zarins et al. 1984). Such artefacts are unknown, however, farther south on the Gulf. During the Jemdat Nasr (3100–2900 BC) and Early Dynastic periods (2900–2300 BC), Mesopotamia saw the emergence of powerful local dynasties whose economic reach expanded outside the south

ED I versd Lagoh

ED I
Abqaiq

Piesinger
1984

Mesopotamian alluvium (for a review see Bauer et al. 1998). At this time, trade
with the northeast Arabian littoral is attested by ceramics found in graves at
Sabkha Hammam near the modern oil town of Abqaiq and in settlement contexts at Umm ar-Ramadh near Hofuf and Umm an-Nussi in the Yabrin oasis
(Bibby 1973: 48; Larsen 1983: 145–146; Potts 1991a: 89–92; Zarins 1989b). The
tiny island of Tarut, joined to the Saudi mainland today by a 6-kilometer-long
dual carriageway, has also revealed spectacular evidence for occupation during
this period. In addition to Early Dynastic Mesopotamian ceramics and numerous softstone vessels (Zarins 1978), limestone statues smaller than life size were
recovered (Burkholder 1971, 1984; Crawford 1998: 45–50; Potts 1993a: 184); see
Text Box 7.

Softstone vessels are of particular interest for understanding some of the
economic networks that may have underpinned settlement on Tarut and the
Eastern Province during these centuries (Zarins 1978). In addition to simply
decorated examples that belong to the série ancienne vessels as first classified by de Miroschedji (1973), elaborately decorated examples in the so-called
Intercultural Style were found at these sites. Kohl's (1978) analysis of the iconography and mineralogy of the Tarut examples of Intercultural Style vessels
positioned them within a larger trade network that encompassed eastern Arabia,
Mesopotamia and Iran and suggested that Tarut was part of the production system for these and other types of softstone vessels. In part this was based on
x-ray diffraction of softstone samples, which speaks more to the mineralogy of
each sample than to the exact geochemical source. More recently Potts (2005)
has challenged the idea of Tarut as a potential source of série ancienne production, particularly as a centre for the so-called Susa–Adab–Persian Gulf group.
Pointing out the wealth of softstone production around Tepe Yahya and the
recent discoveries of softstone at Jiroft, he argues that the série ancienne vessels
from Tarut were likely imports from southeastern Iran (Potts 2005: note 6).

ED II
vessel

RIME!

Ebla
Dilmun TIN

Regardless of the mechanisms by which softstone vessels reached the island
of Tarut, their presence indicates that eastern Arabia was playing a central role
in the movement of goods through the Arabian Gulf. As noted earlier, the
toponym 'Dilmun' was already known in the Late Uruk period. During the
Early Dynastic period it becomes more common and the region is noted as
supplying materials, including copper, to Mesopotamia (Potts 1991a: 85–89).
By 2500 BC, Ur-Nanshe, the first ruler of Lagash, boasts in several inscriptions
of the ships of Dilmun bringing timber to Lagash for temple construction
(Potts 1991a: 88; Sollberger and Kupper 1971: 46). The texts make clear that
the timber was not from Bahrain, and it can be assumed that the timber was
coming from Iran or South Asia. The occurrence of the terms 'Dilmun copper' and 'Dilmun tin' in texts dating to the same period at Ebla, an ancient city
about 50 kilometers southwest of Aleppo, suggests the extent of the merchant
network at this time (Potts 1991a: 88). The term 'Dilmun shekel' is also found

TEXT BOX 7. SOFTSTONE AND 'INTERCULTURAL STYLE' VESSELS

Softstone is, as the name suggests, a soft metamorphic rock that is formed when continental or ocean crusts collide. It is common in the many mountain ranges that are formed during this process and was available for carving and working in various regions of Arabia and adjacent regions in antiquity. It was also an important element of craft traditions in Crete, Nigeria, the Shetland Islands in the United Kingdom, Scandinavia, Cyprus and parts of the northeastern United States.

Softstone is known by a variety of names, some of which reflect its dominant mineralogy and others its physical characteristics. 'Soapstone' is, for example, commonly used in the United States to describe the feel of the material, while 'softstone' is used elsewhere to describe the ease with which the material can be carved. The term 'steatite' is also used to refer to the presence of talc or magnesium silicate. 'Chlorite' refers to the presence of four phyllosilicate minerals: clinochlore, chamosite, nimite and pennantite.

The excavations undertaken by Professor Lamberg-Karlovsky at the site of Tepe Yahya in Kerman (Iran) fundamentally altered our knowledge of the production of and trade in softstone vessels across the Arabian Gulf and Indo-Iranian borderlands during the late fourth and third millennia BC. As early as the 1930s, researchers such as Mackay had recognized that a distinctive group of carved softstone vessels were found at numerous sites across this region. They were carved in a distinctive style that incorporated naturalistic, architectural and zoomorphic motifs, and they were distributed from Central Asia to eastern Arabia. In a pioneering study, Kohl (1978) attached the term 'Intercultural Style vessel' to this type of vessel. It wasn't until the excavation of Tepe Yahya in the late 1960s that one centre for production could be isolated with certainty. A workshop belonging to Period IVB1 at the site contained evidence of debitage and unfinished

vessels, suggesting that the inhabitants of this rather small settlement in the Soghun Valley produced artefacts that were desired by those who were buried in the Royal Graves of Ur as well as those who lived on Tarut island in eastern Saudi Arabia and Umm an-Nar off the coast of Abu Dhabi (Figure 4.3).

Subsequent excavations in the Arabian Gulf, Mesopotamia, South Asia and Central Asia revealed further examples of Intercultural Style vessels, and our knowledge of third millennium BC trade expanded accordingly. In 1982 the potential importance of Intercultural Style vessels for understanding regional interaction in the ancient Near East came to the fore again when the Sumerologist Piotr Steinkeller brought attention to the existence of two softstone bowls, one from Ur and one unprovenanced in the Vorderasiatisches Museum, that contain inscriptions of the Akkadian king Rimush commemorating his victory against Elam and the region of Marhashi, the location of which had perplexed scholars for decades. Both vessels are decorated in the Intercultural Style and comparisons could be drawn to examples from Tepe Yahya. Steinkeller (1982: 254) concluded: 'Although none of the presented data constitutes an iron clad proof for locating Marhashi to the east of Elam, their cumulative effect is such, I believe, as to make this proposition very likely.'

The site of Tepe Yahya could not alone explain the attention garnered by the Akkadian kings or the extensive production of Intercultural Style vessels. In the 1990s a much clearer picture emerged when unseasonal flooding in the Jiroft plain in southeastern Iran revealed a number of tombs that were looted by locals, and the objects they found quickly entered the antiquities market. This looting was brought to the attention of the authorities by Hamideh Choubak of the Iranian Cultural Heritage Organization, and it led to the recovery of thousands of looted objects, which Yousef Majidzadeh

(continued)

Text Box 7 (*continued*)

subsequently published in a catalogue. Included in this catalogue, and revealed by subsequent excavations at a number of sites, were thousands of Intercultural Style vessels as well as ceramic, alabaster and stone artefacts. These have been labelled the 'Jiroft Civilization' by some researchers, and they leave little doubt that this area was the ancient Marhashi, a region known as the supplier of exotic minerals to Mesopotamia and the first

softstone vessels that were widely exported across the Arabian Gulf.

In the centuries following the appearance of Intercultural Style vessels at sites in southeastern Arabia, an indigenous industry in softstone carving emerged. Distinctive vessel forms and decorative motifs developed and were to remain a key feature of southeast Arabian material culture for three millennia.

Figure 4.1. Hafit tombs, Ras al-Khaimah, United Arab Emirates. Photo: William Deadman (University of Durham).

right

in texts at Ebla but its meaning is still debated (Archi 1987; Michalowski 1990; Potts 1991a: 88; Zaccagnini 1986).

The occurrence of the term 'Dilmun' during the first half of the third millennium BC is at odds with the archaeological record from the island of Bahrain. Except for the occasional sherd, archaeological evidence for occupation of the island at this time is virtually non-existent. There are several possible explanations for this discrepancy. The most likely is that during these centuries the term 'Dilmun' refers to the eastern and northeastern coasts of Saudi Arabia, where Early Dynastic material is well known (Crawford 1998:

4–6; Howard-Carter 1987; Potts 1991a: 85–86; Potts et al. 1978: 9). Another possibility is that the term 'Dilmun' itself is used in Mesopotamian texts less to denote a specific geographical region than to indicate an ill-defined southern region. This idea gains credibility when we consider that 'Dilmun' is contrasted with 'Subir' or 'Subartu', a generic term for the north of Mesopotamia (Michalowski 1986) in a text dating to the middle of the third millennium BC from Ebla in Syria (Crawford 1998: 4). As Michalowski (1999: 6) has noted, although this specific text is from Syria it concerns the god Nisaba and is written from a Sumerian, or south Mesopotamian, perspective, indicating that Sumer is 'sandwiched between two general areas: Subartu and Dilmun'.

Regardless of how we choose to identify Dilmun during these early periods, the term itself was used for a region from which exotic goods, including copper, were being shipped. The east and northeast Arabian littorals were, therefore, already playing a critical role in the trans-shipment of goods in a manner that was to become one of the defining elements of east Arabian Bronze Age society.

THE EMERGENCE OF OASIS SETTLEMENT

Another feature that was to define Bronze Age eastern Arabia was the development of sedentary oases in which agriculture was practised alongside the sheep, goat and cattle husbandry that had defined the Arabian Neolithic. There is frustratingly little evidence for these developments from eastern Saudi Arabia. Although dry farming is obviously impossible, some of the most important aquifers in all of Arabia are located in this region. In the middle of the twentieth century, flow analysis of the six main artesian wells around Hofuf indicated a total discharge of 93,300 gallons (about 350,000 liters) per minute (Twitchell 1944: 384). For purposes of comparison: the Ain-es Sultan spring that feeds the oasis of Jericho in Palestine has an estimated flow rate of 1,000 gallons (about 3,800 liters) per minute. Unfortunately, however, too little is known of the prehistoric settlements to make any detailed statement on subsistence strategies, although the finds from Tarut discussed earlier clearly indicate that there was settlement in this region at this time.

Moving southeast across the deserts and vast coastal *sabkha* of Saudi Arabia and through the Jabrin oasis, we find very little evidence of prehistoric occupation until we come to the al-Ain oasis in the UAE. Here clear evidence has been revealed for early third millennium BC occupation of southeastern Arabia. Located on the edge of the oasis is Jebel Hafit, one of the highest mountains in the UAE, which gives its name to a distinctive form of burial that dates to this period and was discovered by the Danish archaeologist P. V. Glob in 1959 and excavated a few years later (Glob 1959). The so-called Hafit tombs are stone-constructed single-chamber tombs, often with a beehive shape (Figure 4.1). They are known throughout southeastern Arabia, from the tip of the Musandam peninsula down to the edges of the Sharqiyah sands (see Deadman 2012; Giraud 2009; Vogt 1985). It has been argued that they are collective tombs for a small group of people, possibly families of extended kin. Those that have not been robbed provide evidence for the first use of ceramics in this part of Arabia, as they contain imported Mesopotamian jars. On the basis of Mesopotamian parallels, these imports begin in the Jemdat Nasr period (3100–2900 BC) and continue throughout the Early Dynastic period (Frifelt 1975; Méry and Schneider 1996; Potts 1991a: 75–76). Locally made copies of these jars also start to appear during this time frame. Small amounts of copper objects are known, although one could not insist that this reflects the beginning of a local copper industry. Square ivory beads from several of these tombs point to connections with Iran, and it is perhaps that region that we should also look to as a potential source of copper (Potts 1993a: 183).

Whereas the finds from Hafit tombs speak of economic interaction with Mesopotamia, there is still little evidence about the local economy of southeastern Arabia's inhabitants during this time. Only Hili 8 in the al-Ain oasis provides evidence that people were transitioning from the pastoral existence that had defined earlier millennia to a sedentary agricultural regime. Today, this site is located on the northern edges of the al-Ain oasis in a rich alluvial setting that marks this oasis as one of the most important agricultural areas in southeastern Arabia. A final publication of the excavations undertaken between 1977 and 1984 by the French archaeologists under Cleuziou (1982, 1989a, 1989b) is awaited, but preliminary reports and specialized studies have provided much information on the growth and economy of the settlement (Figure 4.2). Period I is defined by the construction of a square, mudbrick building (III) and a smaller ancillary building (VI). A defensive function is assumed for this building, and one could envisage that it was surrounded by smaller structures made from organic remains such as palm fronds. The chronology of this early phase at Hili 8 is based upon two ^{14}C dates on brushwood which date the construction of the tower to between 3300 and 2900 BC (Cleuziou 2009: 729). Several types of necked jars with distinctive rims found in later deposits are paralleled in Early Dynastic I and II contexts in southern Mesopotamia, indicating continued occupation through the first half of the third millennium BC.

Agriculture at Hili 8 is attested by the recovery of emmer wheat (*Triticum dicoccum*), bread wheat (*T. aestivuum*), two-row (*Hodeum distichon*) and six-row (*Hodeum vulgare*) hulled barley and six-row naked barley (*Hodeum vulgare* var. *nudum*). Wild oats (*Avena* sp.) and jujube seeds (*Zizyphus* sp.) were collected, while fruits included melons (*Cucumis* sp.) and dates (*Phoenix dactylifera*) (Cleuziou and Costantini 1980; Cleuziou and Tosi 1989). Archaeozoological evidence indicates that sheep, goat and cattle were herded, and donkey and dog were present (Uerpmann and Uerpmann 2007). Dromedaries were also noted in the archaeozoological material, but, as discussed in more detail in

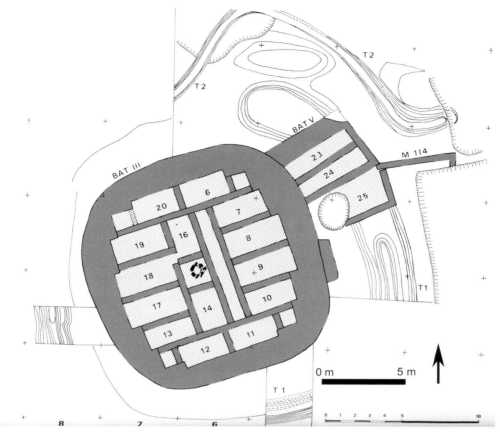

Figure 4.2. Plan of Hili 8, al-Ain oasis, United Arab Emirates. After Cleuziou 1989a.

Chapter 7, these are the remains of wild dromedaries, which were hunted for meat and skins.

Cleuziou and Tosi (1989: 25) claim that the agricultural regime also included millet (*Sorghum bicolor*). If correct, this would be quite important, since its presence at Hili would significantly antedate its initial domestication in Africa (Rowley-Conwy et al. 1997). Also contentious are the claims of Cleuziou and Tosi (2007) concerning the method of irrigation employed at Hili 8. A series of grooves on anthrosols near the site are interpreted as remains of an extensive irrigation system that included underground canals resembling later falaj irrigation (see Chapter 9). There is little evidence to support this assertion, and it seems prudent for the moment to emphasize that the well found in the middle of Hili 8 was used directly to irrigate agricultural fields around the settlement and the grooves were no more than distribution channels (cf. al-Tikriti 2010).

For many years, Hili 8 stood alone as a possible example of an early third millennium BC oasis settlement. More recently, excavations by a joint

French-Italian team at Ras al-Jinz in the Sultanate of Oman have identified two sites, RJ-1 (Ras al-Jinz 1) and HD-6 (Ras al-Hadd 6), that provide much-needed information on villages of this period. Still little is known about RJ-1 in this period, since most attention has been focused on the early second millennium BC levels at the site; but as far as one can judge from preliminary reports (Cleuziou and Tosi 2007: 92; Monchablon et al. 2003) the settlement consisted of a number of posthole-supported structures with associated pits and hearths. Artefacts associated with fishing (hooks, shell pendants) and remnants of a bead workshop were found in associated deposits. Only one pottery sherd, probably imported, was found and no ^{14}C samples were recovered. Rather, the excavators date the site to the early third millennium BC on the basis of its stratigraphic relationship with an Umm an-Nar tomb, and therefore the claim that it necessarily dates to the *very* early third millennium BC remains unsubstantiated.

With HD-6 we are on firmer ground. The excavated portion of the settlement consists of several mudbrick buildings surrounded by a stone wall. At least two structures have been published (Cleuziou and Tosi 2007: 93–95), each comprising a number of smaller rooms that adjoin a long central room. The houses are tightly agglomerated, with little space between buildings. Cleuziou and Tosi (2007: 94) suggest that up to 200 people may have lived in such a settlement, considerably more than hitherto attested at any site. The remains of fishing nets (in the form of calcified rope), copper fishing hooks, as well as pins, knives and chisels suggest that the inhabitants of HD-6 exploited the sea. Bead manufacture from shell and locally available steatite also occurred. According to Cleuziou and Tosi, sites such as HD-6 indicate that copper production was already beginning in the early third millennium BC. There is, however, no archaeological or analytical evidence that supports the assertion that these few copper objects were locally produced. In addition, ceramics and other artefacts from sites of this period show some connections with areas of Iran and other regions in which there was already a well-developed copper industry.

The tenuous indications of settlement from HD-6 and Hili 8 hint at a transition towards sedentary agriculture by 3000 BC. However, the extent to which evidence from these two sites can be considered to indicate the emergence of a full oasis economy that subsequently flourished during the Umm an-Nar period (2500–2000 BC) remains an unresolved issue. Ultimately, it is the rock-built cairn burials – the so-called Hafit tombs – that remain the most prominent archaeological remnant of the period between 3000 and 2500 BC. Increasingly it has been argued that the quantity and location of tombs indicate a shift towards an oasis economy. The most detailed argument in favour of this interpretation has been presented by Giraud (2009) based on widespread survey and detailed GIS analysis of thousands of tombs in the Ja'alan region of Oman. Although emphasizing that her hypothesis needs further testing, Giraud suggests that the location of tombs within areas in which date palm cultivation is currently practised indicates the likely presence of small oasis settlements of the first half of the third millennium BC. Cleuziou is more certain and concludes that Hafit cairn burials 'can now be considered as indicating small palm tree gardens usually not visible to archaeologists, tapering springs or wadi gravels at some distance, which would have played a major role in the overall subsistence economy' (Cleuziou 2009: 734). In this manner, Cleuziou sees the beginning of the third millennium BC as experiencing a fundamental shift from the nomadic pastoral lifestyle of the Neolithic to the oasis economy that was to define Arabia for millennia to come.

To scholars working outside Arabia, Cleuziou's arguments have been enthusiastically adopted (e.g., Boivin and Fuller 2009). In this way the transition to the oasis economy within Arabia has been normalized into a broader narrative that emphasizes agriculture as a key component of social change within the broader Near Eastern and South Asian worlds. For example, it has been recently claimed that the beginning of the third millennium BC in eastern Arabia was marked by 'agricultural settlements and artificial irrigation, together with increasing trade and social complexity. Remnants of channels probably linked to wells have been dated to the third millennium BC in interior Oman (Cleuziou and Tosi 2007). It is plausible that these represent precursors to the more complex subterranean channel systems of the falaj (qanat), although the latter are generally believed to have been invented closer to 1000 BC [see later discussion]. By the start of the third millennium BC, settlements, apparently on the later oasis pattern, and burial monuments (so-called "beehive tombs") were widespread in Oman (Cleuziou and Tosi 2007)' (Boivin and Fuller 2009: 142). In fact, evidence for agriculture is very meagre, the assertion of falaj irrigation extremely dubious and any manifestation of 'social complexity' difficult to ascertain.

The enormous number of Hafit tombs spread across the landscape of southeastern Arabia indicates that whatever process the tombs represent was indeed widespread. It is hard to escape the conclusion that the tombs represent a shift in the conceptualization of landownership and use, as argued in Chapter 3 for the cairn tombs of the late fourth millennium BC in Wadi Sana. A return to moist conditions beginning around 3200 BC (Parker et al. 2006) would have (re)opened the inland plains of southeastern Arabia to sheep, goat and cattle pastoralism in a manner that had been impossible throughout most of the fourth millennium BC. This intensified exploitation does not – by necessity – equate to the emergence of the sort of sedentary oases argued by Cleuziou. Opportunistic agriculture, the intensive harvesting of wild plants, or the use of agricultural fields as reserve zones for pastoralism might have also accompanied increased inland exploitation. Indeed, the type of agropastoral subsistence observed in Mahra and Dhofar today in Oman (ElMahi 2001; Janzen 1986; Zarins 1992), which combines agriculture with pastoralism, is an equally valid interpretation of the archaeological data for the early third

millennium BC. In such a scenario Hafit tombs might have played an important role communicating the position and ownership of temporary agricultural
areas. The sedentary, likely year-round occupation attested at Hili 8 might be
the exception to this more established subsistence pattern. Ultimately, however,
further excavation at settlement sites and bioarchaeological analysis of skeletal
data from Hafit tombs are needed to determine the nature of human settlement during these centuries. What can be stated with certainty is that with the
emergence of sedentary oasis economies after 2500 BC, collective burials are
no longer located in a highly visible position but are rather found in the low-
lying plains and coasts. As we shall see, this change accompanies well-attested
massive shifts in the local economy and settlement patterns throughout southeastern Arabia.

THE UMM AN-NAR PERIOD (2500–2000 BC)

Around 2500 BC the human occupation of southeastern Arabia changes in a
profound and long-lasting manner (Figure 4.3). Normally referred to as the
Umm an-Nar period after the island near Abu Dhabi in which remains of this
time frame were found by Danish archaeologists in the 1950s, these 500 years
witness an intensification of sedentary settlement throughout the region.
There is little doubt that sites of this period and their associated material culture represent the most important shift in human occupation of southeastern
Arabia since the beginning of nomadic pastoralism some 4,000 years earlier.

It is hardly surprising that there has been much scholarly debate on the
nature and causes of these changes. As previously discussed, Cleuziou and Tosi
(2007: 90–91) have argued that the Umm an-Nar period represents a continuation and solidification of small-scale oasis agriculture already evidenced
at Hili 8 and HD-6. This emphasis on irrigation agriculture has been taken
to the extreme by Orchard and Stanger (1994, 1999), who argue that the
settlement at Bat in Oman is 400 hectares in size and considerable portions
of it were irrigated by a form of sub-surface to surface irrigation known as
falaj (discussed in more detail in Chapter 8). They see a similar patterning in
the oasis of Bisyah, which, they argue, encompasses an area of between 300
and 350 hectares, and a number of other sites in inland Oman (Orchard and
Stanger 1994: 79). They conclude, 'In contrast to the view that in the 3rd millennium b.c. northern Oman was a land of small villages, 1½ to 2½ hectares
or even 40 to 50 hectares in size, with economies based on flood irrigation
techniques it has been demonstrated that the al-Hajar settlements were substantial oasis towns, sometimes 300 to 400 hectares in extent, watered by
sophisticated channel systems and capable, in a testing transitional climate,
of growing both perennial and annual crops. The architecture of these well-
planned centres was both imposing and varied and formed part of a material
culture which exhibits relations with Mesopotamia and, to a lesser extent,

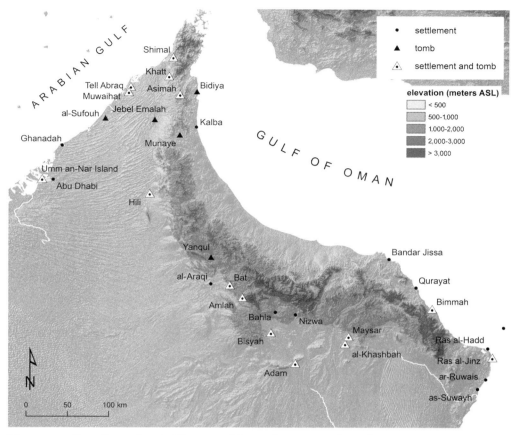

Figure 4.3. Location of main Umm an–Nar settlements and tombs.

Iran' (Orchard and Stanger 1994: 87). Few scholars accept this interpretation, and Potts (1997) has shown that the data for reconstructing the origin, chronology and cultural affiliation of these settlements are much less conclusive than suggested by Orchard and Stanger.

The fact that southeastern Arabia begins to feature in Mesopotamian textual sources during this period has added fuel to the scholarly debate on the origins of Umm an–Nar period settlement intensification. Throughout the later nineteenth century, scholars like Durand and Rawlinson had accepted that the Akkadian toponym 'Magan' referred to a place somewhere in the Arabian Gulf because of its relationship to Dilmun. It was the secure identification by Wellsted (1838) of copper deposits, including some still actively exploited in central Oman, that eventually enabled Kmoskó (1917) to identify southeastern Arabia as the 'Magan' notable for its supply of copper to Ur during the Ur III period (Potts 1991a: 117–125). It is perhaps not surprising, therefore, that great emphasis has been placed on the extraction and export of copper to Mesopotamia as a driver for settlement intensification, a position

that Cleuziou and Tosi reject in favour of an autochthonous origin for Umm
an-Nar culture.

These varied perspectives have continued to cycle in and out of academic
fashion over the past few decades. During this time, intensive archaeological
fieldwork has revealed a diverse array of settlement and mortuary data on
life during the Umm an-Nar period. Numerous settlements are now known,
including Abu Dhabi (De Cardi 1997), Amlah (De Cardi et al. 1976), Asimah
(Vogt 1994), Bat (Brunswig 1989; Frifelt 1976, 1985), Bidya (al-Tikriti 1989b),
Hili 1 (Frifelt 1975, 1979, 1990), Hili 8 (Cleuziou 1982, 1989a; Cleuziou and
Tosi 1989), Maysar (Weisgerber 1981, 1991), Ras Ghanadha (al-Tikriti 1985),
Mowaihat (Phillips 2007), numerous sites around Ras al-Jinz (Cleuziou and
Tosi 2007), Tell Abraq (Potts 1991b, 2000) and Umm an-Nar island (Frifelt
1995). To these should be added the less well published or known sites at
Wadi al-Fajj, Kalba, Bisyah, Nizwa, Adam, al-Khashbah (al-Jahwari and Kennet
2008), Bilad al-Maaidan, Qurayat, Bimmah, Bandar Jissah, Batin and Wadi Ibra
(al-Jahwari 2009: Fig. 1; al-Jahwari and Kennet 2008). In a recent review of the
evidence (al-Jahwari 2009), thirty-one known settlement locations have been
mapped, many of which are likely to include numerous ancient settlements
within a single wadi or alluvial plain. In addition, there is evidence of new
funerary practices centred around the construction of large, collective tombs.
These refine the form already established in the Hafit type of the early third
millennium BC. They are stone-constructed, round and above ground and are

Figure 4.4. Umm an-Nar tomb, al-Ain oasis, United Arab Emirates.

widely distributed: a recent review identified nearly thirty sites with Umm an-Nar tombs, many of them containing multiple examples (al-Jahwari 2009: Fig. 1). They are located near settlements, often within sight of where people lived and in some cases, such as at Hili, were truly monumental and made from well-cut ashlar blocks (Figure 4.4). Dozens of these are known throughout southeastern Arabia, and many have been the subject of detailed and careful excavation (as discussed later).

UMM AN-NAR SETTLEMENTS

The settlements of this period share many architectural features. They are characterized by round towers that range in size from 20 meters in diameter at Bat in Oman to nearly double that size at Tell Abraq in the Emirates of Sharjah and Umm al-Quwain (UAE). One assumes that these towers were at the centre of a much larger settlement that included buildings made from organic materials, such as palm fronds. In some cases, such as Maysar (Weisgerber 1981), there is evidence for substantial domestic architecture near the tower. Bat, in the Sultanate of Oman, is a typical inland Umm an-Nar settlement, even if it is likely one of the larger settlements yet known. It consists of four or five towers and a stone-constructed settlement and is currently under excavation by a team from the University of Pennsylvania. The towers are roughly equidistant from each other and are constructed from locally available material that is hewn into massive blocks, some of which measure 2.5 by 0.75 meters (Orchard and Stanger 1994: 71). A stone-constructed settlement (Bat 1156) has been interpreted as a domestic structure that includes a large circular feature at one end. The area between these towers and settlement encompasses a zone of between 40 and 50 hectares (Cleuziou and Tosi 2007: 146), which may have been irrigated by the control of seasonal flow from the nearby Wadi Sharsah (Fouache et al. 2012).

Residential structures constructed from locally available beach rock, mortar and plaster dominate the settlement on the island of Umm an-Nar (Frifelt 1995). Three individual buildings were partially excavated by Danish archaeologists in the 1960s. The largest of these included a block divided into seven rectangular rooms and measuring 16 by 16 meters. On Umm an-Nar, it is likely that these stone foundations supported organic superstructures likely constructed from date palm fronds. The coastal settlement at Ras al-Jinz 2 on the Oman coast also contains multi-room well-planned buildings (Cleuziou and Tosi 2000, 2007). Here, at least twelve buildings were identified, all constructed from mudbricks. Three buildings were excavated in the southern compound, with Building I consisting of a long 20-meter construction with numerous, similarly sized rooms. The northern compound comprised a courtyard house that was interpreted as a more domestic-oriented structure than those in the southern compound (Figure 4.5).

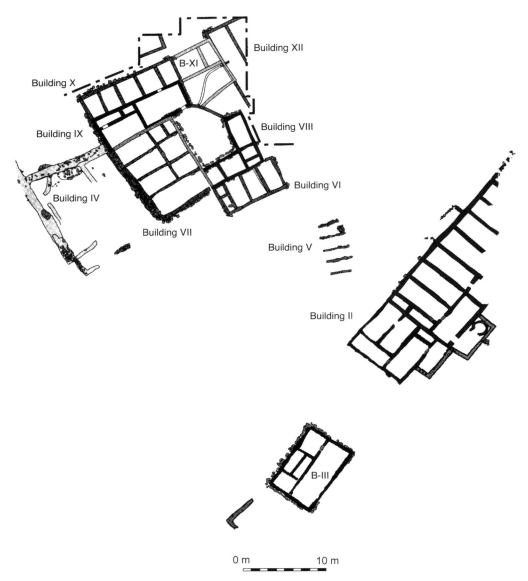

Figure 4.5. Plan of Bronze Age settlement of RJ-2, Ras al-Jinz 2, Sultanate of Oman. After Cleuziou and Tosi 2000: Fig. 5.

UMM AN-NAR SUBSISTENCE

There can be little question, as al-Jahwari (2009) has emphasized in his study of the Wadi Andam in the interior of Oman, that agriculture was an important component of subsistence at Umm an-Nar inland settlements. At Hili 8, a settlement already existing before the Umm an-Nar period, it is likely that the barley, wheat, melon and date palm cultivation that had characterized earlier periods continued (Potts 1993a: 188; Tengberg 1998). Evidence for a similar range of cereal cultivars is found at Tell Abraq in the form of impressions in mudbricks (Tengberg 1998). The actual recovery of archaeobotanical remains is admittedly meagre, but analysis of teeth from inland tombs such as those at Maysar also point to a diet in which cereals played an important role (Kunter 1981: 207, 1983: 340).

Cereal agriculture was thus established in southeastern Arabia during the third millennium BC, and it is likely that this was the result of increasing engagement with those cultures that shared the Arabian Gulf and Arabian Sea. However, the advent of cereal agriculture in eastern Arabia does not mean its inhabitants suddenly transitioned into the role of 'sedentary agriculturalists'. As Smith (2001) has convincingly shown, a perceived duality between non-agricultural and agricultural societies permeates research on ancient food production and '[a]ccompanying this central assumption of duality are a number of implicit correlates that have shaped, to a greater or lesser degree, widespread perceptions of the intervening conceptual and/or developmental territory (if any) that lies between hunter-gatherers and agriculture.... This thin boundary is also often considered to be a one-way membrane. For those crossing over to agriculture, there is no turning back' (Smith 2001: 3). Such epistemological dualities still underwrite research on the ancient Near East by emphasizing the agricultural revolution as a 'no turning back point' which led eventually to the first states (for a more nuanced approach to post-Neolithic northern Mesopotamia see Zeder 1994). As we have already seen, Neolithic Arabia sits outside these frameworks, since components of the canonical Near Eastern Neolithic subsistence package such as sheep, goat and cattle were borrowed and amalgamated *into* existing hunter-gatherer strategies. Moreover, the emergence of cereal agriculture during the third millennium BC does not mean that the inhabitants of southeastern Arabia finally adopted the complete Neolithic package of cereal cultivation and domesticated animals. Detailed analysis of archaeozoological data, particularly by Hans-Peter and Margarethe Uerpmann, highlights that along with domesticated animals a wide range of wild terrestrial and marine resources were still exploited. From region to region, the exploitation of wild and domesticated animals varied considerably according to localized environmental conditions.

In the inland, the exploitation of domesticated animals was a key component of subsistence. From Hili 8 a total of 136 identified specimens indicates that more than 90% of the consumed meat came from domestic animals – cattle provided 60% and the remainder came from sheep and goat (Uerpmann and Uerpmann 2008b: 468). Just as had been the case at the inland site of Jebel Buhais inhabited millennia earlier, hunting played no significant role in the subsistence strategy. Such inland settlements and the coast were separated by the northern extension of the Rub al-Khali, and the distance between them was considerable. The inhabitants of Umm an-Nar island were the most distant from the inland plains that we currently know, and they crafted a subsistence

that exploited their coastal position and desert hinterland. A range of wild terrestrial animals (gazelle, oryx, dromedary) significantly outnumbered domesticated species (cattle and goat) at Umm an-Nar. In fact, domesticated animals
contributed only 2.6% to the meat diet, compared with more than 12% from
the wild terrestrial animals (Hoch 1979, 1995; Uerpmann and Uerpmann
2008b: 475). Sea animals, especially the dugong, clearly were a mainstay of the
diet. Dugong and sea turtle combined contributed more than 70% to the meat
diet of the inhabitants of Umm an-Nar. The fish bones recovered from the
settlement indicate that offshore fishing was also practised. Some of the fish,
such as *Caranx ignobilis* (giant trevally) exceeded 1 meter in length (Uerpmann
and Uerpmann 2005a: 111). As Potts has noted (1991a: 128), the large number
of turtle bones from Umm an-Nar (more than 4,000) attest to the importance
of this animal not only for food but also for leather and shell. A contemporary
text from Mesopotamia records the delivery of turtle products into Ur, and the
Arabian Gulf would be the obvious source of these.

   In the northern part of southeastern Arabia the coastal zones are consid-
erably closer to the inland plains, and a series of wadis carrying alluvial sediments connect both regions. Tell Abraq is located in one such zone in the
Emirates of Sharjah and Umm al-Quwain (Potts 1990, 1991b, 2000). The site
is also located on the edge of what was an active lagoon during the Bronze
Age that linked the settlement with the Arabian Gulf. The inhabitants of Tell
Abraq had at their disposal, therefore, coastal, inland and desert environments.
The extensive archaeozoological remains, comprising 4,447 identified bones,
indicate that during the Umm an-Nar period these varied environments were
all exploited. Wild hunted animals from the desert and desert fringe included
gazelle, oryx and dromedary, with the latter contributing a significant amount
of meat to the diet (Uerpmann and Uerpmann 2008b: 474). Sheep and goat
were the most common domesticated animals. In contrast to the situation in
other coastal sites such as Umm an-Nar and more akin to that in inland sites
like Maysar and Hili 8, cattle (most likely *Bos indicus*) were an important component and when considered in light of meat return constituted a more important part of the meat diet than either sheep or goat (Stephan 1995; Uerpmann
and Uerpmann 2008b). Fish were intensively exploited at Tell Abraq. Most of
the fish isolated to the species level were available from the lagoon that was
adjacent to the ancient settlement (Uerpmann and Uerpmann 2005a). The
recovery of bronze hooks and net sinkers throughout the settlement indicates
that both nets and hand lines were used, but the overall impression is that the
presence of the lagoon negated any necessity to engage in complex, offshore
fishing. Other marine resources included turtle, as at Umm an-Nar, and considerable numbers of the cormorant bird, *Phalacrocorax nigrogularis* (Stephan
1995; Uerpmann and Uerpmann 2008b). A mangrove area also provided a rich
array of food, including the gastropod *Terebralia palustris*, which was an easily
collected source of protein.

Coastal sites facing the Gulf of Oman were, like Tell Abraq, located close to inland alluvial plains and desert environments. The archaeozoological record from sites such as Ras al-Jinz 2 confirms the mixed economy of coastal settlements in this region (Cleuziou and Tosi 2007). Turtle and whale, rather than dugong, which is absent from the Indian Ocean, contributed significantly to the maritime component of the diet. Cleuziou and Tosi (2007: 231) argue that Ras al-Jinz 2 was enmeshed in a broader autochthonous subsistence pattern in which winter occupation of the coast alternated with inland summer occupation. During winter, fish such as yellowfin tuna were heavily exploited. In addition, the green turtle was killed for its meat, oil and shell, and the occasional dolphin or whale that found itself stranded added to food resources. Sheep and goat were much less important to these coastal dwellers and were likely kept in the interior regions, where they were exploited for secondary products, that is, not butchered (Cleuziou and Tosi 2007: 234). These authors also argue that the date palm was not locally exploited in this region and that the few carbonized date stones found at Ras al-Jinz 2 were brought from the interior. Cattle are relatively uncommon at this site, as opposed to Tell Abraq, but donkeys are much more prevalent, perhaps because they are more suited to the gravel plains adjacent to the Omani coast, as opposed to the high sand dune desert interiors of the Arabian Gulf coast.

As we shall see, the coastal position of many Umm an-Nar settlements also provided an opportunity to engage in maritime trade to an extent hitherto unknown in southeastern Arabia. Copper was transported from the interior to the coast for export, and imported foreign goods were funnelled inland. Animals operating as beasts of burden were essential for the maintenance of this intra-regional trade. The dromedary was, however, not yet domesticated. It is possible that cattle were used for transport (Uerpmann and Uerpmann 2008b: 479), but more evidence is needed if this idea is to move from the realm of conjecture. It is likely that the most important development in this regard was the appearance in eastern Arabia of the domesticated ass (*Equus asinus*). As I noted in Chapter 3, the wild ass (*Equus africanus*) was exploited for meat at Jebel Buhais and other Neolithic sites, confirming that Arabia was within its natural range (Uerpmann 1991). By the third millennium BC there is evidence for the exploitation of domesticated ass at Hili 8, Tell Abraq and a number of other sites (Uerpmann and Uerpmann 2008b). The representation of a rider on a domesticated ass from an Umm an-Nar tomb (al-Tikriti 2011) indicates that it was used for transport, while at Maysar 25 in the interior of Oman the bones of domesticated ass exhibited skeletal stress, perhaps related to its use for drawing water or for transporting copper – the extraction and production of which were the raison d'être of Maysar. The possibility that the domestication of wild ass took place within Arabia cannot be completely ruled out, but no evidence is currently available that would support such an hypothesis. DNA analysis (Beja-Pereira et al. 2004) has reinforced a likely African origin for at least some domesticated ass (Clade 1 type), corroborating long-held views based on the early appearance of domesticated ass in Egyptian contexts (Bökönyi 1991; Clutton-Brock 1992). At the same time, however, the possibility that another group (Clade 2) was domesticated from wild ancestors in Africa or Yemen has been signalled by genetic research (Kimura et al. 2010).

Regardless of where it was domesticated, the domesticated ass could move people and goods across the landscape in a fashion hitherto unknown in southeastern Arabia. There can be little doubt that it was critical for the emergence of intra-regional trade networks that engaged in growing regional maritime trade (as discussed later). However, there were still severe barriers to economic integration within southeastern Arabia. It is unlikely that the ass could traverse the Rub al-Khali and desert forelands that separated the inland plains and mineral-rich mountains from the coast. On the Arabian Gulf side, trade between these areas was possible only if one travelled along the flanks of the al-Hajjar mountains to the area located near Ras al-Khaimah where the coastal zone interfaces with the mountains and then down to coastal trading centres like Umm an-Nar and Tell Abraq. This was a lengthy journey that required considerable time, and the rewards would have to have been significant. Only trade in copper and foreign and locally produced durable goods would have provided the necessary incentives. Currently the archaeozoological evidence indicates that food products were not moved across the landscape during this time, and remains of fish and shellfish, which were certainly dried and exported in later periods to the interior, are rare at Umm an-Nar settlements in the interior.

In summary, the archaeozoological evidence from Umm an-Nar settlements throughout southeastern Arabia points to a relatively localized subsistence strategy. This is confirmed by Gregorika's recent analysis of isotopic variation of teeth from Umm an-Nar burials, which showed variations in diet consistent with localized resources at Umm an-Nar island, Mowaihat, Tell Abraq and Shimal (Gregoricka 2011: 331). In short, and perhaps hardly surprising, the factor that most determined subsistence strategy was local availability. With the end of the climatic desiccation of the fourth millennium BC, each environmental niche presented new opportunities for hunting and pastoralism which, although not as bountiful as in the Holocene Moist Phase, were still abundant and conducive to long-term occupation. Cereal agriculture in the third millennium BC was contoured by these already existing patterns of exploitation. It is possible that it became a key component of settlements located in the inland alluvial plains, but even in this zone archaeobotanical evidence is yet to prove a dedicated cereal intensification. It should be remembered that date palm cultivation was likely to have existed in this region for some time, and one could well imagine that cereals were grown in the interstitial zone between trees, just as they were in the recent past (see Tengberg, in press). Indeed, at coastal sites such as Tell Abraq it is hard to imagine that cereals were grown by any other form of cultivation.

It is perhaps useful, therefore, to conceptualize the advent of cereal cultivation within eastern Arabia as part of a long process of selective adaptation to the changing local environment. Cereal crops, just like domesticated sheep, goat and cattle, were integrated within those subsistence strategies that had maintained population groups since near the beginning of the Holocene. When approached in this manner, cereal cultivation sits alongside, rather than initiates, the other aspects of settlement intensification, such as craft specialization, copper exploitation and foreign trade, that characterize the Umm an-Nar period. It is to a deeper investigation of these aspects of Umm an-Nar society that I now turn.

UMM AN-NAR CRAFT PRODUCTION

The most common Umm an-Nar period artefacts recovered in excavations and surveys throughout the UAE and Sultanate of Oman are ceramics. Although occasional production of ceramics, often copying Mesopotamian models, had occurred in previous centuries, the quantity and specialized nature of Umm an-Nar ceramic production mark the advent of an entirely new industry. Two locally produced ceramics, Sandy Red/Orange Ware and Black on Red Ware, dominate production (Méry 1997, 2000; Potts 1991a: 102–110). The former is used in the production of large jars decorated with black-painted wavy lines near the shoulder and sometimes on the rim. It is one of the most common fabrics found at sites of this period, representing between 85 and 95% of the assemblage at Hili 8 (Blackman et al. 1989: 66) and likely produced in that oasis (Frifelt 1990). Black on Red Ware is common in tombs of this period and generally consists of small canister-shaped vessels with black paint on a red ground (Méry 1997, 2000) (Figure 4.6). Geochemical analysis has indicated that both wares are locally produced in the Oman peninsula, although from different geological catchment areas (Blackman et al. 1989; Méry 1997, 2000).

Although both of these wares represent the first widespread local production of ceramics, they are highly standardized in form and decoration and attest to developed technological skills. In her exhaustive study of third millennium BC pottery, Méry (2000) notes that the origins of this industry are to be found in the earlier establishment of 'agricultural' inland oases such as Hili 8. However, the pottery itself 'was inspired by models from the Indo-Iranian region, in particular those of the Keij-Makran region in Pakistan. Not only is the decoration of these vessels inspired by contemporary decorative themes from this region, but the quality of the paste, its fineness and colour are also elements which are similar, together with the shaping technology' (Méry 2007: 160). In a similar vein, Potts (2005) argues that potters from southeastern Iran, particularly the area around Jiroft, emigrated to southeastern Arabia and established the typical Umm an-Nar ceramic repertoire during the later third millennium BC. Neither explanation excludes the other, since it is possible that multiple waves

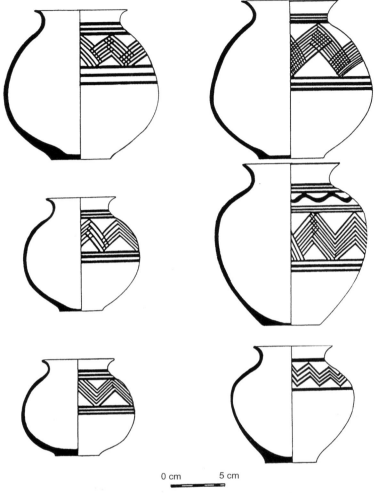

0 cm   5 cm

Figure 4.6. Umm an-Nar Black on Red Ware vessels, Ajman, United Arab
Emirates. After al-Tikriti 1989b: Pl. 39.

of influence, and perhaps potters themselves, moved from the different regions
of the Indo-Iranian region over the course of several centuries. The result was
a ceramic industry which, although located in the inland alluvial oases, served
local funerary and domestic needs across the region. In microcosm these oases
began to reflect fully the absorption and adaptation of a wide range of foreign
inputs: cereal agriculture and sheep, goat and cattle husbandry from the Fertile
Crescent; domesticated ass, possibly from East Africa; and finally craft production from the Indo-Iranian borderlands.

The Umm an-Nar period also witnesses the emergence of a tradition of
softstone working which was to remain one of the most distinctive local craft
traditions in southeastern Arabia until recently. This workable metamorphic

rock is commonly available in exposed seams throughout the al-Hajjar mountains. Hand-carved simple bowl shapes dominate the Umm an-Nar assemblage.
Canisters, often with matching lids, are also known, especially from tomb contexts. Vessels can be plain, but decoration consisting of a dot with two circles or
simple incised lines is common (David 2002; Potts 1991a: 108–110). These were
classed as série récente by de Miroschedji (1973) and are thus distinguished
from série ancienne vessels decorated with animals and naturalistic motifs and
produced in Iran. Umm an-Nar tombs, like that at Hili North, typically contain dozens of softstone vessels (David 2002). On settlement sites they are less
common, perhaps because of issues of preservation, but the general impression
is that their production was geared towards funerary contexts. Their specific
role in such contexts remains unknown, but unpublished examples of canisters
with lids from Jebel Buhais in Sharjah (UAE) contain jewellery, suggesting
their function as containers for precious objects. They were also exported and
were found in the Royal Graves at Ur and Tello in southern Mesopotamia
(Reade and Searight 2001) as well as Bahrain, Tarut, Failaka (Kuwait) and
southern and southeastern Iran (Potts 1991a: 109–110). Whether the vessels
were the main cargo in this trade or simply accompanied other exports, such
as copper, is unknown.

FOREIGN TRADE

As already noted, numerous settlements attest to sedentary occupation of the
coastal zone. The rich biota of the Arabian Gulf and Arabian Sea provided an
important rationale for such occupation, but excavations at a number of sites
have also indicated that foreign trade was of immense importance (e.g., During
Caspers 1971; Potts 1993c).

An Umm an-Nar tomb excavated at Tell Abraq provides a fascinating snap-
shot of international relations during this period (Potts 2000) (Figure 4.7).
Ceramics from Bahrain, Mesopotamia, Central Asia, Iran and South Asia are
all found in some quantity. Amongst the ceramics was a very fine Black on
Grey Ware, often in the form of a miniature jar or straight-sided canister
(Figure 4.8). Such pottery is well paralleled at numerous sites throughout the
Indo-Iranian borderlands, such as Tepe Yahya, Mundigak and Shahr-i Sokhta
(Méry 2000). Geochemical analysis of these vessels confirms a southeastern
Iranian origin (Blackman et al. 1989; Méry 2000). The latter region was also
the likely source of Incised Grey Ware that is also found in a number of Umm
an-Nar tombs.

Numerous ivory combs were also found at Tell Abraq and Ras al-Jinz
(Cleuziou and Tosi 2007: Fig. 253). Although the likely source of these was
South Asia, some of the decorative motifs on the combs are closely paralleled in northern Afghanistan (Potts 1993b, 2000), suggesting that the combs
themselves were the result of complex exchange networks. Several calcite and

Figure 4.7. Umm an-Nar tomb, Tell Abraq, Sharjah, United Arab Emirates.
Photo: Daniel Potts.

Figure 4.8. Black on Grey Ware vessel from Tell Abraq, Sharjah Archaeological
Museum. Photo: the author.

Figure 4.9. Softstone incense burner from Tell Abraq. After Potts 2000: 125.

alabaster vessels from the tomb are paralleled in eastern Iran at Shahr-i Sokhta, and a softstone incense burner or chalice is likely the product of Kerman just across the Straits of Hormuz (Figure 4.9). More than 600 etched carnelian, undecorated carnelian and agate beads were almost certainly produced around Gujarat in India. A small number of gold beads and pendants were also recovered, and although the origin of the gold is not known, some of the beads are paralleled in the Royal Graves of Ur (Potts 2000).

The contents of the buildings at Ras al-Jinz 2 suggest that the inhabitants of this settlement used their position on the easternmost edge of Arabia to engage in regularized maritime trade with South Asia. In addition to locally produced ceramics, softstone vessels (Figure 4.10) and copper objects (Figure 4.11), nearly 300 pieces of bitumen were recovered, most of them coming from Buildings I and II in the southern compound (Cleuziou and

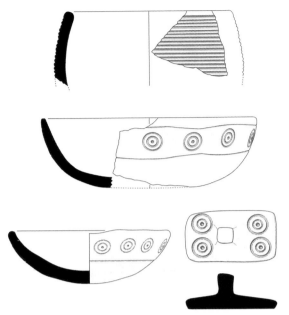

Figure 4.10. Softstone vessels, Bronze Age settlement of RJ-2, Ras al-Jinz 2, Sultanate of Oman. After Cleuziou and Tosi 2000: Fig. 10.

Tosi 2000: 63). Many of them contained the imprint and remains of barnacles and mat impressions, alerting the excavators to their use in caulking boats. Imported Indus Valley stamp seals marked with the Indus Valley script have also been recovered from Ras al-Jinz 2 (Cleuziou and Tosi 2000: 59–61), but it is the plentiful Indus Valley ceramics found at many sites that are the clearest indicator of South Asian trade. One of the most important of these is Black Slipped Micaceous Ware, which has long been linked to the Indian subcontinent and some examples of which carry Indus Valley graffiti (Cleuziou 1992: 97; Cleuziou and Tosi 2007: 172; Potts 1994b: Fig. 53.3). This pottery is found at coastal sites on both the Arabian Gulf and Gulf of Oman but also in considerable quantities at inland centres like Asimah (Vogt 1994). Geochemical analysis (Méry 2000) has indicated that the analysed samples were manufactured at centres on the Indus River, such as Mohenjo Daro, rather than at Harappa. The size and shape of these jars suggest that they were produced and likely exported to southeastern Arabia for the purpose of transporting their contents rather than the vessel itself. Residue analysis has not provided any clues as to what such contents were, but pickled vegetables, dairy products, ghee (clarified butter), wine, honey and indigo have all at one point been suggested (Méry 2007: 201).

Elite Indus Valley ceramic and other objects are also found at a number of sites. These include delicate dish-on-stand forms and several small painted bottles (e.g., at Ras al-Jinz 2; Cleuziou and Tosi 2007: Fig. 182).

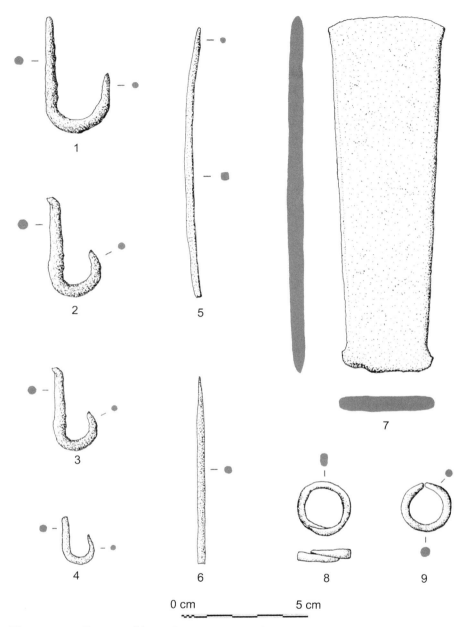

Figure 4.11. Copper objects, Bronze Age settlement of RJ-2, Ras al-Jinz 2, Sultanate of Oman. After Cleuziou and Tosi 2000: Fig. 12.

The presence of several imported Indus Valley weights raises the possibility that the metric system that was common in South Asia had been adopted, or at least employed, in southeastern Arabia and the Gulf. These well-cut chert, agate and softstone weights have been found at Tell Abraq

(Potts 2000: 130) and Shimal in Ras al-Khaimah (Vogt 1996: 118), as well as at Saar (Crawford et al. 1997: Pl. 91) and Qala'at al-Bahrain on Bahrain (Højlund and Anderson 1994: 395) and at Susa (Amiet 1986: 143–144) and Ur (Ratnagar 1981: 184–185). Nearly all of these weights are relevant to the discussion in subsequent chapters because they date to after the Umm an-Nar period. As will become clear, in the early second millennium BC seals and weight systems were employed in the Gulf to facilitate inter-regional trade. The presence of an example from the late Umm an-Nar period at Tell Abraq raises the possibility that the organizational dynamics of trade that characterize the early second millennium BC were already in place, but such an hypothesis certainly could not be insisted upon.

THE COPPER TRADE AND MESOPOTAMIA

While the imported ceramics and other ceramics found at Umm an-Nar sites attest to sustained economic interaction with Iran and the Indus Valley it is the extraction, production and export of copper and copper-based objects that have long been considered the defining characteristic of the Umm an-Nar economy. Systematic exploration by the German Mining Museum in the Sultanate of Oman indicates the intensive exploitation of copper ores from the middle of third millennium BC onwards (Weisgerber 1981). Major mining sites have been noted at several locations throughout the mountains (Weeks 1999, 2003; Weisgerber 1980, 1981), and at Maysar I an extensive settlement was located near an extraction site. Hauptmann (1985: 108) has estimated that total copper production between c. 2500 and 2000 BC was between 2,000 and 4,000 tonnes.

More recently, excavations at al-Moyassar in the Wadi Samad have provided evidence for a primary smelting centre of this period (Weisgerber 2007). This site is occupied through two periods at the end of third millennium BC and contains well-built mudbrick and stone houses, a tower and detailed evidence for smelting, casting and the production of copper objects. A smelting furnace has been reconstructed from the dozens of furnace fragments found at the site, and a hoard of twenty-two bun-shaped ingots illustrated the end result of this first stage of production. Tools and weapons were cast by simple pit moulds. The excavations at al-Moyassar also indicate that copper extraction was not the sole raison d'être of the settlement. The site was located in a potentially rich agriculture area, and evidence for the production of softstone vessels was found at the site. Nevertheless, Weisgerber concludes that 'copper production remained the main industrial activity' (Weisgerber 2007: 253).

The presence of a substantial tower coupled with the diverse industrial practices at al-Moyassar suggests to Weisgerber (2007: 254) that the settlement needed 'competent leaders and the resulting expansion of the economy produced a new elite' (Weisgerber 2007: 254). Such a conclusion speaks to the broader question of how local copper production relates to the efflorescence and growth of Umm an-Nar settlements. There is a chronological correlation between the expansion of the copper trade and intensification of settlement throughout southeastern Arabia. According to Weeks (2003: 24), whose study proved that southeastern Arabia played a key role in the copper trade, evidence for copper production during the earlier Hafit period is 'entirely circumstantial.... Copper production sites of this period are not reported by the German researchers, however an early but undated "trial and error" phase of copper production from Maysar 1 is thought to represent copper extraction prior to the Blütezeit [floruit] of production at the site in the late 3rd millennium BC (Hauptmann 1985: 113)' (Weeks 2003: 24). The site of al-Batin has also indicated potentially precocious copper extraction technology dated by thermoluminesence dating to c. 2500 BC (Weeks 2003: 200).

The most recent analysis (Begemann et al. 2010) of copper and bronze objects and ores from Mesopotamia, Bahrain and Oman confirms that southeastern Arabia was an increasingly significant exporter of copper to Mesopotamia only after the onset of the Umm an-Nar period. In that study, about two-thirds of the analysed Mesopotamian copper artefacts from the Jemdat Nasr, Early Dynastic I and II (i.e., the pre-Umm an-Nar period from c. 3000 to 2500 BC), are compositionally incompatible with sources in Oman (Begemann et al. 2010: 157–159). This situation changes during the Early Dynastic III and Akkadian periods, during which nearly half of the analysed Mesopotamian artefacts are chemically compatible with Omani sources. An increase of Omani-sourced copper from the Akkadian period onwards is also indicated by lead isotope analysis, although it should be noted that at no time does Omani copper dominate the sources used in southern Mesopotamia. According to Begemann et al. (2010: 159), their analyses and previous ones indicate 'that Mesopotamian bronze objects preferentially were made using Indus Valley-Meluhha copper from the Aravalli Hills in southern Rajasthan, in preference to whatever other copper sources may have been utilized in Mesopotamia at the same time.' This is an issue to which I will return later in the chapter.

Textual sources confirm that the large-scale importation of copper into Mesopotamia began only after the middle of the third millennium BC. Significant shipments of copper are noted during the reigns of Lugalanda and Uru-INIM-gina, in the twenty-fourth century BC (Potts 1991a: 182). In these texts, the copper is noted as coming from Dilmun (Bahrain), not Magan (southeastern Arabia), but this simply reflects the fact that the copper was shipped through Dilmun on the route north to Mesopotamia. By the Akkadian period, a specific type of copper mentioned in economic texts may refer to Dilmun copper (Potts 1991a: 184), while several economic texts from Tello and Adab mention copper and bronze objects coming directly from Magan (Potts 1991a: 137).

The emergence of the Akkadian Empire (2300–2100 BC) and subsequent Ur III period in southern Mesopotamia witnesses significant shifts in economic and political organization in southern Mesopotamia (for a review see Liverani 1993; Sallaberger and Westenholz 1999). This political importance of controlling trade with Magan, Dilmun and South Asia is suggested in the inscription of Sargon of Agade (2334–2279 BC), which boasts that the ships of Dilmun, Magan and Meluhha (the Indus Valley) were docked at his quayside in Agade (Gelb and Kienast 1990: 166; Potts 1986, 1991a: 136). It may well have been as a result of this trade that Sargon was able to order the carving of several stelae now in the Louvre in a olivine-gabbro that is geochemically consistent with a source in Oman (Heimpel 1982; Nigro 1998: 85). As Nigro has commented, 'The use of such stone celebrated the establishment of Sargon's supremacy over the southern Mesopotamian city-states, through which he had gained free access to those commercial routes previously controlled by the newly subjugated states (Uruk, Ur, Umma, Lagash)' (Nigro 1998: 86).

Sargon's successors appeared to have taken their control, or claims of control, of Magan to new heights. Manishtushu (2269–2255 BC) claims to have launched a maritime assault on Magan (Potts 1991a: 136; Sollberger and Kupper 1971: 104), while in his Statue A inscription, Naram-Sin (2254–2218 BC) writes: 'Naram-Sin the mighty king, King of four quarters, victorious in nine battles within one year. After he had won those battles he also brought their three kings in fetters before Enlil.... He subjugated Magan and captured Manitan, the "lord" of Magan; he quarried blocks of diorite in their mountains, transported (them) to his city Akkade, made a statue of himself ...' (Gelb and Kienast 1990; Hirsch 1963: 17).

By the Ur III period (2100–2000 BC) textual sources attest to the large-scale importation of copper directly from Magan. The founder of the new dynasty, Ur-Namma, claims in his code and in a number of inscribed clay cones found near Ur that he restored trade with Magan (Jacobsen 1960). His successor, Shulgi, claims to have received gold dust from a King of Magan (Potts 1990: 144). From near the end of the Ur III period, we have several texts of a merchant family who carried out trade with Magan. The father of the family, Pu'udu, shipped barley to Magan in exchange for precious stones. The size of the fleet at his disposal was enormous, comprising eight large ships and six officers, each in charge of sixty men (Steinkeller 2004: 104). From Ur, two texts record the merchant activities of his son, Lu-Enlilla, who had the title of 'sea-faring merchant' (Neumann 1999: 44). One text details the goods provided to him by the Temple of Nanna for the purchase of Magan copper, while the other text is a receipt of copper from Magan (Potts 1990: 145). Since they are from the same year, they likely record the outgoings and revenue from a single trading expedition to Magan. The Mesopotamian goods comprised c. 1,800 kilos of wool, c. 300 kilos of plant material, c. 600 kilos of small fish, c. 1,500 liters of sesame oil, as well as hides and garments. From Magan, Lu-Enlilla received c. 150 kilos of copper, which was almost certainly locally produced. He also received ivory, semi-precious stones and red ochre, which were probably not local. The ivory, perhaps in the form of combs like those found at Tell Abraq and Ras al-Jinz 2 (as mentioned earlier), came from South Asia, while the red ochre (haematite) likely came from the nearby island of Hormuz, just off the coast of Iran, which has considerable haematite deposits that were mined until very recently (Waltham 2008).

These rich textual sources and abundant archaeological remains permit us to make several conclusions about interaction between southeastern Arabia and Mesopotamia at the end of the third millennium BC. Steinkeller has characterized Pu'udu's merchant activity as a sort of 'foreign-trade ministry', since he was clearly well connected with the royal family of Ur (Steinkeller 2004: 104). Not only was one son, Lu-Enlilla, a 'seafaring merchant' but his other son, Kug-Nanna, married into the royal family. Indeed, as Garfinkle (2002) has demonstrated, the community of Ur III merchants was consistently structured around family ties and their connection to the state. Lu-Enlilla was almost certainly acting on behalf of the Temple of Nanna, but like many merchants of the Ur III period he was also a lucrative businessman in his own right (Crawford 2005: 44; Potts 1990: 145). On the return trip from Magan, he presented to the Temple of Nanna 10 liters of Magan onions and 20 liters of an aromatic substance. According to Leemans (1960: 21), this was a tithe that reflected the private gain that Lu-Enlilla made from the Magan transaction. On another occasion he paid a large volume of grain to the state as a 'tithe of sea-faring trade' (Steinkeller 2004: 105). Lu-Enlilla also operated as an arbitrator in economic transactions. In a text from Ur, he authorizes a slave contract (Démare-Lafont 2011: 337; Steinkeller 1989: 302–303) and is referred to by the Akkadian equivalent of 'judge'.

In other words, economic exchange between southeastern Arabia (Magan) and Mesopotamia was orchestrated, from the Mesopotamian perspective, by the state and was in the hands of merchants who were connected to the state not only by their official titles such as 'seafaring merchant' but through powerful family connections. They played an important role in ensuring the supply of foreign goods to the court while at the same time maintaining the economic position of a small number of families. The agricultural-based state in which these families lived was rigidly hierarchical and based on slavery and draconian labour practices (see Englund 1991, 2009). The importation of copper from Magan and elsewhere was critical to the maintenance of this system. Agricultural tools were made from copper (Edens 1992: 126); in one text of the UR III period, 1,083 copper sickles and 60 copper hoes are mentioned as being refurbished from a single storeroom (Postgate 1992: 226). Copper and bronze were also used to produce weapons that were critical for maintaining state control and engaging in military conquests. In other words, control over the copper trade was essential for the maintenance of the political, economic and social order of the UR III state.

TRADE AND SOCIAL COHESION IN THE UMM AN-NAR PERIOD

How did this trade affect southeast Arabian society? In addressing this question we have two sources of information: archaeological data and Mesopotamian texts. Prior to the Ur III period, there are textual indications of a polycentric distribution of power in southeastern Arabia. For example, Manishtushu records that he defeated the '32 Lords of Magan', a term indicating a political landscape consistent with the settlement distribution of the Umm an-Nar period (Edens 1992: 128; Potts 1991a: 137–138). However, less than a century later the political situation in southeastern Arabia is rendered differently in Mesopotamian texts. The significance of the use of the Sumerian term 'en', or 'Lord', to describe a leader of Magan in the inscription of Naram-Sin has been well noted by scholars (e.g., Potts 1991a: 139). In the Ur III period the situation changes again. A king (*lugal*) of Magan is mentioned in one document, and reference to a Nadu-beli as governor (*ensi*) of Magan is noted in another. The implication of the use of this term is unclear; as Potts has noted: 'It is difficult to imagine that the reference to an ensi of Magan during the reign of Amar-Sin can mean that Magan was temporarily part of the Ur III Empire. On the other hand, the dispatch of troops during the reign of Shulgi (2094–2047 BC) must make one wonder whether this might not have been the case, at least for a brief period of time' (Potts 1991a: 148).

It is tempting to read changes in these Mesopotamian texts as evidence of a 'secondary state' in southeastern Arabia, emerging as a result of trade with a more complex neighbour (Edens 1992; cf. Price 1978). Indeed, Reade (2008: 17) has argued that by 2000 BC, southeastern Arabia may 'have been operating as a unified state and perhaps even attempting to impose some form of control over the Gulf'. A more nuanced approach emphasizes that these texts reflect an 'invention of tradition' (Hobsbawm and Ranger 1983) that is an attempt by the states of southern Mesopotamia to render the indigenous kin-based structure of southeastern Arabia (Cleuziou 2002) in an increasingly familiar fashion so as to facilitate intensifying economic interaction. This phenomenon is evident in Assyria's dealings with northern Arabia much later in the first millennium BC (as described later) and is a well-noted phenomenon during contact episodes between asymmetrical political systems in Europe, the New World and Africa millennia later. To interpret the evidence as Reade does is analogous to interpreting the British tradition of calling Australian aboriginal leaders 'kings' and giving them decorated plates as evidence of a monarchical system in indigenous Australia. Not only were such terms irrelevant within local social systems, but the plates themselves soon became socially worthless curios and museum objects (Foley 2007; Troy 1993).

Of course, this does not mean that southeastern Arabia was unaffected by increased demand for copper and its engagement in a regional trade network. Increasing economic interdependence must have resulted at the local and intra-settlement levels. The networked economy, the emergence of specialization and the continuation of generalized production strategies were linked in a dynamic feedback mechanism that fostered settlement growth (Rouse and Weeks 2011: 1589). However, if our 'seafaring merchant' Lu-Enlilla did actually sail with his ships down to Magan in the twenty-first century BC (rather than have his cohorts of terrified slaves and officers make the trip), he would have encountered a society that was fundamentally different from that of Ur. The buildings on Umm an-Nar island or at Tell Abraq had not radically changed in several centuries. Despite the apparent wealth of copper, he would have seen no palaces or elite residences or any overt marker of institutionalized authority at these sites or at any inland settlement. He would have also been struck by the absence of temples in which formalized religion was practised. We might well imagine that when he told the 'locals' that Shulgi, the king of Ur, had decided that he was in fact a god, they would have just chuckled or been bewildered. They would have also been bewildered by the pride he displayed in a cylinder seal which was 'of the extremely rare in-na-ba type' that had been given to him by the king himself (Steinkeller 2004: 104), since cylinder seals had little use in southeast Arabian society at this time (Potts 2010). Similarly, he might have been as astounded as Geoffrey Bibby was 4,500 years later to discover that the meal he ate that night was, in fact, dugong steaks.

How, then, was southeastern Arabia affected by economic and political engagement with its neighbours? In answering this question, we should start with references to the export of barley during this period. Edens (1992: 127) and During Caspers (1989) argue on the basis of a single Ur III text that coastal settlements such as Umm an-Nar became reliant on imported Mesopotamian barley for subsistence. As we have seen already, the inhabitants of coastal settlements had a wide range of foodstuffs available, and analysis of teeth from Umm an-Nar island suggests that cereals were not commonly consumed, even if there was small-scale cereal agriculture in the inland oases (Højgaard 1980). As Potts (1993a: 188) has noted, the idea that these settlements were reliant on barley can be perhaps best described as pure fantasy.

Visible markers of prestige did make their way into southeast Arabian society at this time. Some of these, including wool and textiles that were exported in some quantity from Ur and Girsu, both of which had well-established textile industries (Waetzoldt 1972), are archaeologically invisible (Crawford 1973). Even though the textiles that were exported were apparently of second- ary quality (Potts 1990: 147; Waetzoldt 1972: 72; see Steinkeller 1995), to the inhabitants of Magan they would have carried much socially visible prestige. Linen has also been found in the Umm an-Nar grave at Tell Abraq (Potts and Reade 1993), and although it is not known whether it was imported, there is no doubt that linen was a high-prestige garment (Waetzoldt 1983). Imported gold, silver, ivory, lapis lazuli and etched carnelian personal adornments are found in tombs at al-Safouh, Mowaihat, Tell Abraq, Ras al-Jinz and Hili and on Umm an-Nar island (Cleuziou and Tosi 2007: 129; De Waele and Haerinck 2006; Potts 2000; al-Tikriti et al. 2004: 172). Their presence suggests that a certain segment of society benefited from increased exchange and trade with Mesopotamia and South Asia and may have emulated foreign elites through the display of prestige emblems. These people were almost certainly local – recent isotopic analysis of teeth from burials at Umm an-Nar, Mowaihat, Tell Abraq and Shimal indicates that only three non-locals were identified out of a sample size of 100 individuals (Gregoricka 2011: 327).

The social display of these objects was, however, only one part of a constant and dynamic process of absorption and resistance to foreign cultural inputs. The Umm an-Nar tombs in which the dead were buried with their prestige garments and accoutrements affirm values that are antithetical to the con- temporary sociopolitics of the regions from which these objects came. Umm an-Nar tombs are collective – there is virtually no evidence for differentiated treatment of the individual, regardless of whether or not that individual was adorned with special exotic gifts. The undifferentiated treatment of the dead was an attempt by the living to emphasize the importance of social cohesion in a monument that was both visible to nearby settlements and accessed fre- quently to bury the recently departed. When the latter occurred and a new burial was placed into the tomb, bones were pushed to one side or heaped together in one corner of the tomb, not out of any disrespect but rather as an act of affirmation participated in by both the living and dead. In this way, the inhabitants of Umm an-Nar settlements engaged in an act of collective memory that stretched back not just to their parents and grandparents but to their Neolithic ancestors interred in communal burials such as those at Jebel Buhais (Chapter 3). As Cleuziou and Tosi have commented: 'Once this lifetime was over everybody entered through a complex processing of their physical remains into their world of the ancestors, regulated by the most important cri- terion of social organization: kinship. This strong manifestation of "equality" should not be taken as a witness of a strictly egalitarian society but rather as the ideological affirmation of what should have been beyond the complex- ities of diversity in wealth and power among the living' (Cleuziou and Tosi 2007: 132).

In the Umm an-Nar tomb at Tell Abraq, the treatment of a single skeleton stands in contrast to the normal pattern of interment. A female, 18–20 years of age, was fully articulated within a mass of disarticulated bones (Potts 2000: 92). She had obviously been moved from the place of her original interment, or at the least care was taken to ensure that her body remained articulated, as disarticulated skeletons were placed above and below her. Her skeleton also exhibited several abnormalities that were consistent with a neurological disorder, perhaps polio (Potts 2000: 92). In her life, she would have required constant attention and assistance from her kin. Whether or not this was provided we will never know, and indeed it is not clear that polio was the cause of her death, but the treatment afforded to her skeleton after death reflected an understanding of (ideal) care and attention on the part of the community. Several other cases of incapacitated injuries were noted by Vilos, who concluded that 'members of the Tell Abraq community were valued despite the fact that they were unable or limited in their ability to contribute to the community and may even have placed a burden on the group's resources. The people of Tell Abraq showed compassion and a caring nature toward their own, regardless of what misfortune fell upon their lives' (Vilos 2011: 77). In other words, if our 'seafaring merchant' Lu-Enlilla did bring his flotilla of trading ships to the coastal settlement of Tell Abraq, he would have engaged with a community that was as distant as could be from the oppressive state in which he and his family thrived.

If Lu-Enlilla had been present at Tell Abraq during a burial, he would also have been struck by the rituals associated with the interment of the dead. Animal, and occasionally human, sacrifice was a common feature of elite Bronze Age Near Eastern burials, as seen, for example, in the Great Death Pit at Ur, where both humans and animals were sacrificed during the burial of a member of the royal ruling elite of Ur (Baadsgaard et al. 2011; Pollock 2007). In contrast, there is a striking and nearly complete absence of sacrifice in Umm an-Nar tombs. Occasional finds have been reported, but these can be mostly attributed to later interference or bioturbation (Blau and Beech 1999: 39–40). A single exception to this is the Umm an-Nar tomb in Ras al-Khaimah in the northern UAE in which a complete skeleton of a dog lay alongside the body of a female (Blau and Beech 1999). Blau suggests that the dog was used for hunting or herding and as a domestic animal was integrated within the social framework in which the woman existed. In this sense, the dog was not sacrificed in the same manner as animals and humans were at Ur. To sacrifice an animal, or indeed a human, at the time of interment would be to negate the affirmation of equality by taking a resource that belonged to the community, or at least a segment of it, and 'giving' it to an individual. It would affirm the status of the living individual transformed into the realm of death and the afterlife. In short, it would encourage the loss of social cohesion in the living society.

In many ways, therefore, Umm an-Nar funerary practices consumed foreign elite paraphernalia that filtered into southeast Arabian society and redefined them in a context that emphasized the primacy of communalism over the transitory nature of material wealth. Even for those not engaged in the disposal of the dead, the visibility of these tombs in the settlement landscape communicated this message on a continual basis. This assuaging function of Umm an-Nar tombs became increasingly important as engagement with Mesopotamia accelerated in the last century of the third millennium BC. In her analysis of the construction techniques used in the fourteen Umm an-Nar tombs in the al-Ain oasis, Méry notes an 'almost linear evolution' of the techniques employed (McSweeney et al. 2008: 10). Towards the end of the third millennium BC, carefully worked ashlars are increasingly used in the construction of larger and more elaborate tombs that were more visible in the landscape (McSweeney et al. 2008). By the twenty-first century BC, tombs like that excavated at Tell Abraq contain a wide assortment of luxury goods from Mesopotamia, Iran and South Asia. The correlation between investment in tomb construction and the absorption of elite foreign goods suggests that the resolution of social tension communicated by the tombs became increasingly important as southeastern Arabia absorbed and resisted foreign cultural inputs into its society.

Analysis of the bioarchaeology of Umm an-Nar skeletal material indicates, however, that the message communicated by the tombs did not completely arrest growing social tension. Analysis of nearly 400 individuals in the tomb at Tell Abraq highlights dietary and disease characteristics of the population (Potts 2000), as well as bone deformations consistent with repetitive biomechanical work during the twenty-first century BC (Cope et al. 2005). A remarkable aspect of these data is the unparalleled number of neonatal and pre-term individuals. Of the 127 sub-adults (less than 18 years of age) recovered from the tomb, 22% were third-trimester (pre-term) infants, 9% were neonates and 61% were children under 5. In contrast, children aged 6–18 made up only 7% of sub-adults (Baustian 2010). This demographic profile is without known parallel in ancient Near Eastern contexts. Baustian (2010) suggests that cultural factors such as consanguinity and low marriage age may be responsible for the very high rate of pre-term and neonatal death. The absence of a similarly high incidence of neonatal death in other prehistoric burials (such as at Jebel Buhais, mentioned earlier) suggests that such practices cannot be assumed for all of prehistory. Rather, infection, as suggested by indications of *Staphylococcus* and *Streptococcus*, and nutritional stress in both mothers and neonates and pre-terms are the likely causes of such high infant mortality.

Bioarchaeological data from an Umm an-Nar tomb and associated burial pit at Hili paint a similar picture (Bondioli et al. 1998; McSweeney et al. 2008). A minimum of 300 people were interred in this tomb, and pronounced evidence for high infant and young adult mortality was recorded. In the associated burial pit, a minimum of 600 individuals were identified. In this population, porotic hyperostosis/cribra orbitalia was common, leading the authors to conclude that 'a large proportion of the population suffered from anaemia and/or starvation during childhood. Some of these individuals died in infancy, while others survived into adulthood. Repeated periods of illness or malnutrition during childhood were apparent from the presence of hypoplastic lesions on tooth enamel' (McSweeney et al. 2008: 6).

In short, the increasing wealth generated by trade with Mesopotamia did little to improve the daily lives of the inhabitants of southeastern Arabia. On the contrary, the two collections of bioarchaeological data that are contemporary with accelerated trade and engagement with Mesopotamia at the end of the third millennium BC portray a society in which access to basic foodstuffs was becoming increasingly difficult. Although we do not have bioarchaeological data from the centuries immediately prior, there seems no question that the health of the inhabitants of southeastern Arabia in the very late third millennium BC was not as good as that of their nomadic ancestors who herded sheep and goat 3,000 years earlier and were buried at Jebel Buhais (Chapter 3).

THE END OF THE UMM AN–NAR PERIOD

The sequence of tombs and settlements in al-Ain indicates that mortuary practice and regional economics shifted dramatically by the end of the twenty-first century BC (McSweeney et al. 2008). Hili Tomb N and Hili North Tomb A are critical in this regard, as they span the last centuries of the Umm an–Nar and the beginning of the subsequent Wadi Suq period (2000–1500 BC). The tombs are completely different in structure: Hili Tomb N is a simple pit grave that existed alongside an already existing Umm an–Nar stone tomb (Tomb E), while Hili North Tomb A is a classic Umm an–Nar period circular stone constructed from well-cut masonry and containing multiple chambers. Significant artefactual similarities between the latest Hili North Tomb A levels and the earliest Hili Tomb N layers speak to a intensive cosmopolitan economy during the Umm an–Nar period. Imported Iranian and Indus Valley ceramics and the same range of imported Indus carnelian (etched and undecorated) beads and calcite vessels are found in each tomb.

By the later levels of the use of Hili Tomb N, around 2000 BC, the situation changes dramatically. Some of the locally produced ceramics are no longer wheel-made and exhibit poor control over firing temperatures. The origin of imported material also shifted, with material from Nausharo more common than Indus Valley ceramics. At the same time, carnelian beads from the Indus Valley are now less common than paste beads. Softstone vessels decorated in a fashion typically recognized as Wadi Suq (as described later) are also found (McSweeney et al. 2008).

These changes mirror sweeping regional alterations in settlement throughout southeastern Arabia. Not a single Umm an–Nar type of tomb, or any

above-ground tomb, is known to have been constructed after 2000 BC.
Inasmuch as the construction of these tombs must have played a key role in
social relations within Umm an–Nar society, massive social changes are indicated.
At the same time, many Umm an–Nar settlements are abandoned, and only a
handful show any continued occupation into the second millennium BC.

Attempts to cast these changes as an outcome of centre–periphery relations
with South Asia or Mesopotamia are entirely unconvincing (e.g., Edens 1992).
Even if there were interruptions, trade with Mesopotamia, South Asia and Iran
continued in the early second millennium BC. Climate was also not a direct
cause of these events. Parker's claim that a desiccation event led to the 'end of
the Umm al Nar period' (Parker et al. 2006: 473) does not tally with the archaeological evidence: the lake cores he cites indicate a 'total desiccation' around
2200 BC (Parker et al. 2006: 473), but tombs at Tell Abraq and Hili indicate a
vibrant cosmopolitan economy well into the twenty-first century BC.

CONCLUSIONS

Local adaptation to shifting environmental conditions led to increasing intensification of land use in southeastern Arabia from the early third millennium
BC onwards. This intensification is particularly marked during the Umm an–
Nar period (2500–2000 BC). The causes of this are unclear, but Mesopotamian
demand for copper, while an increasingly important part of the economy, was
not directly responsible. Increasing demand for copper did result in economic
changes, and trade connections brought new and exotic artefacts into the cultural fabric of the society. In many societies this would have created the potential for increased social and political stratification, and it is indeed clear that
southeast Arabian society, forged by millennia of adaptation to the desert environment, struggled with these foreign inputs. The allure of such prestige goods
and their implied authority were mitigated by collective burials in which individuals who had access to gold, carnelian, ivory, silver and lapis lazuli during their lives were interred alongside those who were buried with a simple,
locally made pot. Increased community labour and skill were dedicated to
their construction as these collective tombs became increasingly important in
communicating social cohesion towards the end of the Umm an–Nar period.

The abandonment of Umm an–Nar lifeways must be situated within these
developments and within a longue durée perspective on the occupation of
southeastern Arabia. We have seen in the textual sources that by the twenty-
first century BC the Ur III state attempted to transform the sociopolitical
organization of Magan into a hierarchical framework that reflected its own.
The importation of visible social markers of prestige, such as textiles and some
personal adornments, had the potential to play into the desired fraying of the
social fabric. The increasing investment in larger and more elaborate Umm
an–Nar tombs, which operated as affirmation of the counter-value of social

cohesion, suggests increasing societal tension. Might it be, perhaps as a response to the rise of an individual who did indeed claim the title of 'king' or the increasing potential that this might occur, that the inhabitants of southeastern Arabia took the ultimate step in affirming the tribal values that had defined their society for generations and simply abandoned their increasingly tension-ridden permanent settlements? The archaeological evidence makes it clear that such an abandonment did take place, but as an explanatory mechanism the scenario just described remains no more than an attractive hypothesis which requires further investigation. As we shall see in Chapter 6, however, in sub-sequent centuries those regions of Arabia, such as Bahrain, that had been in closer cultural contact with Mesopotamia moved through this societal thresh-old and transitioned to hierarchical states.

CHAPTER 5

THE BRONZE AGE IN WESTERN ARABIA

INTRODUCTION

At the end of Chapter 3 I examined the mechanisms by which the inhabitants of western Arabia responded to the climatic deterioration of the fourth millennium BC. These are to some extent paralleled in eastern Arabia, where, as we saw in the preceding chapter, widespread sedentary occupation emerged by c. 2500 BC. It is thanks to the initial discovery of a Bronze Age in Yemen some thirty years ago (de Maigret 1984a) that a similar process can be traced for the Arabian southwest, even if many of the details are still unclear. De Maigret's discovery prompted intensive research, particularly in the Yemeni Highlands, where initial experimentation with agriculture permitted a subsequent adaptation to the more arid regions surrounding the Ramlat as-Sabatyn and coastal environments. The result was the development of substantial settlements well before the emergence of the Sabaean Federation in the eighth century BC. This process did not, however, result in fundamental shifts in subsistence throughout all of western Arabia. Evidence for the central and northern regions indicates that varied lifeways were pursued in the highly demarcated regions of the Asir, Hijaz and Nafud. In this chapter I will bring these currents of evidence together, in the hope of painting a broad picture of developments in one of the least-studied time periods in Arabian archaeology.

HIGHLAND SETTLEMENT AND THE EMERGENCE OF AGRICULTURE

Archaeological evidence for the emergence of agriculture in southwestern Arabia is scarce and reliant on data from just a handful of sites (Figure 5.1). Wheat, barley, lentils, peas, chickpeas, figs and possibly broomcorn millet are present at Jubabat al-Juruf and Hayt al-Suad in the Dhamar region during the late fourth and early third millennia BC (Boivin and Fuller 2009: Table 2; Ekstrom and Edens 2003; Harrower 2008: 498). In total, the sample

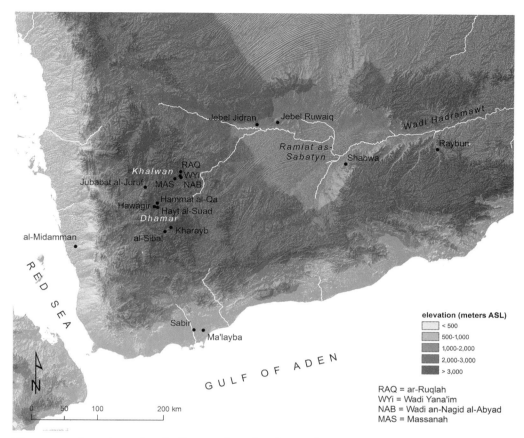

Figure 5.1. Location of main Bronze Age sites in southwestern Arabia.

from these two sites comprised more than 1,400 charcoal fragments, making the discoveries incontestable evidence of early agriculture (Charbonnier 2008).

With its piedmontane valleys and sufficient rainfall, the Dhamar region provided the ideal area for the emergence of agriculture. Indeed, evidence for possible terracing dated to the sixth and fifth millennia BC has been noted at al-Hadabah (Ghaleb 1990) and Sedd adh-Dhraa (Harrower 2006: 91; Wilkinson et al. 1997). Further investigations are required before it can be concluded that these terraces were necessarily agricultural in function; a role in promoting wild plant growth for fodder for domesticated animals is also possible (McCorriston et al. 2005). Nevertheless, there can be little doubt that with the cessation of the Holocene Moist Phase the Highlands were a refuge for occupation, in much the same way that coastal regions were in southeastern Arabia (Chapter 3). Although reduced, rainfall was still higher than that in adjacent zones. Palaeosols that had been formed principally during the earlier Neolithic continued to be generated, perhaps as a result of feedback initiated by the presence of vegetation and human activity (Wilkinson 2009: 56). In a sense, these environments can be viewed as an aspect of niche construction in which human activity created conditions that expanded optimal zones for agriculture (Wilkinson et al. 2012). With the availability of domesticated crops from the late fourth millennium BC, the Highlands became the ideal location, therefore, to experiment with new food production strategies.

This resulted in a massive increase in the number of permanent settlements throughout the Dhamar region. In total, fifty-one sites of the third and early second millennia BC have been recorded in one of the most extensive surveys yet conducted in Yemen or, for that matter, anywhere in Arabia (Edens and Wilkinson 1998; Wilkinson 2009; Wilkinson and Edens 1999; Wilkinson et al. 1997). There is great variation in the size of settlements, but by the second millennium BC they reach a maximum size of 15–20 hectares. The earliest well-documented site is al-Sibal, dating from 2900 to 1700 BC (Edens 1999b: 107) or 2600 to 1900 BC (Edens and Wilkinson 1998: 79) on the basis of ^{14}C samples. The site was located on the edge of a montane plain and presents a picture of a large, complex ancient settlement. It is between 1 and 2 hectares in size and appears to have experienced several phases of building. In the northeast of the site, there is evidence for a town wall surrounding the settlement. Long single-room structures were evident on the surface, while a large multi-room structure, which was identified as some type of elite building, was located near the centre of the settlement (Wilkinson 2009).

Hammat al-Qa is slightly later than al-Sibal and is more representative of typical Highland Bronze Age settlement (Edens et al. 2000; Edens and Wilkinson 1998: 80; Wilkinson 2009: 54). On the basis of ^{14}C samples, this 4-hectare settlement dates to the end of the third and beginning of the second millennium BC. Located on top of a plateau, it is surrounded by a massive and gated boulder-constructed wall (Wilkinson et al. 1997: 111) (Figures 5.2 and 5.3). Limited excavations have revealed a dense residential zone in which two basic types of buildings can be discerned. The first consists of a simple rectangular room accessible from the longside and often containing small annexes and internal benches (Figure 5.4). The second is a multi-room structure that appears to have been arranged around a courtyard (Edens et al. 2000).

As Edens and Wilkinson note (1998: 81), the size and organization of Hammat al-Qa are unmatched throughout southwestern Arabia (Figure 5.5). Indeed, the Dhamar region, and more generally the high plateau, provides the most abundant archaeological evidence for Bronze Age settlement. This may be because this region was in fact the most densely occupied at this time, or it may be an artefact of archaeological research (Wilkinson 2009: 59). It has been one of the most extensively surveyed in Yemen and, unlike adjacent areas in the east and on the edges of the desert early settlement, has not been obscured by later sedimentation and building activity.

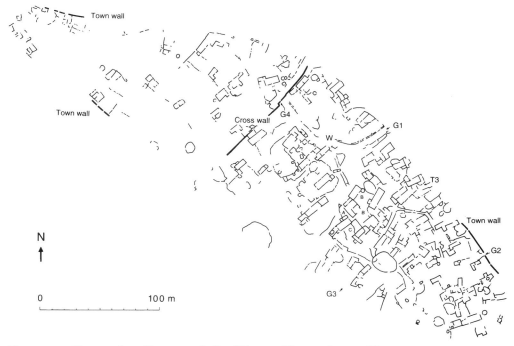

Figure 5.2. Bronze Age Hammat al-Qa, Dhamar, Yemen. Image: Tony Wilkinson.

Figure 5.3. Town wall remnants, Hammat al-Qa, Dhamar, Yemen. Photo: Tony Wilkinson.

Figure 5.4. Residential architecture, Hammat al-Qa, Dhamar, Yemen. Photo: Tony Wilkinson.

Figure 5.5. View of Hammat al-Qa, Dhamar, Yemen. Photo: Tony Wilkinson.

There can be no doubt that the emergence of agriculture was key to the development of large sedentary settlements in this part of southwestern Arabia. On the basis of the discoveries at Hayt al-Suad and Jubabat al-Juruf, it can be concluded that the agriculture regime of the Dhamar region comprised a mix of cultivars that reflected the geographical position of southwestern Arabia. Lentils, chickpeas, peas, figs and barley were all 'founder crops' of the Neolithic Levant and Fertile Crescent. Boivin and Fuller (2009: 146) suggest that the dominance of hulled emmer wheat (*Triticum dicoccum*) in Yemen points to an African origin, and this contrasts with the dominance of bread wheats (*Triticum aestivum*) in eastern Arabia. The emergence of agricultural settlements in eastern and western Arabia reflects, therefore, environmental factors combined with the varied geographical orientation brought about by the position of Arabia between South Asia, Africa and the Middle East. The introduced cultivars were differentially exploited in accordance with the rainfall regimes of eastern and western Arabia. The presence of broomcorn millet (*Panicum miliaceum*) at Jubabat al-Juruf is of particular significance since, as a summer crop, it would have provided the basis for double cropping and increased agricultural yield. Such cultivation was not possible in the Umm an-Nar settlements of southeastern Arabia.

As I noted in Chapter 2, the Highlands are not an homogenous ecological environment, and while agriculture became cemented within the subsistence strategy of Dhamar, the inhabitants of adjacent regions deployed a subsistence strategy that responded to more challenging environments. The Khawlan region of the Highlands, where Bronze Age settlement was first discovered (de Maigret 1990), is characterized by deeply incised narrow valleys that cut through the Precambrian basement rocks and present limited opportunities for cultivation. This contrasts with the Dhamar region with its large intermontane cultivable plains as well as plateaux that provide access to these valleys and protection. Rainfall accentuates these differences as it decreases dramatically from west to east. Dry farming is thus possible in many of the regions of the central Highlands, but on the arid margins and in the Khawlan region, sayl irrigation (the capture of seasonal runoff) was critical to agricultural success.

The inhabitants of the Khawlan adapted to this environment. A survey in this important watershed revealed thirty-eight settlements situated within a narrow ecological range. Small excavations were conducted at al-Massanah site 1 (MASi) and a site in the Wadi an-Nagid al-Abyad (NABvii), while more extensive excavations were conducted in the Wadi Yana'im (WYi) and ar-Ruqlah (RAQi) (de Maigret 1990). Despite the various appellations given to these sites and their cultural remains (e.g., Wadi Yana'im culture, the Khawlan Bronze Age culture), a similar layout is found at most settlements. They are small, normally less than 1 hectare (de Maigret 1984a, 1990; Edens and Wilkinson 1998: 73–75), and consist of rounded, stone-constructed compounds with central sub-circular rooms.

That these settlements were engaged in agriculture is evident from barley, wheat, oat, sorghum, millet and cumin impressions on ceramics from Wadi Yana'im, al-Masannah and Wadi al-Is (WUiv) (Costantini 1990). The presence of sorghum in the Khawlan is noteworthy. A summer crop, like millet, it would have permitted double cropping in this region. However, the fact that it is attested in only four ceramic impressions (Charbonnier 2008; Costantini 1990), is absent in the larger archaeobotanical collection from Dhamar and is occurring at a very early date in comparison with the evidence for its domestication in Africa raise the possibility that the plant may be present in a wild form or that a re-evaluation of this identification may be necessary. An alternative possibility is that it was introduced to southwestern Arabia from South Asia, but that is not an hypothesis that could be insisted upon given the present evidence (Boivin and Fuller 2009: Table 1; Fuller 2003).

Upon the discovery of the Khawlan Bronze Age, de Maigret speculated that the settlements he uncovered were located on the edge of a region in which a much more intensive agricultural regime was present (de Maigret 1990: 217; Edens and Wilkinson 1998: 79). The discoveries in the Dhamar region of significantly larger sedentary settlements would appear to confirm this hypothesis. Whereas sites such as al-Sibal and Hammat al-Qa are large, well-organized and fortified, the Khawlan settlements might be more accurately described as 'small agro-pastoral villages or even hamlets' (Wilkinson 2009: 59). The pastoral component of the Khawlan settlements was likely very pronounced, with sheep and goat dominating pastoralism. Wilkinson notes also that cattle are more common in the central Highlands as opposed to the Khawlan, in line with the more fertile setting (Wilkinson and Edens 1999: 28).

Nevertheless, throughout the third millennium BC these two regions were in contact with each other. The architecture of Talaba, Abent and Hamat Liban al-Kebir in the Dhamar (Wilkinson et al. 1997: 111, 117) displays clear similarities with that of Khawlan Bronze Age settlements. They also shared a new technology of fundamental importance: ceramic production. The Bronze Age pottery from Yemen has not been subjected to the same detailed geochemical analysis as Umm an-Nar pottery, but it seems likely that local clay sources were exploited to make a series of simple functional shapes, the decoration of which is limited to burnishing and incised decoration. Aspects of the pottery from the earlier settlement of al-Sibal in the Dhamar are not always shared by possibly contemporary settlements in the Khawlan region, perhaps because of chronological differences or a lack of interaction between the two zones. By the later third and early second millennia BC, however, a 'single tradition' is in existence and strong formal, morphological and functional ties emerge between the two assemblages, even if the temper of each assemblage is specific to the basic geology of each region (Edens 1999b).

DIVERGING SETTLEMENT SYSTEMS

Differences in the size, organization and number of settlements in the Khawlan and Dhamar regions increase during the second millennium BC. In the Khawlan no new settlements are known even if the sites of WRAii, WUiv, GAi and MAAii are said to continue into the early second millennium BC (de Maigret 1990: 35, 39–40). In contrast, the 3- to 4-hectare site of Kharayb in the Dhamar area was sounded by Edens and Wilkinson and dates to this period (Edens 1999b; Edens and Wilkinson 1999). The architecture consists of clusters of stone-constructed, long narrow buildings with internal divisions (Figures 5.6 and 5.7). Excavations focused on one stone-constructed building

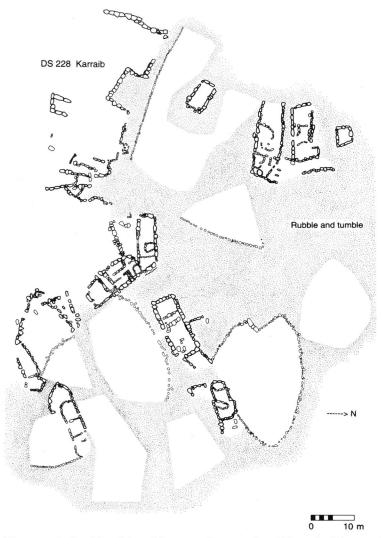

Figure 5.6. Residential architecture, Bronze Age Kharyab, Dhamar, Yemen. Image: Tony Wilkinson.

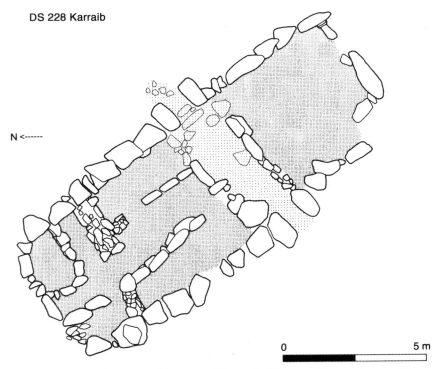

Figure 5.7. Residential architecture, Kharayb, Dhamar, Yemen. Image: Tony Wilkinson.

measuring 13.9 by 5.4 meters (Figure 5.8). Four ^{14}C dates were obtained from this building. The two early dates are considered by Edens to represent sediment that was incorporated into the settlement from an earlier site or settlement phase at the site. The main occupation of the settlement and the many ceramics excavated within the rectilinear building are fixed by the two later dates. When combined, this evidence suggests that the settlement was occupied during the second half of the second millennium BC, if not earlier. The ceramics from Kharayb show similarities with the earlier Khawlan and central Highland assemblages (Edens 1999b: 117–121). The parallels to earlier material suggest some form of continuity in material culture production that may, or may not, reflect a broader cultural continuity in the occupation of the Highlands. However, the new forms that define the late second millennium BC Kharayb assemblage are not paralleled in the Khawlan, which leads Eden to concur with de Maigret's contention that the Khawlan was depopulated at this time (Edens 1999b: 121). At the same time, the central Highlands continue to experience settlement growth, and one of the largest settlements yet known in this region emerges. Hawagir is nearly 15 hectares in size and breaks with the tradition of hilltop settlement in that it is located in the alluvial plains of the Qa Jahran (Wilkinson and Edens 1999). The loss of defensive ability

Figure 5.8. Excavation of a stone-constructed building, Kharayb, Dhamar, Yemen. Photo: Tony Wilkinson.

associated with such a location was obviously compensated by the economic benefits of cultivating a more expansive and accessible area.

In summary, intensive agriculture resulted in rapid settlement growth in the Highlands from c. 3000 BC onwards. The question of where the domesticated crops came from is not resolved, but contacts with eastern Africa must have played an important role. The key development that ensured continued occupation of this region was irrigation technology that likely included sayl (runoff) control, ghayl (spring flow) irrigation (Varisco 1983), as well as managed dry farming through the use of terracing in the central Highlands (Edens and Wilkinson 1998: 88). From a longue durée perspective it would seem that the third millennium BC was critical in the consolidation of these technologies. The size of sites in the Dhamar region and the development of a settlement hierarchy suggest that these technologies were perfected by the second millennium BC. However, just as in southeastern Arabia the demarcated environment resulted in varied settlement trajectories: Dhamar and the central Highlands prospered, whereas a mixed farming and pastoral regime was implemented in the more challenging environments of the Khawlan region. Agriculture was, however, established in southwestern Arabia and altered not just Highland occupation but occupation of the desert fringes and coastal zones, to the examination of which I now turn.

DESERT ADAPTATION

At the same time that the inhabitants of the central Highlands were experimenting with agriculture, nomadic pastoralists continued to exploit the interior

deserts and fringes of the Ramlat as-Sabatyn. In this inland sand sea, thousands
of tombs have been noted along the ridges of Jebel Jidran and Jebel Ruwaiq
(Braemer et al. 2001). These tombs, like those in the Wadi Sana in Yemen and
in southeastern Arabia (Harrower 2008), were likely important markers of territoriality for groups exploiting adjacent environments in a seasonal pattern
of pastoralism. In Jebel Ruwaiq, the tombs are clustered in a density of about
thirty per hectare. They consist of circular stone constructions between 4 and
5 meters in diameter and vary between 2.5 and 3 meters in height. A single
chamber lies within, but in some cases a circular tomb adjoins the main tomb.
A series of stone arrangements running in a linear pattern from the main tomb
have also been noted. Four of these tombs were excavated by a French team
in the 1990s, and two of these were very well preserved (Braemer et al. 2001).
Several ^{14}C dates obtained from bones confirmed that they are the earliest
Bronze Age occupation yet discovered in the Arabian southwest. Two groups
of ^{14}C dates were obtained: the first, represented by eight samples, cluster in
the first half of the third millennium BC, while two other dates belong to the
first half of the second millennium BC. The number of individuals in each
tomb varied from two to seven, and in several tombs children as well as adults
were buried. In one well-preserved tomb (no. 81), food offerings, including
the remains of a sheep, were found inside vessels. Despite the fact that many
of the tombs had been robbed, a wide range of artefacts was recovered. These
included ceramic vessels; beads of carnelian, ceramic, bone and softstone; and
bronze awls. While there is little difference in the types of goods found in the
tombs, the amount of goods differs considerably. This is particularly the case
with the beads (Braemer et al. 2001: 34).

There are no known settlements associated with these tombs, but it is clear
from the associated grave goods of softstone, carnelian, bronze and pottery
that the people who were buried maintained contacts with the Highlands to
the west. Of particular significance are the ceramics that indicate that these
nomadic pastoralists engaged with, or occasionally seasonally occupied, the
settlements in the Khawlan region. Engagement with this region provided
an opportunity for the spread of newly developed subsistence technologies
towards the arid margins of the Highlands and, subsequently, the edges of the
Ramlat as-Sabatyn. Brunner's (1997) ^{14}C dating of irrigation sediments near
the large mounded settlement of Hagar Yahirr provides evidence for such on
the very western edge of the Ramlat as-Sabatyn. Hehmeyer (1989) has also
documented irrigation agriculture during the second millennium BC in this
zone, suggesting increasing intensification of one of the wadi systems that was
to emerge as a political centre in the first millennium BC.

Such innovation was, however, not limited to the western edges of the
Ramlat as-Sabatyn. The most important sequence for the Bronze Age in the
southeast of the Ramlat as-Sabaytn comes from the large (15-hectare) stratified
site of Shabwa, the later capital of a kingdom centred in the Hadramawt. A

deep sounding at the site revealed layers of ash in its lowest levels (Level I) and, immediately above in Level II, the remnants of mudbrick architecture associated with ceramics (Badre 1991). Two ^{14}C dates from this level suggest a date in the first half of the second millennium BC (Breton 1996). A series of mudbrick buildings of uncertain design and function and beaten earth floors continue up until Level IV. Judging by the ^{14}C dates on either side of this level, these remains should be dated to the second half of the second millennium BC. The limited amount of ceramics from this sounding indicate continuing traditions of incised decoration from the earliest ceramics onwards. Burnishing, common elsewhere towards the end of the second millennium BC, is not found in the Shabwa sequence. Changes in ceramic technology, in particular the addition of chaff as temper in Level IV, have been noted (Badre 1991), and these might relate to agricultural practice. Although the details are scanty, the presence of substantial buildings and a ceramic industry likely indicates the presence of an agricultural regime similar to that which existed in later centuries in Shabwa (Gentelle 1981).

Moving eastwards from Shabwa into the mouth of the Wadi Hadramawt, the first major tributary wadi one encounters is the Wadi Do'an. About 20 kilometers into this wadi lies Raybun, a site investigated by Russian archaeologists in the 1980s. Critical for understanding the first millennium BC Hadrami religious architecture, their research also revealed evidence of Bronze Age occupation. The earliest levels at Raybun contain mudbrick architecture and a distinctive red-burnished and red-painted pottery. Sedov (1996: 70–71) also noted the existence of this pottery at Safa I and II elsewhere in the Wadi Do'an and at as-Safil II and III in the Wadi Idim, farther along the Wadi Hadramawt. He labelled this assemblage, dated by a series of ^{14}C dates, the 'Ancient Wadi Hadramawt Culture' (Sedov 1996: 86). In discussing it, Sedov (1996) draws parallels to Late Bronze Age ceramics from the southern Levant, especially the red-burnished decoration. Given the subsequent discovery of contemporary Bronze Age culture in the Highlands and the coast and the concomitant development of irrigation technology, an alternate perspective which emphasizes the autochthonous origins of Raybun and its economy might be entertained.

Farther west in the Wadi Hadramawt and the Jol, the situation is much less clear. Shi'b Munayder in the Wadi Idim, surveyed and excavated by McCorriston in the 1990s (McCorriston 2000), consists of stone-constructed houses, terraces, water-diversion walls and enclosures, and a single ^{14}C date confirms an occupation in the second half of the second millennium BC. The population was considered to be at least semi-sedentary and probably engaged in pastoralism. A recent survey in Dhofar suggests a rich Bronze Age landscape characterized by numerous 'tombs with tails' (as discussed later), but settlements are also known (Newton and Zarins 2000). Future research there is crucial for understanding how the inhabitants of this verdant zone of southern Arabia adapted to shifts in the Holocene climate.

COASTAL ADAPTATION

As noted in Chapter 3, pastoral nomadism and intensive marine exploitation characterized human settlement in the coastal zone, especially the Tihama, during the Neolithic. By the late third millennium BC, a commonality in subsistence strategies and material culture can be found at a wide variety of sites stretching from Sihi on the Saudi Arabian coast to Sabir on the southern Yemeni coast. The importance of irrigation agriculture along with interaction with African neighbours appears to be critical to the longevity of these settlements.

All the known major coastal settlements of the second millennium BC are located in areas in which dry farming was not possible. They are, however, located at the embouchement of significant wadi systems that could be tapped using sayl irrigation systems, just as they were up until the development of electric pumps (Varisco 1983). The northernmost large settlement is Hodeidah, which although unexcavated is estimated to be 25 hectares in size and contains artefacts that clearly link it to well-dated assemblages elsewhere (Edens and Wilkinson 1998: 104). The site is located on the alluvial fan of the Wadi Urq, which discharges sediment and water from the mountains. Farther south is the recently discovered settlement of Kashwaba, which is situated on the 'highly cultivable land' between the Wadis Badwah and Ajji (Khalidi 2005: 122–123). Although known for some time (Ciuk and Keall 1996), a recent survey indicated that the site was much larger than originally thought and stretched over an area of 1 by 2 kilometers (Khalidi 2005: 123). Just to the south lies the large alluvial fan of the Wadi Zabid, on which the settlement of al-Midamman is located. Although I discuss the settlement in more detail later, it suffices to note here that artefacts confirm that agriculture was an important part of subsistence (Giumlia-Mair et al. 2002: 196).

It is, however, the excavations at Ma'layba and Sabir near the Gulf of Aden that have revealed the chronology and economy of coastal Bronze Age culture. Both sites are located near the embouchement of the Wadi Tuban, which today ensures that the nearby oasis of Lahij is one of the most important agricultural centres in southern coastal Yemen (Maktari 1971). The small tell of Ma'layba contains 6 meters of cultural deposits that were split into Phases Ia, Ib, Ic and II (Vogt et al. 2002; Vogt and Sedov 1998). The architecture typically consists of posthole remains and the occasional burnt wooden post that likely represent the remains of barasti structures. The excavators also note that the remains of agricultural fields were stratigraphically interspersed between the architectural remains. Nine ¹⁴C dates were obtained from the sequence at Ma'layba, and these show a nearly continuous occupation beginning around 2000 BC and ending around 1300 BC.

Sabir lies near Ma'layba and is approximately 1 by 2 kilometers in size (see Figure 5.9). Although known since the 1950s, the site was assumed to date to

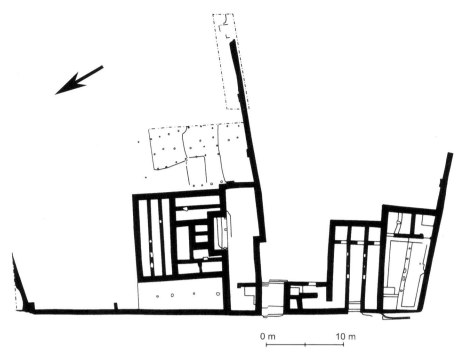

Figure 5.9. Plan of Bronze Age settlement of Sabir. After Vogt and Sedov 1998: Figure 1.

the later first millennium BC until joint German-Russian excavations began there in the 1990s. Their excavations revealed 4–5 meters of archaeological deposit (Vogt and Sedov 1998: 262) and a wide horizontal exposure of architecture dating to the late second millennium BC. Most of the settlement was characterized by barasti structures (Vogt and Sedov 1998: 262), but large areas of substantial mudbrick buildings were also found. The latter include industrial areas in which pottery and bronze were produced. Most spectacular was an area (Sabir 5) of architecture measuring 55 by 40 meters (Vogt and Sedov 1998: 262–264). Three individual buildings (A, B and C) were revealed in this area. Building C consists of a large hall with a central platform accessible by stairs. Two long narrow rooms or storage galleries adjoined the building. Vogt and Sedov (1998: 263) suggest that this plan anticipates the plan of classic south Arabian temples.

A rich artefactual assemblage was found in these buildings and other areas of the site. A red micaceous ware with mineral or shell temper dominates the ceramics, but a steatite-tempered ware is also known (Figure 5.10). The pottery is normally slipped or burnished and occasionally incised. Vessel forms include deep bowls, hole mouth jars and canisters. Of particular note are several hemispherical baseless vessels with holes or windows. These have been interpreted as incense burners and parallel those that appear a century or two later in southeastern Arabia (Chapter 9). The use of these within buildings that

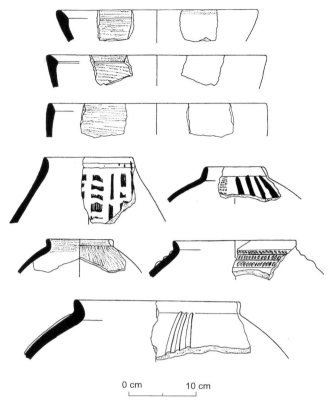

0 cm   10 cm

Figure 5.10. Bronze Age Sabir culture ceramics, Ma'layba, Yemen. After Vogt and Sedov 1998: Figs. 3 and 4.

formally anticipate later south Arabian religious architecture is an important indicator of the emergence of indigenous ritual practice in this area.

Three buildings excavated at Sabir are tightly dated by numerous ^{14}C samples suggesting that the buildings came into existence in the thirteenth century BC, thus correlating with the end date of the sequence at Ma'layba. Three ^{14}C samples from the destruction level of the site calibrate to within the tenth century BC. Assuming that the organic material represented by these samples exited the carbon cycle shortly before the destruction of the settlement, it can be concluded that Sabir was destroyed in that time. The occupations of Sabir and Ma'layba when combined thus cover most of the second millennium BC.

Although archaeobotanical remains from these settlements are extremely limited, there can be little doubt that the settlements' subsistence included agriculture (Boivin and Fuller 2009: Table 2). Located within the flood zone of the major wadi systems that run from the mountains to the sea, these settlements were able to trap sediment and episodic runoff in much the same manner as desert fringe settlements. The limited nature of the archaeobotanical record from these sites precludes a detailed discussion of the range of cultivars grown, but one could envisage that the cereals (wheat, barley) that had been grown for a considerable time at this stage in the Highlands were, perhaps after adaptation to the arid fringes of the latter region, suitable for cultivation in coastal settlements. The date palm was likely critical to the development of subsistence in these settlements, as it provided a canopy and micro-environment for small-scale agriculture in harsh coastal environments, as well as a bountiful fruit supply. The foliage and branches were also critical to the development of barasti architecture, since the fronds are strong yet permit the movement of air. Such construction is common along the Tihama coast today. As discussed in Chapter 3, archaeobotanical evidence suggests that eastern Arabia was one potential source of the domestication and cultivation of the date palm. Evidence for its presence in Bronze Age contexts in the west of Yemen is limited to two impressions from sites in the Khawlan region (Charbonnier 2008: Table 1). Given the fact that it was not present on the African side of the Red Sea until the Middle Kingdom (Murray 2000), one might well suppose that it was introduced from eastern Arabia to western Arabia sometime during the second millennium BC. The impact that it had on coastal settlement in the Tihama can hardly be exaggerated.

In addition to agricultural settlements, numerous shell midden sites have been identified on the coastal zone. Typically deflated and with few visible structures, these middens have been dated by the appearance of typical Sabir-like ceramics or by direct ^{14}C dating of shells. One such midden, Sihi, provides the northernmost evidence for the spread of coastal Bronze Age culture (Zarins and Badr 1986; Zarins and Zahrani 1985). The site consists of a wide scatter of middens and hearths with artefactual debris. Ceramics and bronzes from the site parallel material from al-Midamman and Sabir. The ^{14}C data from this site have been collated by Edens and Wilkinson (1998: Table XI). The calibration of the shell dates from Sihi requires an assessment of the 'deviation from the global reservoir' effect that is not factored into their assessment of the dates. When averaged, two pre-bomb known age samples from the Red Sea suggest that 116 ± 31 should be added when the Sihi samples are calibrated. This brings the samples into close alignment with those from Sabir. Numerous other shell middens dating to the Bronze Age have been found in the Tihama survey conducted by Khalidi (2005), and some of these provide evidence for the primary production of obsidian (Khalidi 2009).

Sites with megaliths have been long noted in the Tihama, although until recently little evidence on their chronology was available. This situation has now been rectified with the excavation of al-Midamman by Canadian archaeologists. As previously noted, this large settlement lies on the edge of the Wadi Zabid drainage and contains prehistoric remains spread over 4 square kilometers. A residential area has been revealed by wind erosion where ceramics, obsidian stone tools and copper implements are visible on the surface. The deflated nature of the deposits means, however, that it is difficult to define the settlement spatially and chronologically. Nevertheless, Keall (1998, 2005; Weeks et al. 2009) has identified two major phases of occupation. The first, 'Monumental Phase 1', consists of the residential area and clusters of standing stones, some of which appear to be oriented towards the mid-winter sunset. In 'Monumental Phase 2', domestic occupation continues at the site but the pillars are reused in a number of buildings, including temples, and graves. The excavators note that the ceramics and stone tools from both phases are indistinguishable from each other, suggesting a close chronological relationship.

A single ^{14}C sample on a burnt palm date found in a Monumental Phase 2 deposit suggests that this phase dates to the last quarter of the second millennium BC. This is supported by ceramic parallels to material from Sabir. The close artefactual links between Monumental Phases 1 and 2 and the single ^{14}C date led the excavators to suggest that the standing stones date immediately prior to Monumental Phase 2. This is significantly later than hitherto had been supposed for this type of structure but in the absence of any conflicting data must be accepted.

An important component of Monumental Phase 1 at Area HWB at al-Midamman was a line of in situ megaliths oriented towards the mid-winter sun. Their orientation and the observation that they were reused in the construction of a temple support the assertion that they had a ritual function. The ritual association of the standing stones is also suggested by the recovery of three caches of eighteen bronze objects that were found in association with a large obsidian core (Weeks et al. 2009). The excavators date this horde, which consisted of blades, adzes, points, razors and spatulae, to Monumental Phase 1 at the latest. Initial assessments of the typology of the artefacts linked them with Levantine objects of the Middle Bronze Age. More recent analysis (Giumlia-Mair et al. 2002: 196, 206–207) has highlighted parallels to the well-dated assemblage from Sabir. Analysis of these artefacts revealed three compositional groups: tin-bronze, with between 2 and 3.5% tin; arsenical copper, with 1–2.5% arsenic; and a relatively pure copper (Giumlia-Mair et al. 2002: Table 1). Lead isotope analysis of the cache objects and five artefacts from the residential area yielded important results about the origin of the copper used to make these objects. Objects from the settlement site contained different lead isotope signatures than material from the caches. To Weeks et al. this indicated 'a re-orientation of exchange systems and/or developments in the technology of metal mining and smelting in the region' (Weeks et al. 2009: 587) across the second millennium BC. More important, however, was the issue of absolute provenance. The lead isotope data from the al-Midamman bronzes are not consistent with a source in either the Levant or eastern Arabia, both of which had well-established bronze-producing industries in place by the second millennium BC. Rather, these data point to a source in the Arabian Nubian Shield which includes southwestern Arabia and the adjacent regions of eastern Africa. At the least, therefore, copper objects from al-Midamman are the product of a production and exchange system that is centred on the southern reaches of the Red Sea. A possible source of some of this copper has been recently discovered at Kutam, located in the middle of the central Highlands just inside the Saudi border and only 60 kilometers from the entrance to the Tihama near Faifa. This site has been described as 'marked at the surface by ancient trenches and pits in a zone 500 meters long and 100 meters wide. Slag piles, estimated to contain about 50 000 tonnes of material, lie in the southwest flank of the ridge and in the adjacent valley' (Saudi Geological Survey 2007, quoted in Weeks et al. 2009: 594).

Other aspects of material culture hint at the African orientation of Bronze Age coastal culture. Several sherds from Sabir with incised decoration in-filled in different pigments have striking parallels with the Nubian C-group and Pan Grave cultures (Vogt and Sedov 1998). The general style of decoration has parallels in pre-Axumite materials in Ethiopia as well. Such connections are also suggested by the excavations at Adulis in the Eritrean coast (Paribeni 1907) that revealed ceramics comparable to those from Sabir (Edens and Wilkinson 1998: 104; Fattovich 1985). The discovery of Bronze Age remains in the Farasan Islands may indicate the importance of these islands in the maintenance of such trade routes (Bailey et al. 2007; Demarchi et al. 2011).

By the late second millennium BC, therefore, the coastal Bronze Age culture of Yemen encompasses a vast area. Sabir and Sihi are separated by 600 kilometers of coastal plain which can be 50 kilometers wide (Vogt and Sedov 1998). Whether this entire zone is densely occupied is unknown, and most settlements consisted of organic structures made from date palm. Nevertheless, as a discrete ecological zone, the Yemeni coastal zone is comparable to an area as large as the Levantine coast from Gaza to the Hatay province in Turkey. The position of the largest settlements strongly suggests that agriculture played a key role in the coastal economy, and the earlier Highland development of irrigation technologies, such as controlling runoff, may have been key to these developments (Vogt and Sedov 1998: 267). At the same time, connections across the Red Sea and Gulf of Aden were critical. The tantalizing glimpses of northeast African trade provided by ceramics and bronzework will undoubtedly be filled out in future years as research resumes around the Horn of Africa. It is likely that this research will shed new light on the interconnections between Egypt, northeastern Africa and Arabia and the role played by the enigmatic country of Punt, fabled in Egyptian records as the home of incense and other exotica. Whether or not this affirms the use of the term 'Afro-Tihama' culture (Kitchen 2002) or 'Afro-Arabian' culture (Fattovich 1997) remains to be seen.

Currently, there is little question that such trade is embedded within the broader intensification of coastal Bronze Age culture that includes irrigation agriculture and megalithic ritual centres. In the recent past, studies of contemporary sayl irrigation in the Wadi Tuban (Maktari 1971) and Wadi Zabid

(Varisco 1983), both of which were centres of Bronze Age occupation, have emphasized the role of authority and power in water allocation. However, the propensity of scholars to characterize these Bronze Age developments in terms of 'hierarchies' and incipient sociopolitical complexity (e.g., Boivin and Fuller 2009) must be avoided if we are to fully understand the transformation of society from the earlier Neolithic pastoral mode. Models that assume a trajectory towards socioeconomic complexity because earlier Neolithic occupation was pastoral and later Iron Age polities can be characterized as 'states' are based on reductionist paradigms that do not take into account the minimal evidence for social structure during these millennia.

SETTLEMENT IN THE HIJAZ

Agricultural intensification and inter-regional interaction were not limited to the southern stretches of western Arabia during the Bronze Age. The archaeological site of Tayma is well known from numerous textual sources of a later period when it served as one of the main caravan stations on the overland trade network that linked Arabia and the rest of the Near East (Chapter 9). During the Holocene Moist Phase, a 13-meter-deep lake is hypothesized to have existed near the site where the sabkha is still present today (Engel et al. 2011). Snails from the lake depression have been ^{14}C-dated to c. 4500 BC (Eichmann et al. 2006a: 164), but by c. 2000 BC the lake would certainly have been dried out (Figure 5.11). Episodic rainfall, then as now, would have rapidly recharged the water table. Currently, fresh water is available at a depth of only 1–2 meters in the sabkha and about 4 meters in palm groves (Eichmann et al. 2006a: 165), and there is no reason to believe that a similar situation did not exist during the Bronze Age.

The archaeological remains of Tayma are spread out over 800 hectares (Edens and Bawden 1989), making it an ancient settlement with few comparisons in the rest of the ancient Near East. Recent excavations by Saudi archaeologists (Abu Duruk 1989, 1990, 1996; al-Hajri 2006; al-Hajri et al. 2005) and a joint Saudi-German team (Eichmann et al. 2006a, 2006b) have fundamentally altered our understanding of the history of the settlement and proved that Tayma's canonical entry into Near Eastern archaeology in the first millennium BC masks a complex Neolithic to Bronze Age trajectory that parallels many developments elsewhere in Arabia. Recent ^{14}C and OSL dating of the massive 14-kilometer-long fortification wall of the city confirms that the initial stages of the wall date from the early second millennium BC (Eichmann et al. 2006a, 2006b; Intilia 2010; Klasen et al. 2011) (Figure 5.12). This wall was reconstructed throughout the second millennium BC until, by the late second millennium BC, the various construction phases measured more than 10 meters in height (Intilia 2010). In addition, recently discovered bronzes from Tayma attest to its

Figure 5.11. Tayma, Saudi Arabia, surface of the sabkha north of the oasis (from southeast). Photo: DAI Orient Abteilung, A. Hausleiter.

occupation by the early second millennium BC. These include a fenestrated axe and a ribbed dagger that are well paralleled in Middle Bronze Age contexts in the southern Levant (Hausleiter 2010).

Given the climatic conditions that existed in the Hijaz following the Holocene Moist Phase, the construction of such a substantial city wall suggests the existence of a large sedentary community in which agriculture played an important role. Irrigation was the sine qua non of such developments. While it is difficult to draw comparisons to the modern economy of the region given the current use of industrial technologies for irrigation, it is clear from early Islamic sources that the Hijaz had immense agricultural potential with traditional irrigation methods. In the seventh century AD the region produced wheat, barley, sorghum and alfalfa (Heck 2003: 564). All of these cultivars were available in Arabia by the second millennium BC (Potts 1994a). At the same time, the recent discovery of a cartouche of Ramesses III engraved on a mountain near Tayma suggests interaction with northeastern Africa (Eichmann and Sperveslage 2011). Continued excavations at Tayma will clarify the relationship between foreign trade and subsistence intensification in explaining the growth of this extraordinary Bronze Age city.

Figure 5.12. Tayma, Saudi Arabia, outer city wall, Square W18 (from west); sandstone foundation and mudbrick construction; preserved height c. 6 m. Photo: DAI Orient-Abteilung, S. Lora.

ROCK ART, MENHIR, KITES AND CAIRNS

Thus far, our examination of the Bronze Age of western Arabia has emphasized agricultural and sedentary settlement after the cessation of the Holocene Moist Phase. The wide distribution of rock art, carved stones and megalithic dolmens suggests that non-sedentary existence also remained a key component of ancient lifeways throughout western Arabia. Although some scholars (e.g., Newton and Zarins 2000) have examined this evidence in toto, it is important to explore how each class of evidence individually illuminates human–environmental dynamics.

As noted in Chapter 3, rock art is found throughout those areas of western and northwestern Arabia in which the Arabian Nubian Shield has created a series of mountains, terraces and piedmonts. That some of this rock art might date to the Bronze Age, and is thus relevant to our immediate discussions, was reinforced by Anati's (1968a, 1968b, 1972, 1974) detailed analysis of photographs supplied by the Philby-Ryckmans-Lippens expedition to central Arabia, especially the area around Jebel Qara. Although he never visited the rock art, Anati used his impression of the super-position of drawings and some distinctive weapon types to assign his 'Realistic-Dynamic' style, which included images of people hunting a variety of animals, among them dromedaries, to the Bronze Age of the third and second millennia BC (Anati 1968b: 23–24). The appearance of a lunate pommel-handled dagger was critical for this dating scheme. He compared these to examples from southern Mesopotamia and Egypt that were dated independently to the third and second millennia BC. A more recent analysis by Newton and Zarins (2000) on the basis of a wide variety of parallels to these daggers largely supports Anati's conclusions. Newton and Zarins note that this dagger type is also found on a number of menhirs (see Chapter 3), or stone stelae, found in the Yemeni Jol and Mahra regions. They conclude: 'Their distribution across the Arabian peninsula and occurrence in Mesopotamia and Egypt suggest a time line of use for over a millennium from 2500 to 1500 BC. They are clearly Bronze Age weapons identified as status markers and should be associated with Semitic-speaking pastoral people of the Arabian peninsula in its largest sense' (Newton and Zarins 2000: 161).

Although Anati's work established a framework for interpreting Arabian prehistoric rock art, research since then has expanded the geographical and possibly chronological range of some of his styles, as well as incorporating in more detail the relationship between text and image (e.g., Achrati 2006). In Yemen, Garcia and Rachad's research in the Saada region has revealed rock art styles similar to those identified by Anati (Garcia and Rachad 1989, 1990, 1997; Inizan and Rachad 2007). That some of the rock art identified as Bronze Age by Anati might date to earlier periods has been indicated by several researchers. Lézine (2010), for example, has tied the appearance of bovids in rock art to the earlier Holocene Moist Phase. As noted in Chapter 3, Khan and others (e.g., Bednarik and Khan 2005; Khan 2008) endorsed this earlier chronology for rock art at Jubbah and Shuwaymas in northern Saudi Arabia. Ultimately the dating of rock art in Arabia will remain as uncertain as it is throughout the world until reliable chronometric methods are available. In the meantime, the strong parallels between representations of the lunate pommel-handled dagger and archaeologically recovered examples suggest that a Bronze Age date is likely for at least *some* of the representations of hunting found throughout southwestern, western and northwestern Arabia.

Evidence for a non-agricultural intensification of land use after the cessation of the Holocene Moist Phase may be indicated not only in the rock art just noted, but also in the proliferation of mass-kill traps across the northern and central Arabian deserts. These unique stone features, first labelled 'kites' by RAF pilots flying from Jordan to Baghdad in the early twentieth century, have been a matter of much debate amongst archaeologists. Examples from the Negev, Jordanian and Syrian deserts are well studied (Helms and Betts 1987; Holzer et al. 2010; Legge and Rowley-Conwy 1987; Van Berg et al. 2004), and there appears to be some consensus that they date from c. 4000 BC to 1000 BC. A discrete bone assemblage of Persian gazelle from Tell Kuran in Syria dated to the end of the fourth millennium BC, recently published, has been

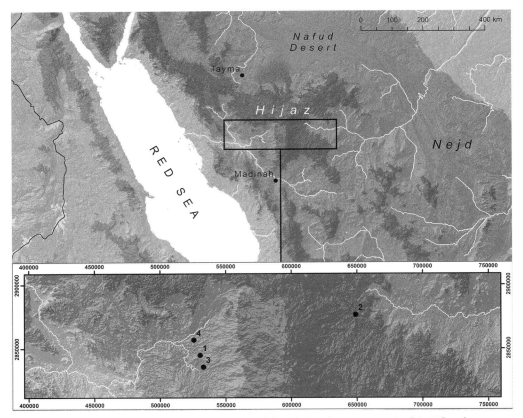

Figure 5.13. Location of Tayma and 'kite' sites in western Arabia. The dots indicate the presence of large kite systems after Kennedy and Saeed 2009.

characterized as resulting from a single hunting episode that occurred at one of these kill traps (Bar-Oz et al. 2011).

The current emphasis on kites as a feature of the Syrian and Jordanian deserts merely reflects the visibility of these from known aerial routes of the early twentieth century. More recently, satellite images have documented an astonishing array of desert kites well within Saudi Arabia (Figure 5.13). To these should be added those noted by Parr (1978: 39) at the edge of Wadi Sirhan in northern Saudi Arabia and the enigmatic stone circles noted in Zarin's survey in the Central Province (Zarins et al. 1979: 25). Just 100 kilometers northeast of Medinah, in the Harrat Khaybar, 239 kites in a wide array of shapes and sizes have been documented (Kennedy and Saeed 2009). Many of these kites are comparable to those found in Syria and Jordan. Enigmatic stone 'wheels' with multiple compartments are also found in both regions. How far south kites are found is unknown, but an analysis of satellite imagery of a region similar in size, 400 kilometers to the south in the hinterland of Jeddah, revealed no kites but more than a thousand enigmatic stone structures ('pendants') that also possibly served as mass-kill traps (Kennedy and Bishop 2011).

Nearly one thousand burial cairns were also noted in the Saudi satellite data. Although little can be said about the chronology of these, it is likely that they represent a symbolic configuration of the landscape in much the same way as has been noted in southwestern Arabia (Braemer et al. 2001) and eastern Saudi Arabia (Chapter 4). Excavations of a potentially comparable tomb around the area of Tayma (al-Hajri et al. 2005; as-Samiya 2006) suggested connections to the Chalcolithic of the southern Levant, although such connections remain to be demonstrated for the region more broadly. Recent research around Kharj in central Arabia has clarified the existence of enormous cairn fields that were originally noted as part of the comprehensive survey undertaken by the Saudi Department of Antiquities in this area (Zarins et al. 1979). Excavation of one cairn by a Saudi team revealed bronze weapons comparable to those from the early second millennium BC elsewhere in Arabia (Schiettecatte et al. 2013).

Rock art, kites, pendants and cairns, although still enigmatic in many ways in combination, suggest an intensification of settlement throughout the steppic areas of southern, central and northern Arabia. That this occurs during the Bronze Age and earlier seems likely on the basis of multiple strands of chronological evidence. Without clearer evidence from these sites and the broader cultural landscape in which they are situated, it is difficult to come to any firm conclusion about their subsistence practices and economy. That hunting was important seems likely. Hunting outposts are known from slightly earlier periods in the Near East, such as at Umm Dabaghiyah in the steppic regions of northern Iraq (Kirkbride 1974, 1975). Indeed, the multi-compartment 'wheel' structures noted in the Central Province may be comparable to the cellular buildings excavated at Umm Dabaghiyah which have been interpreted as temporary storage areas for hunting activities.

Whether such hunting was tethered to sedentary agricultural settlements or was carried out by specialized nomadic hunters is not known. Ethnohistoric accounts of the Solubba as specialized nomadic hunters of northern Arabia are well known from the recent past. The description of their activities provided by Barker (1876: 267–268; see also Simpson 1994) is worth quoting in full:

> During the summer months, when these animals come up from the south of Arabia in numerous herds – thousands together – the whole tribe go out to hunt. They gather stones, and build a low wall two miles long in the shape of a semicircle. This wall is just high enough to prevent gazelles jumping over it. In the middle of the semicircle they break it down a little, but not entirely; and on the other side they excavate a pit as large as they can make it. When everything is ready the whole tribe go out, and stretching away on the plains, drive the gazelles into the semicircle. The animals come to the wall and run along it, and when they come to the broken place

in the wall the leader jumps over, and then every one of the herd follow his example. Here there are men ready, who slaughter them, skin them, and salt the meat, which is then dried in the hot sun for the winter's provision. *This tribe has no other means of subsistence than this hunt, which never fails them, because there are thousands of herds, and the gazelle cannot possibly escape.* (Emphasis added)

Whether or not the proliferation of kites, rock art, and other enigmatic stone structures attests to this form of specialization will be revealed only by further surveys and excavations along the flanks of the Asir and Hijaz. For the moment, this evidence reminds us that adaptation to Arabia's post–Holocene Moist Phase climate was not limited to experimentation with agriculture and sedentarization.

CONCLUSIONS

In less than twenty years our knowledge of the Bronze Age in western Arabia has increased dramatically. Excavations and surveys in Yemen have highlighted that at the end of the Holocene Moist Phase favourable ecological niches such as the Highlands were the focus of experimental and ultimately successful adaptive strategies based on agriculture. These innovations were differentially employed in the sharply demarcated environments of the Highlands. As the evidence currently stands, it seems likely that these innovations were then adapted to the arid conditions on the edges of the Ramlat as-Sabatyn and the coast. The resultant expansion of settlement is reflected not only in the number of settlements but also in the increased exploitation of raw materials such as copper and possibly aromatics. Although the evidence is less detailed, a similar picture is emerging from the Hijaz in northwestern Arabia. Contrary to the dominant narrative that sees Tayma emerge as a result of Mesopotamian interaction, it is now clear that a massive walled 'city' existed from the early second millennium BC.

Alongside this evidence for agriculture-based settlement, there are tantalizing glimpses of an increased exploitation of the deserts and steppic environments that became even less conducive to pastoralism following the end of the Holocene Moist Phase. Here we face the inevitable problems of rock art chronology, but a combination of several strains of evidence suggests that hunting intensified in these regions. In this manner, the desert economy may have been increasingly segregated from fertile regions, and vice versa, since the domesticated animals that were a component of the latter's economy were ill-suited to pastoralism in the harsh desert conditions.

Accessing the social fabric of these societies is difficult given our current state of knowledge. We know too little about funerary practices, and no settlement has been excavated to the extent that questions about activity patterning and social organization can be addressed. It is tempting to see in some of the larger second millennium BC Highland settlements the beginnings of the hierarchical use of space, unlike anything from the Arabian southeast, and these might presage the developments that take place throughout southwestern Arabia at the beginning of the first millennium BC. To insist upon such a scenario, however, is to streamline cultural change in a fashion that is not supported by the current evidence. Only future excavations and surveys will throw more light on this issue.

CHAPTER 6

EASTERN ARABIA FROM 2000 TO 1300 BC

INTRODUCTION

In Chapter 4, I outlined some tentative ideas concerning the disappearance of the Umm an-Nar culture in southeastern Arabia around 2000 BC. As we shall see later in this chapter, these changes brought about an entirely new phase of occupation normally referred to as the Wadi Suq period (2000–1500 BC) and Late Bronze Age (1500–1300 BC). It is still difficult to understand these periods fully given the relative paucity of settlements, but it is clear that the intensification of settlement that characterized the Umm an-Nar period gave way to an archaeologically less visible exploitation of the landscape. At the same time, changes in settlement patterns in the middle and northern parts of the Gulf accelerated in the opposite direction. By 2000 BC, the island of Bahrain witnesses the emergence of the first state in prehistoric Arabia. The origins and character of these divergent trajectories across eastern Arabia, as well as the reasons for their occurrence are the focus of this chapter.

THE EMERGENCE OF THE DILMUN STATE

Although archaeological remains are present at Qala'at al-Bahrain prior to the establishment of the 'Early Dilmun' phase, our knowledge of these is minimal (Højlund and Andersen 1997: 14–15) (Figure 6.1). The first major extensive building phase occurs during the Early Dilmun period (Periods I–II, c. 2200–1800 BC) and is marked by the establishment of several large constructions (Højlund and Andersen 1994, 1997). The so-called Early Dilmun Palace consists of three stone-constructed buildings, of which only Building I is complete in plan. It consists of a tripartite structure with a central long corridor and ancillary rooms on either side. A single entrance on the western side provided direct access to the central corridor. The 'fine execution' of the masonry and the size of the building (16 by 22 meters) led the excavators to argue that Building I was part of a palace along with the adjacent, but only partially

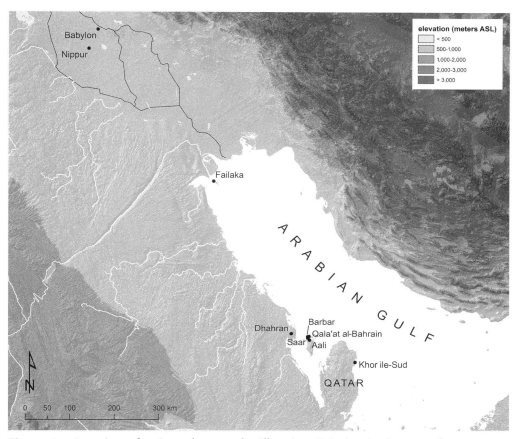

Figure 6.1. Location of main early second millennium BC sites in the central and northern Arabian Gulf.

excavated Buildings II and III. All were likely constructed according to an overall plan (Højlund and Andersen 1997: 16).

Locally made ceramics dominate the limited number of artefacts recovered from the Early Dilmun Palace. A distinctive ceramic ware called 'Chain Ridged Ware' utilizes a highly calcareous local clay source that results in visible lime spalling due to high-temperature firing. Given the fact that the earlier pottery found at al-Markh is likely imported from Mesopotamia (Potts 1991a: 154), the pottery traditions discovered in the Early Dilmun levels of Qala'at al-Bahrain reflect the emergence of an indigenous pottery tradition that exploited distinctive clay beds on Bahrain to make unique vessel forms. At the same time, the material culture assemblage from these levels indicates that Bahrain was already engaged in trade with its neighbours in the Arabian Gulf. A number of sherds that appear to belong to the Umm an-Nar 'Black on Red' tradition are found in Periods I–II (Højlund and Andersen 1997: 37–39). Several soft-stone vessels, which judging by their shape and decoration are almost certainly imported from southeastern Arabia, are also found (Højlund and Andersen

1997: 38–39). Southeastern Arabia was also the likely source of the copper that was processed and worked in the crucibles and moulds found in these levels (Højlund and Andersen 1997: 35).

Whether or not the Early Dilmun buildings on Qala'at al-Bahrain can be classed as a palace, it is abundantly clear that they served a supra-kin based function. They speak of a monumental manifestation of power and authority unlike anything in southeastern Arabia during the same period. Emerging societal differences can also be seen in the archaeozoological record from Qala'at al-Bahrain and adjacent sites. The Uerpmanns (1997) have noted that differences in food resources between the nearby domestic settlement of Saar and Qala'at al-Bahrain are greater than any differences they noted within Saar itself. Furthermore, systemic differences in the size of the sheep from Qala'at al-Bahrain and from Saar suggest that a different breed, similar in size to those from southern Mesopotamia, was kept at the former site. It is interesting that goats from Saar and Qala'at al-Bahrain, which were kept primarily at a household level, were similar in size (Uerpmann and Uerpmann 1997: 305). Only a small portion of Qala'at al-Bahrain has been excavated, however, and a reconstruction of Early Dilmun society on the basis of these excavations alone would be perilous. Fortunately, other evidence from Barbar and Saar, the thousands of burials for which Bahrain is well known, the widespread use of glyptic and the overseas activities of Bahrain have augmented our understanding of a society that was experiencing a vastly different trajectory than its neighbours to the south.

The deep stratified deposits at Qala'at al-Bahrain make it difficult to ascertain the layouts of any domestic buildings of the Early Dilmun period. Saar, to the south of Qala'at al-Bahrain, has provided expansive and detailed information. The London-Bahrain Archaeological Expedition excavated nearly half of Saar, which measured up to 2.3 hectares, in the 1990s (Killick and Moon 2005). Eighty-four buildings were isolated, of which sixty-eight were excavated. On the basis of ^{14}C dates and the chronological inference of artefacts, it was concluded that the site was occupied from c. 2050 to 1750 BC and was therefore in existence during Periods I–II at Qala'at al-Bahrain and when the Barbar Temple was being constructed and used (as discussed later). Nearly all Saar buildings are simple residential structures with two or three rooms. 'Main Street' divides the settlement in half, and a number of alleyways and squares radiate in lateral directions. The houses are grouped in identifiable quarters, each of which contains a few houses (Figure 6.2). A temple revealed near the centre of the excavated area was nearly 15 meters long and underwent several phases of rebuilding and renovation. In the earliest phase, an altar was located against the southeastern wall of the temple and was reworked in later phases (Figure 6.3).

The objects found within these buildings reflect the daily lives of the inhabitants of Saar in a fashion that is unparalleled at any site of this period

Figure 6.2. Main residential area, early second millennium BC settlement of Saar, Bahrain. Photo: National Museum of Bahrain / London–Bahrain Archaeological Expedition.

Figure 6.3. View of temple, early second millennium BC settlement of Saar, Bahrain. Photo: National Museum of Bahrain / London–Bahrain Archaeological Expedition.

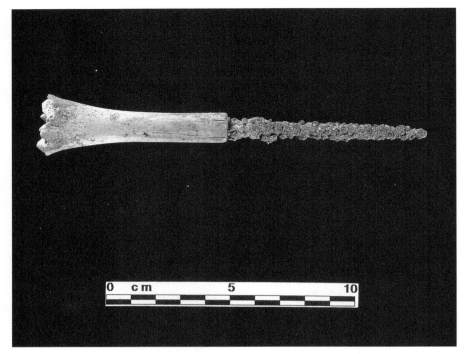

Figure 6.4. Bronze needle with bone handle, early second millennium BC settlement of Saar, Bahrain. Photo: National Museum of Bahrain / London-Bahrain Archaeological Expedition.

in the Gulf. More than 200 copper objects were found in the residential buildings. Weapons are rare but awls, fishhooks, adzes, hoes and rings are common, many of which indicate the varied subsistence strategies practised by the inhabitants. Bronze needles with bone handles (Figure 6.4), beads of semi-precious stone, steatite and clay, as well as some clay zoomorphic figurines were also found. Bitumen was used for containers and for making baskets. Dozens of carved softstone vessels almost certainly imported from southeastern Arabia were also found (Killick and Moon 2005: 208–212) (Figure 6.5). Southeast Arabian ceramics are, however, uncommon in the ceramic corpus, which is dominated by locally produced storage vessels and cooking pots (Figure 6.6). The most common imported pottery is from the Indus Valley civilization. In particular, pottery from the Late Sorath Harappan phase dominates the imported material, which in total accounts for less than 0.5% of the corpus, in strong contrast to the situation at Qala'at al-Bahrain, where it is closer to 3% (Carter 2005b: 262). Carter notes that this 'reflects Saar's rural setting, in contrast to the cosmopolitan, urban status of Qala'at al-Bahrain' (Carter 2005b: 266).

Uerpmann and Uerpmann's detailed archaeozoological analysis (2005b) indicates that the people of Saar ate large amounts of fish, especially sha'ari fish

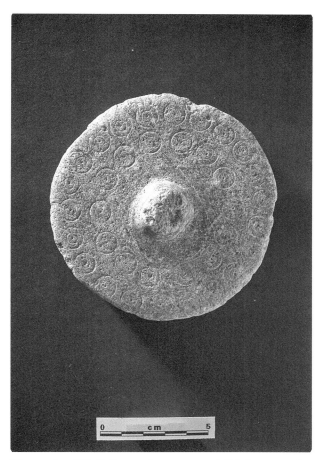

Figure 6.5. Wadi Suq softstone vessel lid from southeastern Arabia, early
second millennium BC settlement of Saar, Bahrain. Photo: National Museum
of Bahrain / London-Bahrain Archaeological Expedition.

(*Lethrinus nebulosus*) and hammour (*Epinephelus coioides*). They hunted some
wild animals, including dromedary, oryx and gazelle, but these were probably
less important than the cattle, sheep and goat that were herded in several different cycles and at different levels of specialization across the island (Olijdam
2000). Analysis of sheep bones from Saar and Qala'at al-Bahrain indicates
that the people at Qala'at al-Bahrain kept a sheep breed similar to that from
Mesopotamia (Uerpmann and Uerpmann 2005b: 305), while at Saar the sheep
which were herded and consumed 'may represent the local stock, which is
known from older sites in the general area such as Tepe Yahya on the northern
side of the Lower Gulf, and at al-Buhais 18, Hili 8 and Tell Abraq on its southern side' (Uerpmann and Uerpmann 2005b: 306). This may be indicative of a
difference in the cultural orientations of the inhabitants of these two sites, and
I return to this broader issue in more detail later.

Figure 6.6. Local pottery, early second millennium BC settlement of Saar, Bahrain. Photo: National Museum of Bahrain / London-Bahrain Archaeological Expedition.

THE BARBAR TEMPLE

European archaeologists have known about the archaeological site of Barbar since Captain Durand visited Bahrain in 1878 (Durand 1880). It was not until the 1950s, however, that Danish archaeologists began to excavate a site that typifies the unique and important material culture of Bahrain (Andersen 1986; Andersen and Højlund 2003). Between 1954 and 1961 a sequence of three superimposed temples was discovered, the first two of which had multiple building phases (Andersen and Højlund 2003). Barbar Temple I consists of a large rectangular platform measuring approximately 25 by 18 meters, which was placed on an earlier oval platform. Poorly preserved temple buildings were revealed on top of the platform. The buildings were made from locally available uncut farouche (consolidated beach sediment) blocks and constructed in a depression containing a natural artesian spring, the water from which was collected into a pool (Andersen and Højlund 2003: 80). A layer of clean clay was laid down below the lowest levels of the temple complex and probably represents a foundation deposit for the entire structure. Found within or on the clay were a great variety of artefacts, including at least fifty ceramic beakers, stone vessels and vessel fragments, as well as fragments of gold band, lapis lazuli and carnelian beads. It is, however, the large number of copper and bronze objects that reveals the important role that the metals trade played on Bahrain at this time.

More than twenty bronze blades, spearheads, adzes and knives were found, along with at least two bronze ingots. These objects were very poorly made, and the weapons had not been strengthened or properly cast. The likelihood that these bronzes were never actually used, in addition to the recovery of ceramic beakers in this deposit, suggests that the objects are the remains of a libation ritual that marked the inauguration of the temple's construction (Andersen and Højlund 2003: 257). These objects and the ceramics found in Temple I, including two Umm an-Nar imports from southeastern Arabia, suggest a date for its construction in the twenty-first century BC, equivalent to Qala'at al-Bahrain Phase Ib or IIa.

A massive investment in the temple results in the construction of Temple II towards the end of the twenty-first century BC. The oval platform terrace walls are reworked and large ashlar limestone blocks used for the construction of a platform upon which a large double circular altar and other buildings are constructed (Figure 6.7). Much of this stone was probably imported from the island of Jiddah on the northwestern coast of Bahrain (Andersen and Højlund

Figure 6.7. Main altars in the Barbar Temple Phase II, looking southwest, 1956. Photo: Moesgaard Museum.

Figure 6.8. Bull's head from the Barbar Temple. Photo: Moesgaard Museum.

2003: 81). It is to this period of the temple's use that a large copper head of a bull belongs (Figure 6.8). Likely affixed to some sort of stand, it is considered to represent some form of cult object. During-Caspers (1971) drew attention to strong parallels that exist in Early Dynastic Mesopotamia cultic paraphernalia, but it should also be noted that the head is that of a *Bos indicus*, the species of cattle most exploited in the Arabian Gulf and South Asia. In either case, its workmanship is indicative of the developed bronze- and copperworking technology existing on Bahrain at this time.

During the use of Temple II, a large pool was constructed to the southwest of the oval platform. Constructed from cut limestone blocks, the pool measured 5 by 6 meters in plan and was sunk into the ground to a depth of several meters (Figure 6.9). A stone-constructed staircase linked the temples to the pool and gave access to the water table, which was still present when the pool was first excavated in the 1960s (Figure 6.10). Temple III, probably constructed in the early twentieth century BC, was massively disturbed by the later removal of stones and demolition. It is clear that it represents a significant reworking of the temple complex, although the Temple II pool and staircase continued to be used.

Figure 6.9. Barbar Temple, the pool of Phase IIb, looking southwest, 1960.
Photo: Moesgaard Museum.

The discovery, excavation and eventual publication of the Barbar Temple complex generated much debate among Near Eastern archaeologists. Because of its religious and monumental character, it has been discussed as a component of broader Near Eastern archaeological discourse on Mesopotamian religion and religious practice. In fact, interpretations have centred on the worship of Mesopotamian deities at Barbar. Initial interpretations by Mortensen (1986) emphasized parallels with Early Dynastic temple architecture in southern Mesopotamia. Alternatively, the presence of a well pool led Andersen to argue that the temples were dedicated to Enki, a god of Eridu and closely associated with (subterranean) water (Andersen 1986). Comparisons between the layer of clay that separated the *abzu* (the subterranean freshwater abode of Enki) from the world of humanity in the Mesopotamian myth of Enki and Ninmah and the layer of clay laid down to mark the inauguration of the temple strengthened this argument (Andersen and Højlund 2003: 330). Furthermore, the myth of Enki and Ninhursag mentions that Enki provided fresh water to Dilmun upon the request of his daughter, Ninsikilla. A less Mesopotamia-centric view has been proposed by Potts (1991a: 172), who argued that the toponym 'Barbar' relates to the Sumerian word for those temples dedicated to Utu, the sun god, whose Akkadian equivalent, Shamash, enjoyed popularity through much of pre-Islamic Arabia. In the absence of any inscriptions from the Barbar Temple, all of these theories remain complete conjecture.

Figure 6.10. Barbar Temple, staircase of Phase IIa, looking west, 1959. Photo: Moesgaard Museum.

UNDERSTANDING EARLY DILMUN SOCIETY

The debates surrounding the Barbar Temple have occasionally overshadowed the broader implications of it and the Early Dilmun buildings on Qala'at al-Bahrain for our understanding of Early Dilmun society. In their monumentality and the massive labour investment required for the movement of ashlar limestone blocks from Jiddah to Barbar, these two sites alert us to a critical development on the island of Bahrain. For the first time in Arabian prehistory, a monumental construction visually reminded the population of the authority and power of a small group within the population. Differential access to foodstuffs on Qala'at al-Bahrain and the importance of water access at the Barbar Temple indicate that there was a materialist component to this authority. In other words, the kinship that had reinforced social cohesion since the Neolithic was beginning to fray on the island. I argued in Chapter 4 that collective burials played an important part in reinforcing such social cohesion in southeastern Arabia, and it

Figure 6.11. Late-type burial mounds at Aali with the Royal Mounds in the background, looking north, c. 1960. Photo: Moesgaard Museum.

is telling that the clearest indication of the loss of such cohesion on Bahrain is reflected in the unique burials that cover large areas of the island.

As previously noted, the existence of thousands of burials on Bahrain attracted archaeologists to the island from the nineteenth century onwards (Figure 6.11). The mound fields are scattered in clusters in the north of the island around Isa Town, Barbar, Rifa'a, Hajjar, Saar, Aali, Dar Kulaib and Umm Jidr to the south. By the 1950s archaeologists noted that there were so many burial mounds on the island that it seems that 'the rugged surface is due to a natural phenom-enon, a seething mass of sand, stiffened at the beginning of time and not the work of Man' (Glob 1960: 14, quoted in Højlund 2008: 7). The exact num-ber of these large visible mounds is unknown: Bibby suggested approximately 100,000, whereas Laursen (2008) put the figure closer to 170,000. Regardless of how many existed before the construction and economic boom that has defined Bahrain for the past forty years, it is likely that today there are no more than 20,000 extant burial mounds (Højlund 2008: 7).

Numerous excavations have provided a snapshot of burial customs in the late third and early second millennia BC. The picture that emerges stands in stark contrast to the contemporary Umm an-Nar burial practice of south-eastern Arabia. Most Bahrain tombs contain only one or two individuals, as opposed to the hundreds of individuals that were interred in an undifferenti-ated mass in Umm an-Nar tombs. Remains of animals, especially sheep and goat, have been noted in Bahrain tombs, and the cut marks recovered on the bones suggested to Kveiborg (2007) that the animals were slaughtered at the graveside and portioned for consumption as part of the burial custom. As I noted in Chapter 4, funerary offerings of animals are almost completely absent from Umm an-Nar tombs in southeastern Arabia. The societal implications of these differences in burial customs is heightened when we consider how the Bahrain tombs change from the late third to early second millennium BC.

Detailed mapping of the extant tombs and a synthesis of excavated examples suggest to Højlund three main periods of use during which the tombs operate as proxies for significant shifts in the sociopolitical organization of the island. In Period I, from 2200 to 2050 BC, burials are in simple small mounds with little evidence of differential access to grave goods or investment in tomb con-struction. In Period II, 2050–1750 BC, elite two-storey tombs are dispersed at a number of burial fields across northern Bahrain. By the nineteenth and eighteenth centuries BC, the concentration of these elite tombs shifts towards a single site: Aali, which can be considered a 'royal burial' field (Figure 6.12). Two other general trends characterize Period II tombs in northern Bahrain: the general wealth of the tombs increases, but concomitantly, disparity in the quality and quantity of grave goods also increases. For Højlund, it is not a coin-cidence that these changes occur at the same time as the establishment of a fortification system around Qa'alat al-Bahrain, the construction of the Barbar Temple and the codification of glyptic (discussed later) across the island. He concludes: 'The evidence from the burial mounds thereby supports and adds new substance to the conclusions drawn from studies of Qa'alat al-Bahrain. The Barbar Temple and the settlements at Saar and Failaka: the Early Dilmun Society expanded dramatically and became vastly wealthier from period II through period IIb and IIc. This process of change was probably related to an intensification of trade through the Gulf with Mesopotamia, caused by an increasing demand for foreign commodities and raw materials and a monopo-lization of this trade by Dilmun' (Højlund 2008: 136).

Laursen (2008) has gone further and argued that the so-called ring mounds – circular tombs with an external ring wall which are in existence throughout most of the last three centuries of the third millennium BC – reflect the existence of a semi-stratified elite and multiple small sociopolitical orga-nizations. The end of the third millennium BC witnesses 'the emergence of a new social hierarchy that was centrally controlled by one or more dynas-tic lineages. This is manifested in the southern, middle and finally, northern

Figure 6.12. Royal Mounds at Aali, 1956. Photo: Moesgaard Museum.

clusters at Aali. Assuming that the Aali mounds mirror a securely established power structure maintained in the hands of one lineage for numerous generations, I choose to label this organisational stage "dynastic"' (Laursen 2008: 166). He has speculated that the Dilmunite king who receives a special gift from Shamshi-Adad (1813–1781 BC) (as described later) is likely buried in one of the large ring tombs at Aali.

TRADE, ADMINISTRATION AND FOREIGN RELATIONS OF THE DILMUN STATE

By the beginning of the second millennium BC, portions of Dilmun society had moved towards a political structure that was similar to those common throughout the ancient Near East. The emergence of a royal lineage that interacted with other kings in the Middle East marks a complete contrast with the picture from southeastern Arabia at the same time. What caused these changes and to what extent did they permeate all of Dilmunite society?

Most scholars agree that the answer lies, at least in part, with the role that Dilmun played in the trans-shipment of copper to Mesopotamia. When Magan (ancient southeastern Arabia) disappears from Mesopotamian texts in the early second millennium BC and the Umm an-Nar culture comes to an end, Dilmun emerges as a powerful economic centre in the Arabian Gulf. From Ur, and dating to the Isin-Larsa period (essentially the first two centuries of the second millennium BC), texts record the importation from Dilmun of a range of exotic goods, including gold, semi-precious stones, ivory and copper (Potts 1991a: 220). There can be little doubt that copper was of particular importance in this trade system. By the nineteenth century BC, a group of traders referred to as alik Tilmun, or 'Dilmun traders', are known from Ur, and it is possible that private capital played an increasingly important role in this trade (Crawford 2005). One such Dilmun trader was called Ea-naṣir, and a series of economic documents belonging to him were found in his house at Ur. One text records 611 talents (18.33 tonnes) of copper in one shipment alone (Potts 1991a: 224–225). According to Begemann et al. (2010) this is equivalent to the staggering figure of between 10,000 and 18,000 copper ingots.

As noted in Chapter 4, Weeks's analytical work on copper and copper-alloy objects from southeastern Arabia and the central Arabian Gulf confirms that at least some, if not most, of this copper was coming from the al-Hajjar mountain range of southeastern Arabia (Weeks 2003: 199). This has been confirmed by Prange (2001) and by Begemann et al.'s (2010) more recent study, which included lead isotope and compositional analysis of artefacts from a number of sites. Those who inhabited the central buildings at Qala'at al-Bahrain and were buried in the tombs at Aali either organized the expeditions to southeastern Arabia to obtain this copper or purchased it from Magan traders, who brought not only copper but other luxury goods from South Asia, and then sold the goods to the traders who sailed south from Mesopotamia or farther north (Eidem and Højlund 1993).

ARABIAN GULF GLYPTIC

The international commerce that developed as goods were transported across regions where different languages were spoken posed obvious logistical problems. It is hardly surprising, therefore, that one of the most distinguishing characteristics of late third and early second millennium BC Bahrain is the development of an indigenous style and form of glyptic. The first examples of such glyptic have been referred to by a number of names, including 'Persian Gulf' seals and 'Arabian Gulf Type' (Kjærum 1980, 1983, 1994) but in the most recent literature are simply called 'Gulf Type' seals (Laursen 2010). They are engraved with representations of animals on the face and a perforated circular knob or boss on the reverse. They are made from a variety of materials, including semi-precious stones and ivory, but are most commonly made of steatite. A sub-set of these seals is inscribed with Indus Valley script, the importance of which we will return to later. The presence of Indus Valley script and the recovery of numerous examples at Indus Valley sites led some scholars to argue initially that the seals were from the Indus Valley (Gadd 1932; Hallo and Buchanan 1965). However, Glob's excavations at Qala'at al-Bahrain in the 1950s resulted in the discovery of numerous examples and led him to identify them as an important and unique component of Dilmun culture (Glob 1959).

For many years the chronology of these seals rested upon less than secure contexts in the Indus Valley and Mesopotamia. More recently, a reanalysis of published and unpublished Gulf Type seals has secured their chronology beyond doubt (Laursen 2010). Of particular importance is one seal which, because of its use of Linear Elamite, can be dated to the reign of Puzur-Inshushinak, the last king of Anshan and a contemporary of Ur-Namma (2112–2095 BC), founder of the Ur III dynasty. This chronology correlates with that observed from the Royal Graves at Ur, with their occurrence on Qala'at al-Bahrain IIa and with their relative paucity (in comparison with later Dilmun-type seals) at the settlement of Saar. All of this evidence combined suggests that Gulf Type seals were produced and in use from c. 2100 to 2000 BC (Laursen 2010), thus marginally predating, or coinciding with, the establishment of the Aali royal cemetery.

Most of the 121 Gulf Type seals known thus far were found on Bahrain, but examples have also been recovered throughout the Indus Valley, southeastern Iran, Failaka (Kuwait), southeastern Arabia and southern Mesopotamia (Laursen 2010). The widespread adoption of this glyptic in those regions in which Bahrain was actively engaged in trade suggests a link between them and the mercantile activity of Dilmun society. Furthermore, by the beginning of the second millennium BC, the Dilmun weight measure, referred to in an Old Babylonian text from Ur, was compatible with those from southern Mesopotamia, the Indus Valley, Egypt and parts of Syria (Ascalone and Peyronel 1999; Peyronel 2000; Zaccagnini 1986) (see Text Box 8). Mesopotamian and Indus Valley weights have also been found in Bahrain and southeastern Arabia. When combined, the evidence points to the existence of a cosmopolitan group of merchants whose economic activity spread through the Indian Ocean and into the Arabian Gulf.

The presence of Indus Valley script on twenty-eight Gulf Type seals has focused scholarly attention on the identity and geographical origin of these merchants. One possibility is that they were acculturated South Asians who used their 'heritage' script to render a geographical or personal name in the native language of the Arabian Gulf (Laursen 2010). Specific quarters or settlements containing 'Meluhhans' (i.e., those who originate from the Indus Valley) might have existed in southern Mesopotamia at this time. One such example is the town of Guabba, an important harbour city for Lagash in which it has been argued that 'Meluhhans' resided (Vermaak 2008), some of whom had Sumerian names (Parpola et al. 1977). The possibility that a similar group of traders were similarly attracted to the 'rising centre of trade on Bahrain' (Laursen 2010: 131) cannot be ruled out.

TEXT BOX 8. THE DILMUN WEIGHT AND INTERNATIONAL EXCHANGE

Anyone who has ever moved to the United States, or any American who has ever moved to Europe, knows that one of the most difficult challenges of daily life is adjusting to the different metrological systems employed in grocery stores. Eventually most people will round the difference between a US pound and a metric kilo up or down according to a simple equation: a pound is *about* half a kilo and a kilo *about* two pounds. The problem with this approximation is that it is *very* approximate and can lead to all sorts of over-purchases precisely because the weight systems employed in each region have no simple conversion point (i.e., 1 US pound = 0.453 metric kilo, not 0.500 kilo). Eventually one adapts to eating larger or small portions than one was used to.

The intense maritime trade that characterized the Arabian Gulf in the early second millennium BC incorporated at least three different regions: Mesopotamia, the Arabian Gulf and the Indus Valley, each of which had its own metrological systems. When large amounts of copper or small amounts of precious metals were being traded across these great distances, the weight system that was employed must have been flexible enough that merchants from different regions were satisfied they were fulfilling their contracts and purchasing correct amounts. Fortunately, research conducted in the past few decades on the weight systems employed in Mesopotamia, the Gulf and the Indus Valley indicates that such a system did emerge during this period. In discussing this, it is best to start with the weight system employed at Ur, from which the most extensive evidence derives.

Three basic units were employed in Mesopotamia: the mina, the shekel and the talent. The metrology was sexagesimal; that is, there were 60 shekels to a mina and 60 minas to a talent. The weight of the Ur mina during the period of Arabian Gulf trade can be calculated on the weights found at Ur by Woolley. In total, sixty-five stone weights were found at Ur (Roaf 1982), of which sixty-two came from graves (Peyronel 2000). Based on an average weight of a Mesopotamian shekel as approximately 8.4 grams, the weights varied from ⅓ shekel to 3 shekels. The high frequency of weights discovered in graves reflects the importance that these had in the economic lives of those interred. Indeed, in two of the graves, balance pans from scales were also buried. In some cases, what might be considered a nearly complete set of weights was also recovered. For example, in Grave LG 45 at Ur, seventeen weights were found in association with the balance pans. These weighed ⅓, ⅓, ½, ⅔, ⅔, 1, 1, 1, 2, 2, 2 and 3 measures of an 8.4 gram shekel (Peyronel 2000: 183).

Detailed metrological analysis has shown how the Ur weight system related to that employed in other regions. In particular, the ratio between the Ur mina and that employed in Dilmun is provided by a text of the merchant Ea-naṣir from Ur (see main text). The text records the dispersal of copper coming from Dilmun to Ea-naṣir and several other investors. The amounts are given in Dilmun mina, and the entire amount is recorded in Ur minas (= 60 shekels). Analysis of this tablet provides an exchange factor of 1 Dilmun mina = 2⅔ Ur minas, or 1 Ur mina = ⅜ Dilmun mina. In other words, the ratio of the Ur to Dilmun mina was 8/3. Based on an average weight of the Ur mina of 500 grams, the Dilmun mina would thus equal approximately 1,350 grams.

Roaf (1982) reported the existence of seven stone weights from Bahrain which confirmed the existence of this weight system. These weighed 1.8, 13.5, 13.9, 27, 171, 670 and 1,370 grams and are thus in ratio agreement with the weight of a supposed Dilmun mina of 1,350 grams. In other words, the weights (excluding the lightest weight) are approximately $\frac{1}{100}$, $\frac{1}{100}$, $\frac{1}{50}$, $\frac{1}{8}$, $\frac{1}{2}$ and 1 unit of a Dilmun mina. Zaccagnini (1986) has taken the analysis of Dilmun and Mesopotamian metrology further. She suggested, on the basis of the weights found on Bahrain but excluding the lightest, which she considered irrelevant to the weight system, that unlike the sexagesimal Mesopotamian weight system, the Dilmun mina was based upon factors of 8 and 10. In other words, the Dilmun mina had two basic 'units': one was a $\frac{1}{100}$ unit of 13.5 grams, while the other was a $\frac{1}{80}$ unit of 17 grams. If Zaccagnini is correct, and no subsequent discoveries have challenged her conclusions, the Dilmun mina achieved something that the US and metric systems have never resolved: a common conversion point between different metrological systems. To explain: The unit of $\frac{1}{80}$ of a Dilmun mina (17 grams) was *more or less* equivalent to 2 Mesopotamian shekels of 8.4 grams.

In other words, traders coming to Dilmun to purchase pearls would be able to weigh their purchases in the local weight system and simply convert the amount to their own system. However, the Dilmun weight system appears to have been even more conducive to international exchange. The other 'unit' of the Dilmun mina ($\frac{1}{100}$) was approximately 13.5 grams, which comes very close to the average weight of 13.6 grams employed as the basic unit for metrology in the Indus Valley and is double the skekel weight of 6.5 grams attested elsewhere in the Near East outside of Mesopotamia (Zaccagnini 1986: 21–22). Thus, the metrology of the Dilmun weight, in combination with the discovery of Mesopotamian and Indus Valley weights on Bahrain and elsewhere in the Arabian Gulf, attests to the central role that the island played in the movement and exchange of goods across southwest Asia.

Bibby's excavations in Qala'at al-Bahrain indicated that Gulf Type seals gave way to a different glyptic tradition around the twentieth century BC. This new type, called 'Dilmun seals', is differentiated from the earlier type by dotted circles on the boss, a variety of human and animal figures on the face and the absence of any inscription (Crawford 2001) (Figure 6.13). They emerge from a type of intermediate seal style, sometimes called 'Proto-Dilmun Type' (Kjærum 1994). The chronology of Dilmun seals proper is fixed by the use of one to seal a tablet from the tenth year of the reign of Gungunum of Larsa (1923 BC) (Hallo and Buchanan 1965). There seems little doubt that Dilmun seals, like the earlier Gulf Type, were used for sealing vessels and tablets. Examples of sealings have been found at Barbar (Kjærum 2003: 296) and Saar (Crawford 2001: 32–38, 76–106) on Bahrain, on Failaka (Barta et al. 2008: Fig. 14) as well on the tablet from Larsa previously noted. Although many remain unpublished, close to 1,000 seals have so far been discovered in the Arabian Gulf (S. Laursen, personal communication), and perhaps nearly half of these come from Failaka. They have also been found at Ur and Tell Ischali in Iraq, Susa in Iran, Gardan Reg in Afghanistan, Lothal in India and several sites in Saudi Arabia and the UAE (Potts 1991a: 199–200).

Figure 6.13. Dilmun stamp seal in Style IA from Tell F6 on Failaka, Kuwait-Danish excavations in 2011. Photo: Hélène David-Cuny, courtesy Moesgaard Museum.

The large number of Dilmun seals and their widespread distribution leave little doubt that the first three centuries of the second millennium BC witnessed a massive expansion of economic activities centred upon Dilmun. The large number found on Bahrain and on Failaka suggests that these activities were an important component of the Dilmunite state, and they must be viewed, therefore, as an administrative measure similar to that which had been employed by other Near Eastern states since the fourth millennium BC. At the same time, their form and iconography set them apart from canonical Near Eastern glyptic, which had been dominated by the use of cylinder seals since the Uruk period. Indeed, as Potts (2010) has pointed out, cylinder seals are relatively rare in Gulf contexts: only eighteen dated to between c. 2500 and 1800 BC have been recovered, and thirteen of these are from Bahrain or Failaka.

FAILAKA AND THE NORTHERN ARABIAN GULF

In the preceding discussion much mention was made of Failaka, the small island off the coast of Kuwait that witnesses a rapid emergence of settlement

Figure 6.14. Tell F6 on Failaka, Kuwait, with (*left*) the 'palace' excavated by a Danish mission c. 1960, (*right*) the temple excavated by a French mission in the 1980s and (*middle*) the new trenches by the Kuwait-Danish mission, 2008–2009. Photo: Yves Guichard, courtesy Moesgaard Museum.

at the end of the third millennium BC. Excavations by numerous international teams have revealed a long history of occupation through the second millennium BC (Calvet and Gachet 1990; Calvet and Salles 1986; Højlund 1987; Salles 1983). Our knowledge about Failaka in this period comes principally from the Danish and French excavations at F3 and F6 (Figure 6.14). For our present discussion, Periods 1–3A are of most importance, as they cover the end of the third and the first three centuries of the second millennium BC (Højlund 1987, 2010). A series of stone-constructed houses define Period 2. The material culture found within these dwellings is entirely compatible with that found on Bahrain during the City II period, or the nineteenth and eighteenth centuries BC. In the subsequent period, a large – clearly non-domestic – building was constructed. Although incomplete, it measures nearly 25 by 25 meters and contained a large central hall with stone columns. A number of smaller ancillary rooms surrounded this room. The walls were made of semi-dressed stone, and stone slabs were set into the floor. The building is generally considered to represent a palace or some type of elite building.

The large number of Dilmun seals and sealings found in these buildings (probably more than anywhere else in the Gulf) and the homogeneity of material culture with that of Bahrain have led scholars to see this occupation of Failaka as the result of colonization. More recent excavations at the site al-Khidr in the north of Failaka have confirmed strong ties to Bahrain on the basis of ceramics and glyptic; the importation of copper/bronze objects and softstone vessels from southeastern Arabia is also likely to have been carried out via Bahrain (Barta et al. 2008). Analysis of the stamp seals found in the Period III palace has suggested that specific forms of glyptic were employed in this building (Abu Laban 2010; Højlund 2010), lending credibility to the notion that these settlements were a deliberate attempt by the Dilmun state to establish a trading colony at the critical point of access to the Shaṭṭ al-Arab and Tigris-Euphrates river systems. Today, Failaka lies just 10 kilometers from the Khor as-Subiyah tidal inlet that gives access to the southern Iraq marshes, and any traffic to and from that system must pass by the island.

That contact with southern Mesopotamia was important for Failaka's inhabitants can be assumed. However, the ceramics from all areas of occupation remain strongly within the Bahraini tradition until the end of Period 2 (Højlund 1987). By Period 3A (the eighteenth century BC), Mesopotamian-inspired or –imported pottery increases to nearly 50% of the corpus (Højlund 1987). It would be tempting to see this and subsequent developments on Failaka as evidence for the influx of people from Mesopotamia (Potts 1991a: 291; cf. Højlund 1993) who submerged an existing Dilmunite population. However, the interplay between material culture, colonialism and mercantile activity is very complex. If one envisages that the initial settlers of Failaka came from Bahrain with the express purpose of trading with southern Mesopotamia, then familiarity with the latter area may have led to processes of acculturation and eventual adoption of cultural traits. The most recent discoveries at Failaka add to the uncertainty: excavations below the Period 2 palace have revealed an earlier house structure in which Mesopotamian material culture dominates (Højlund 2010). How this can be configured into the narrative of colonization that has dominated studies of Failaka remains to be seen.

In summary, the archaeological evidence from Failaka and the emergence of glyptic combine with evidence from Bahrain to paint a picture of a state whose principal economic activity was the control of traded goods in the Gulf. Textual sources and archaeological evidence indicate that copper, semi-precious stones, wood, ivory and gold were the objects of this trade (Potts 1991a: 220). The shipment of copper from southeastern Arabia, and possibly other areas, was of particular importance (Carter 2003; Leemans 1960; Oppenheim 1954; Potts 1991a). The control of this trade resulted in fundamentally new forms of political authority on Dilmun which spread from its centre on the island of Bahrain to the northern reaches of the Arabian Gulf.

DILMUN: AN ARABIAN STATE

Why did this occur on Bahrain when, in the centuries prior to these developments, southeastern Arabia had played the same role in Gulf trade and, moreover, was actually the source of much of the traded copper? Laursen (2009) has raised the possibility that southeastern Arabia's relationship with Marhashi (southern and southeastern Iran) meant that it became economically sidelined when the Ur III state clashed with the latter region and Dilmun took advantage of this economic vacuum. These events led to a 'general organizational decline' in southeastern Arabia (Laursen 2009: 137) that contrasts with a new social hierarchy based on lineage on Bahrain (Laursen 2008: 166).

Setting aside the issue of southeastern Arabia's connections with Iran, which were of no greater importance than connections with other regions in the Arabian Gulf, Laursen's explanation presupposes that existing societal differences led to divergent trajectories in Bahrain and southeastern Arabia in the early second millennium BC. Indeed, the burial mounds of Bahrain that date to the two centuries before the emergence of the Dilmun state leave little doubt that some of the inhabitants of the island were already organized in a hierarchical fashion that was quite unlike anything in southeastern Arabia. Why was this the case? Is it possible that contact with Mesopotamia during the late fourth and early third millennia BC at sites such as Tarut and Dhahran and the Mesopotamian importation of Dilmun copper challenged the social order established during the Neolithic (Chapter 3)? Aspects of the emerging Dilmun state did indeed emulate concepts of Mesopotamian social order. For example, Højlund (2000) has drawn attention to the fact that the shape of the Dilmun seal mirrors those of the royal cap worn by Mesopotamian rulers of the late third millennium BC. This cap was a sign of divine right and power and thus its adoption as one of the mechanisms that ensured that the new Dilmun 'economic system was legitimised, a system in which the ruler seized the right to direct and profit from the trade, a right which earlier, before the kingdom was formed, had been with the heads of individual families' (Højlund 2000: 19).

Did this emergence of political authority, invested in the control of trade and legitimized through monumental buildings, result in 'the genealogy of enslavement and alienation' and 'the advent of public repression' as it did elsewhere in the Near East (Bernbeck 2009: 57), or did the millennia of social formation and adaptation to the arid coastal zones of eastern Arabia result in something uniquely 'Arabian' about the Dilmun state that differed from that in Mesopotamia?

In Chapter 4, I suggested that if the 'seafaring merchant' Lu-Enlilla sailed from Ur to southeastern Arabia in the twenty-first century BC he would have found a society that was organized in a fundamentally different fashion from his own. What would the 'Dilmun trader' Ea-naṣir, also travelling from Ur but to Dilmun and three centuries later, have thought about the island kingdom he was visiting? Fortunately, we know more about Ea-naṣir than Lu-Enlilla so we are in a better position to understand his experiences as a merchant in the Arabian Gulf. Ea-naṣir lived in one of the larger houses in what Woolley called 'AH' block at Ur. The entrance to his house was an alleyway just off 'Old Street', and the house contained five rooms which encompassed a courtyard. The floors were made of baked brick, and the house consisted of two storeys, or at least access to the roof, and a separate lavatory. Two rooms contained vaulted tombs and altars (Dunham 2007: 274). Although unexcavated, these were likely dedicated to members of Ea-naṣir's family. Ea-naṣir's daily life in and around his house would have reinforced the stratified and segmented nature of Ur society. He was aware that even within the AH area there were stark differences in house size, wealth and occupation. When he walked south of Carfax and Straight Street in AH block, he would have noticed that the houses were smaller: 40 square meters on average, as opposed to the opulent 72 square meters per house in the area where he lived (Van De Mieroop 1992: 124). His neighbours' activities were similar to his: those who lived on Church Lane and Niche Lane were silver traders (Van De Mieroop 1992: 128), some of whom might have provided the *tadmiqtu* loans that were a critical part of his business (Potts 1991a: 223). When Ea-naṣir took a longer walk, about 500 meters to the west and over the canal, he would have encountered the Nanna Temple complex, the administrative and religious centre of Ur. Just to the south lay the EM block, where the powerful high administrators and cult personnel for the temple lived. He might have been aware that here at No. 7 Quiet Street lived the family of temple archivists, who perhaps kept records of his dealings with the temple (Van De Mieroop 1992: 125). He might have wondered, nervously, if they had heard about his unhappy customers, especially Nanni, who in the text known as UET 5.81 complains about the quality of copper he has brought and asks, 'Who is there amongst the Dilmun traders who has treated me in this way?' (Leemans 1960: 52).

These vignettes of daily life in Ur would have stayed with Ea-naṣir as he set sail to Dilmun to organize a shipment of copper. Upon arrival on Bahrain he probably would have visited Qala'at al-Bahrain and paid his respects to the political authority of the island. Although the city was smaller than anything he would have seen in Ur, he would have felt familiar with its layout. He would have recognized from their fine masonry and monumentality that the buildings in the central area of the settlement were the seat of power. Perhaps he would have visited the Barbar Temple, where he would find familiar the obvious labour and investment that had gone into its construction. In other words, there was much to recognize on Bahrain even if the scale was much smaller than he was used to. On our imaginary trip, we might give cause for Ea-naṣir to move outside his 'comfort zone' and visit the settlement of Saar, just a few kilometers to the south of Barbar. Initially walking up Main Street, he might have found the town familiar. But it would have dawned on him that it was fundamentally different than Ur, not just in size but in organization as well.

Indeed, the excavation of Saar has revealed a settlement that is structured in a very different fashion than that which existed at Ur at this time. The vast majority of houses (about 80%) are simple two- to three-room dwellings distributed evenly throughout the settlement (Killick and Moon 2005: 149–150). The building sizes and layout were generally stable, and most buildings contained a similar range of food preparations and storage facilities: each had a small clay oven (*tannour*), a hearth, a cooking pot support, a storage pit and a workbench. Only three or four houses might be considered elite or of high status (Killick and Moon 2005: 348). Building 53 contained numerous rooms, two large walled courtyards and fragments of many storage jars and imported high-status vessels. Buildings 220 and 35 also contained more than the normal number of rooms, and the former contained many seals and seal impressions. Killick and Moon (2005: 348) conclude that these three buildings, and possibly one other, are candidates 'for the residences of the wealthier members of Saar society'.

The growth and elaboration of these buildings bear witness to how certain sections of society benefited from the intense trade in which Dilmun was engaged. However, in each case these buildings started as very simple dwellings that expanded and incorporated adjoining buildings only by the last phase of the settlement. The social and economic differentiation to which these buildings attest does not appear to have deep social roots. Buildings 220, 53 and 35 are scattered across the entire settlement. In other words, there was no wealthy quarter at Saar comparable to the northern section of the AH block at Ur in which Ea-naṣir lived. The newly rich of Saar shared party walls with those who lived in the simplest two- and three-room dwellings. Similarly, although there was a small temple at Saar, there was no quarter comparable to the EM block at Ur that housed the temple functionaries. The buildings alongside the temple at Saar incorporated a wide range of types, including simple two-room dwellings (see Figure 6.3). If, on our imaginary journey, Ea-naṣir had had the opportunity to see the cemetery at Saar, he too would have been struck by the agglomeration of single burials packed tightly against each other, completely unlike anything he had seen in Ur or even the huge tumuli burials at Aali. We might ascribe to him the thoughts one has today when looking at these burials: in death the people of Saar maintained the close-knit and cohesive community that they experienced in life.

I am not arguing that the people of Saar lived an egalitarian existence that was threatened by the emergence of nouveau rich traders in the late nineteenth century BC. Excavations at Saar did reveal clear indications of differential access to resources, particularly in reference to terrestrial meat and large versus small fish, especially emperors (*Lethrinus* sp.) (Uerpmann and Uerpmann 2005b). Since this accumulated evidence is likely the result of numerous meals over many years, the social differences that they attest to are probably long-standing (Uerpmann and Uerpmann 2005b: 300). However, at Saar this social ranking does not appear to correlate with other durable forms of social status. For example, Building 208, which provides evidence for access to larger fish, is in fact smaller than Building 207, the inhabitants of which had access only to smaller fish. The lack of permanent indicators of social status at Saar, the relative homogeneity of building types and the simple burials might indicate that, in opposition to the monumentality that dominated Qala'at al-Bahrain and Barbar, a degree of social cohesion was maintained by certain sections of Dilmun society.

THE DEMISE OF EARLY DILMUN

If competing modes of social organization did indeed exist in nineteenth century BC Dilmun, then developments in the coming decades would have accentuated differences between them. A series of letters from Mari in Syria dating to the first two decades of the eighteenth century BC detail the existence of a caravan(s) travelling from Dilmun to Syria, presumably via the Euphrates, and the lengths to which the north Mesopotamian king Shamshi-Adad went to protect it (Potts 1983: 392–396, 1991a: 226; Reade 1983: 327–330). One of these texts contains the first cuneiform reference to the existence of a king of Dilmun (Potts 1991a: 229). Eidem and Højlund's (1993) analysis indicates that the letters probably refer to a single high-level diplomatic mission between Mari and Dilmun which was driven in part by a desire on the part of Shamshi-Adad to portray himself as a successor to the earlier Akkadian kings. They conclude that the texts 'represent a long awaited textual confirmation of the theory, based on the archaeological finds, that by this time Dilmun was a kingdom. Like other kingdoms in the Near East the Dilmun state may obviously have found it expedient to establish connections with the major political power of the day' (Eidem and Højlund 1993: 447).

By the early eighteenth century BC, therefore, control over the movement of copper and other luxury goods through the Arabian Gulf and into Mesopotamia finally brought the new elite of Dilmun onto the world stage of Near Eastern states and monarchies. This control was to prove as precarious as it was beneficial. A text dated to 1745 BC, the fifth year of the reign of Hammurabi's son Samsu-iluna, records the importation into Babylonia of a wide variety of precious and semi-precious metals, including '12 mina refined copper of Alashiya and of Tilmun' (Millard 1973: 212). Alashiya can almost certainly be identified as Cyprus, and although Cypriot copper is noted in earlier Mari texts, this document marks the first time that Cypriot copper is mentioned in Babylonia proper and the last time that Dilmunite copper is mentioned in the Old Babylonian period (Potts 1991a: 226). Millard (1973: 213) argued that Hammurabi's northern conquests opened up a

Syrian-Levantine-Mediterranean corridor for goods to be funnelled through to southern Mesopotamia, thus rendering Gulf sources of copper no longer necessary. Although some trade between Susa and Dilmun continued, the effect on the elite institutions of Dilmun was dramatic. In the second half of the eighteenth century BC, the large Aali tombs are no longer constructed and the palace on Qala'at al-Bahrain and the Barbar Temple fall into disrepair or are abandoned (Højlund 2008: 127). The political capital derived from control of the copper trade had been key to the authority of the new dynastic rulers of Dilmun. The speed with which they collapsed furthers the impression that their legitimacy was based purely on economic power and had not penetrated deeply into the ideology and social fabric of Dilmunite society. It is perhaps from this perspective that we can understand why the inhabitants of Saar decided to leave their settlement at this same time.

FOREIGN INTERVENTION AND THE RE-EMERGENCE OF DILMUN

After an hiatus of uncertain length, the Early Dilmun Palace on Qala'at al-Bahrain is reoccupied in the middle of the sixteenth century BC (Højlund and Andersen 1997: 50). This phase of occupation, referred to as Periods IIIa and IIIb1 (or the Middle Dilmun phase), witnessed the rebuilding of floors and walls in both Buildings I and III (Højlund and Andersen 1997). French excavations in a nearby part of the site have also revealed a large palatial structure of this period (André-Salvini and Lombard 1997). Just as in the Early Dilmun period, a city wall surrounded the settlement. Prima facie, the reutilization of earlier monumental constructions might be viewed as indicating a renaissance of the Early Dilmun state. However, the nature of political complexity on Bahrain had shifted considerably from what it had been in previous centuries (Højlund and Andersen 1997: 49). Whereas Early Dilmun political authority appears to have had an autochthonous basis centred on the control of Gulf trade, the emergence of the Middle Dilmun kingdom seems to have been directly related to political hegemony exercised by the Kassite dynasty of southern Mesopotamia. Long before the excavations at Qala'at al-Bahrain, Goetze's (1952) publication of two texts, dated to the reign of the Kassite king Burnaburiash (1359–1308 BC), from Nippur raised the possibility that the 'brother' of the governor of Nippur was the governor of Dilmun. Although debate ensued as to whether or not an actual governor of Dilmun is mentioned, the matter was put to rest by the publication of a cylinder seal in the British Museum that mentions a governor of Dilmun (Potts 1991a: 310).

The emplacement of a governor on Dilmun explains the presence of several cuneiform texts on the island at this time. Nine texts are known from the Danish excavations (Eidem 1997), and the French Archaeological Mission discovered a cache of nearly fifty tablet fragments (André-Salvini and Lombard

1997). The earliest of these date to the reign of Agum III in the early fifteenth century BC, that is, from the beginning of Kassite control over Bahrain. The tablets discovered by the Danish mission were all found in Building I of the palace, the so-called 'Kassite warehouse', and are concerned with the admin-istration of rations and other activities associated with the palace. The brief publications on the discoveries by the French mission paint a similar picture: all the texts seem to be administrative or ration texts, and two actually mention the palace itself (André-Salvini and Lombard 1997). The recovery of eleven Mitanni style and two Kassite cylinder seals (Potts 2010: 22) and 114 sealings (Olijdam, in press) highlights that the foreign governor of Dilmun brought with him the full range of administrative and economic mechanisms employed by his contemporaries in Babylon.

The level of infiltration of Kassite influence beyond the upper echelons of Dilmun society is difficult to assess. Veldhuis (2000) maintains that two texts from the Danish excavations (Eidem 1997: Nos. 319, 320) were school texts for the learning of cuneiform. Eidem (1997: 80) is less confident about this interpretation for one text, but the presence of the remaining text and a pos-sible Sumerian-Akkadian lexical text from the French excavations (André-Salvini and Lombard 1997: 166) indicates a process for teaching cuneiform on Bahrain. It is unlikely, however, that this process extended beyond those individuals tasked with record keeping and ration control in the palace. Kassite influence is also marked in the ceramics of the Middle Dilmun phase at Qala'at al-Bahrain, especially in the appearance of pedestal-footed goblets (Højlund 1987) and imported Kassite ceramics, pendants and seals in tombs at al-Hajjar and al-Maqsha (Denton 1994, 1999; Rice 1988). On the basis of the tomb con-tents, Denton (1999: 155) raises the possibility of actual migrations of people from southern Mesopotamia to Dilmun. As with the school texts, however, here again we are probably dealing with only the elites of the island who lived in the capital and were buried in monumental tombs. Excavations at Dhahran (Frohlich and Mughannum 1985; Potts et al. 1978: 9) in Saudi Arabia have also revealed second millennium BC material, including Kassite, or Kassite-influenced material, which has also been found farther south at Khor-ile Sud on Qatar (Edens 1999a; Potts 1993a: 197–198), although this is more likely the result of trade, perhaps with Bahrain itself.

Beyond the veneer of Mesopotamian influence, subsistence strategies in the central and northern Arabian Gulf continued to exploit the local distinc-tive environment. Excavations at Qala'at a-Bahrain and on F6 at Failaka have revealed the first *madbasas*, or date presses, yet discovered in Arabia (Højlund 1990). Madbasas were used to extract the syrup (dibs) of the date fruit: large quantities of dates were piled onto the madbasa, and over time the force of gravity caused liquid to be expressed and to run down indented channels to a pot or plastered sump. They were a common feature of traditional archi-tecture in eastern Arabia until the very recent past. The largest published archaeozoological data set for this period comes from the northern wall and monumental building area of Qala'at al-Bahrain (Uerpmann and Uerpmann 1997). This indicates a mixed faunal economy that included sheep, goat, cattle and, naturally, the exploitation of marine resources such as fish and turtle. Hunted wild animals included oryx and gazelle. Comparison of the faunal assemblages from the seaward-facing northern wall excavations and the central monumental buildings indicates some differences in subsistence strategies that likely relate to the different social and political statuses of the inhabitants of both of these areas. This included differences in the slaughtering ages of animals, the proportion of meat versus fish consumed and differences in the proportion of hunted animals (Uerpmann and Uerpmann 1997).

In summary, Kassite political control over Dilmun is at odds with prior Mesopotamian engagement with the central Arabian Gulf. The installation of a high-ranking official on an island which, at that time, was not a critical entrepôt for trade seems at first puzzling. Kassite concern about increasing Elamite control over the eastern edge of the Arabian Gulf and the establishment of Liyan on the Bushire peninsula, in which the Elamite king Humban-numena constructed a high temple to the goddess Kiririsha, might at first seem a possible reason for control over Dilmun. However, Potts (2006) has convincingly argued that throughout most of the thirteenth century BC, a political détente was achieved between the Elamite and Kassite realms through dynastic marriages. He concludes that the inter-dynastic marriage system 'offers an interesting context in which to consider the coexistence of Elamites and Kassites in the Persian Gulf, particularly with respect to probable Elamite attitudes towards Kassite hegemony in the western Persian Gulf. Although an apparently important base, possibly even a main port of trade, was maintained by the Elamites at Liyan, it may be suggested that the Elamites respected the Kassite sphere of influence in the western Persian Gulf, just as the Kassites respected the Elamite sphere of influence in the eastern Persian Gulf' (Potts 2006: 118). This might well be the case, but the limited archaeological evidence at our disposal does not permit us to address why the Kassite dynasty considered the control of Dilmun to be so important. 'Dilmun dates' are noted in several texts in southern Mesopotamia (Potts 1991a: 301, notes 11 and 12), but these could have grown within southern Mesopotamia itself. Olijdam (1997b) has raised the interesting possibility that control over Dilmun was important for the movement of lapis lazuli from Afghanistan to Babylon, where it was used as an important diplomatic gift within the 'Brotherhood of Kings' (see Podany 2010) that had emerged throughout the Near East by the fifteenth century BC. In this context, it is also interesting to consider the recently published archive of King Ayadaragalama of the First Sealand Dynasty in Babylonia, which predates by a few decades the consolidation of Kassite control over Dilmun. In this archive, five occurrences of the name Anzak, the patron god of Dilmun, are found, suggesting to Dalley

(2013: 181) that people who had close ties to Dilmun or Magan were already living in southern Mesopotamia at the end of the sixteenth century BC. Such evidence hints at the possibility that economic connections between southern Mesopotamia and the Arabian Gulf remained strong even after the assumed collapse of the copper trade at the end of the eighteenth century BC. It is hoped that future excavations on Bahrain will provide further information on these still poorly understood centuries.

KASSITE CONTROL AND THE AHLAMU

Whatever the reason for increased Mesopotamian engagement, it is very clear from the excavations on the island of Failaka (Calvet and Gachet 1990; Calvet and Salles 1986; Højlund 1987; Salles 1983) that the northern Gulf experienced Mesopotamian control and/or acculturation to an even greater extent than Bahrain. Højlund (1987) has demonstrated that by the middle of the second millennium BC southern Mesopotamian material dominates the material assemblage on the island. This includes elite materials, such as glass and glazed ware, as well as everyday ceramics. Of particular importance is a large temple platform from F3 (Period 3B) that contains an altar and series of columns. The entire platform, dated by ceramics as well as Kassite and Mitannian cylinder seals, may be identified with a temple noted in a number of cuneiform inscriptions found elsewhere on Failaka (Glassner 1984; Potts 1991a: 270–272). In fact, the use of cuneiform at Failaka is greater than at any other location in the Arabian Gulf. Forty-six inscriptions were published by Glassner in 1984, and several additions to this corpus were made with the publication of the French excavations in the late 1980s and 1990 (see Glassner 1999). Many of these inscriptions are found on the numerous Kassite cylinder seals that have been found on Failaka (Kjærum 1983; Potts 2010). When this evidence is combined with the overarching Mesopotamian character of the material culture, it leaves little doubt that Failaka was part of the Kassite realm, perhaps a 'dependency' (Potts 2010: 22), a conclusion reinforced by recent excavations at al-Khidr and other sites on the island (Barta et al. 2008).

Kassite political control over Bahrain comes to an end by the second quarter of the fourteenth century BC, and at Qala'at al-Bahrain a destruction level dates to this period. Three published letters sent from the governor of Dilmun, Illi-ipashra, to the governor of Nippur, Illiliya, indicates that by the middle of the fourteenth century BC internal problems on the island challenged Kassite control (Olijdam 1997a). A troublesome group, the Ahlamu, are identified as the main culprits. In the first letter, Illi-ipashra writes, 'The Ahlamu who surround me have taken away the dates and as far as I am concerned there is nothing I can do' (Olijdam 1997a: 200). Soon after, the situation has deteriorated: Illi-ipashra writes, 'The Ahlamu certainly speak words of hostility and

plunder to me. When I asked them for Belu-hebil, they did not hand him over'
(Olijdam 1997a: 202). As Olijdam notes, the latter section might indicate that a
high-ranking Kassite official has been taken hostage.

The identity of these Ahlamu has puzzled scholars for decades. Some have
argued that they are the forerunners of the Aramaeans, who are certainly
referred to by that term in the first millennium BC. Olijdam, overturning
Kupper's (1957) identification of them as agricultural labourers, suggested they
were mutinous soldiers who had once served the Kassite governor. Both interpretations, however, are based on contextual analysis of the meaning of the
word in Babylonian and later texts. As Van De Mieroop (2007: 64) has cautioned, it is important not to focus too much on the identification of the
Ahlamu as a single group, but rather recognize that the term was a generic and
somewhat contemptuous one for 'nomads'. A striking analogue is the manner
in which the term 'Bedouin' was sometimes applied in nineteenth-century
England to describe the homeless who survived on the streets of London.
For example, Goerge Sala in his *Twice Round the Clock, or The Hours of the Day
and Night in London* (1859) writes of children in Covent Garden at 6 A.M. as
follows: 'Wretched-looking little buyers are they, half-starved Bedouin children, mostly Irish, in faded and tattered garments, with ragged hair and bare
feet.' It was likely that an aspect of alterity was pronounced on Bahrain, where
there appears to have been an elite, urban Babylonian ruling clique, living in
an environment that was vastly different from that in southern Mesopotamia.
From this perspective, it is interesting to consider the possibility that the term
'Ahlamu' simply refers to the 'native' pastoral nomads who occupied Bahrain
and the adjacent east Arabian coast at that time. If this was the case and if the
destruction of Qala'at al-Bahrain is attributable to the Ahlamu, then the end of
Kassite control of Bahrain and the subsequent 'occupational enigma' (discussed
later) can be viewed in a different perspective: one that emphasizes the inevitable tension that arose between a ruling Babylonian and pro-Babylonian clique
and a restive local population. Such a social dichotomy finds an obvious prec-
edent in the stark contrast I discussed earlier between the organization of the
settlement of Saar and the palatial constructions of Qala'at al-Bahrain during
the Early Dilmun period.

Following these events, settlement on Bahrain and Failaka is less archaeologically visible for several centuries. In the case of the small island of Failaka,
which has now been systematically surveyed by numerous archaeological
teams, it is difficult to escape the conclusion that the presence of only a
single Iron Age burial amidst the extensive remains from the Bronze Age and
Hellenistic periods confirms a virtual abandonment of the island until c. 300
BC. Archaeologically visible settlement on Bahrain is scarce from c. 1300 to
1000 BC. However, the chronology and character of this period are obfus-
cated by the tendency of archaeologists to use evidence for Mesopotamian

interaction with the island as a proxy for actual economic activity. The lack of Mesopotamian references to Dilmun between the thirteenth and eighth centuries has led some scholars to suggest an occupation enigma throughout these centuries (cf. Kervran et al. 1987). Attempts to explain this enigma by the infiltration of date-stealing nomads from the east Arabian mainland before they continued their ravages north in the Sealand of Mesopotamia seem misguided, given the relative paucity of evidence. Small traces of occupation have been found at Qala'at al-Bahrain, and the island of Bahrain and the adjacent east Arabian littoral were certainly not abandoned. What was abandoned was the social order and concomitant monumentality that had developed during the early second millennium BC and was subsequently imposed by foreign control. That these developments were relatively unique within, and in the Kassite case extra-local to, the social forces that had shaped Arabian society can be seen no more clearly than by examining the archaeology of the same period from Dilmun's immediate neighbours in southeastern Arabia.

SOUTHEASTERN ARABIA FROM 2000 TO 1600 BC

The disappearance of the term 'Magan' from Mesopotamian sources and the rise of Dilmun as a powerful economic centre in the Arabian Gulf correlate with a shift in settlement patterns in southeastern Arabia (Figure 6.15). The subsequent seven hundred years are sometimes generically referred to as the 'Wadi Suq' period (e.g., Carter 1997), but it is now clear that this time period should be divided into two distinct phases, which Velde (2003) has labelled the 'Wadi Suq' (2000–1600 BC) and 'Late Bronze Age' (1600–1250 BC). Though it was once thought of as a period of decline following the collapse of the Umm an-Nar culture, it is now clear that during these centuries many of the economic activities characteristic of the Umm an-Nar period continue but within a reoriented settlement and social system that stands in contrast to the rise of the Dilmun state just to the north.

As previously noted, the rise of the Dilmun state was due in no small part to the control of copper trade with Mesopotamia. There can be little doubt that much of this copper was mined and processed within southeastern Arabia. Evidence for imported Bahraini ceramics at Tell Abraq and a number of coastal settlements both in the UAE and on Qatar indicates the existence of a number of 'way stations' that facilitated the movement of copper and other goods (Carter 2001). Included in these other goods were more than forty softstone vessel fragments and lids from Saar (Killick and Moon 2005: 205) and numerous similar examples from Qala'at al-Bahrain and in tombs, all of which were produced in southeastern Arabia. Whether these vessels were themselves objects of trade or contained a precious substance is unknown.

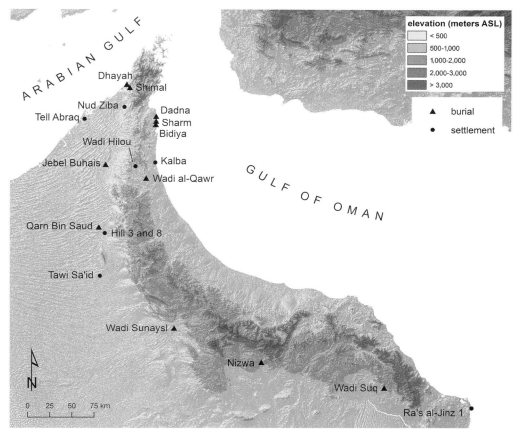

Figure 6.15. Location of main Wadi Suq period sites in southeastern Arabia.

WADI SUQ METALWORK AND CRAFT TRADITIONS

The copper industry within southeastern Arabia was not, however, completely oriented towards an export market. Tombs of the Wadi Suq period contain bronze weapons and tools that are equal in number to, if not more abundant than, those found in the preceding Umm an-Nar period. These differ significantly from those produced in the Umm an-Nar period and exhibit a distinctive craftsmanship and technology. Weapons include novel types of spearheads, which were probably used for throwing (Potts 1998), and swords (Velde 2003), examples of which are known from tombs throughout the peninsula. The number of weapons discovered in Wadi Suq contexts is significant, especially when one considers that most of these tombs were robbed at some stage in antiquity (Figure 6.16). The possibility that this represents a more 'war-like' existence during the Wadi Suq period must be tempered by the fact that these weapons were buried – and were thus out of use. Potts (1998), following Härke (1997), has gone as far as to suggest that the number of weapons found

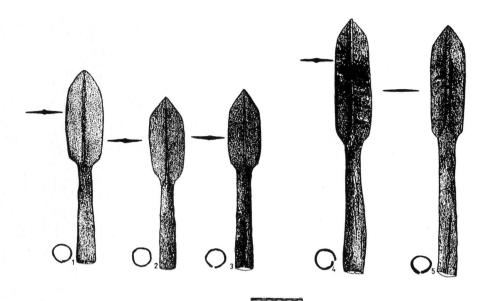

Figure 6.16. Wadi Suq bronze weapons, Jebel Buhais burials, early second millennium BC. After Jasim 2012: Fig. 12.

in burials has a ritual significance during a time of relative peace, and the relative lack of trauma in the few analysed skeletons of second millennium BC
date might support this assertion (Blau 1999: 199).

It can be assumed that the copper with which these objects were made was
mined and processed in the al-Hajjar mountains and on the island of Masirah.
Recent excavations in the inland area of Wadi Hilou in the Emirate of Sharjah
(UAE) has revealed a copper processing site dated on the basis of a ^{14}C date
to between 1900 and 1700 BC (Kutterer et al. 2012). It is worthy of note that
there is little evidence for Umm an-Nar processing in the area of Hilou, and
one might conclude that the picture drawn by early researchers of a relative
decline in the copper industry in the Wadi Suq period (e.g., Hauptmann 1985:
Fig. 1) simply reflects the fact that copper mining took place at different locations than it did in the Umm an-Nar period and substantial Wadi Suq period
sites are still to be found.

A similar reimagining of craft traditions is attested by softstone and ceramic
production during the Wadi Suq period. Distinctly decorated softstone vessels
are very common at sites. Their forms and decorative schemes developed out
of the Umm an-Nar série récente style through an intermediate phase known
as série intermédiaire into a distinctive série tardive (Potts 1991a: 249–250)
(Figure 6.17). As David (1996) has noted, these terms, which are derived from
de Miroschedji's (1973) analysis of Iranian vessels of the third millennium BC,
should perhaps be replaced by explicit local terms such as 'Umm an-Nar' and
'Wadi Suq'. She concludes that softstone production in the Wadi Suq is greater

Figure 6.17. Wadi Suq softstone vessels, Jebel Buhais, Sharjah, United Arab Emirates. After Jasim 2012: Fig. 49.

Figure 6.18. Wadi Suq painted beakers, Jebel Buhais, Sharjah, United Arab Emirates. After Jasim 2012: Fig. 21.

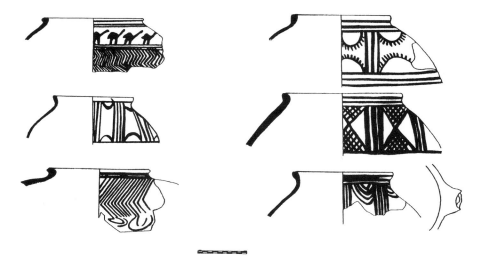

Figure 6.19. Wadi Suq spouted and storage jars, Jebel Buhais, Sharjah, United Arab Emirates. After Jasim 2012: Fig. 39.

than that in the Umm an-Nar period and exploits a wider range of geological sources. Wadi Suq ceramic production follows a similar pattern. Vessels are still made from a well-levigated clay, but new clay beds are now exploited to produce vessels that are formed and decorated in a completely different fashion than those of the Umm an-Nar period (Méry 1991: 73). A common type is a tall beaker form made in 'céramique semi fine', as defined by Méry (2000: 249–271), which is decorated with a wide variety of painted schemes (Figure 6.18). A diverse array, quite unlike the somewhat limited Umm an-Nar ceramic repertoire, of painted and unpainted spouted vessels and storage jars is also produced. Some of these seem to have a specifically domestic function (Méry 1991: 72–73) (Figure 6.19).

WADI SUQ PERIOD SETTLEMENTS, SUBSISTENCE AND FUNERARY PRACTICES

Metalwork and softstone and ceramic production follow, therefore, a similar trajectory in which production is diversified and the foreign models that had influenced production in the third millennium BC are rejected in favour of a local and distinctive repertoire (David 1996: 44). These changes accompany a radical reorientation of settlement location and subsistence. Wadi Suq period settlements have been excavated or surveyed at Ras al-Jinz 1 (Cleuziou and Tosi 2007), Tawi Sa'id (de Cardi et al. 1979), Hili 8 (Cleuziou 1979), Hili 3, Kalba (Carter 1997), Nud Ziba (de Cardi et al. 1994; Kennet and Velde 1995; Velde 2003), Tell Abraq (Potts 1990, 1991b, 2000) and Wadi Hilou (Kutterer et al. 2012). In some cases, this occupation is characterized by a modification of existing Umm an-Nar buildings. This is the case at both Tell Abraq and Kalba in the northern UAE (Carter 1997; Potts 1991b). At Tell Abraq, several retaining walls were constructed around the Umm an-Nar tower to create level surfaces upon which organic structures, such as barasti huts, were built. At Kalba retaining walls were constructed around the substantial third-millennium buildings during the phase that Carter (1997) labels 'the classic Wadi Suq', which he dates from 2000 to 1500 BC. Continued occupation of earlier Umm an-Nar towers appears also to be the case at Hili 8 in the al-Ain oasis.

Newly found settlements are also known from the French–Italian excavations on the Ras al-Jinz peninsula. RJ-1, located on top of the plateau overlooking the beach at Ras al-Jinz, consists of agglomerations of small, semi-circular and rectangular houses (Cleuziou and Tosi 2007: 262). Little is known about the material culture of this settlement, as the excavators have conducted only minimal excavations at what is clearly a heavily deflated site (Monchablon et al. 2003). The inhabitants of RJ-1 relied on fishing, and there is some evidence for the consumption of sheep and goat. Cleuziou and Tosi argue that the seasonal pattern of inland migration continues in this period, although the evidence for such is scant. In addition, and unlike what has been found for the earlier third millennium BC, there is very little, if any, evidence of foreign contact and trade.

The relative lack of Wadi Suq sites and their rather ephemeral nature led Cleuziou (1981) to suggest that the Wadi Suq period was characterized by a reversion to a nomadic lifestyle centred on the exploitation of the domesticated dromedary. Research since then has proved that domesticated dromedary does not appear in this part of Arabia until c. 1000 BC, although this has not apparently dissuaded Cleuziou and Tosi from continuing to link desedentarization and dromedary nomadism in subsequent publications (Cleuziou and Tosi 2007: 271). As I discussed in reference to the early third millennium BC in southeastern Arabia, approaches that dichotomize sedentary and nomadic modes ignore lifeways that strategically employ a wide range of fixed and mobile food production strategies. Although our evidence is still very limited, this seems to be precisely the case with the Wadi Suq period. Dozens of large shell middens, largely absent from the Umm an-Nar period, have been discovered alongside the ancient lagoon shore near Tell Abraq (Magee et al. 2009). These are also known farther north around Shimal, and the analysis of archaeozoological data (Glover 1991, 1998; Vogt and Franke-Vogt 1987) indicates a diet focused upon marine resources. Isotopic analysis of skeletal material from tombs in Shimal confirms this picture (Grupe and Schutkowski 1989).

Whether or not the people who left these shell middens were living at the same place all year round is unknown. Palaeoclimatic evidence (Parker et al. 2006) indicates that Lake Awafi in Ras al-Khaimah is re-established at this time, indicating increased winter rainfall. It is indeed possible that a more active nomadic pastoral component may have exploited the more verdant grasslands that would have resulted. There may be a hint of this at Tell Abraq, since the contribution to the diet made by cattle, which were less suited to nomadic pastoralism in southeastern Arabia than sheep or goat, decreases from the beginning of the Wadi Suq to the Late Bronze Age (Stephan 1995: 53–54, Fig. 4). At the same time, the growing of cereals and date palms during the Wadi Suq period is attested by the numerous grinding stones and date seeds found at sites like Tell Abraq (Potts 1991a: 256–257). Recent isotopic analysis of teeth from Shimal and Sharm on the east coast of the UAE confirms that at least some of the inhabitants of those regions were eating C3 plants such as wheat, barley and dates (Gregoricka 2011: 337–338).

Wadi Suq period subsistence strategies exploited, therefore, the diverse resources of the southeast Arabian landscape. Too little is known about this period or the preceding Umm an-Nar to formulate how such exploitation quantitatively differed from that practised previously, but it is clear that some shifts did take place and the centuries after 2000 BC witnessed an extensification of settlement that cannot be classed as fully 'sedentary' or 'nomadic'.

These changes in settlement and subsistence are accompanied by a massive shift in funerary practices. By 2000 BC the large, above-ground monumental

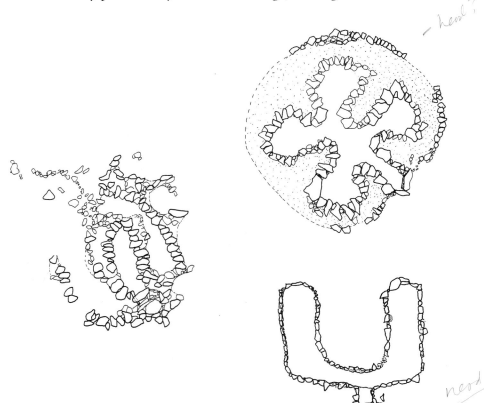

Figure 6.20. **Various types of Wadi Suq tombs, Jebel Buhais, Sharjah, United Arab Emirates. After Jasim 2012: Figs. 27, 46, 55.**

tombs of the Umm an-Nar period give way to elaborate subterranean or semi-subterranean tombs that are normally elongated and sometimes consist of multiple connected chambers. Such tombs have been excavated in the wadi which gives its name to the culture (Frifelt 1975), Dadna (Benoist and Ali Hassan 2010), Bidiya (al-Tikriti 1989a), Jebel Buhais (Uerpmann et al. 2006), Shimal (de Cardi 1988; Velde 2003; Vogt and Franke-Vogt 1987), Wadi Sunaysal (Frifelt 1975), the Wadi al-Qawr (Phillips 1987, 1997) and Sharm (Blau 1999). A recent publication of those excavated at Jebel Buhais in Sharjah (UAE) provides information on the diversity of tomb forms (Jasmin 2012) (Figure 6.20). A total of eleven massive stone-constructed tombs have thus far been published, although many more are known. They consist of a variety of forms, including ring tombs that are largely above ground, horseshoe-shaped tombs, single elongated chamber tombs, U-shaped tombs and an unparalleled clover-shaped tomb.

IDENTITY AND AUTONOMY IN THE WADI SUQ PERIOD

As a whole, the archaeological record from the Wadi Suq period stands in contrast to that which existed in the Umm an-Nar period. For the first time, craft production is focused completely upon locally derived forms and decorative repertoires. The old tower-centred settlements which by the end of third millennium BC had become the focus of increasing social tension are either abandoned or remodelled. Subsistence strategies embrace the varied potential of the landscape. Umm an-Nar tombs, which played a key role in communicating the importance of the collective over the individual, are abandoned for collective tombs that are no longer visible markers on the landscape and therefore no longer served to mitigate increasing social tension. At the same time, the great diversity of Wadi Suq burial forms would seemingly indicate a decline of collective (regional) identity, perhaps in the face of increasing tribalism. At the same time that these changes were taking place, southeastern Arabia continued, if not increased, its export of copper to Mesopotamia via Bahrain. For Bahrain this trade resulted in the emergence of a centralized, but structurally fragile state. For southeastern Arabia, this trade was subsumed into a reaffirmation of local identity and ideologies which had maintained the society for millennia.

SOUTHEASTERN ARABIA FROM 1600 TO 1000 BC

The period from 1600 to 1000 BC can be treated as a single phase of occupation even though it comprises the Late Bronze Age (1600–1300 BC; Velde 2003) and Iron Age I period (1300–1000 BC; Magee 1996b) (Figure 6.21). Only a handful of Wadi Suq settlements continue to be occupied during these centuries. New settlements are very rare, but an exception seems to exist in the northeast of the UAE. Around 1500 BC a series of stone buildings are

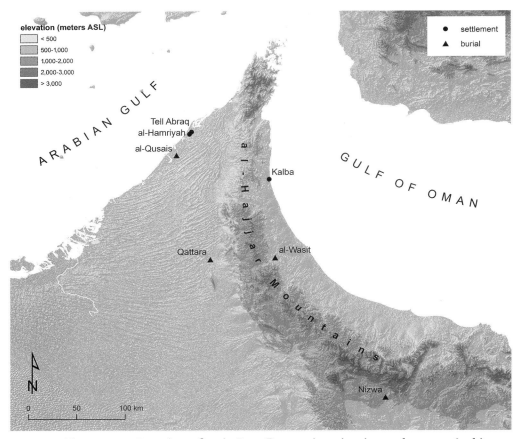

Figure 6.21. Location of main Late Bronze Age sites in southeastern Arabia.

constructed at Shimal at the edge of the Wadi Haqil (Velde 2003). Evidence of intensive marine exploitation was found at nearby shell middens to the west of Shimal and at Hamriya, while the deeply stratified sites of Tell Abraq and Kalba continue to be occupied (Potts 2000). Burials, which were such a common feature of the archaeological record a few centuries earlier, become increasingly less archaeologically visible; only four are known from this period: Nizwa, Qattara, Qusais and al-Wasit.

The data for this period are so limited that it is difficult to assess subsistence and settlement patterns. On the basis of ceramics, a shift towards a less intensive production mode appears to take place. In the assemblages from Shimal and Tell Abraq, 'céramique semi fine' of the Wadi Suq period is absent. Coarse gritted pastes dominate the Late Bronze Age repertoire of simple bowls and storage jars (Velde 1991, 2003) (Figure 6.22). A pedestalled goblet with string-cut base, the shape of which recalls contemporary ceramics from Kassite Mesopotamia, is also common (Figure 6.23b, c). Imported Mesopotamian vessels (Figure 6.23a) and vessels containing or coated with bitumen (Figure 6.23d) are also known

Figure 6.22. Late Bronze Age pottery, Tell Abraq, Sharjah, United Arab Emirates. Photo: the author.

Figure 6.23. Late Bronze Age pottery, Tell Abraq, Sharjah, United Arab Emirates: (a) imported Mesopotamian vessel fragment; (b, c) local goblets with string-cut base; (d) local pottery with bitumen. Photo: the author.

Figure 6.24. Iron Age I pottery, Tell Abraq, Sharjah, United Arab Emirates. Photo: the author.

from Tell Abraq. The high degree of metric and formal variation combined with a clear decrease in the technology invested in local ceramic production suggests a move towards part-time or even 'household' production (cf. Rice 1981). This continues into the Iron Age I period when Coarse Handmade Ware, which is distinctive in its fabric, lack of decoration and uneven firing, domi-nates ceramic production in the northern UAE (Magee 2011) (Figure 6.24). Geochemical analysis of sherds from Hamriya, Tell Abraq and Sharm suggests that the Wadi Haqil in Ras al-Khaimah is one of the main production centres for this pottery. The ceramics were distributed, in either raw material form or finished form, through the wadi systems and flanks of the al-Hajjar moun-tain range that are easily traversed with donkeys. It is not surprising that this coarse ware is unknown in the central UAE around al-Ain and in the Sultanate of Oman.

Paradoxically, bronze production continues to flourish during these cen-turies. One of the richest tombs yet discovered in southeastern Arabia, at al-Wasit, dates to this period (Weisgerber 2007) and contains nearly sixty spearheads, swords and daggers. A similarly rich assemblage was found in the Warrior's Grave at Nizwa in Oman (al-Shanfari and Weisgerber 1989). Several innovations in bronzework also occur with long swords, which are almost cer-tainly Iranian in inspiration (Lombard 1985), and short swords or daggers are now produced. The introduction of the bronze arrowhead is a marked feature of Late Bronze Age culture (Figure 6.25). Whether this indicates increased inter-tribal violence or is associated with increasing hunting is unknown. As

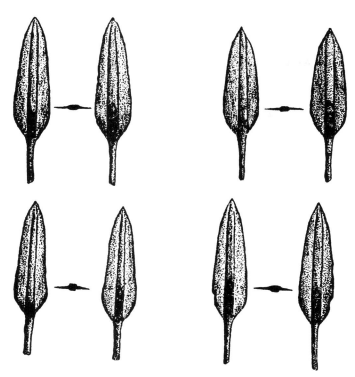

Figure 6.25. Late Bronze Age arrowheads, Jebel Buhais, Sharjah, United Arab Emirates. After Jasim 2012: Fig. 58.

Potts (1998) has pointed out, neither can be excluded, since pre-Islamic poetry focuses on the use of the bow and arrow for hunting, while rock art portrays its use in battle. In light of the earlier discussion and the pronounced evidence for the placement of weapons in burials, it is interesting to note that most arrowheads are found in tombs. Numerous examples of these arrowheads are incised after manufacture with simple liner decorations on the midrib (Magee 1998). Three decorative elements are known: straight lines, chevrons and stars or asterisks. The decorative elements occur in three main configurations: 'XI>', 'XIXI>' and '>>'. The distribution of each configuration is not geographically restricted, since each can be found in tombs in the north of the UAE down to the central part of the Oman peninsula, suggesting that they are not 'wasm', or tribal marks (contra Vogt 1994). The possibility that they were used in belomantric rituals or games of chance has been suggested by this author but is an interpretation that could certainly not be insisted upon (Magee 1999).

Excavations at Kalba and Tell Abraq indicate that occasional trade with the area around Minab in southeastern Iran increases during the Late Bronze Age and Iron Age I period (Magee and Carter 1999). The construction of a large mudbrick platform at Tell Abraq indicates another important aspect of growing international contacts. The platform is made from sun-dried rectangular

Figure 6.26. Late Bronze Age floor with postholes, Tell Abraq, Sharjah, United
Arab Emirates. Photo: the author.

mudbricks and covers the entire summit of the mound. There are no identifiable structures on the platform, nor was any substantial occupation debris
layered above it. The only other local parallel for this platform is found at
Kalba on the east coast of the UAE and dates to approximately the same time
(Magee and Carter 1999). In Central Asia such platforms are a distinguishing
feature of Late Bronze Age (Namazga VI) and Early Iron Age (Jaz Depe I) cultures, particularly in the oases north of the Kopet Dagh in present-day south
Turkmenistan and Uzbekistan. Well-known examples are found at Kuchuk
Tepe, Kyzyl Tepe and Tillya Tepe (Magee and Carter 1999: note 63). The brick
sizes of these platforms are the same as those from Tell Abraq (60 by 30 by 10
centimeters) and are close to those at Kalba (50 by 30 by 8 centimeters). It is
difficult to explain these similarities over the vast distance of 1,500 kilometers
that separates southeastern Arabia from Central Asia.

On the lower edges of the mounds at Tell Abraq a series of floor levels with
postholes attest to continued occupation, most likely in the form of barasti
structures, through the second half of the second millennium BC (Figure 6.26).
Recent excavations have revealed the existence of a large fortification wall surrounding the settlement during this period. There is no evidence for a gap
between phases of occupation, and the Iron Age I habitation is functionally
coeval with Late Bronze Age architecture (Magee and Carter 1999). A similar
situation is evident at Shimal, which also contained significant Late Bronze

Age deposits (Velde 1991). There, the Iron Age I occupation follows directly upon the earlier deposits with no hiatus. A stratigraphic and architectural configuration noted at Kalba on the east coast is similar to that noted for Tell Abraq, as mentioned earlier (Magee and Carter 1999). Also on the east coast, excavations at Sharm have revealed Iron Age I ceramics in a multiple-reuse tomb (Barker 2002). The tomb was oval and subterranean, with a stone superstructure. Because the burial was disturbed, it was not possible to assign a discrete use of the burial to this phase.

Even if our knowledge of Late Bronze Age and Iron Age I subsistence strategies is extremely limited, data from Tell Abraq suggest a preponderance of sheep and goat over cattle and the hunting of a wide variety of wild animals. Some of these, such as dromedary, become increasingly rare towards the end of the eleventh century BC (Uerpmann and Uerpmann 2002), perhaps indicating they are overhunted. At the same time, there is a clear decrease in specialization of many aspects of the economy, especially ceramic production. That this represents a shift towards a more extensive use of the landscape is possible, but further research on the elusive remains of this period is needed.

CONCLUSIONS

Between 2000 and 1300 BC, the inhabitants of eastern Arabia exploited their environment and engaged with their neighbours in a dynamic, and sometimes divergent, manner. An increased demand for copper from Mesopotamia led the inhabitants of the central and northern Arabian Gulf towards a recognizable form of state-level complexity from the very beginning of the second millennium BC onwards. All of the trappings of social complexity are manifested on Bahrain at this time, including elite burials, palace structures and complex methods of mercantile control. The familiarity of these sociopolitical devices should not mask, however, what are glimpses of another reality on Bahrain. Indications of strong social bonds are present at the large settlement of Saar and throw light on the broader question of divisions within the island as a whole and how foreign influence and control operated. By the fifteenth century BC, the trappings of the state can be maintained only by direct foreign intervention in the form of a governor appointed directly by the ruling Kassite dynasty of Babylon. The possibility that the subsequent eclipse of Kassite rule had its origin in internal divisions within the island must be considered, even if our knowledge of these centuries is scanty at best.

The rise of Dilmun and the eclipse of Magan as the source of copper imports into Mesopotamia is a symptom rather than a cause of the significant changes that occurred in southeastern Arabia following c. 2000 BC. The relative dearth of permanent settlement masks what is a complex economic system in which copper export to Bahrain continues alongside craft production that resonates with local and innovative modes of production. An understanding of the factors that drove and sustained these changes, and in particular the extent to which the society re-engages with nomadic pastoralism, has thus far remained elusive to researchers, but there is no denying that Wadi Suq material culture carries with it an affirmation of local identity and ideology. How this changes throughout the second millennium BC is still unclear. It is hoped that renewed excavations at multi-period sites such as Tell Abraq (Magee et al. 2009) will shed light on this period, as will the expeditious publication of already excavated sites such as Kalba.

CHAPTER 7

HUMANS, DROMEDARIES AND THE TRANSFORMATION OF ANCIENT ARABIA

INTRODUCTION

The previous four chapters were concerned with the widespread and dynamic human exploitation of Arabia from c. 9000 BC to 1000 BC. The thousands of artefacts, settlements and tombs dating to this time frame reinforce the central hypothesis of this book that human occupation of Arabia was neither static nor homogenous. Absent from these millennia of occupation are the caravans of dromedaries, interest in which has so often defined Arabia's entry into mainstream Near Eastern archaeology. Indeed, since its earliest Western occurrence in the fourteenth-century romance poem 'Kyng Alisaunder', the word 'dromedary' has become synonymous with caravans transporting exotica, such as incense, from the depths of Arabia to centres of power and civilization. That this approach still permeates much thought is no more evident than in the recent burgeoning of scholarship purporting to highlight trade between the southern Levant and northern Arabia (e.g., Artzy 1994; Finkelstein 1988; see also Chapter 9).

Dromedaries were a natural part of the Arabian landscape throughout the Holocene and earlier. The domesticated sheep, goat and cattle that were present in Arabia from the Neolithic onwards were introduced from more fertile regions. The dromedary was the only native Arabian animal to come under the control of humans and inhabited an entirely different ecology than other domesticated animals. The decision to embark upon domestication must, therefore, be contextualized within the long history of human–environmental relations *within* Arabia, especially following the end of the Holocene Moist Phase. Investigating this history of interaction, rather than assuming that domestication was brought about by a desire for trade, illuminates human adaptation to the rich and varied resources of Arabia.

FROM HUNTING TO HERDING

It can be assumed that wild dromedaries were present in Arabia from the beginning of the Holocene onwards and thus formed an integral part of

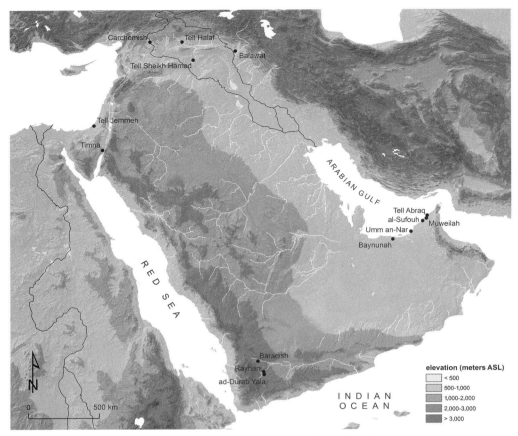

Figure 7.1. Location of main sites mentioned in this chapter.

human–environmental dynamics (Figure 7.1). The earliest Holocene evidence for the hunting of wild dromedaries is found at the Neolithic site of Jebel Buhais 18 in Sharjah (UAE). Their contribution to the meat diet was not insignificant, and if one accepts that the 'unidentified very large animal' category from this site includes dromedaries, as suggested by the Uerpmanns (Uerpmann and Uerpmann 2008a), they contributed more than any other wild animal to the meat diet. In gauging the diet overall, however, it is important to note that wild dromedaries represent an amount equivalent to about 4% of the meat supplied by sheep, goat and cattle. These domesticated animals also supplied milk to the diet, however, something that wild dromedaries could not do. In other words, the relatively optimal conditions of the Holocene Moist Phase favoured the use of domesticated animals over the benefits of hunting large game such as dromedaries.

After the cessation of the Holocene Moist Phase around 4000 BC, the hunting of wild dromedaries intensifies across Arabia. Although the remains of wild dromedaries are virtually absent from those sites located in the inland alluvial plains of southeastern Arabia such as Hili 8 and Maysar, wild dromedaries were an important food source at settlements interfacing with the desert foreland of southeastern Arabia. On Umm an-Nar island, for example, wild dromedaries accounted for an amount equivalent to nearly 400% of the meat supplied by domesticated animals (Uerpmann and Uerpmann 2008b: 475). They were so significant that they were initially considered to represent domesticated animals (Hoch 1979; cf. Uerpmann and Uerpmann 2002). At Tell Abraq, a site also located on the edge of the desert but with easier access to alluvial grazing zones, wild dromedaries were also important, accounting for an amount equivalent to nearly 50% of the meat supplied by domesticated animals.

Discoveries made in the past ten years in the UAE confirm the importance of hunted dromedaries for subsistence during this period. Excavations between 2001 and 2004 at al-Safouh, located just outside the modern city of Dubai, revealed a Bronze Age mass-kill site from which an extraordinary 17,812 bones of wild dromedaries have been recovered (von den Driesch et al. 2008). Carbon-14 dating of bones suggests that the site was visited periodically by humans with the intention of hunting wild dromedaries from the end of the third millennium BC until the third quarter of the second millennium BC. The ancient ecology of this part of the UAE coast explains why dromedaries chose to return to this location on an annual basis. Shells indicate that al-Safouh was on an ancient lagoon that contained extensive halophytic vegetation. This type of vegetation serves as an ideal fodder for grazing dromedaries that would seasonally alternate between exploiting coasts and inland dune areas. As the excavators of al-Safouh note: 'It is easy to imagine that the local hunters, who knew this behavior well, waylaid the grazing animals and encircled one or more suitable individuals, when the wild dromedaries of al-Safouh were visiting the khors [lagoons] in order to meet their requirements for salt. While a group of hunters possibly threw lassos at this animal other members of the hunting party may have attacked it with arrows and other weapons....After the animal was exhausted it was pulled down and killed by a deep cut through the throat. Hunting down the animal in this way may have been relatively easy, because in the muddy environment the prey could not run away quickly' (von den Driesch et al. 2008: 494–495).

The large number of wild dromedary bones found at al-Safouh and the more recently discovered site of Baynunah (Beech et al. 2009) and the nearly complete absence of other animal remains indicate the existence of specialized hunting zones. The presence of numerous fireplaces and the size of the slaughtered animals suggest that they were killed on-site and the meat consumed and/or transported to nearby settlements. As this meat might have been transported 'off-the-bone', perhaps dried and salted like gazelle meat prepared by the Solubba (Chapter 5), it is possible that wild dromedaries actually contributed more to the diet of those in surrounding settlements than the archaeozoological evidence suggests (the so-called *Schleppeffekt*). One could not insist upon such an idea, however, given the extreme heat of the region and the health risks inherent in transporting raw meat any distance. Nevertheless, the lagoons on which al-Safouh was located were quite common throughout the northern UAE during the Bronze Age. There is every reason to believe, therefore, that al-Safouh represents one of many such kill sites that existed along the interface between the desert and coast.

Rock art from western, central and northern Arabia also indicates that hunting wild dromedaries was an important part of subsistence strategies in those regions. At Jebel Qara and the other areas visited by the Philby-Ryckmans-Lippens expedition, numerous representations of humans killing dromedaries with spears, bows and arrows and throwing sticks are known (Anati 1968b: 47–80). As noted in Chapter 7, Anati dates these representations to the third and second millennia BC on the basis of the lunate pommel-handled dagger depicted in many of the drawings. Similar representations are known in the Saada region of Yemen and in northern Saudi Arabia at Shuwaymas near Jubbah (Bednarik and Khan 2005).

If Anati's dating is correct and the evidence from southeastern Arabia is an accurate representation of subsistence strategies from the Neolithic into the Bronze Age, then the period from the late fourth millennium to the end of the second millennium BC witnesses an intensification of dromedary hunting along the desert frontier across Arabia. As noted in Chapter 6, kites and mass-kill traps used to hunt gazelle in the western and northern parts of Arabia also date to this period. A shift to more intensive hunting throughout Arabia is indicated, and it is tempting to view this as a response to the climatic changes that accompanied the end of the Holocene Moist Phase. Prior to this, relatively optimal conditions had permitted sheep, goat and cattle pastoralism in regions in which rainfall created suitable vegetation, as at Neolithic Jebel Buhais. With the termination of the Holocene Moist Phase, the ecological niches in which introduced domesticates could be pastured became restricted. In contrast, the native dromedaries and gazelle were able to survive in adjacent arid ecological niches. Where these niches interfaced with the coastal and piedmont zones occupied by humans, dromedaries became a ready source of meat and hides.

The long stratigraphic sequence at Tell Abraq in the northern UAE provides an opportunity to assess the relative importance of dromedary hunting through the third and second millennia BC. In the middle of third millennium BC, wild dromedaries contributed an amount equivalent to nearly 50% of the meat supplied by domesticated animals. By the end of the third millennium BC, wild dromedaries decline to nearly 25%. In the early Wadi Suq period (c. 2000–1800 BC) they represent no more than c. 15%, and by the Late Bronze Age less than c. 5% (Uerpmann and Uerpmann 2002). According to the Uerpmanns (in press), the declining proportion of wild dromedaries is consistent with overhunting of the local population. The possibility of intensifying other food procurement strategies was limited by the natural environment, since all available ecological niches (grazing plains and the sea) were likely fully exploited. In addition, the absence of dromedaries as a beast of burden meant that food resources from other ecological niches, such as the inland plains or mountains, could not so easily be moved around the landscape. It is against the potential dietary stress brought about by these conditions that the move towards controlling and herding dromedaries must be contextualized.

IDENTIFYING DOMESTICATED DROMEDARIES IN THE ANCIENT NEAR EAST

This emphasis on the use of dromedaries for trade and transport across desert environments has meant that scholars have been quick to identify any representation or remains of dromedaries as evidence that (a) they were domesticated and (b) they were used for trade. On this basis, Ripinsky (1975, 1985) argued that dromedaries were used for trade in Egypt by the Old Kingdom. Midant-Reynes and Brawnstein-Silvestre (1977) showed that none of the evidence cited by Ripinsky actually demonstrated that dromedaries were used for transport or as beasts of burden (see also Rowley-Conwy 1988). In much the same way, archaeozoological approaches to dromedary domestication in the ancient Near East have relied upon sporadic finds of bones from individual sites with little or no attention to the demographic, morphological and/or size characteristics that would illuminate whether or not dromedaries were domesticated and what function they served in the ancient economy. The most commonly cited research on this issue, that of Wapnish (1981, 1984) on the remains from Tell Jemmeh in Palestine, epitomizes many of these problems. Not only are there serious stratigraphic problems with Petrie's excavations but, as Wapnish herself notes (Wapnish 1981: note 15), there are no morphological, demographic or size characteristics that would indicate the presence of domesticated, as opposed to wild, dromedary. Despite these caveats, Tell Jemmeh is often cited in support of an early and/or widespread use of dromedary caravans in the southern Levant. Artzy, for example, points to the existence of dromedary bones from Tell Jemmeh as evidence for an intricate overland trade network that connected Tell Nami with southern Arabia in the fourteenth and thirteenth centuries BC (Artzy 1994: 135). In fact, only five bones of dromedaries are known from these levels, and there is no evidence that they are of domesticated dromedaries. Similarly, Borowski claims that 500 dromedary bones were found at Tell Jemmeh, 'the majority of which belong to the Neo-Assyrian and Neo-Babylonian periods' (Borowski 1999: 121) and that these were evidence of the use of dromedaries for military transport. Fewer than 40 dromedary bones are actually assigned to strata of this period (Wapnish 1981: Table 1).

Horwitz and Rosen's (2005) review of dromedary remains from the southern Levant indicates that decreasing numbers of dromedary bones are noted from the Chalcolithic to the end of the second millennium BC. They argue that the near absence of dromedary bones at the time when it is assumed that dromedary caravans were in operation (the late second millennium BC) can be explained by taphonomic and cultural choices. They write that dromedaries 'represented valuable animals, neither readily consumed (due to their expense) nor kept in abundance, especially not in farming or urban settlements. Moreover, if they were primarily raised by nomads for sale, then only a few animals would have been kept by the herders close to their residence, while the majority would have been left to graze further afield. Together with the average longevity of camels (up to 40 years), this greatly reduces the chance of finding their remains in a site. Furthermore, as they appear to have been primarily exploited as beasts of burden in trade, they can be classified as mobile elements' (Horwitz and Rosen 2005: 127–128). Horwitz and Rosen's assumption that dromedaries were used for trade and that this meant they were not consumed is not only questionable given evidence from elsewhere in the Near East, but also negated by their own evidence: the rapid increase in the number of dromedary bones after 1000 BC suggests that dromedaries did make their way into the archaeological record, presumably as a result of consumption.

Epigraphic evidence for the use of domesticated dromedaries carries its own problems associated with translation and etymology. Whether it is the dromedary or Bactrian camel that is referred to in ancient sources is a recurrent problem. This critical difference is rarely emphasized to the extent that it should be, presumably because it has been assumed that if humans were able to use the Bactrian camel for trade and transport, then they could do the same with the dromedary, even if both animals are adapted to vastly different environments and have divergent histories of human exploitation. Finkelstein, for example, relying on an outdated reading of the text on the Broken Obelisk argued that 'the large scale use of camels in the southern trade developed late in the second millennium' (Finkelstein 1988: 247). The relevant word for camel on the Broken Obelisk (*udrate*) almost certainly refers to Bactrian camels (Heimpel 1980; Potts 2004) and is, in fact, probably an Old Iranian loan word (Redard 1964).

The same confusion arises when we consider Mesopotamian textual sources. Camels are noted in a series of lexical texts called the *URRA=hubullu* lists, which are essentially bilingual concordances between Sumerian and Akkadian. List XIII consists of animals, most of which are domesticated (Heide 2011). The lists were copied in the first millennium BC but are believed to represent earlier, but largely incomplete texts. In these texts, three terms are used to describe camels: *am.si.kur.ra*, *am.si.HAR.ra.an* and *anše.a.ab.ba*. Although all three are translated in the texts as *Akkadian ibilu*, or 'dromedary camel', it is generally accepted that the first two refer to Bactrian camels. It is the meaning of the third term, translated as the 'donkey of the sea' that is of interest for our discussion. In a Neo-Babylonian *URRA=hubullu* text, *anše.a.ab.ba* is equated to

Akkadian ibilu (= dromedary). Since there is no question that dromedaries are domesticated by this period, the text is hardly controversial. Three earlier precursor texts carry variations of these lists, and these have the potential to provide important information on dromedary domestication. A Middle Assyrian (thirteenth century BC) and a thirteenth-to twelfth-century BC example from Ugarit have been reconstructed to carry the term *anše.a.ab.ba*. On the basis of this evidence, it might be concluded that domesticated dromedaries are known in Syria during the thirteenth and twelfth centuries BC. Lambert (1960) has gone further and raised the possibility of an early second millennium BC date based on the observation that these texts are believed to represent versions of text originating in the Old Babylonian period.

However, the incomplete nature of the texts and the fact that readings of earlier documents are often based on later, but more complete versions stand in the way of any certainty on this issue. To complicate the matter, an *URRA=hubullu* text from thirteenth-century BC Emar does not contain the term *anše.a.ab.ba* in list XIII, where it typically occurs, but rather in list XI, which details the skins and hides of animals. In any case, as noted by Lambert (1960), the *URRA=hubullu* documents do not exclusively contain references to animals that are under human control: there are references to feral or possibly wild animals, including the *anše.edin.na*, or 'donkey of the desert'. In other words, the textual sources provide little certainty as to when dromedaries were domesticated.

Ultimately archaeozoological data provide the most direct evidence for determining when dromedaries were domesticated. The archaeozoological detection of this process is, however, not straightforward. In addition to the use of complex genetic markers, which may not always be accessible in the archaeological record (Zeder 2006a, 2006b), two methods are generally employed to illuminate the stages and process of domestication (Uerpmann and Uerpmann, in press). The first is based on the demography of the ancient animal population. Put simply: if a specific animal population is hunted in the wild and the remains are brought back to the settlement and eventually excavated and studied, these will reflect the natural demography of the species in terms of sex, age and size. If, however, the animal is herded (i.e., domesticated), it is likely that selective slaughter to further the health and economic benefit of the herd was practised. For example, one might expect differential slaughtering between males and females, since only a few males are needed to ensure continued reproduction in the flock. The early domestication of goats in the Zagros mountains of Iran provides an example of selective breeding that is detectable in the archaeological record (Zeder and Hesse 2000).

The second approach emphasizes morphological and size changes in the domesticated animal population. Morphological changes – for example, in the shape and size of goat horns – reflect direct human intervention in the form of selective breeding. More generally, however, the size of animals appears to

decrease once they are domesticated. The reasons for this are not fully understood, but it has been empirically observed for dogs, sheep, goats, cattle and
horses. It has been argued by Zeder and Hesse, however, that the size of animals may reflect the specific environment and ecology in which the animal
population subsists (Zeder and Hesse 2000: 2254) and thus may not be a sensitive index of domestication. To overcome this problem, it is necessary to examine an archaeozoological sequence from a single area over a lengthy period of
time. In that way, some control is exercised over the variable of local ecology,
assuming that no dramatic changes in climate occur during that time frame.

NEW EVIDENCE FROM SOUTHEASTERN ARABIA

It is for the reasons already outlined that the southeast Arabian sites of Tell Abraq
and Muweilah are critical to this discussion. Following the slow decline in the
quantity of wild dromedaries at Tell Abraq (as previously mentioned) there is
a sudden increase in their number in the Iron Age II period (1100/1000–600
BC) (Uerpmann and Uerpmann 2002). During this time, dromedaries equate
to more than 10% of the weight proportion of domesticated animals at Tell
Abraq, while at Muweilah this figure is even higher and close to the per-
centage of wild dromedaries during the Bronze Age. Log size indices consistently indicate that these dromedaries are smaller than those of the Bronze
Age (Uerpmann and Uerpmann 2002). As noted earlier, a decrease in size is
associated with domestication in other animals and, when combined with the
increase in the number of dromedaries, is highly suggestive of the presence of
domesticated dromedaries beginning around 1000 BC. The recovery of nearly
900 dromedary bones at Muweilah has provided a much-needed demographic
profile for these Iron Age II dromedaries. On the basis of a comparison with
the earlier Bronze Age data, epiphyseal fusion of the bones suggests that '[a]t
Sufou 2 less than 10% of the animals were killed at an age under 12 months,
while at Muweilah more than one-third of the animals did not survive this age.
After this kill-off of juveniles, the survival curve for Muweilah flattens, probably indicating the exploitation of life-time products – labour and possibly
milk – of the adults reaching ages of four years and beyond. It is obvious that
the pattern of dromedary exploitation changed from al-Sufou 2, where a wild
dromedary population was extensively hunted, to Muweilah, where domestic
dromedaries were utilized for their respective products together with domestic
sheep, goats and cattle' (Uerpmann and Uerpmann, in press).

The combined evidence from Tell Abraq and Muweilah confirms that
domesticated dromedaries were present from c. 1000 BC onwards. That their
presence follows a slow decline in the number of hunted wild dromedaries
suggests, on a theoretical level, a causal link between early attempts at domestication and the use of dromedaries as a food source. It is important, however,
to reiterate that the evidence from Tell Abraq and Muweilah is related only to

the *presence* of domesticated dromedary. To confirm that the complex process of domestication occurred *within* southeastern Arabia requires careful analysis of archaeozoological evidence for the centuries leading up to 1000 BC. Unfortunately, excavations at Tell Abraq are yet to reveal extensive archaeozoological remains for the period from 1300 to 1000 BC, that is, those centuries that must be considered critical for the interface between the hunting of wild dromedary and the herding of domesticated dromedary. A renewed program of excavation has begun at this site, and it is to be hoped that new evidence will be forthcoming.

It is indeed possible that dromedaries were domesticated elsewhere and were introduced into southeastern Arabia. Currently, however, there is no compelling archaeozoological data in support of such an hypothesis. Several population centres in northwestern Arabia are located near zones of transition to deserts where wild dromedaries flourished. One such site is Tayma in the Hijaz, which, as noted in Chapter 6, was a centre of Bronze Age occupation on the margins of the Nafud desert. Unfortunately, there are as yet no published archaeozoological data on the presence of dromedaries at this site. Timna in the Negev is also important in this regard, and a recent publication (Grigson 2012) has detailed the remains of seventy-nine dromedary bones, more than half of which had butchery marks, from Area 30 at this site (Grigson 2012: 88). Given their size, these dromedaries are probably domesticated and they compare well with the dromedary remains from Tell Abraq and Muweilah (Grigson 2012: 87). Grigson's (2012: 87) comment that these remains may be earlier than those from Tell Abraq and Muweilah, thus raising the possibility that this region was a centre for initial domestication, is not borne out by the evidence. The combined average of three charcoal ^{14}C samples from Area 30 calibrates at 2-sigma to 1081–922 BC, while the date on a dromedary bone calibrates at 2-sigma to 1019–514 BC. These dates do not predate the beginning of the Iron Age II period in southeastern Arabia, which the relevant Tell Abraq deposits date to, nor the earliest occupation thus far attested at Muweilah.

Another possible centre for initial dromedary domestication is southwestern Arabia. The excavation of ad-Durayb Yala in Yemen provides abundant archaeozoological data from four strata dating to the late second and early first millennia BC. Dromedary bones were found in Stratum B dated from 1050 to 800 BC (Fedele, in press). The upper (later) levels of this stratum contained seventeen dromedary bones that are consistent in their size with domesticated dromedaries in southeastern Arabia. The lower (earlier) levels of Stratum B also contained dromedary bones that were, however, unmeasurable. On the basis of these data, Fedele has concluded '[t]hese bones thus establish the presence of dromedaries in a domestic context at Yala during the second half of the ninth century BC, or at a cautious minimum date of about 800 BC' (Fedele, in press). It is significant that the bones showed evidence of butchering, indicating that they formed part of the subsistence diet at the settlement. Other sites confirm a similar chronology for the appearance of domesticated dromedaries in the Arabian southwest. A total of sixty-two dromedary bones were found in the ninth to seventh century BC levels at Rayhani, and Fedele (in press) attributes these to domesticated dromedaries. Dromedary bones were also recovered from ^{14}C-dated layers in probes along the city wall at Baraqish. The earliest examples date to the eighth and seventh centuries BC, and Fedele considers these a mixture of both wild and domesticated.

Thus, no site in Arabia has yet provided data that detail the transition to domestication comparable in either quantity or chronological breadth to the data from Tell Abraq and Muweilah. Regardless of where initial domestication took place, the increase in domesticated dromedaries at Iron Age settlements in southeastern, southwestern and northwestern Arabia and the presence of butchery marks leave little doubt that the consumption of dromedary meat was an immediate benefit of dromedary domestication. When viewed in light of the long history of wild dromedary hunting in Arabia and the clear importance that this played in subsistence strategies, it is tempting to argue that initial domestication was driven by this subsistence need at the end of the second millennium BC. Palaeoclimatic evidence (Parker et al. 2006) indicates a decline in the major sources of rainfall throughout Arabia at this time, placing further stress on existing forms of subsistence. The impact of dromedary domestication would have been revolutionary in terms of food procurement. For the first time after the Holocene Moist Phase a terrestrial animal that was native to Arabia, and thus able to subsist in regions where introduced domesticates such as sheep and goat could not compete for resources, became a stable and reliable part of subsistence. The desert, which had become increasingly negligible in subsistence strategies other than hunting since the end of the Holocene Moist Phase, was transformed into an important component of lifeways.

The importance of this development was not limited to the meat supplied by dromedaries. The evidence from Muweilah is highly suggestive that the procurement of milk was an important benefit of domestication. As noted in Chapter 3, sheep, goat and cattle milk supplied much-needed hydration for the inhabitants of prehistoric Arabia. With the termination of the Holocene Moist Phase and the shrinking of pastoral ranges for these animals, this resource would have become less available. In numerous ways, dromedary milk provided benefits that exceeded that of sheep and goat. Although the amount varies according to climate, fodder and access to water, an average dromedary can produce anywhere from 4 to 15 kilograms of milk per day (Horwitz and Rosen 2005: 124). In addition, the composition of dromedary milk is significantly different from that of cow's milk and provides, for example, three times as much vitamin C – a factor that is critical in regions in which fruits high in vitamin C are not readily available.

FROM FOOD TO TRANSPORT

If we momentarily accept the hypothesis that the immediate benefits of dromedary domestication were food and milk, then the issue of when dromedaries began to be used for trade and transport should be addressed separately. On the one hand, it cannot be assumed that domestication led to dromedaries being used as beasts of burden quickly, since there is nothing intuitive or obvious about riding dromedaries. It might be considered intuitive to use the animal for unmounted transport – but that hardly permitted the traversing of deserts by human population groups. On the other hand, the Bactrian camel had been domesticated for some millennia (Potts 2004), and there is no doubt that by the end of the second millennium BC it was used for riding and transport. The possibility that this provided a model, or inspiration, for training dromedaries for trade and transport must be considered. While these two animals inhabit vastly different ecological niches, there are points at which their use might have overlapped.

One of these points lies at the very northern edge of the Arabian desert at the interface with the apex of the Fertile Crescent. The recent publication of camel remains from Tell Sheikh Hamad, on the left bank of the Khabur River in Syria, confirms that Bactrian camels were present in this area (Becker 2008). At least nine bones of metrically identified Bactrian camels were recovered in the Middle Assyrian levels (c. 1300 BC) at this site. There can be no doubt that these Bactrian camels were used for trade and transport, and indeed their presence in Syria likely resulted from Assyrian royal policy. As Assyria expanded towards Iran and areas east, access to, and the flow of, Bactrian camels to the west increased. In the eleventh century BC, the Assyrian king Assur-bel-kala (1074–1057 BC) sent merchants to acquire female Bactrian camels, almost certainly from Iran (Potts 2004: 153). The inhabitants of northern and western Syria would, therefore, have been familiar with the use of Bactrian camels as beasts of burden and mounts, well before dromedaries were apparently domesticated, or introduced, to these regions.

After 900 BC, Bactrian camel bones are very rare at Tell Sheikh Hamad (one from the residential and four from the palace area) (Becker 2008). At the same time, however, sizeable quantities of dromedaries are known: 96 (or 5.7% of 1,671 domesticated animal bones) are found in the Neo-Assyrian residential and 150 (or 0.16% of 12,881 domesticated animal bones) in the palace area (Becker 2008). Butchery marks indicate that these were eaten, providing 24.2% of the bone weight from the residences and 9.52% of the bone weight from the palace area. The appearance of dromedaries at Tell Sheikh Hamad thus follows from an existing knowledge of the use of Bactrian camels for trade and transport. In considering the possibility that it was in this zone that dromedaries were initially employed for trade and transport, it would have to be acknowledged, however, that Tell Sheikh Hamad is the exception to what is otherwise a relative lack of dromedary remains in an environment that lay on the very margins of the natural ranging zones for dromedaries.

The other zone of potential overlap between the Bactrian and dromedary camels is in southeastern Arabia, where, as we have seen, the most complete record of the appearance of domesticated dromedaries and the disappearance of wild dromedaries exists. Bactrian camels are unknown in the prehistoric archaeozoological record from southeastern Arabia. However, through most of the Bronze Age, this region was in close economic contact with areas of southern and southeastern Iran and Central Asia. Some of this exchange was likely down-the-line trade in which people from southeastern Arabia never actually travelled to distant regions, but it is very likely that there was movement of both people and goods from southeastern Iran to southeastern Arabia since at least the middle of the third millennium BC. As noted in Chapter 4, Potts (2005) has gone as far as to suggest that the Umm an-Nar ceramic industry was the result of immigrant potters from southeastern Iran. The Bactrian camel is suited to the east Iranian environment, and evidence for its presence is known from the Bronze Age onwards. The merchants who sailed back and forth across the Arabian Sea and Straits of Hormuz would likely have seen it being used for transport, and thus it might be assumed that the inhabitants of southeastern Arabia were familiar with the use of camels for transport and trade since at least the third millennium BC. Parenthetically, the lack of any evidence for dromedary domestication during these centuries strengthens our hypothesis that initial dromedary domestication was not motivated by a desire to use the animal for trade and transport, since the population of southeastern Arabia was likely aware of this potential for centuries before finally embarking upon the process of domestication.

Although in theory archaeozoology might provide evidence for when dromedaries were first used for trade and transport, our current perspectives on this issue are limited to artistic and coroplastic evidence. Several reliefs from sites on the northern interface of the Syrian desert show clear evidence for dromedaries being ridden from the ninth century BC onwards. The first of these comes from Tell Halaf, a settlement located farther up the Khabur from Tell Sheikh Hamad (Figure 7.2). A 65-centimeter-high low-relief sandstone orthostat from the Palace of Kapara, son of Khadianu at Tell Halaf, clearly shows a person riding a dromedary while sitting on a boxlike saddle. The saddle is secured by ropes that run across and under the belly of the dromedary. The rider sits askew, that is, rides side-saddle. Unfortunately, the date of construction of the palace and, indeed, the reign of Kapara remains unclear, but a date in the late tenth or ninth century BC seems likely.

From the same general region comes another representation of a domesticated dromedary. A limestone plaque measuring 1.22 meters in height and 1.53 meters in width was found in Woolley and Lawrence's excavation at Carchemish. Although the top portion is broken, it clearly shows a person

Figure 7.2. Relief showing dromedary and rider from Tell Halaf, Syria. Photo: Walters Art Museum.

riding a dromedary in much the same fashion as the Tell Halaf relief. It is, however, more detailed and shows a harness that 'consists of a beech stirrup, a square cut saddle secured by a broad girth, stirrups consisting of a cord looped from the saddle, a broad collar and, apparently, a guide rope attached to the collar' (Hogarth et al. 1914: 186). The rider is bearded and either is wearing a helmet or has a thick mass of hair. In his left hand he carries a bow. He rides the dromedary askew. The dating of this relief is also problematic, however. The dromedary relief was found in the 'Herald's Wall' at one end of a sequence of four limestone plaques. Mallowan (1972) argued that these four plaques are homogenous in style and should be dated to the time of Katuwas, son of Suhis II, who likely ruled in the early ninth century BC. This was endorsed by Genge (1979), but Winter (1983: 179) dates them slightly earlier, to the reign of Suhis II. In any case, a date in the late tenth or early ninth century BC correlates with the evidence from Tell Halaf. The chronology of the Carchemish regents remains sufficiently unclear, however, that such a conclusion cannot be insisted upon. Lastly, Shalmaneser III's construction of cedarwood gates capped with bronze reliefs at Balawat (ancient Imgur-Enlil; see Schachner 2007) provides a clear representation of a dromedary with a pack being led by a rope. The person leading the dromedary is identified as coming from Dabigu in Bit Adini on the Euphrates, a town that had been captured by Shalmaneser III in 856 BC (Mitchell 2000: 190).

Textual sources confirm that dromedaries were used for transport by the ninth century BC in the region of Syria and northern Mesopotamia. The earliest Mesopotamian reference that implies that dromedaries were being ridden and used for transport is Shalmaneser III's record of the defeat of Gindibu the Arab, who had joined a coalition of Syrian and Levantine kings who rebelled against Assyrian control in 853 BC. In his account outlining the defeat of this coalition, Shalmaneser III records the seizing of 1,000 dromedaries from Gindibu the Arab. Given the artistic evidence from Carchemish and Tell Halaf and the representations on the Balawat gates that refer to Bit Adini, it would seem that the dromedary-borne inhabitants of the north Arabian desert were playing an increasingly important role in political affairs and were thus very worthy of mention in Assyrian annals. It is implied in the inscription that the dromedaries captured by Shalmaneser III were under the control of Gindibu and were thus likely to have been used either as mounts or for transport. The date of Shalmaneser III's victory (853 BC) fits well with the representational evidence previously discussed.

These artistic representations and textual references refer largely to nomadic and semi-nomadic groups in northern Arabia. The use of dromedaries by these groups was an important feature of their independence, and thus references to them by the sedentary agricultural centres of power, like Assyria, carried a clear message of control over desert frontiers (see Chapter 9). In assessing the use of the dromedary for trade and transport, it is important to also focus on 'indigenous' manifestations that may reflect an everyday or commonplace familiarity with the dromedary. Clay figurines are one such set of evidence that since the beginning of the Holocene have provided important information about the use of domesticated animals throughout the Near East (e.g., Matthews 2002).

The earliest securely dated clay figurines showing dromedaries being used for trade and transport are found in the Arabian southeast. The most complete examples come from Muweilah, a site that has also provided the most domesticated dromedary bones yet discovered in the Near East (as mentioned earlier). One such complete figurine exhibits what is either a load or a saddle on its back and is decorated with painted lines on its legs and torso (Figure 7.3). The saddle is decorated with cross lines in a fashion not dissimilar to the Tell Halaf relief and an early example of a clay figurine from Tayma in the Hijaz (Figure 7.4). Numerous other incomplete examples are known from Muweilah and other sites dating to between c. 1000 and 600 BC (Magee 1996b). The

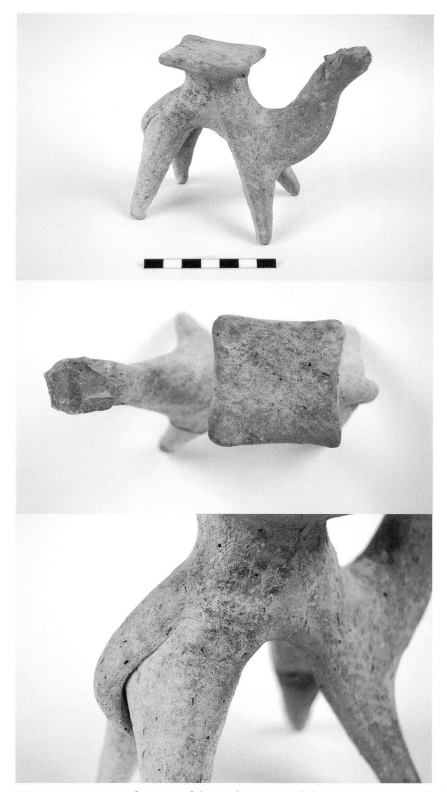

Figure 7.3. Ceramic figurine of dromedary, Muweilah, c. 1000–700 BC, Sharjah, United Arab Emirates, with detail showing painted decoration and saddle. Photos: the author.

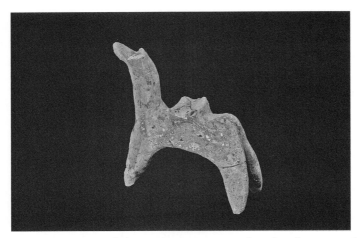

Figure 7.4. Painted dromedary terracotta figurine from a multiple burial (early to middle first millennium BC) from Tayma, Area S/Tal'a. DAI Orient-Abteilung. Photo: M. Cusin.

Muweilah examples are more precisely dated within this time frame. More than forty ¹⁴C samples date the construction, rebuilding and destruction of the settlement from the tenth until the eighth century BC. It is not possible to place these dromedary figurines into any particularly time frame within these centuries, but it can be stated with certainty that their occurrence is not limited to the later phases of occupation. Indeed, since the raison d'être of the settlement seems to have been overland trade, there is every reason to believe that the figurines date to the earliest phases of settlement. In chronological terms, these clay figurines date to the same phase of settlement (Iron Age II) in which archaeozoological evidence for the presence of domesticated dromedary in southeastern Arabia is found, and the renewed excavations at Tell Abraq indicate that figurines of domesticated dromedaries are absent from the immediately earlier Iron Age I levels (1300–1100 BC). Not only does the date of the figurines correlate with the archaeozoological evidence on the appearance of domesticated dromedaries, but it is worth emphasizing that figurines of other well-known domesticated animals such as cattle, sheep and goat are virtually absent from the coroplastic repertoire of the southeast Arabian Iron Age. It is, therefore, tempting to view representations of dromedaries being used for trade and transport as a reflection of their relative novelty within the region.

CONCLUSIONS

Artistic, textual and archaeozoological evidence from across the Near East provides important information on the human exploitation of dromedaries. Intensification of wild dromedary hunting is indicated in several regions of Arabia and attested by various forms of evidence from the fourth to the middle of the second millennium BC. If the evidence from southeastern Arabia can be considered symptomatic of the Arabian Peninsula as a whole, the population of wild dromedaries suffered as hunting intensified. By the middle of the second millennium BC the mass-kill site of al-Safouh was no longer used, and wild dromedaries became increasingly rare at Tell Abraq. As it stands, the evidence suggests that an initial benefit of domesticating dromedaries was their use as a food resource. Whether or not this drove domestication cannot be examined given the current state of evidence. However, it should be emphasized that the inhabitants of southeastern Arabia and northern Arabia were likely familiar with the transport capacity of Bactrian camels from the middle of the third millennium BC onwards, but this knowledge did not motivate any attempt at domestication, which occurred only 1,500 years later.

For the inhabitants of prehistoric Arabia the implications of dromedary domestication were multitudinous. Three thousand years after the end of the Holocene Moist Phase had turned the desert zones of Arabia into a landscape in which pastoralism and agriculture were difficult, humans were able to re-engage with these environments. Dromedary pastoralism meant a steady supply of milk and meat which, if we accept the analogy of the modern Rwala in Jordan, was sufficient to maintain subsistence (Lancaster and Lancaster 1990). These activities could be grounded in new settlements such as Muweilah which occupied frontier zones that were previously uninhabitable (as discussed later). Furthermore, the use of dromedaries as beasts of burden permitted the inhabitants of Arabia to move foodstuffs and goods across a landscape that had proved increasingly resistant to the (re-)establishment of the type of regional integration that had existed during the Arabian Neolithic. The newly exploitable deserts also operated as buffer zones against sedentary agriculture states and permitted the inhabitants of prehistoric Arabia to render anew those interactions that hitherto had operated through maritime routes only. In this way, the domestication of the dromedary permitted the political, economic and social consolidation of ancient Arabia and its subsequent engagement with the rest of the Near East. The next two chapters are dedicated to an examination of these trends.

CHAPTER 8

INTENSIFICATION AND CONSOLIDATION: ARABIA FROM 1300 TO 800 BC

INTRODUCTION

In the millennia following the end of the Holocene Moist Phase there is very little evidence of inter-regional contact or movement of peoples across Arabia. As a result, scholarship has tended to demarcate regions within Arabia into separate fields of study. It is for this reason that Chapters 4, 5 and 6 are regionally specific, as opposed to Chapter 3, which offers an overall perspective on the Arabian Neolithic. In this chapter, I argue that as a result of centuries of experimentation with irrigation technology and dromedary domestication, large parts of Arabia (re-)experience similar patterns of growth and expansion during the early first millennium BC. It is instructive to examine in detail how these shared processes of adaptation resulted in new social formations that drew upon existing traditions but responded to opportunities for environmental adaptation and subsistence. In some ways, these processes led eventually to the emergence of a material culture koine towards the end of the first millennium BC, a detailed discussion of which lies outside the scope of this book.

SETTLEMENT INTENSIFICATION IN SOUTHEASTERN ARABIA

Unparalleled settlement intensification occurs throughout southeastern Arabia during the Iron Age II period (1000–600 BC) (Figure 8.1). Initially, researchers such as Humphries (1974: 53–54) suggested that these developments were closely linked to political and cultural developments in Iran, especially the rise of the Achaemenid Empire (538–332 BC). It is now abundantly clear on the basis of ^{14}C dates from numerous sites (Magee 2003) that settlements emerged at least 500 years earlier and most ceased to be occupied by c. 600 BC.

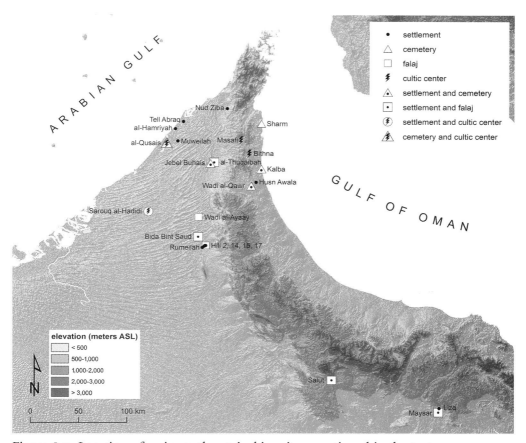

Figure 8.1. Location of main southeast Arabian sites mentioned in the text.

THE FALAJ IRRIGATION SYSTEM

Archaeological research conducted since the 1990s leaves little doubt that the use of the falaj irrigation system was responsible for this massive expansion of settlement. This system of irrigation involves tapping aquifers by means of a long, human-constructed tunnel and transporting the water underground to lower-lying areas where cultivation is possible (Figure 8.2). The tunnels can run for several kilometers and contain access holes throughout that permit cleaning and repair work. While dating these systems remains problematic, numerous examples of ancient falaj have been found alongside well-dated Iron Age II settlements. A falaj labelled Hili 15, which emerges near the settlement of Hili 17 and a fortified component known as Hili 14 in the al-Ain oasis (Boucharlat and Lombard 1985; al-Tikriti 2010), was the first of these to be discovered. It consists of a long subterranean tunnel that was accessed by a series of holes that were apparent in the excavated portion of the tunnel. The tunnel provided water to channels that were controlled by stone slabs and water

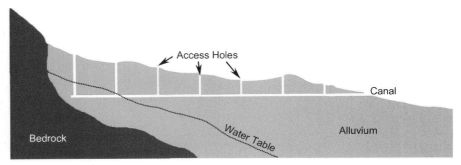

Figure 8.2. Cross section of a falaj system tapping a mountain aquifer. Aflaj can also tap low-lying aquifers in wadi systems and depressions.

diverters, which in turn led to surface channels. The water source tapped by this system was located to the east of the archaeological zone in an area where field reconnaissance was not possible. Recent excavations 1.5 kilometers to the northeast of Hili have revealed, however, sections of the same falaj system (al-Tikriti 2010). The date of its use is fixed by the recovery of Iron Age II pottery from within it, as well as its location near the independently dated sites of Hili 17, Hili 14 and Rumeilah (Boucharlat and Lombard 1985).

Numerous other examples of falaj systems have recently been excavated just to the north of al-Ain at Bida Bint Saud. The environment of this site consists of rolling low sand dunes with no evidence of recent occupation. Service holes for a falaj system were found near a single Iron Age II building consisting of a large central room with column bases and several smaller ancillary rooms containing large storage jars. The layout mirrored that found at Rumeilah and Muweilah (as described later). The falaj comprised an underground water gallery that emptied into a large mudbrick-lined depression accessed by a series of steps. The association between the irrigation system and Bida Bint Saud led al-Tikriti to refer to the latter site as Beit al-Falaj (the House of the Falaj). Continued research in this region has revealed the presence of falaj systems in association with Iron Age II occupation at Jebeeb, Wadi al Ayaay and Dhahret al-Hasa (al-Tikriti 2010).

Farther to the north in the al-Madam area, excavations have revealed a falaj system associated with the settlement of al-Thuqaibah (Córdoba 2003). This falaj, which is tall enough that a person can walk through it, consists of a completely covered underground tunnel more than 120 meters in length with five visible access holes. It probably taps the nearby Wadi Yudaiyah (Córdoba 2003). Lastly, in the Omani interior a falaj system has been revealed alongside the settlement of Salut in the Wadi Bahla (Avanzini and Phillips 2010). The falaj consists of a 2.6-kilometer underground gallery that runs towards the Iron Age settlement. Of particular interest for this falaj is the date of the earliest occupation of Salut. There are indications that the settlement is one of the earliest known Iron Age II settlements (Avanzini and Phillips 2010), and if the falaj system is associated with the initial settlement it would push the date of falaj use in southeastern Arabia back towards the end of the second millennium BC.

These discoveries fundamentally challenge the narrative on falaj irrigation that has dominated Near Eastern archaeology since Henri Goblot (1979) published his seminal book on the subject. According to this narrative, the falaj was an imperial technology that was 'invented' in the eighth or seventh century BC in Iran, where it was seen by Sargon II in his campaign against ULHU (e.g., Laessøe 1971; Lightfoot 2000: 215). According to this view, the technology was then transferred to Arabia and the rest of the Middle East during the period of the Achaemenid Empire (538–332 BC). Ultimately, a reference in Polybius (X, 28) is used to justify the view that this important hydraulic technology was spread to the 'less developed' areas of the Middle East. In fact, Polybius writes only that the Achaemenids granted people who provided water to previously unirrigated lands by means of these channels the right to work the land for five generations. He does not state that the Achaemenids spread the technique itself. Aurel Stein, one of the first scholars to conduct systematic field research in Iran and who was aware of Polybius's text, noted that no 'direct archaeological evidence has, as far as I know, been advanced as yet for the determination of a terminus post quem as regards the introduction of this characteristic feature into the agriculture of Iran' (Stein 1934: 124).

Stein's typically critical view of the textual sources appears to have eluded more recent scholarship (e.g., Bulliet 2011: 12; Lightfoot 2000), and the connection between the Achaemenid Empire and falaj is still commonly accepted despite the complete absence of any supporting archaeological evidence and a rereading of the relevant Sargon inscription, which indicates that falaj are not mentioned (Salvini 2001). Even when reference has been made to the existence of pre-Achaemenid falaj in southeastern Arabia, scholars are unwilling to accept an indigenous origin. Lightfoot, for example, writes, 'There may have been a few qanats in Oman predating the Achaemenid era (as early as 1200 BC) possibly introduced from the Iranian side of the Gulf as part of a normal process of contact and trade' (Lightfoot 2000: 221). There is, however, no evidence that falaj were known in southeastern Iran in this period, and indeed the only known and excavated settlement in this region, Tepe Yahya, is abandoned from the middle of the second millennium until the eighth century BC (Magee 2004).

Whether or not the falaj system was invented in southeastern Arabia remains an open question. There can be little doubt, however, that when viewed within the longue durée of southeast Arabian prehistory the use of the falaj around 1000 BC, the earliest yet attested anywhere in the Near East, represents a culmination of experimentation with extracting sub-surface water and responding to environmental changes. The expansion of settlement in the third millennium BC and Umm an-Nar period was due largely to the ability of the inhabitants

Figure 8.3. Shallow wells at Muweilah, Sharjah, United Arab Emirates, c. 1000–800 BC. Photo: the author.

of southeastern Arabia to create continuous flow from artesian wells to the surface and then transport water to small plots of land. This has been most clearly demonstrated at Hili 8 in the al-Ain oasis, where Cleuziou (1997) uncovered evidence for a well and irrigation canals around the site. During the second millennium BC, when the climate appears relatively favourable, one could well imagine that springs, which are known throughout the al-Hajjar mountains of southeastern Arabia, were employed to irrigate small agricultural fields. Coastal occupation at this time also relied upon wells that tapped thin lenses of fresh water which overlay denser salt water. Such was the case at Tell Abraq, where a well existed through the middle of the Umm an-Nar tower. The nearby Iron Age site of Muweilah has also revealed a number of shallow wells which are interconnected by a series of rock-cut channels and which seem to form an elaborate system for accessing and collecting fresh water in an environment where salt water was relatively close to the surface (Figure 8.3).

By the beginning of the Iron Age II period, therefore, the inhabitants of southeastern Arabia had employed a variety of techniques to obtain fresh water. These would have generated a body of knowledge on the mechanics of aquifer flow and the impact of rainfall on recharge and well productivity. This knowledge was key to survival, especially when rainfall patterns changed as they did at the very beginning of the Iron Age II period. Around 1000 BC, palaeoclimatic proxies (Parker et al. 2006) indicate a sudden decrease in rainfall throughout the region. Declining rainfall would have affected aquifer recharge throughout the mountains and alluvial plains, resulting in a declining water table and the cessation of spring activity. The falaj is an obvious solution to this problem; it essentially accesses the declining level of the spring by creating a tunnel. How such an action could eventually lead to the creation of a falaj has been observed in a recent ethnographic study in Khorasan, Iran. Semsar Yazdi and Labbaf Khaneiki (2010) record visiting a village that had traditionally received its water from a natural spring. After a severe drought the inhabitants of the village extended a horizontal tunnel to 'follow the spring'. Over the next twenty years the tunnel was extended by about 30 meters a year, which resulted in the creation of a falaj with two well shafts (Semsar Yazdi and Labbaf Khaneiki 2010: 62).

Whether or not the inhabitants of southeastern Arabia were the first to solve the problem of a declining water table by the use of a falaj is unknown, and indeed multiple centres of origin may exist. It is clear, however, that current archaeological evidence from southeastern Arabia offers the clearest and earliest example of the impact of falaj irrigation on arid zone settlement. This is particularly evident on the western flanks and alluvial plains of the al-Hajjar mountain range, where a massive increase in permanent settlement characterizes the Iron Age II period. The first indications of this were found in the al-Ain oasis: a previous centre for Umm an-Nar occupation that had become increasingly abandoned by the end of the second millennium BC. At the beginning of the Iron Age II period around 1000 BC, when falaj systems are constructed near Hili 15, Bida Bint Saud, Jebeeb, Wadi al-Ayaay and Dhahret al-Hasa (al-Tikriti 2010), this pattern of decline is reversed and a densely occupied oasis polity emerges. This was first revealed by excavations in the 1970s of remarkably well-preserved houses constructed from mudbrick and/or pisé at Hili 2 (ur-Rahman 1979). Although this site was excavated as an individual site, in the Iron Age it represented a dispersed domestic quarter for a polity that stretched over much of the al-Ain oasis. The excavation of Rumeilah (Boucharlat and Lombard 1985) provided solid chronological information on the emergence of this polity. Five mudbrick or pisé structures, perhaps clusters of houses, were excavated by a French archaeological team between 1981 and 1983 and were the main focus of a magisterial PhD completed by Lombard at the University of Paris (1985). The buildings at Rumeilah follow a variety of plans, including examples with courtyards and long narrow rooms, possibly for storage (Figure 8.4). The

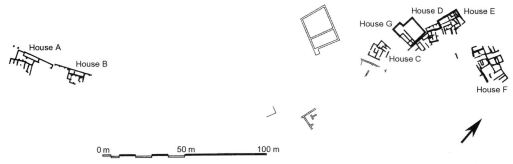

Figure 8.4. Plan of Iron Age II settlement, Rumeilah, al-Ain oasis, United Arab Emirates. After Boucharlat and Lombard 1985: Fig. 1.

excavations focused on only a portion of the site, and survey suggested that remains covered an area of about 1.6 hectares. Excavations at Hili 17 revealed houses with a layout similar to that of houses at Hili 2, along with evidence for a ceramics kiln and associated wasters. Widespread evidence for comparable settlements which are probably part of the same oasis polity has been found just to the north of al-Ain, where mudbrick-constructed houses are found in a series of wadi fans that now extend well into the desert. These include the sites of Bida Bint Saud, Wadi al-Hamam, Wadi al-Ayaay and Dhahret al-Hasa (al-Tikriti 2010). Some of these sites have revealed substantial mudbrick buildings of various functions, while others remain enigmatic in their layout due to the dense dune cover in this area. Nevertheless, the associated ceramics and other finds are consistent with an Iron Age II date (al-Tikriti 2010).

Surveys and excavations in the fertile al-Madam plain of Sharjah have revealed a similar expansion of settlement associated with the use of a falaj (Boucharlat 1997; Córdoba 2003, 2010). Excavations during the 1980s by the Sharjah Directorate of Antiquities and Heritage at al-Thuqaibah revealed evidence for Iron Age II houses comparable to those in al-Ain. Recent intensive surveys and excavations by a Spanish archaeological team have revealed further evidence for domestic structures that are linked by a thin mudbrick surround wall. Although the houses were abandoned and do not reveal a complex stratigraphic sequence such as that found on a 'tell' site, careful excavation has revealed that these two houses and the surround wall underwent several phases of rebuilding and construction (Córdoba 2003, 2010).

South of al-Ain, the alluvial plain widens into the Dakhiliya region of the Sultanate of Oman. Although this region has been less systematically explored than the UAE, there is no question that major Iron Age II settlements are an important feature of a landscape that has traditionally been exploited through the use of falaj irrigation. Examples of falaj are known in association with an Iron Age II settlement at Maysar (Weisgerber and Yule 1999: 101), and a system has been investigated more recently at Salut near modern-day Nizwa

Figure 8.5. View of the Iron Age settlement of Salut, Wadi Bahla, Sultanate of Oman. Photo: the author.

(as mentioned earlier), where excavations have revealed a highly fortified settlement atop a rock outcrop in the Wadi Bahla (Figure 8.5). Excavations are continuing at this site, but published results already suggest it is a site of significant interest for reconstructing residential and ritual life during the Iron Age I and II periods (Avanzini and Phillips 2010). Numerous settlements are also located inside the wadi systems and low-lying mountain ranges nearby, and these were also likely supported by falaj irrigation.

Uneven survey brought about by political borders has hampered attempts to assess the number of Iron Age II sites in these alluvial plains. Systematic survey in the area of central Oman provides some impression, however, of the extent of settlement intensification during the Iron Age II period. Around the Wadi Bahla no fewer than thirty sites have been recorded (Schreiber 2010: Table 1), and a similar density has been recorded in the Wadi Andam (al-Jahwari and Kennet 2008). One could not insist on an actual number, but there is little doubt that settlement density during the Iron Age II period surpasses anything during the Bronze Age and, indeed, was rarely matched up until the present day.

Given the current state of evidence, there seems little doubt that this extraordinary expansion of settlement was due to falaj irrigation. The provision of fresh water for consumption would have been one of the benefits of this system, but since research began in this region it has been assumed that Iron Age falaj were used to expand and intensify agricultural production. Until recently, however, frustratingly little evidence was available on the agricultural regime of inland Iron Age II settlements. In part, this was due to the differential preservation of seed remains in the dry Arabian environment, but the lack of systematic flotation at many sites should also be noted. Recent analysis of pollen and seed remains from Salut in central Oman has finally provided a more detailed picture of falaj oasis agriculture during the Iron Age II period. That study indicated the cultivation of wheat, date palms, sesame and basil (Bellini et al. 2011). It could be envisaged that this range of cultivars were grown in close proximity to each other, with the date palm tree used as a canopy – a practice that still prevails among farmers in the Wadi Bahla today.

SOUTHEAST ARABIAN CRAFT TRADITIONS

This intensification of settlement along the flanks of the al-Hajjar mountains was accompanied by a reinvigoration of craft industries throughout the region. Iron Age II ceramics are the most obvious indication of this and consist of a distinctive range of bowls and storage jars that are decorated and shaped in a manner quite unlike anything that had existed earlier in southeastern Arabia (Figures 8.6 and 8.7). Geochemical and petrological analysis has indicated that the al-Ain oasis, which was flourishing because of falaj irrigation, was a centre for ceramic production (Benoist and Méry 2012; Magee 2011; Magee et al. 2002). A distinctive fabric called 'Sandy Ware' was produced here, probably at Hili 17, and was exported in a variety of shapes across southeastern Arabia. It is very likely that other production centres were also active in this period in the north of the UAE around al-Khatt, but geochemical and archaeological evidence has yet to confirm this hypothesis. A distinctive form of the Iron Age II period is the bridge-spouted vessel, which indicates influence from Iran. Examples are both locally made in Sandy Ware and in a fine, well-levigated painted version that might be an import from Iran (Figure 8.8) (Magee 2011).

Figure 8.6. Iron Age II storage jar, Muweilah, Sharjah, United Arab Emirates. Photo: the author.

Figure 8.7. Iron Age II bowl, Muweilah, Sharjah. United Arab Emirates. Photo: the author

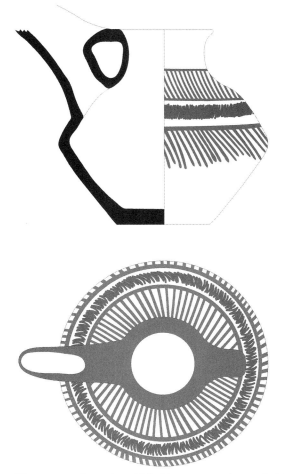

Figure 8.8. Iron Age II bridge-spouted vessel, Muweilah, Sharjah, United Arab Emirates. Drawing: Bryn Mawr College Archaeological Project in the United Arab Emirates.

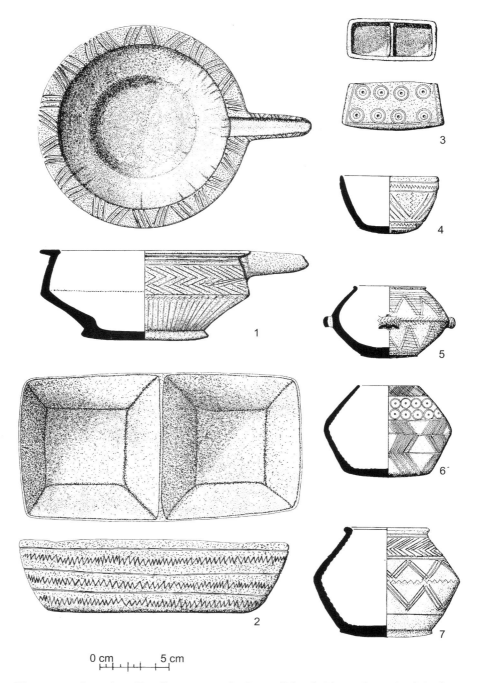

Figure 8.9. Iron Age II softstone vessels, Rumeilah, al-Ain oasis, United Arab Emirates. After Boucharlat and Lombard 1985: Fig. 3.

Softstone vessel production also continues in the Iron Age II period with new shapes and decorative schemes in which the dot and circle motif employed extensively in the previous millennia gives way to linear design (Figure 8.9). Bronze production, which occurred throughout the second millennium BC, also expands during this period. Raki 2 and Bilad al-Madain in the central Oman mountains provide evidence for the large-scale extraction of copper during the Iron Age II period (Hauptmann 1985). A survey by a team from the German Mining Museum around Bat has revealed numerous Iron Age II settlements, tombs and mining zones. One such settlement, al-Banah, is surrounded by massive stone-constructed fortification walls and towers and has been described as the largest known Iron Age fortification in Oman (C. Thornton, personal communication). The recent discovery of the bronze production site of as-Safah on the edge of the Rub al-Khali near Dhank in Oman suggests that copper was shipped from mining sites to production centres in a complex local trade system. We return to the importance of bronzeworking to the regional economy later.

IRON AGE MOUNTAIN SETTLEMENT

Settlement intensification was not limited to the alluvial flanks of the al-Hajjar mountains. Numerous examples of mountain settlements dating to the early first millennium BC have been excavated throughout the UAE and Sultanate of Oman. These include several settlements excavated in the Wadi al-Qawr in southern Ras al-Khaimah (Phillips 1987), Husn Awhala in Fujairah (Potts et al. 1996), Husn Madhab (Corboud et al. 1994: 22–24), Manal in the Wadi Sumayl in Oman (ElMahi and Ibrahim 2003) and several sites, such as Qarn al-Mu'allaq, behind Sohar (Costa and Wilkinson 1987). For the most part, these consist of stone-constructed buildings encompassing an area on the edge of a wadi system. On the whole, the settlements are quite small, but they are often located in a strategic area that maintained views up and down the wadi system. The excavations at Husn Awhala in the Emirate of Fujairah provide the most detailed information on any of these settlements in the northern stretches of the al-Hajjar mountains. A well-constructed stone fort was revealed immediately under a more recent mudbrick construction. The gateway into the fort is particularly notable for its defensive and well-constructed nature (Petrie 1998; Potts et al. 1996). The ceramics from inside consist almost entirely of very large collar-rimmed jars, suggesting that the storage of water or perhaps cereals was an important activity. Communication with the coast is indicated by the recovery of shells that included typical mangrove species such as *Terebralia palustris*. In the southern reaches of the al-Hajjar mountains, excavations and surveys have revealed numerous similar settlements. Few are excavated, but many have been surveyed and have revealed typical Iron Age II pottery (Costa and Wilkinson 1987).

Although our knowledge of the ecology of these settlements is poor, it can be assumed that small-scale agriculture and sheep and goat pastoralism were the main subsistence strategy. The use of falaj technology is very likely, but has not been demonstrated, and in many locations simple wells dug into the wadi bed would have provided water. The numerous and varied geological resources (copper, softstone, basalt for grinding stones) of the mountains were also exploited.

THE DROMEDARY AND THE INTEGRATION OF AN IRON AGE LANDSCAPE

In some respects, the settlement intensification that characterizes the Iron Age II period is not too different from that of the earlier Umm an-Nar period. At that time, coastal settlements also existed and played an important role in the export of copper to and import of luxury goods from South Asia, Iran and Mesopotamia. By the Iron Age II period, settlement dynamics in southeastern Arabia had radically shifted in two fundamental ways. Firstly, southeastern Arabia is absent from Mesopotamian sources until the seventh century BC, and although there is some evidence that copper was being shipped via Bahrain during the late eighth and seventh centuries BC (Potts 1991a: 340), copper export to Mesopotamia was not an important part of the southeast Arabian economy. The existence of coastal sites, therefore, was not predicated on their role in the trans-shipment of goods. Secondly, the presence of domesticated dromedaries permitted an economic alignment between coastal and inland sites throughout southeastern Arabia. For the first time, it was possible to efficiently move goods across the desert frontier separating mountains from coasts in southeastern Arabia. This fundamentally altered the role of coastal settlements, as they were now able to receive goods from inland settlements in an efficient fashion. For the transport of foodstuffs such as cereals grown in the falaj-based inland settlements, time was a key issue. Assuming a daily rate of around 40 kilometers for a dromedary caravan, in two days large amounts of goods, including food, could be transported from the inland to the coast. At the same time, coastal resources could be moved inland. These included shellfish, which became more common at inland sites, such as Husn Awhala (Potts et al. 1996), and dried fish, which were important not only as food but also as fodder. Imported ceramics and other luxury items from Iran, Mesopotamia and Bahrain were transported via these coastal towns as well.

Coastal sites expanded considerably as a result. In the northern UAE several important settlements have been excavated. In the Iron Age II period at Tell Abraq, occupation expands across the settlement. Judging by the extensive patterns of postholes recovered at the site, the typical form of occupation in this period was barasti structures, as in the Iron Age I period. An expansion of settlement is also seen just to the south of Tell Abraq at Hamriya. The possibility that both 'sites' represented a single ancient settlement is indicated by their proximity to each other and their similar occupation histories. Archaeological remains consisting of shell middens, scattered shell deposits and hearths are spread over an area of at least 1.4 by 1.8 kilometers at Hamriya, equivalent to an area of approximately 250 hectares. Detailed surveys and excavations revealed evidence for multiple phases of occupation, including Wadi Suq, Late Bronze Age and Iron Age; however, the vast majority of the shell middens date to the Iron Age II period (Magee et al. 2009). Archaeozoological data indicate that a mixed economy was practised: cattle, sheep, goat, donkey and dromedary are attested in the limited faunal data. Wild animals included hare, fox and gazelle, but the largest number of bones – 2,298 specimens in total – belong to fish, with Sparidae (sea breams) being most frequent.

Other evidence for coastal occupation facing the Arabian Gulf is limited. This is most likely due to the rapid modern development of cities such as Dubai and Abu Dhabi. The work carried out on the islands off the modern coast of Abu Dhabi is an exception. Excavations at Rufayq, which lies on one of these islands, yielded several hearths with lenses of ash. Two sites were focused upon for ^{14}C dating: RU-2 consists of at least six hearths with several other anthropogenic features buried under nearby dunes, while RU-5 consists of at least twenty hearths. In each case, the hearths are constructed from local stone (Hellyer and Beech 2001) and date to the Iron Age II period.

Analysis of ceramics from Hamriya (Fritz 2007) and Tell Abraq provides important information on the coastal economy of the Iron Age II period. Intensive interaction with regional neighbours, including Iran, Bahrain and Mesopotamia, has been recorded from each site. However, the most important interaction was with the new, developing falaj polities of the inland. It is from these that the inhabitants of the coastal zone received their ceramics as well as their bronze tools and weapons and softstone vessels. Compositional analysis of ceramics from Hamriya and Tell Abraq indicates that considerable amounts were produced in the inland oasis of al-Ain, quite probably at Hili 17 (Magee 2011). This pattern differs from that evident in the preceding Iron Age I period, when the inhabitants of Tell Abraq received their ceramics from the northern plains and wadi systems of Ras al-Khaimah.

Occupation of the desert fringes and inland dune fields that separate the coast from the alluvial plains is also completely transformed as a result of domesticated dromedary. The discovery and excavation of Muweilah and Sarouq al-Hadidi are of particular importance in this regard. Muweilah, in the Emirate of Sharjah, is about 15 kilometers from the present-day coastline and has been excavated by the author since 1994 (Magee 1996a; Magee et al. 2002). Archaeozoological and archaeomalacological data indicate that when the settlement was occupied a lagoon coming in from the coast must have been located within a few kilometers of the settlement. The site consists of cultural remains spread over an area

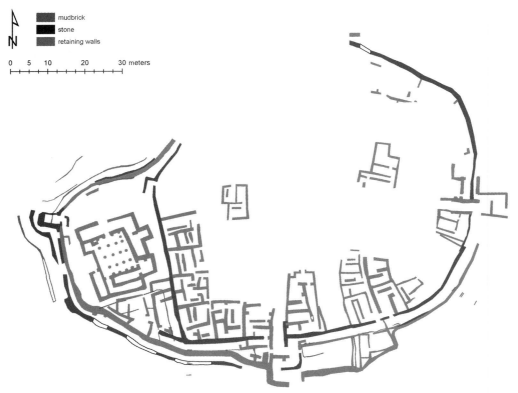

Figure 8.10. Plan of Iron Age II settlement at Muweilah, Sharjah, United Arab Emirates. Bryn Mawr College Archaeological Project in the United Arab Emirates.

of about 500 meters east to west and 450 meters north to south, or about 22 hectares. The vast majority of this area comprises campsites with ceramic, shell and faunal remains. Excavation of one of these indicated that it was occupied both prior to and during the establishment of a massive walled compound at the centre of the settlement called Area C (Figure 8.10).

Area C at Muweilah is one of the largest and most densely occupied Iron Age settlements in southeastern Arabia. It is also one of the most tightly dated sites yet excavated in the region. More than forty ^{14}C samples date the construction, reorganization and catastrophic destruction of the settlement to the first three centuries of the Iron Age II period. The phasing of the site also provides an insight into the rapid pace of change in southeastern Arabia at this time and the concomitant social tension created by the potential for new forms of wealth and legitimacy.

The development of Area C begins towards the end of the tenth century BC when a large stone wall enclosing an area of about 1 hectare was constructed. Three gateways, each of which is oriented towards the cardinal directions, provided access to the interior of the settlement. Shortly after the construction of this wall, if not at the same time, a number of pisé buildings were constructed up against the southwest interior of the surround wall. These consisted of multi-room dwelling compounds with shared walls. Hearths, cooking features and storage areas were common in all compounds. At this stage the compounds enclosed a large courtyard. Beginning in the middle of the ninth century BC, buildings are constructed in this central area. These free-standing structures are arranged in similar fashion to other buildings at the site and contain evidence for domestic occupation. At this stage of the settlement's history there is no evidence for internal differentiation of any kind, and the size of the rooms and their layout are remarkably standardized.

During the ninth century BC, buildings were constructed against the south-eastern interior face of the surround wall. These are larger than those to the south and contain evidence of elaborately plastered floors, drainage systems from the roof, as well as food production and bronze casting in open work spaces. Sometime in the ninth century BC, the settlement undergoes a massive change. A series of stone-lined ditches and then a large 1.5- to 2-meter-wide fortification wall are constructed around the settlement and enclose the earlier surround wall. In the south and east, the gateways are reconfigured so that they now represent a complex defensive arrangement that funnels those who enter the settlement through a narrow access point. In the south of the settlement, new buildings are constructed in the space between the fortification wall and the earlier interior wall. These include kitchens, storage areas and a large room that appears to be an animal enclosure.

In the south of the settlement also important changes occur during the ninth century BC. The new fortification wall encloses an area in which a free-standing building is constructed. Labelled Building II, it consists of a large central room measuring 10 by 12 meters that contains the remains of twenty column bases arranged in a five by four pattern (Figure 8.11). In this central room, several large storage jars were found, including one that measured more than 150 centimeters in height. Ancillary rooms in the same building include evidence of a kitchen and a bronzeworking area in which 1,500 pieces of production refuse and just-cast arrowheads were recovered (Figure 8.12). In a small room adjoining the main room, nearly fifty painted bridge-spouted vessels that are well paralleled in Iran were recovered alongside Mesopotamian jars, softstone vessels and numerous iron weapons and tools that when discovered represented the earliest securely dated evidence for the use of iron in southeastern Arabia (Magee et al. 2002).

The high degree of preservation of so many artefacts is in no small part due to the massive destruction that is wreaked upon the settlement. Whole carbonized dates were found in the destruction layer, and it is likely that these exited the carbon cycle just before the destruction of the settlement. Carbon-14 analysis of these dates indicates that there is a 74% chance that the destruction of the settlement occurred between 799 and 750 BC. In other words, Area C

Figure 8.11. Columned building, Iron Age II settlement at Muweilah, Sharjah, United Arab Emirates. Photo: the author.

Figure 8.12. Bronze production refuse, Iron Age II settlement at Muweilah, Sharjah, United Arab Emirates. Photo: the author.

dates to wholly within the Iron Age II period and is likely to have been occupied from the beginning of this period to sometime in the eighth century BC or a little later. The excavations provide a snapshot of life in the desert fringes during these centuries. Exchange with regional and inter-regional partners is attested by imported ceramics from Iran, Mesopotamia and Bahrain. Copper was imported from the mountains, and bronze objects were produced within the settlement. Geochemical analysis of ceramics indicates that Muweilah was receiving local pottery from a number of oasis centres and then redistributing it in the northern areas of the Peninsula (Magee 2011). The discovery of a three-letter inscription in the Sabaean Monumental script (Müller 1999) suggests the possibility of overland trade with southwestern Arabia.

As noted in Chapter 7, Muweilah has provided the largest and most tightly dated corpus of domesticated dromedary bones of any Iron Age site in the Near East. Terracotta figurines of dromedaries also attest to the familiarity with the animal. The faunal data indicate that dromedaries were secondary only to sheep and goats as providers of meat and five times more important than cattle. Oryx and gazelles were the main hunted terrestrial animals, but foxes and wolves were also hunted. Exploiting the local lagoon was an important part of the subsistence strategy practised at this site as well. Shellfish, particularly *Terebralia palustris* and *Marcia*, were consumed along with large numbers of fish and the Socotra cormorant.

The preponderance of dromedary bones, the position of the settlement and the amount of imported materials highlight the role that Muweilah played in the transport of goods across southeastern Arabia. The location of imported material, bronzeworking and iron weapons and tools within the columned hall at Muweilah suggests that the control of this trade was an important aspect, if not the raison d'être, of Muweilah's existence. In this sense, it may have operated as a gateway community, as defined by Hirth (1978). The complex of defensive systems suggests that it increasingly benefited from this role throughout the ninth century BC.

The construction of a columned hall in which rare imported objects were located marks the apex of the settlement's growth in the late ninth and early eighth centuries BC. Columned halls are also known from settlements associated with falaj in the inland (as discussed later), and they are stylistically similar to the examples noted in western and northwestern Iran during the same period (Magee 2007). It has been pointed out by several researchers, however, that ascribing the origin of the southeast Arabian examples to Iran is fraught with geographical and chronological problems. Even the columned halls from central west Iran, like those at Godin Tepe, are nearly 1,400 kilometers from southeastern Arabia. In addition, the Godin Tepe example and the example from Tepe Nush-i Jan date to the seventh century BC, too late to have provided inspiration for the well-dated examples at Muweilah and Rumeilah. The columned halls from Hasanlu are early enough to have provided a model for the southeast Arabian examples, and Burnt Building II at that site does show remarkable similarities to the example from Muweilah, but Hasanlu is nearly 1,700 kilometers away. Stronach (2003) suggested that the appearance of columned halls in southeastern Arabia indicates that Fars, which borders the Arabian Gulf in southwestern Iran, might have played a critical role in the origin and dispersal of the columned-hall tradition. Only future excavations in that region can confirm such an hypothesis; for the moment the diffusionary path by which columned halls appear in southeastern Arabia remains a mystery.

Despite the apparent Iranian stylistic origins of columned halls, there is little doubt that their function was rooted in an Arabian economic and symbolic context. A large, highly decorated, semi-ovoid incense burner with a painted figurine of a humped zebu bull was found in a columned hall at Muweilah (Figures 8.13 and 8.14). Although this is by far the most elaborate incense burner from the site, other examples, including those with bird and dromedary figurines (Figure 8.15), are also known. The presence of an inscription at Muweilah might suggest that southeastern Arabia was in contact with the distant and increasingly important south Arabian kingdoms, from which the frankincense to be burnt in such vessels could have been transported on recently domesticated dromedaries. The shape of the incense burners also recalls examples from the late second millennium BC levels at Sabir in Yemen, reinforcing the connections to that region.

Recent excavations at Sarouq al-Hadid in the Emirate of Dubai also attest to new opportunities for economic exploitation of the desert regions during this period. The site is located nearly 50 kilometers from the modern-day coast and almost the same distance from the oasis of al-Ayaay, which contained an

Figure 8.13. Incense burner, Iron Age II settlement at Muweilah, Sharjah, United Arab Emirates. Photo: the author.

Figure 8.14. Detail of incense burner, Iron Age II settlement at Muweilah, Sharjah, United Arab Emirates. Photo: the author.

Figure 8.15. Incense burner with figurine of camel, Iron Age II settlement at Muweilah, Sharjah, United Arab Emirates. Photo: the author.

Iron Age II settlement and falaj system (as described earlier). Excavations have revealed a highly dispersed site with a large amount of metalworking slag on and within the mobile sand dunes that characterize the northern extension of the Rub al-Khali (Nashef 2010).

While no clear 'settlement' has been revealed at Sarouq al-Hadid, the site has provided one of the richest assemblages of metal artefacts yet discovered in prehistoric Arabia. In addition to elaborately decorated iron spears and swords, the assemblage is dominated by points and blades, some of which contain bronze hilts with iron additions (Nashef 2010). Until the excavation of these objects, iron was virtually unknown in the southeast Arabian Iron Age, with the only published examples coming from Muweilah. Dozens of bronze objects, including many weapons, were also found. Of particular interest was a highly decorated bronze tripod, 31 centimeters in height and containing an open shallow bowl and zoomorphic feet. A detailed analysis by Potts (2009) draws convincing parallels to bronze tripods from Assyria and Urartu. He entertains the possibility that the piece in question was imported from one of these centres, but it is equally likely that the tripod was manufactured at Sarouq al-Hadid for export but, for some unknown reason, was never shipped. One of the most puzzling aspects of the site is the massive amount of evidence for bronze and iron production, despite being located at least 60 kilometers from the nearest copper source.

A variety of factors are likely to explain why an industrial site was located in the middle of this desert environment. An acacia forest was probably located near the site in antiquity. Such forests are known in the region today and provide a wealth of important resources, including fuel for metalworking and fodder for animals. They are typically located in areas where water is easily accessed, and several wells are present at Sarouq al-Hadid (Nashef 2010). Such a forest, together with the presence of domesticated dromedary, would have permitted Sarouq al-Hadid to flourish. Its equidistance between the inland oases and coasts meant that it could also transport and then refine copper from the mountains and return bronze objects to local and regional markets (such as the bronze tripod discussed earlier). Ironworking would have relied on imported raw materials, perhaps via coastal settlements like Tell Abraq and Muweilah or perhaps via inland desert trade routes from the rest of Arabia (Chapter 9). In addition to imported materials, other coastal resources such as dried fish and shellfish are likely to have been transported through this area. The result was that Sarouq al-Hadid quickly became a critical node between coast and inland.

Whereas excavations at numerous sites in southeastern Arabia have highlighted the production and consumption of traded goods, Sarouq al-Hadid highlights the social and economic power derived from the movement of luxury goods across the desert landscape. We have already characterized Muweilah as a 'gateway community' that exploited local resources and the movement of goods into and out of the desert foreland. Sarouq al-Hadid differs in some respects from this model. Its rapid emergence in the Iron Age II period can be best explained by the transit (and further processing) of goods. Bandy's (2004) analysis of trade and social power in the southern Titicaca Basin of Peru and Bolivia documents the emergence of 'transit' communities and provides a compelling analogy to this situation. As he notes: 'Broadly speaking, analyses of trade are usually concerned with macropolitical and macroeconomic processes in producing and consuming regions. Communities that occupy territory through which trade routes and trade goods must pass, if organized in a decentralized and stateless fashion, are normally relegated to the margins and footnotes of treatments of exchange. However, groups occupying these strategic positions, which we may term "transit communities," are often profoundly affected by the trade passing through their territories' (Bandy 2004: 97).

The diversity and value of objects from Sarouq al-Hadid indicate the social power and wealth that resulted from its role as a 'transit community'. In addition to highly decorated metal objects, including some made of iron, a not yet fully published assemblage of gold and electrum jewellery, beads, coils and leaf was discovered (Nashef 2010). These are almost certainly imported from elsewhere in Arabia, and the excavators have drawn parallels to finds from Saudi Arabia and Jordan. A series of metal plates interpreted as scales were found in association with some gold objects, indicating that the site regulated the movement of precious metals across the landscape. It is significant that the gold jewellery and decorated bronze and iron objects are the only vestiges of the social power that the inhabitants of Sarouq al-Hadid derived from their critical role in Iron Age trade. There is no evidence for substantial buildings or temples at the site, and as far as one can judge the inhabitants lived in simple barasti structures.

NEGOTIATING COHESION IN THE SOUTHEAST ARABIAN IRON AGE

Falaj technology and domesticated dromedary permitted unparalleled settlement intensification throughout all the environmental zones of southeastern Arabia. The ability to move goods across these environments and create an integrated regional economy was an important component of this process. Structurally, southeastern Arabia at this time is comparable to southern Mesopotamia during the fourth millennium BC, where, it is argued, the Mesopotamian advantage of both agricultural potential and the ability to transport goods set in train amplifier effects that ultimately led to the creation of the Uruk city-state (Algaze 2001). In southeastern Arabia, there is clear evidence that both of these factors gave rise to potential alterations in the distribution and deployment of power within society as a whole. However, a nuanced approach to the archaeological record illuminates efforts to modify these processes and ensure the maintenance of social cohesion at an intra-polity and regional level.

NON-RESIDENTIAL ARCHITECTURE OF THE IRON AGE II PERIOD

Unique non-residential buildings are found at numerous sites during the Iron Age II period. The first category consists of heavily fortified stone-built constructions located on top of mountains. Examples have been found at Jebel Buhais (Boucharlat 1992), Husn Madhab (Corboud et al. 1994) and Lizq (Weisgerber 1981: 226–227). As Potts (2001: 49) has noted, 'The purpose of these fortresses, it may be argued, was to safeguard the agricultural settlements associated with them, particularly their precious aflaj, and the concentration of power in such centres is an important social and political phenomenon.' However, whether they were places of refuge in times of conflict or actual centres of power remains debatable, as few have been fully excavated.

Another more prominent category of non-residential buildings is found near falaj systems on the alluvial plains. In al-Ain, a large fortified building (Hili 14) was located next to the Hili 15 falaj. Although the building has not been excavated, its outline was discernible on the surface and consisted of an almost square building with thick fortification walls measuring between 50 and 60 meters in length. Limited probes revealed very large storage jars in some rooms (Boucharlat and Lombard 1985). The presence of these jars, the location of the building and its fortified structure naturally led to the conclusion that its function was tied to the administration of the falaj system (al-Tikriti 2002: 124). A building with a potentially similar function has been excavated at Bida Bint Saud (al-Tikriti 2002, 2010). In this case, the pillared building (or columned hall) referred to by al-Tikriti as the House of the Falaj consists of a single mudbrick building measuring 10 by 13 meters. According to Benoist (2010: 130–131) a 3.8-meter staircase runs from this building into a narrow room, which opens into the falaj itself (Benoist 2010: 130–131). In addition, numerous and very large storage jars at both sites raise the possibility that these buildings operated as control and redistribution centres. As previously discussed, a similar example has been revealed in the excavations at Muweilah. In that case, several very large storage jars were also found along with imported and traded goods.

These unique buildings and storage facilities have been interpreted as evidence for the emergence of elites whose control over water reinforced their authority and power. However, further research at these buildings and associated settlements has yet to reveal any form of status wealth or administrative systems such as glyptic within these buildings. Benoist has argued convincingly that these buildings with their large open spaces were used episodically for meetings, possibly by the 'elders' of the settlement. As she notes: 'Questions related to water rights probably were the subject of regular discussions between different members of the community, those who benefited from parts of water, and those who were in charge of water administration. Some of those discussions

might well have been taking place inside pillared buildings. But those questions were probably not the only ones which might have been debated....
[O]thers such as alliances, weddings, manufacture and trade rules, policing, war,
all questions involving the community might have also have occurred' (Benoist
2010: 131–132). In this sense, Hili 15 and the columned buildings at Bida Bint
Saud and Muweilah are more akin to the *majlis* of traditional Islamic society
in which a tribal leader would meet with community members on a regular
basis to discuss matters of concern to the community at large. This would
have provided an opportunity to maintain social cohesion and avert political
and economic disharmony within a settlement. It is tempting, therefore, to
recast discussions of the emergence of 'elites' during this period and emphasize
individuals or groups of individuals who did not hold absolute authority but
whose political role was similar to that of the idealized form of the *mukarrib* of
southwestern Arabia discussed in more detail later.

In addition to the ability to access water through falaj, the other component
of southeast Arabian Iron Age settlement intensification was the movement of
goods by dromedary across the landscape. As this increased, the potential for
controlling and restricting access to burgeoning trade routes must have arisen.
It is the tension created by this development that explains one of the most
novel aspects of the Iron Age: the practice of highly symbolic and shared ritual that linked producers, consumers and transit communities through central
places. Sites that may be identified as 'cultic' or possibly pilgrimage centres are
located in each of the major transit zones that linked the east to the west coast
(see Figure 8.1). These include al-Qusais (Taha 1983) on the west coast, Sarouq
al-Hadid (Nashef 2010) in the desert, Masafi (Benoist 2010) in the centre of the
al-Hajjar mountains and Bithna (Benoist 2007) at the interface of the mountains and the east coast.

The artefacts at each of these sites are compellingly similar and, judging by
their unique design and function, were used in rituals. Ceramics with appliqué
snakes are one of the most common examples of such finds. At al-Qusais these
are found in a long rectangular building constructed from local beach rock
and labelled 'the Mound of the Serpents'. At this and at other sites, appliqué
snakes are found on a wide variety of ceramics, including lids, storage vessels
and bridge-spouted vessels. This last form is relatively uncommon during the
Iron Age and appears to be concentrated at sites of ritual or administrative significance. Dozens of vessels with appliqué snakes, including several complete
storage jars measuring more than 50 centimeters in height, were also found at
Sarouq al-Hadid (Nashef 2010). Several of these vessels were decorated with
multiple snakes, all typically on the upper face of the exterior of the vessel.

The site of Masafi is located at a midpoint in the wadi system that still
provides one the most common transit routes across the al-Hajjar mountains.
Excavations at the Iron Age II settlement have revealed several ritual buildings
in which ceramic vessels with appliqué snakes are common (Benoist 2010).

These include a whole range of vessels, including bridge-spouted vessels. A similar range of artefacts is found in a number of buildings, platforms and open-air altars at the nearby site of Bithna. Although badly damaged by later building and recent graves, careful excavation revealed several different phases of occupation, all dating to the Iron Age II period. The artefacts found in association with these buildings complement the material from al-Qusais, Sarouq al-Hadid and Masafi: more than fifty-six examples of vessels with appliqué snakes were discovered. In most cases, the snakes are on the upper body of the vessel and appear to represent the same type of snake found at the other sites. A number of unique vessels from Bithna are worthy of specific mention. These include pedestalled chalices with appliqué snakes and the figurine of a human holding an open bowl on which a snake crawls.

At each of these sites, representations of snakes are not limited to ceramic vessels. Cast bronze snakes, often highly decorated, are also found in a variety of shapes and sizes. From the Mound of the Serpents at al-Qusais, no fewer than nineteen bronze snakes have been reported (Taha 1983). An unknown number were excavated at Sarouq al-Hadid (Nashef 2010), while at least 34 examples are known from Masafi (Benoist 2010).

Representations of snakes are not the only common element at these sites. The ceramic repertoire includes chalices and pouring vessels that are uncommon at residential sites. The possibility that these were used in banqueting and feasting is furthered when we consider the large amounts of animals that have been recovered from Bithna. The refuse of bronze production, including casting spillage and slag, has been found at Masafi and Bithna, and in the most recent excavations at the former site more than fifty complete ingots of copper or bronze were recovered from a single storage vessel (A. Benoist, personal communication) buried into the middle of one of the cultic buildings. Taha (1983) reports that hundreds of bronze arrowheads were also recovered from the Mound of the Serpents at al-Qusais, and while no definitive number is available from other sites, it is clear from preliminary publications that they exceed the quantities typically found at Iron Age II residential settlements.

Various aspects of the same ritual paraphernalia, but not in the same quantity, have been found at other Iron Age sites. Bronze snakes are known from Salut and vessels with appliqué snakes are known from Muweilah, Tell Abraq, Asimah, am-Dhurra, Salut and Rumeilah (Benoist 2007: 34). Incense burners have also been found at many of these sites. None, however, display the complete range of ritual materials, bronze snakes and evidence for bronzeworking evident al-Qusais, Sarouq al-Hadid, Masafi and Bithna. For this reason, the latter sites should be considered cultic centres, and their positions as strategic end points and midpoints along the east to west trade route suggest a functional link between trade, ritual practice and the production of bronze.

Numerous scholars have attempted to discern a formal religious background to these rituals, especially by focusing on representations of the snake. To Benoist, 'the representations of snakes at Bithnah – and on other sites in the Oman peninsula – strongly suggest that the snakes depicted were vipers, and most probably a species present in the region. This recalls one of the elements present in the symbolism of the snake in the Levant: the toxicity of its poison as a source of power over life. Thus, a meaning related to healing comparable to that suggested in the Levant may also have existed here' (Benoist 2007: 51). Potts (2007: 72) has cast a wider net and, in reviewing the evidence from southeastern Arabia and Bahrain, suggests a Vedic origin for the snake cult. Potts also notes that the snake was the symbol of the chief Minaean moon god, Wadd (Potts 2007: 65). The Kingdom of Ma'in was one of the five kingdoms that emerged in the early first millennium BC in southwestern Arabia, and bronze snakes have also been interpreted as votive offerings in south Arabian temples (Potts 2007: 65). Nevertheless, snakes are not the only ritual aspect at these sites. The evidence for bronzeworking suggests a functional connection between the production of bronze objects and weapons and cultic activity. As already noted, Raki 2 and Bilad al-Madain, located in the central Oman mountains, provide evidence for the large-scale extraction of copper during the Iron Age II period, and it is likely that primary copper from these sites was transported to regional centres for secondary refining and the production of objects (Hauptmann 1985). The evidence for bronzeworking at cultic sites suggests that they played a key role in such activity.

PILGRIMAGE, TRADE AND SOCIAL COHESION

The location of Masafi, Bithna, al-Qusais and Sarouq al-Hadid along a common west to east trade route and the commonality of paraphernalia found at each of them suggests that pilgrimage was enmeshed within cultic activity (Benoist 2010). In this regard, the establishment of cultic centres served to normalize the new economic order in southeastern Arabia brought about by agricultural intensification of the inland through falaj technology and the development of intra-regional trade following the domestication of the dromedary, but it did so in a fashion that emphasized the importance of social cohesion. As Kantner and Vaughn (2012: 66) have recently argued in their examination of pilgrimage at Chaco and Nasca in the American Southwest, pilgrimage 'serves as a costly signal of the pilgrims' commitment to the religious system and the beliefs and the values associated with it; this in turn facilitates cooperation and other prosocial behaviors among pilgrims who otherwise might be strangers'. It is likely that our currently emerging knowledge of cult, ritual and pilgrimage in the southeast Arabian Iron Age will develop further as fieldwork expands beyond those areas that had traditionally been the focus of archaeological investigation.

Ultimately, the analysis of Iron Age II burials holds the potential to provide detailed insights into the changing social relations that accompany these developments. However, our knowledge of Iron Age funerary customs, unlike that regarding such customs in the Umm an-Nar period, is paltry and no regional assessment of Iron Age II burials has been conducted until now. A number of Iron Age burials have been found throughout the Oman peninsula and east Arabian littoral. On the whole, they are marked by a great diversity of both form and contents. In al-Qusais, located in the modern city of Dubai, excavations revealed evidence of numerous chamber graves that had been cut into hardened sabkha deposits. Although still not published, the material on display in the Dubai Museum includes bronze objects, Iranian-inspired painted spouted vessels, alabasters and softstone vessels. The graves were associated with a ritual area that contained bronze snakes and vessels with appliqué serpents. The most complete published assemblage of Iron Age II burials is from Jebel Buhais, in the inland of the Emirate of Sharjah (Uerpmann et al. 2006). Excavations have revealed several Iron Age II graves, including single rock-constructed, semi-subterranean tombs, graves located on the mountain itself and graves that exploited natural rock crevices halfway down the mountain face. Bronze arrowheads and beads of semi-precious stone, including carnelian, are also common. Carved softstone vessels are plentiful and often outnumber ceramic vessels. As well, graves discovered in the Wadi al-Qawr have revealed dozens of complete examples of delicately carved vessels. Here, the graves consist mostly of large stone-constructed communal burials continuing the tradition of earlier Bronze Age burials. However, analyses of the quantities and types of goods deposited in these graves have failed to highlight any evidence of differential access to materials or any difference in the type and size of grave structure (Fritz 2010).

In summary, the southeast Arabian Iron Age witnessed immense changes in human–environmental relations. The development of falaj technology and the presence of domesticated dromedaries opened the landscape to increasing intensification and trade. The potential for social, economic and political differentiation as a result of these developments was marked. The social cohesion that had maintained human settlement in this region for millennia was, however, reaffirmed and communicated to the population by innovative displays of ritual and pilgrimage. It is thus possible to compare these ideological affirmations to the function of Umm an-Nar tombs during the late third millennium BC when southeastern Arabia also experienced rapid settlement intensification.

SOUTHWESTERN ARABIA

As noted in the introduction, the rise of the Sabaean Federation has been the subject of scholarship which emphasizes the monumentality of major sites, the

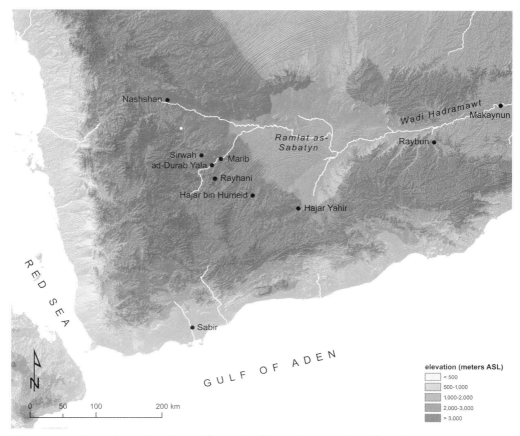

Figure 8.16. Location of main southwest Arabian sites mentioned in the text.

development of writing and the economic benefits of long-distance overland trade from the eighth century BC onwards (see Breton 2000; de Maigret 2002; Hoyland 2001). The published scholarship on these issues has drawn on the rich corpus of South Arabian inscriptions, biblical references and later classical sources. I do not intend to examine and review the archaeology of the Sabaean Federation here, since numerous excellent works already exist. A brief outline is, however, required if we are to understand how these developments fit into the broader cultural sequence throughout southwestern Arabia in the late second and early first millennia BC (Figure 8.16).

The centre of the Sabaean Federation was Marib in the Wadi Dhanna at the edge of the Ramlat as-Sabatyn, where, as detailed in Chapter 5, agricultural settlement had already existed for several millennia before the eighth century BC. Neo-Assyrian kings, such as Sargon II and Sennacherib, recognized that a powerful king who sent a gift of aromatics and precious stones to the Assyrian court had lived here during the eighth and seventh centuries BC (Hoyland 2001: 39; Robin 1991: 56). An even earlier inscription, discovered more recently, refers to the activities of merchants of Saba around the middle Euphrates region of Suhu (Chapter 9). These brief foreign glimpses of the Sabaean Federation are less important, however, than the hundreds of inscriptions written in the South Arabian script in a language called Sabaic (Macdonald 2000) that provide important information on the history of the Sabaeans and how they constructed their own cultural identity.

Short inscriptions and a single recently discovered lengthy one from Sirwah (Nebes 2007) inform us that a variety of mukarribs, or 'federators' (Robin 1996: Nos. 1150–1153), ruled Marib during the eighth century BC. As Breton (2000: 33) has noted, mukarribs were 'never invested with absolute authority or autonomy; instead, the sovereign made important decisions in consultation with several other important figures represented in "councils" or "assemblies" whose main concerns were typically related to irrigation'. In this sense, 'mukarrib' must be differentiated from the term used by Assyrian kings to describe the rulers of this region. Recent discoveries have indicated that towards the end of the eighth century BC, one of these mukarribs is Yita amar Watar bin Yakrubmalik. He is probably to be identified with It'amra from Saba, who is mentioned as paying tribute to the Assyrian king Sargon II in 715 BC (Nebes 2007: 25). The discovery of a massive inscription of his at the Temple of Almaqah at Sirwah confirms his importance during this period (Nebes 2007) alongside others whose names we know from shorter inscriptions (Breton 2000: 33).

Marib was, however, not the only powerful oasis polity at this time. The ancient city of Nashshan, modern al-Bayda in the Jawf, extracted considerable wealth from the control of irrigation in the Wadis Madhab and Kharid. It was ruled by an individual called Sumhuyafa and his descendants at the end of the eighth and early seventh centuries BC (Avanzini 1996; Bron 2010). One inscription makes it clear that these leaders pledged alliance with the mukarrib of Saba (Avanzini 1996: 65). The other oasis polity about which we have some information at this time is Awsan. Located on the edge of the Wadi Markha, its capital is possibly to be identified with the site of Hajar Yahirr (Breton 1994). Awsan derived considerable power from its position, since it lay between Saba and the Wadi Dhanna to the west and the Wadi Hadramawt, which provided access to the coast and sources of frankincense and on the edge of which was located the powerful city of Shabwa.

In the early seventh century BC, the Sabaean mukarrib, Karib'il Watar, describes in two lengthy inscriptions at the Temple of Almaqah at Sirwah his actions that brought the various polities of southwestern Arabia into a single confederation. The fact that these deeds were recorded at a temple to Almaqah is very significant. Almaqah was the principal god of the Sabaeans. The people of Saba thought of themselves as the progeny of Almaqah, and as the power of Saba spread, the worship of Almaqah expanded across southwestern Arabia (Breton 1991: 21, 2000: 120).

Karib'il Watar's Sirwah inscriptions (normally referred to as RES 3945–3946) describe eight military conquests of extraordinary scope. The first took place in the highlands to the immediate west of Marib. There he claims to have captured 8,000 and killed 3,000 of his enemy. He then turns his attention to Awsan, which, as we noted earlier, was of critical importance for communication routes around the Ramlat as-Sabatyn. Sixteen thousand were killed and 40,000 taken prisoner. Karib'il Watar claims to have destroyed the capital of Awsan, probably Hajar Yahirr. In his third and fourth campaigns he attacked the low-lying hills at the edge of the coastal strip facing the Gulf of Aden. The settlement of Sabir, discussed in Chapter 5, may have been one of those cities he attacked in these two campaigns. Nashshan, which as we noted earlier was one of the most powerful rivals of Saba in the eighth century BC and whose leader, Sumhuyafa, had entered into an alliance with the Sabaeans, bore the brunt of the fifth and sixth campaigns. Perhaps because of Nashshan's importance, Karib'il Watar describes a harsh defeat for Nashshan and other allied cities in line 16 of the Sirwah inscription: '[He] destroyed the fortified town of Nashshan to the point of saving it from any looting that it might have otherwise suffered had it been spared from the flames; he inflicted a similar destruction on the Afraw palace and the city of Nashshan; he imposed a tribute on the backs of their citizens, hitting the priests in particular; he ordered the massacre of all Nashshanites who hesitated to show devotion to the divinities; demanded of King Sumhuyafa and Nashshan that Saba be established in the city of Nashshan and that Sumhuyafa and Nashshan build the temple of Almaqah' (translated by Breton 2000: 37 from the French text of Robin 1996: 1121–1123). Karib'il Watar's conquest of southwestern Arabia was concluded by attacks against the Tihama coastal region and the Najran region to the north of Jawf.

Following these victories, the Sabaean mukarribs ruled over large areas of southwestern Arabia. For the next two centuries they attempted to impose their culture and language throughout southwestern Arabia, and the inscriptions of various mukarribs speak of their building programs, especially religious and irrigation works. These centuries and the subsequent rise of Qataban in the Wadi Beihan at the end of the sixth century BC lie well outside the scope of this work. Approaches to understanding the rise of the Sabaean Federation are, however, germane to the broader themes developed in previous chapters. In particular, the relative importance given to external stimuli versus autochthonous developments has been a constant theme in discussions of the Sabaean Federation. On the one hand, scholars have long emphasized the importance of the Marib dam, which controlled flow through the Wadi Dhanna and diverted water and sediment into the northern and southern oases of Marib (see Brunner 1983; Gerig 1982; Hehmeyer 1989; Hehmeyer and Schmidt 1991; Schaloske 1995). At their maximum extent, the southern oasis comprised 3,750 hectares and the northern oasis 5,700 hectares (Breton 2000: 19). The dating of the dam is unclear, but there is little doubt that from the beginning of the first millennium BC it was a critical component of the economy of the Sabaean Federation and was indeed built upon centuries of irrigation technology that had been perfected in the Wadi Dhanna (Francaviglia 2000).

On the other hand, our knowledge of much of the Sabaean Federation comes from inscriptions written in a script that, in one fashion or another, points to external influence. The most common languages employed in these inscriptions may be classed under the rubric 'Ancient South Arabian' (Macdonald 2000: 30). For our purposes, the most important is Sabaic written in Monumental South Arabian script. Once these languages were established in southwestern Arabia, their use in monumental inscriptions and, as has recently been discovered, minuscule writing on the midribs of palm fronds (Ryckmans 2001) became a critical element of the maintenance of political, religious and social ideology.

Questions on the origins of this alphabetic script and language resonate with the broader issues of this book. Two traditions dominated alphabetic writing systems in the ancient Near East: Northwest Semitic and Arabian, of which Ancient South Arabian is a part. Northwest Semitic and Arabian alphabetic sequences are found at Ugarit on the Syrian coast in the late second millennium BC (Dietrich and Loretz 1988; Macdonald 2000: 31–32; cf. Healey 1991). The minor occurrence of an Arabian alphabetic sequence at Ugarit has led scholars to assume that it was a common script somewhere else in the Near East during the second millennium BC. Knauf, in particular, has argued that the emergence of the original alphabet took place in Syria-Palestine and is attested in the Late Bronze Age. Indeed, the discovery of an abecedary in cuneiform script listing letters in South Arabian order at Beth Shemesh in Palestine supports this view (for a discussion see Healey 1991: 73). Knauf's strong conclusion that '[b]oth the signs and the letter order of the south Semitic alphabet derive from Southern Palestine during the flourishing of the "first Mediterranean world economy" and the Midianites in northwestern Arabia played a key role in the transmission of the alphabet into Arabia' (Knauf 1989: 84–85) stands in contrast to Macdonald's more cautionary conclusion that 'there is as yet no firm basis for dating the origins of the Arabian alphabet' (Macdonald 2000: 32). Furthermore, to researchers such as Knauf (1989: 86), the foreign origin of the South Arabian alphabet is inexorably tied to the origins of the Sabaean Federation. It is argued that once the Sabaeans began to trade with the states of the Fertile Crescent, they reaped considerable economic benefits and began to move towards a more complex political structure. The language could then be employed as a mechanism by which the state was legitimized and maintained.

This alphabet was employed mostly in western and southwestern Arabia and not in the east, although for what reasons we do not know. As Macdonald

(2000: 38) has cautioned, 'This apparent difference may in part be due to an imbalance in the amount and type of research which has so far been devoted to the two sides of the Peninsula. The study of the ancient history of both the northwest and southwest is still dominated by epigraphy, and the results of the archaeological work of the last twenty five years are only now beginning to change and fill out the traditional picture.' It should be remembered that at least one example of the use of the South Arabian script has been discovered in a ninth- or eighth-century BC context at Muweilah in the UAE (Müller 1999), and although this example is indeed 'isolated' (Avanzini 2010: 11), it was discovered because every sherd from the excavation was kept and studied – a practice that is not undertaken on every excavation in the region. Who knows how many more examples of South Arabian might be discovered in the future? In addition, we need to keep in mind the practice of miniscule writing on organic materials, which has only recently come to light in southwestern Arabia but which may also have existed in eastern Arabia but simply has not been preserved. Regardless of these caveats, no one would deny that the use of South Arabian for propagandistic statements is a critical part of statecraft limited to southwestern Arabia during this period.

THE SABAEAN FEDERATION IN THE LONGUE DURÉE

Although the language in which these inscriptions are written reflects broader connections to the regions north of Arabia, when viewed from a longue durée perspective the developments that take place in the early first millennium BC in southwestern Arabia can be understood as the culmination of a process of human adaptation that began millennia before. Intensive sedentary agriculture in southwestern Arabia is already known from the third millennium BC in the Highlands. As discussed in Chapter 6, this permitted the development of large villages in optimal environmental niches. As technology developed, agriculture based on trapping runoff and dams spread to other regions of Yemen, including the desert fringes, Wadi Hadramawt and coasts. In the following discussion, we will focus on the substantial settlements that appear near the interface between the mountains and Ramlat as-Sabatyn in the centuries immediately prior to the emergence of the Sabaean Federation. These include the sites of ad-Durayb Yala, Rayhani, Hajar bin Humeid and Raybun. Shabwa, which was discussed in Chapter 7 in reference to its important second millennium BC occupation, appears to have been abandoned from the middle of the second millennium BC to c. 600 BC (Badre 1991).

ad-Durayb Yala is located in the Wadi Yala on the eastern edge of the Ramlat as-Sabatyn, 30 kilometers from the Sabaean capital of Marib. Excavations conducted by Italian archaeologists led by Alessandro de Maigret revealed a 2.3-hectare walled town in which multiple phases of occupation were evident (de Maigret 1988; de Maigret and Robin 1989) (Figure 8.17). The settlement

Figure 8.17. View of late second millennium BC settlement of ad-Durayb Yala, Yemen. Photo: Missione Archeologica Italiana nella Repubblica dello Yemen.

comprised a semi-circular town, more than 200 meters in diameter, surrounded by a large buttressed stone wall which would have stood about 4.5 meters in antiquity (de Maigret 1985: 348) (Figure 8.18). The town was entered though a gate guarded by two large rectangular towers (de Maigret 1985: 351). Excavations along the city wall and inside one very well-preserved house (House A) revealed four phases of settlement from the twelfth to the eighth century BC (Figure 8.19). Although excavations were limited, there was some evidence on the surface remains for internal differentiation in the arrangement of domestic and other structures. The excavations in House A indicated that the settlement had been destroyed by fire, along with the rest of the settlement, in the eighth century BC.

ad-Durayb Yala is positioned between the Ramlat as-Sabatyn and the eastern edge of the Khawlan region that was a centre for Bronze Age occupation. Like those of the Bronze Age settlements, the inhabitants of ad-Durayb Yala practised agriculture, and a standard assemblage of cultivars (wheat, barley and possibly millet) can be assumed even if detailed archaeobotanical evidence is absent. The size of ad-Durayb Yala leaves no doubt, however, that the agricultural regime by which the city was fed was based on significant irrigation systems, much larger than those employed during the Bronze Age in the Khawlan. These consist of dams and terraces that have been documented at al-Jafnah near the site (de Maigret 2005). ad-Durayb Yala has also provided evidence for the appearance of domesticated dromedary by the ninth century

Figure 8.18. View of the town wall of ad-Durayb Yala, Yemen. Photo: Missione Archeologica Italiana nella Repubblica dello Yemen.

Figure 8.19. House A, ad-Durayb Yala, Yemen. Photo: Missione Archeologica Italiana nella Repubblica dello Yemen.

Figure 8.20. Early South Arabian inscriptions from ad-Durayb Yala, Yemen.
Photo: Missione Archeologica Italiana nella Repubblica dello Yemen.

BC. Although dromedary was never significant in the faunal diet, the fact
that it complemented existing subsistence strategies and was used to integrate
settlements with other regions is an issue that we will return to below. Fedele
has noted that 'between about 850 and 650 BC dromedaries had become common animals in the domestic stock of this part of Yemen, even at a distance
from the famed Frankincense Road. Yala is interesting in this context precisely
because it lies away from the routes employed by long-distance caravan trade.
By the late ninth century BC the dromedary, although on occasion appreci-
ated at the table, had in fact acquired the complete multiplicity of roles that
was to be its lasting distinction' (Fedele, in press: 7). ad-Durayb Yala is also critical for understanding the emergence and use of South Arabian script. Several
ceramics with inscribed personal names were found in strata ^{14}C-dated from
the twelfth to the ninth century BC (de Maigret 2005) (Figure 8.20). These
graffiti emphasize the importance of the indigenous development of this script
in the centuries prior to Karib'il Watar's conquest and the beginning of the
Sabaean Federation.

Rayhani, in the Wadi Jubah about 40 kilometers south of Marib, lies in an
environmental location similar to that of ad-Durayb Yala. Excavations by a US
team have focused on two settlement sites: Rayhani itself, which measures
3 hectares, and the smaller site of al-Tamra (Blakely 1985, 1996; Glanzman
1987, 1994, 2004, 2005; Glanzman and Ghaleb 1987). The former site has provided a long stratigraphic sequence that stretches from the late second into the
early first millennium BC. Of particular interest are Strata VII and VI, which
include the second and third occupation phases. Several ^{14}C results from these
phases confirm a date from the late second into the early first millennium
BC. Unlike those of the Occupation Phase 1, these strata contain architecture. Sherds inscribed with South Arabian script are known from Occupation

Phase 2 at Rayhani, thus echoing the evidence from ad-Durayb Yala. By Occupation Phase 3, monumental inscriptions are known and a large city wall is constructed.

Detailed sedimentary and geomorphological research has provided insights into the agricultural regime of Rayhani. Higher levels of phosphates have been noted near the settlement than elsewhere, perhaps indicating the use of manure for fertilizer. Irrigation channels and ridges demarcating fields have also been recorded from this area. Archaeobotanical research (Stewart 1987, 1996) indicates the presence of a large amount of *Zizyphus*, but barley, wheat, dates, peas, chickpeas, bitter vetch, pomegranate and flax are also noted. The archaeozoological data portray an animal economy similar to that of ad-Durayb Yala, with a preponderance of sheep, goat and cattle and small amounts of dromedary that increase significantly by the second quarter of the first millennium BC (Edens and Wilkinson 1998: 106).

Prior to the excavation of ad-Durayb Yala and Rayhani, Hajar bin Humeid was the key site for understanding developments from the late second into the early first millennium BC. The publication of this site, excavated by William Foxwell Albright in the 1950s, provided the first detailed analysis of ceramics for the late prehistory of southwestern Arabia (Van Beek 1969, 1997). The site is located in the Wadi Beihan, 80 kilometers to the south of Marib, and is thus in a similar position to the sites discussed earlier. Regrettably, however, the level of detail paid to matters of subsistence was below par in Albright's excavations. Impressions on ceramics indicated the presence of barley, oats, broomcorn millet and African teff, flax, sesame, cumin and possibly grape. Archaeozoological research was largely absent from the excavations.

All these sites have common economic and ecological characteristics. Located in wadi systems that extend from the Highlands, they were able to develop significant agricultural production. Although the data are uneven, a wide range of cultivars were grown from the late second millennium BC onwards. Unlike their Bronze Age ancestors, who occupied more fertile regions in the Highlands, the inhabitants of these settlements perfected irrigation systems to sustain settlements that were, by south Arabian standards, considerable in size. In this manner, the developments in the late second and early first millennia BC foreshadowed the large-scale constructions that define the Sabaean Federation in terms of both irrigation systems and buildings. The integration of this region into a single federation during the seventh century BC is also foreshadowed by the material culture commonalities found during the late second and early first millennia BC. Ceramics, in particular, attest to the emergence of a regional material culture identity that has been named the 'Sayhadic Iron Age' (Edens and Wilkinson 1998). A series of distinctive shapes characterize this assemblage, including bowls and bases with flared stands decorated with a burnished red slip and the occasional use of incision. In its earliest manifestation dating to the late second millennium BC, this assemblage is already found at Rayhani, ad-Durayb Yala and Hajar bin Humeid. There can be little doubt that the presence of domesticated dromedary at these sites was critical for this material culture integration.

Even with the use of the dromedary, however, the highly demarcated environment of southwestern Arabia continued to create material culture boundaries during these centuries. There is little evidence for the penetration of the Sayhadic material culture assemblage across the Highlands or the Ramlat as-Sabatyn until later in the first millennium BC. In Chapter 6, we outlined the spread of the Sabir culture across the Tihama into the southern coastal zone of Yemen in the second millennium BC. Evidence of a distinctive Highland culture has been found as well, but further research is required to clarify the chronological and spatial limits of Highland Iron Age culture.

Excavations in the Wadi Hadramawt have revealed a distinctive late second to early first millennium BC ceramic assemblage that also clearly differs from the Sayhadic tradition. Raybun in the Wadi Doan is of particular importance in this regard, as is the recently excavated site of Makaynun (Schiettecatte 2007). A burnished ceramic, often with painted decoration in bands near the rim, is the most characteristic aspect of this 'ancient Wadi Hadramawt culture' and has been dated from the thirteen to the eighth century BC (Sedov 1996). Sedov has suggested that the origins of some of these new pottery traditions can be found in Palestine or northwestern Arabia. While there are indeed some generic parallels to those regions, the desire to seek allochthonous origins for emerging south Arabian culture must be weighed against the overwhelming evidence for the importance of indigenous processes. In the Wadi Hadramawt, the development of irrigation systems was as critical as it was elsewhere in southwestern Arabia at this time. As Schiettecatte has demonstrated (2007), springs that had supported earlier settlements such as Shi'b Munaydir in the Hadramawt dried up by the middle of the second millennium BC. Settlements like Raybun, Makaynun and al-Safil emerged as the ability to trap and divert water on the lower reaches of the wadi floor developed. These new settlements were strategically located to tap the episodic flow of as many wadi systems as possible. Detailed archaeological and geomorphological research at Makaynun, located at the junction of four tributaries of the Wadi Masila in the Hadramawt, has indicated that during the early first millennium BC these irrigation systems developed rapidly. By the seventh century BC, Makaynun 'became the center, the meeting point, for the agricultural communities that had developed in parallel in the lower part of the surrounding tributary valleys. Each community had built up a cultivated area and an irrigation network which, when linked together, formed the agricultural territory on which the emergence of a center such as Makaynun was based, together with the prosperity of its political and religious elite…. The emergence of a regional center seems in that case to originate in a very local process founded in a territory defined by the watersheds of tributary valleys' (Mouton et al. 2011: 163).

In summary, by the beginning of the first millennium BC, well-developed regional cultural facies, each relying on irrigation, had developed throughout the highly demarcated environment of southwestern Arabia. Contact between these regions was increasingly facilitated by the use of the domesticated dromedary. Considerable wealth was generated in each of these regions, but by the late eighth century BC, one polity centred in the Wadi Dhanna had grown to such an extent that it began to incorporate the others. Why this occurred at this location and at this time is still not entirely clear. Theories that emphasize the importance of trade with the Fertile Crescent overestimate the wealth that this generated during these early phases of the incense trade. Ultimately, it must have been the agricultural potential of the Wadi Dhanna and the rich benefits that resulted from controlling and harnessing its floodwaters after millennia of experimentation. As Breton has commented: 'The supremacy of Saba was due in large part to a superior level of agricultural prosperity. The sheer size of the Marib oasis and its exploitation through intensive farming gave the region a clear advantage over its neighbors in terms of resources.' This was particularly important in the late second and early first millennium BC, when, as we have already described, there is compelling evidence for a decline in the summer monsoon rainfall (Lückge et al. 2001). Agricultural prosperity was in itself, however, not enough, and Breton concludes that '[t]his advantage was optimized by the highly organized collective known as Saba. Tribal cohesiveness was perhaps the single greatest reason for Sabaean dominance over its neighbors' (Breton 2000: 40).

The resultant political configuration, the Sabaean Federation, differed significantly from other Near Eastern states during this period (cf. Knauf 1989). We have already discussed the term 'mukarrib' and how it reflected the importance of consultation as a part of political authority. In later textual sources the social structure over which the mukarrib 'ruled' is well known. The basic social unit was the *bayt*, or 'house', which according to Korotayev (1994) can be defined as a 'clan community' that is bound by kinship even if internally structured by gender and social relations. These much later textual sources are likely to carry some distant echo of the social structures that were translated through the massive changes taking place in the late second and early first millennia BC. As McCorriston has noted: 'We can be reasonably certain that the fundamental metaphors and motifs of social constitution in Arabian states reflect and manipulate shared habitus. The basic social roles and relationships in ancient Southern Arabian states, then, are transpositions of preexisting ethnic, territorial tribal social relations' (McCorriston 2011: 69). One might see in the structure of the Sabaean Federation, therefore, an echo of the tribal structure and assabiya that had been mediated through adaptation and social formation since the Neolithic.

NORTHWESTERN ARABIA

Thus far we have focused on the changes brought about by agricultural intensification and the introduction of domesticated dromedary in the southern half
of Arabia. A rich but less explored archaeological record is known from the
northern areas of Arabia during the same period. Beginning in the second half
of the second millennium BC, the various oases of northern Arabia experience
a rapid transformation in settlement density and economy (Figure 8.21). In
discussing these, it is convenient to move from oasis to oasis, but it is important
not to lose sight of the general picture of settlement intensification that characterizes this region as a whole.

Tayma was already discussed in reference to its considerable Bronze Age
occupation. During Occupation Phase IV, which dates from 1200 to 900 BC
(Eichmann et al. 2006a: 169–170), the settlement grows substantially. A massive
public building is constructed in the northwestern part of the Qraya zone of
the site. Stone-constructed and measuring 12 by 9 meters, it was surrounded

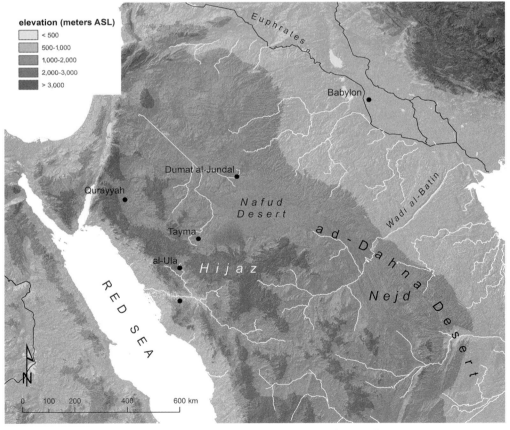

Figure 8.21. Location of main late second/early first millennium BC sites in
northern Arabia.

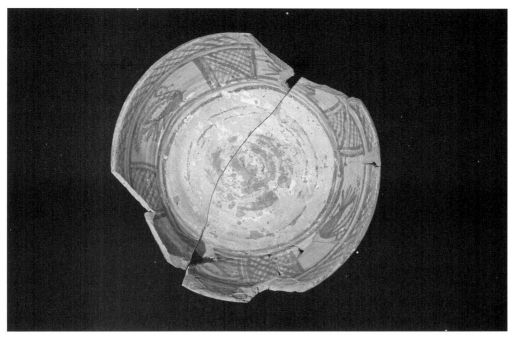

Figure 8.22. Tayma, Area O, painted pottery bowl (diam. c. 28 cm) with representations of birds (late second to early first millennium BC), Qurayyah Ware. DAI Orient-Abteilung. Photo: M. Cusin.

by what appears to be a colonnade or row of pilasters. Numerous small drinking vessels, as well as inlaid bone and wood, faïence, ivory and glazed objects, have been found in this building. The building has few parallels in Arabia, the Near East or the eastern Mediterranean. Nevertheless, it seems clear that it had some public function, and the consumption of liquids and possibly banqueting were an important component of activities (Hausleiter 2010). Few other remains of this period have been excavated at Tayma – only one small annex attached to the defensive wall in Area A can be dated to Occupation Phase IV on the basis of the associated ceramics.

Occupation Phase IV ceramics from Area O consist of wheel- or lathe-turned pottery. Most common forms include large open bowls, but small wheel-made chalices are also known. They are decorated with a white slip and painted with polychrome (red, black, brown) decoration. Stylized birds are painted on the interior face of the vessels, indicating some similarity with Qurayyah Ware (Figure 8.22). However, there are significant differences in the style and technology of Qurayyah Ware, such that each should be considered a regional specialism (Hashim 2007).

Although no single area of Tayma has so far provided a complete sequence through the Iron Age, it is apparent on the basis of ^{14}C dates that occupation continues at Tayma from the ninth century BC into Occupation Phase III,

Figure 8.23. Tayma, Area S/Tal'a, painted pottery beaker and small bowl ('Sana'iye' pottery) from a child's grave (early to middle first millennium BC). DAI Orient-Abteilung. Photo: M. Cusin.

which dates approximately from 900 to 550 BC. This continuity in occupation is attested in the funerary complexes at Tal'a and Sana'iye (Abu Duruk 1990). These consist of large stone tombs constructed in a single complex and used for multiple burials. The graves and their associated finds are overridingly local in origin. Building remains of this phase are, however, scarce, and the only possible building that might date to it is located in Area F. The distinctive painted pottery from this area dates to the first half of the first millennium BC (see al-Ghazzi 2000; Hashim 2007) and was labelled 'Tayma Painted Ware' by Edens and Bawden (1989) (Figure 8.23). According to Hashim (2007) citing al-Ghazzi (1990), this pottery is also found at a number of other sites in northern and eastern Saudi Arabia, as far east as Dhahran.

During Occupation Phase III, Tayma begins to feature in Neo-Assyrian records. In one of his summary inscriptions, Tiglath-Pileser III describes his subjugation of Shamsi, queen of the Arabs, and notes how the people of Tayma brought tribute (Byrne 2003: 12). At about the same time, Tayma is mentioned in the inscriptions of the governor of Suhu on the middle Euphrates, which are discussed in more detail later. In the reign of Sennacherib in the early seventh century BC, the people of Tayma are also noted as bringing gifts to the 'desert gate' of Nineveh (Potts 1991c: 11). The possibility that a god of Tayma is mentioned in inscriptions at Kuntillet Ajrud in the northern Sinai has also been noted, although this reading is not accepted by all (Dalley 2013: 183). A fragment of a sandstone relief currently in the Louvre does provide, however, important information on the occupation of Tayma at this time. The relief contains depictions of a date palm, grapevine, offering table and vessels. An extensive review of contemporary iconography led Potts to conclude that the relief was the product of a provincial artist operating within the Assyrian realm (Potts 1991c: 18). Specific parallels to Tell Halaf suggested to him that the 'artist would have been more at home in the north Arabian/Syrian region than he would have been on the banks of the Tigris' (Potts 1991c: 18). But it is the chronology of the stele that is of such importance for understanding Tayma: if Potts's attribution is accepted then Tayma had already begun to develop a distinctive artistic tradition in the first half of the first millennium BC (Potts 1991c: 19).

The oasis of Qurayyah is most important because of its association with so-called Midianite ceramics, which Parr prefers to label 'Qurayyah Painted Ware' or simply 'Qurayyah Ware' (1988). Our knowledge of the ancient settlement is, however, very limited because of the nature of research conducted at the site. A kiln, which may be linked to the production of Qurayyah Ware, has been noted in the literature (Ingraham et al. 1981: 73; Parr et al. 1970: 240). Furthermore, Parr has pointed out that 'there are strong reasons for believing that other archaeological features reported at Qurayyah, especially the fortification walls and an extensive irrigation and field system, date to the same period as the surface sherds' (Parr 1996: 214). These strong reasons have never been outlined, but it appears increasingly likely given the archaeological discoveries at Tayma that Qurayyah may have indeed experienced settlement growth during the second half of the second millennium BC. At the same time, it should be noted that the Midianite pottery used to date Qurayyah has recently been the subject of reanalysis, raising the possibility that it dates only to the very end of the second and early first millennium BC (Tebes 2007).

While best known as the centre for the Lihyanite tribes from the sixth century BC onwards, there is tantalizing evidence that the oasis of al-Ula (ancient Dedan) was already an important economic centre at the turn of the second millennium BC. According to the most recent excavations conducted by a Saudi team (al-Said 2010), the ancient settlement, which measured approximately 300 by 200 meters, was occupied from the second millennium BC onwards. The importance of agriculture in the growth of al-Ula in the early first millennium BC is tentatively indicated by al-Nasif's (1980, 1981) hydrological and archaeological survey. On the basis of local histories and pre-Islamic topographic sources, he argued that falaj of some antiquity are known in the oasis of al-Ula (al-Nasif 1980: 158). In addition, Wissmann and Müller interpreted a series of short Dedanitic inscriptions found at al-Ula as describing a falaj system (cf. Scagliarini 2002: 574). Scagliarini very cautiously accepts this reading but notes that other possible readings also exist. She dismisses a possible pre-Achaemenid dating of the inscriptions and the falaj on the basis of the assumption, now proved incorrect, that falaj were introduced into Arabia by the Achaemenids in the fifth century BC. As we saw in the preceding chapter, falaj technology already existed in the early first millennium BC in southeastern Arabia, and it cannot be ruled out, given the possibility of trans-Arabian movement brought about by the domestication of the dromedary, that the technology was introduced into northwestern Arabia at this time. In any case, much more research must be conducted before we fully understand al-Ula prior to its rise to prominence in the sixth century BC. For the moment, it is tempting to see a settlement trajectory similar to Tayma: settlement growth and expansion in the second millennium BC based on irrigation agriculture, and economic expansion in the first millennium BC based on dromedary-borne trade, leading to increasing attention from Mesopotamian powers.

The oasis of Dumat al-Jandal (ancient Adummatu) also began to assume some regional importance during the first half of the first millennium BC. It is mentioned in an inscription of the Assyrian king Sennacherib in the early seventh century as a place to which Telhunu, queen of the Arabs, fled after their defeat at the hands of the Assyrian army (Eph'al 1982: 41). It continues to feature in Assyrian inscriptions in subsequent centuries. From southern Mesopotamia, contact with Dumat al-Jandal is indicated by the presence of the personal name Adumma in a letter excavated at Nippur (Cole 1996: 15). Recent archaeological excavations conducted by a joint Saudi-Italian-French team have as yet uncovered no remains that date to this period (Loreto 2012; see also al-Dayel and al-Shadukhi 1986). It is hoped that continued excavations at this site will illuminate the occupation of this oasis at what was undoubtedly an important period in its development.

Just as in southwestern Arabia, a key feature of the development of these north Arabian oases was the use of the writing. Although a number of terms have been used to describe the language and scripts employed by the inhabitants of north Arabian oases, the general term 'Oasis North Arabian' captures the varied languages which existed at al-Ula, Tayma and Dumat al-Jandal. The vast majority of short inscriptions in this language date to well after the limits of this book. However, as Macdonald (2000: 43) has noted and as discussed in more detail in the next chapter, a reference to a language that may be read as

'Taymanitic' in an inscription of a palace official from Carchemish in Syria suggests that the language may already have existed, and been recognized as important, in the eighth century BC. The occurrence of Oasis North Arabian on seals in Mesopotamia (Sass 1991) supports this chronology. If that is the case, the use of the language correlates with the growth of settlement throughout northern Arabia and increasing engagement with neighbours.

Much more research remains to be done on the early history of north Arabian oases. Substantial settlements like Dumat al-Jandal were clearly important enough to come to the attention of Assyrian kings, and it is to be hoped that a new program of archaeological research at that site will fill out the details of its early history. Nevertheless, the archaeological data as they currently exist indicate expansion of settlement in northern Arabia from the second half of the second millennium BC until the Neo-Babylonian period. This stands in contrast to the long-held views of some scholars, such as Parr (1993), that Egyptian imperial rulers during the nineteenth and twentieth dynasties created towns and settled nomadic people in order to control the caravan trade from southern Arabia. According to Parr, when the power of the twentieth dynasty declined, this area was abandoned, and as a result the local population reverted to its 'natural' nomadic lifestyle. He argues that with the renewed interest in the Hijaz under the Neo-Babylonian and Achaemenid kings, particularly Nabonidus, urbanism once again emerged. The new data from northern Arabia, especially Tayma, fundamentally challenges this reconstruction of settlement history. The inhabitants of Tayma were constructing large fortification systems and living within them by at least 2000 BC, or 700–800 years before Egyptian intervention in this area. The stimulus for sedentarization cannot, therefore, be sought in external factors but must rather be looked for in the processes of environmental adaptation that we have seen elsewhere in Arabia. The development of irrigation technologies, particularly towards the end of the second and beginning of the first millennium BC, when both of the weather systems that brought rainfall to Arabia changed, had the potential to fundamentally alter the human occupation of northern Arabia. While it is difficult to draw comparisons to the modern economy of the region given the use of industrial technologies for irrigation, it is clear from early Islamic sources that the Hijaz had immense agricultural potential with traditional agricultural methods. In the seventh century AD the region produced wheat, barley, sorghum and alfalfa (Heck 2003: 564), and as previously noted, the substantial aquifer near Tayma provided the basis for various forms of irrigation in the very recent past (Hamann et al. 2008). The possibility that these technologies permitted settlement growth in zones outside the main oases of northern Arabia remains to be investigated. In this regard, however, it should be noted that according to Hashim (2007) remains dating to this same period have also been reported from Zubaidah near the Wadi ar-Rimmah in central Arabia, and Tayma-type pottery has been found at many sites in northern and eastern

Saudi Arabia. An important Iron Age site (204–137) was also noted in the Wadi Tharbah, 35 kilometers northwest of Madain Salih during the comprehensive survey (Gilmore et al. 1982: 17). Further research at these sites is critical for our understanding of settlement growth during the Late Bronze and Iron Ages.

CONCLUSION: PAN-ARABIAN SETTLEMENT INTENSIFICATION OF THE LATE SECOND MILLENNIUM BC

The simultaneous settlement intensification that occurs in southeastern, southwestern and northern Arabia suggests a systemic ecological adaptation to the climatic shifts that affected the Peninsula as a whole during the late second and early first millennia BC. In each of these regions, this adaptation built upon centuries of experimentation and innovation. In the Arabian southwest, this included the use of dams and terraces from the third millennium BC onwards, culminating in the monumental irrigation works at Marib. In southeastern Arabia, falaj technology stood at the end of a long line of technologies that utilized groundwater from wells and springs and transported it to agricultural fields. In northwestern Arabia, our evidence is slight but the substantial aquifers that characterize this region must have provided the basis for new irrigation technologies that fed expanding oasis polities at Tayma, al-Ula, Qurayyah and, possibly, Dumat al-Jandal. The resultant expansion of settlement coincided with the newly acquired ability to move goods across the landscape. In southeastern Arabia this resulted in greater economic integration between the various ecological niches that characterize the landscape. In southwestern Arabia, transport and movement permitted the emergence of the Sayhadic Iron Age that foreshadowed the Sabaean Federation.

In none of these cases, however, was the new political and economic configuration of society comparable to that which existed elsewhere in the Near East. The social cohesion that had formed in the previous millennia, although undoubtedly challenged by new potential forms of wealth, was reinforced through ritual and pilgrimage or transformed into new political roles such as that of the 'mukarrib' in southwestern Arabia. Simultaneously, the domesticated dromedary permitted these newly emerging centres to engage with the rest of the Near East in ways that fundamentally differed from those in previous millennia. It is to these events that we turn in the next chapter.

CHAPTER 9

EXPANSION AND ENGAGEMENT:
ARABIA AND THE ANCIENT
NEAR EAST

INTRODUCTION

Arabia's inhabitants traded and engaged with adjacent peoples in Mesopotamia, Africa and South Asia from the Neolithic onwards. This activity, such as the obsidian trade between the Tihama and northeastern Africa and the importation of Ubaid ceramics into eastern Arabia, was episodic. At other times, intensive economic engagement lasted a few centuries and had profound effects upon social and economic organization, such as on Bahrain in the early second millennium BC. In most cases, this trade was conducted via maritime trade routes across the Red Sea, Arabian Gulf or Arabian Sea. The states and polities in adjacent regions extracted considerable wealth from this trade, as is most clearly seen in the movement of copper from southeastern Arabia in the late third and early second millennia BC. The rulers of these adjacent regions also derived considerable domestic political authority by claiming control over this largely maritime exchange system.

In this penultimate chapter, I argue that just as the domestication of the dromedary shifted internal economic dynamics within Arabia, it also profoundly affected Arabia's relationship with its neighbours. Although the importance of dromedaries has been long recognized by scholars, I argue that those who have addressed this issue have approached it from only one side of the trade equation. I argue that for the first time in Arabia's prehistory, the domestication of the dromedary permitted the inhabitants of Arabia to control both the *method* of transport and the *location* in which exchange took place. In turn, this led to a fundamental shift in the 'polarity' of inter-regional exchange and geopolitical interaction throughout the entire Near East (Figure 9.1).

ARABIAN OVERLAND TRADE TO THE LEVANT

From the late second millennium BC onwards, the inhabitants of Arabia interacted with the emerging empires and secondary states of the Near East at a level

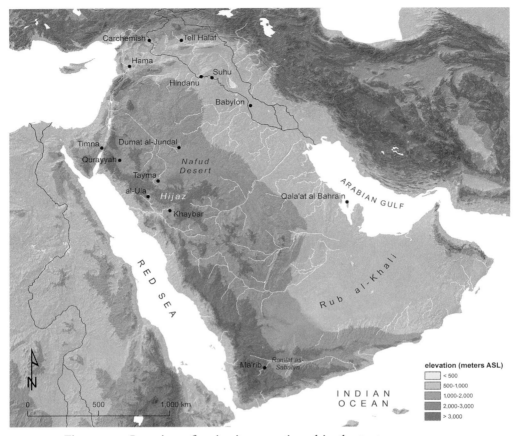

Figure 9.1. Location of main sites mentioned in the text.

that was unparalleled in previous millennia. This was to continue through the first millennium BC into the late pre-Islamic period and then culminate in the emergence and spread of Islam in the seventh century AD. It is widely recognized that the domestication of the dromedary, which was available as a means of transport by the ninth century BC, was critical to this phenomenon.

Examining this sustained economic interaction provides an entry point into Arabian archaeology for many scholars whose main focus otherwise is the Iron Age Levant or Assyria (e.g., Artzy 1994; Bienkowski and van der Steen 2001; Finkelstein 1984, 1988; Finkelstein and Perevolotsky 1990; Wapnish 1981). According to these scholars, dromedary caravan trade erupts when a unique configuration of factors coalesces in the twelfth century BC. These include the cessation of maritime trade in the eastern Mediterranean, the decline of New Kingdom Egypt and the reconfiguration of new political systems in the southern Levant (e.g., Artzy 1994). Characteristic of this approach is an absence of any detailed examination of the economic and social configuration of *Arabian* society (beyond simplified models of nomadism), and thus the dromedary

caravan is reduced to a deus ex machina that can be used to explain economic and political processes in the southern Levant (e.g., Finkelstein 1988)
or Assyrian imperial policies (Wapnish 1981). I refer to the assumptions that
underpin this approach and the epistemological framework in which this
research is conducted as the 'overland Arabian trade model'. According to its
adherents, overland trade became a commodity that was controlled by the sedentary polities of the southern Levant and was exploited for their economic
and political benefit from the twelfth century BC onwards.

The actual archaeological evidence in support of this model is decidedly
weak. In Chapter 7, I suggested that dromedary transport did not occur before
the very beginning of the first millennium BC and that dromedary remains are
especially rare in the southern Levant until some centuries later. Nevertheless,
a persistent interpretation that aromatics were transported from southwestern
Arabia into the southern Levant at the end of the second millennium BC continues to contour much research. So-called Midianite pottery has also played
a key role in this model, as it is considered an important proxy for the last
stage of this trade between northwestern Arabia and the areas north of Aqaba
from c. 1300 BC onwards. This pottery has received its most extensive treatment by Rothenberg in his excavations at Timna (Rothenberg and Glass 1983)
and by Parr in his surveys in the Hijaz (Parr et al. 1970). Both scholars argue
that Midianite pottery is an identifiable type that is characterized by distinct
forms and, in particular, highly decorative painted patterns. The pottery is also
called 'Qurayyah Ware' on the basis of its abundance at that site in northwestern Arabia (Ingraham et al. 1981; Parr 1988), although it has also been noted at
Wadi Sharmah and Wadi Aynuna, in the al-Bad area and at Tayyib al-Ism in the
northern Hijaz (Ingraham et al. 1981: 74). In the Arabian overland trade model,
Midianite pottery serves a dual function. Firstly, it is taken as symptomatic of the
existence of a group of nomadic traders and raiders who feature, albeit negatively,
in the biblical tradition. This is most clearly articulated in Rothenberg's excavations at the copper mining and processing site of Timna, where it is argued that
the concentration of Midianite pottery in certain areas of the camp indicates
the physical presence of Midianites who had been coerced to work by their
Egyptian overlords (Rothenberg 1972; Rothenberg and Glass 1983). Secondly,
Midianite pottery is seen as evidence of trade in itself (e.g., Bienkowski and van
der Steen 2001: 26; Singer-Avitz 1999: 48–52) on the basis of the assumption
that Midianite pottery comes from northwestern Arabia. When it is discovered in association with other ceramics, it thus highlights the interconnected-
ness of northwestern Arabia and the southern Levant during the late second
millennium BC. In the discussion of pottery from a single house at Khirbet
el-Meshash in the northern Negev, Fritz, for example, concludes that the discovery of Midianite pottery alongside northern coastal ceramics 'demonstrates
extensive contact with the Philistines on the coastal plains, the Phoenicians in
the northern coast, and also groups in the Arabian desert' (Fritz 1981: 68).

Midianite pottery is neither evidence for the presence of Midianites nor evidence for trade between Arabia and the southern Levant. To some extent, it is not necessary to detail why Midianite pottery should not be associated with Midianites per se. That attaching ethnicity to ceramics is methodologically fraught is well established in archaeological scholarship. In addition, the chronology of Midianite pottery seems sufficiently elongated so as to more likely represent a lengthy stylistic tradition than any single group of nomads. Although it was initially dated on the basis of Egyptian imported material at Timna to the thirteenth and twelfth centuries BC (Rothenberg and Glass 1983), its chronology has been since extended considerably. Bienkowski and van der Steen note that it has been found at Barqa el-Hetiye in contexts ^{14}C-dated to the ninth century BC and in seventh- to sixth-century contexts at Tawilan in Jordan (Bienkowski and van der Steen 2001: note 2), while recent excavations at Timna have adjusted the chronology of the relevant parts of that site to the very end of the second (Tebes 2007), if not the early first millennium BC (Ben-Yosef et al. 2012).

Equally problematic is the provenance of Midianite pottery. The large quantities of it noted by Parr at Qurayyah have certainly played an important role in discussions, but the scientific evidence presented by Rothenberg and Glass (1983) is most commonly cited in support of a Hijazi origin. In that paper, they presented a petrographic analysis of limited amounts of Midianite pottery from Timna and Qurayyah and very limited quantities from other sites in Israel, such as Tell Masos. The stylistic similarity (decoration, form, technology) of the ceramics is noted as evidence of a single source throughout their discussion. Thin-section analysis indicated similarities in the addition of both shales and quartz to the fabric, indicating to the authors a single production centre in northwestern Arabia. The certainty of Rothenberg and Glass's conclusions is at odds with the inherent difficulties of ascribing provenance on the basis of mineralogy. For the study to carry weight, it would have to have been demonstrated that the inclusions found within Midianite pottery are not found in other common ceramics of that time frame – this was not attempted in the research. Furthermore, as described in a rarely cited paper (Gunneweg et al. 1991), geochemical work cast doubt on the accepted origins of Midianite pottery. Instrumental neutron activation analysis of Edomite pottery from the southern Levant and Midianite pottery from camps at Timna indicated that ten of the fourteen sherds of Midianite pottery were geochemically consistent with locally produced Negebite and Edomite wares of the Negev (Gunneweg et al. 1991: 249–250).

The questionable attribution of Midianite pottery combined with the lack of large-scale evidence for domesticated dromedary in the southern Levant (Chapter 7) throws doubt on the existence of extensive overland trade between Arabia and the southern Levant in the late second and early first millennia BC. In part, the willingness of scholars to persist with the Arabian overland trade model derives from the systemic biased view of ancient Arabia and its inhabitants that we discussed in the opening chapter. In this model, the inhabitants of ancient Arabia are cast as static players with little or no agency or control of their economy. Trade is reduced to a simple economic phenomenon in which rare and luxurious commodities from Arabia are imported into the Levant and serve to legitimize new political and social order in emerging states such as ancient Israel. In essence, therefore, while the biblical narrative of the visit of the Queen of Sheba to the court of King Solomon is now widely regarded as anachronistic in its composition (e.g., Singer-Avitz 1999), this story continues to contour archaeological interpretations of trade in the very early first millennium BC. Furthermore, later Roman period trade is often used as an uncritical analogue in justifying the existence of these earlier forms of trade. As noted by Edens and Bawden, this has affected our broader understanding of Iron Age trade mechanics: 'The central importance of South Arabian incense to both the Biblical and the classical accounts of the western Arabian trade on the one hand and the stasis, broadly speaking, of geographical constraints on the trade on the other have together induced an essentially non-historical attitude which projects conditions reflected in classical writings backward across the previous thousand years. This attitude is indefensible in the face of the historically known variability of social conditions in northern Arabia, of the multiplicity of possible communication and transportation routes, and of the existence of raw materials and commodities in addition to southern aromatics known to have entered the western Arabian trade' (Edens and Bawden 1989: 85).

Finally, the proponents of the Arabian overland trade model have rarely addressed the question of how the inhabitants of Arabia benefited from trading with, and allowing their trade to be controlled by, the early Iron Age polities of the southern Levant. It is an unstated assumption that the dromedary caravans that travelled from the Hijaz to the southern Levant received much-needed supplies or foodstuffs to alleviate their presumably dire subsistence. This was clearly not the case: the inhabitants of northwestern Arabia were able to engage with large oasis towns, such as Tayma, that were as well resourced with agricultural supplies as any town in the southern Levant. Early Iron Age southern Levantine polities did not have access to precious metals or luxury goods that might have been desired by the inhabitants of Arabia. Copper was obviously available in the Negev and played an important role in the economy, but this was also directly available from southern Arabia, where, as we have seen in Chapters 4 and 5, indigenous copper industries developed in both the southwest and southeast.

In short, there was no need for dromedary caravans coming from northern Arabia to engage with the southern Levant. Furthermore, to insist that dromedary caravans could easily be controlled by polities that would, in turn, derive considerable economic benefit from them is to misunderstand the fundamental transformative role that dromedary domestication played in the ability of

Arabia's inhabitants to engage with their neighbours. For the first time, the inhabitants of Arabia controlled the means of trade. Knowledge of where this 'ship of the desert' could rest and travel was idiosyncratic to those populations who had lived in the desert and adapted to desert life for millennia before. The inhabitants of settlements throughout the Fertile Crescent lacked this knowledge and were largely unable to access the desert trade routes employed by dromedaries. That the inhabitants of Arabia skilfully exploited this advantage to their own economic benefit is abundantly clear from the first detailed evidence we have of engagement between Arabia and the Fertile Crescent in the ninth century BC.

THE EMERGENCE OF OVERLAND TRADE

Textual references and archaeological evidence from the northern arc of the Fertile Crescent and the Assyrian heartland indicate that it is with this region, rather than the southern Levant, that the inhabitants of Arabia engaged from the ninth century BC onwards. The region around the middle Euphrates and the Khabur headwaters provides some of the most convincing evidence for such trade, and I have already discussed the orthostat reliefs from Tell Halaf and Carchemish as some of the earliest unequivocal representations of a human riding a dromedary.

A more explicit indication that dromedary caravans from Arabia were active in this area is found in an eighth-century BC text from Carchemish. This Hieroglyphic Luwian text concerns Yariris of Carchemish, who boasts of the number of languages and scripts he can understand. One of these can be identified as Taymanitic, the Oasis North Arabian language centred on Tayma (Macdonald 2000: 40–42). Yariris also notes his ability with the languages of Tyre and Assyria, and if we accept, as seems likely, that Yariris's linguistic abilities are a proxy for economic interaction, Carchemish is placed at a central node, with Phoenicia the main maritime merchant power to the west, Assyria the main political power to the east and Tayma the main power to the south (Livingstone 1999: 233–236; Macdonald 2000: 42).

The existence of actual trade and dromedary caravans linking southwestern Arabia, northern Arabia and the arc of the Fertile Crescent is indicated by both archaeological data and a series of documents discovered at Sur Jur'eh on the middle Euphrates. The archaeological evidence is slim but impressive: a Period III grave at Hama in Syria contained an ivory beaker with a standing ibex on the rim. Avanzini has shown that this piece fits perfectly within the corpus of archaic artworks from Yemen (Avanzini 2005; Potts 2003; Scigliuzzo 2003). The significance of this object extends well beyond its discovery far from its place of manufacture. The ivory cup is delicate and cannot have been an easily transported commodity. It is more likely a special gift destined for an individual at Hama who was of some importance, either politically or economically, possibly a merchant. The fact that this person chose to have the vessel placed in his or her grave indicates that it was as cherished as it was unique.

The Sur Jur'eh texts date to the eighth century BC and concern the local governor of Suhu, called Ninurta-kudurri-usur, and his father, Samas-resa-usur. The text mentions a dromedary caravan coming from southwestern Arabia via Tayma and entering the town of Hindanu on the western border of Suhu. The texts inform us that Ninurta-kudurri-usur waited with his cavalry and chariots at Azlaiianu and ambushed the caravan when it left Hindanu. When they attacked the caravan they seized 200 dromedaries, iron, precious stones and 'all kinds of goods' (Byrne 2003: 15; Cavigneaux and Ismail 1990; Liverani 1992). This account is extremely important because it not only provides the earliest secure textual evidence for an overland trade route that linked southwestern Arabia, northwestern Arabia and the Fertile Crescent, but also highlights important aspects of how this trade was conducted. Hindanu, the town in which the dromedary caravan stopped, lay on the very edge of Assyrian control for most of the first half of the first millennium BC. It had been brought into submission by Shamshi-Adad V (823–811 BC) after it had revolted against Ashurnasirpal II and Shalmaneser III (Postgate 1975: 415–416). Postgate believes that it enjoyed an almost independent status by 648 BC and that it surrendered to Nabopolassar in 616 BC. Although technically in the territory of Suhu, which itself had revolted against Assyria between 774 and 745 BC, Hindanu thus exercised its autonomy from any regional control for most of the eighth century BC, if not longer.

To the dromedary-borne traders of Arabia such cities would have been ideal trading places: enthusiastically on the edge of imperial and even regional control, they were safe havens in which informal trade could take place unencumbered by the threat of taxes and seizure of goods or dromedaries by state and imperial powers. Mastery of the dromedary was key. A dromedary caravan could sit near the edge of town and wait for an appropriate moment to enter and conduct business. Unless regional authorities had dromedaries, they would be unable to intercept the caravan whilst it was travelling in the desert. In the case of Hindanu, it appears that the caravan had just left and was likely in an environment in which horses, and perhaps donkeys, could manoeuvre. It is surely not a coincidence, therefore, that Ninurta-kudurri-usur records that the seizure of dromedaries was just as important as the seizure of the goods being transported by the caravan.

It is likely that this sort of furtive trade had already commenced in the ninth century BC when the Assyrian kings Tukulti-Ninurta II and Shalmaneser III received aromatics (including myrrh) as tribute from Suhu, Hindanu and other areas of the middle Euphrates (Edens and Bawden 1989: 91). These most likely came from southwestern Arabia via Tayma. The same caravans that carried these aromatics were also, it seems, engaged in intra-regional trade within the middle Euphrates region. A letter from Marduk-apla-usur, the ruler of Suhu, to

Rudamu/Urtamis, king of Hama, speaks of common trading interests between the two cities and seeks reassurance that third parties will not engage in such trade (Parpola 1990). Trade between these cities would typically have occurred down the Euphrates where it was easily controlled by Assyria or one of the polities controlling Syria at this time. An overland dromedary route would have been more direct, crossing just north of the city of Palmyra, which was in later times to assume such economic importance. Travel along this overland route could be conducted without the threat of taxation and control from state or imperial powers.

The routes taken by these dromedary caravans coming from Arabia to the Fertile Crescent has exercised numerous scholars. To Na'aman (2007) and Byrne (2003) the goods seized by Ninurta-kudurri-usur indicate that the caravan travelled from Tayma to the Negev and then from the southern Levant to Syria before crossing eastwards to the Middle Euphrates. They argue that the blue-purple textiles, iron and semi-precious stones amongst the trafficked goods could not have come from Arabia. Na'aman (2007: 112) also argues that the presence at Beersheba of a cylinder seal from Suhu, dedicated by Rimut-ilani, son of Adad-idri, to Apla-Adad, confirms this western trade route.

The dyed textiles in Ninurta-kudurri-usur's booty are indeed unlikely to have come from Arabia. But their existence in the dromedary caravan does not necessitate the view that the caravan stopped at or interacted with the southern Levant. Not only is evidence for interaction between Arabia and the southern Levant decidedly weak, but the cities of Tell Halaf, Hama and Carchemish with which dromedary caravans were engaged had strong connections with Phoenicia, the likely origin of dyed textiles. Traders might have exchanged aromatics for these textiles (Macdonald 1997: 335–337) with the intention of bringing them back to Arabia, where, although some cotton cultivation was possible (Bouchaud et al. 2011), they were not commonly available. Alternatively, these traders might have acquired them with a view to transporting them to areas farther east and southeast through the Syrian desert. Such 'middleman' trade would have been lucrative for sellers and buyers alike, since the only other mode of transport down the Euphrates river was easily controlled and taxed, particularly around the island of Ana. This freedom of movement made dromedary caravans a threat to the role that economic control played in imperial strategy – a reality no more clearly seen than by the fact that Ninurta-kudurri-usur boasts so proudly of his capture of just one, relatively small caravan. Finally, the iron transported by the dromedary caravan captured by Ninurta-kudurri-usur was likely acquired in the region of Hama or Carchemish. Since the production of iron is limited throughout the first millennium in southwestern and southeastern Arabia, it is entirely possible that these caravans provided a major conduit for the transport of this precious metal into the Peninsula.

So what trade route did the Suhu dromedary caravan take from Yemen to the Fertile Crescent? It likely proceeded from Yemen to Najran and then Yathrib (Medina). At Yathrib, the caravan could have headed northeast via Hail to southern Babylonia, but it chose to go to Tayma, probably via Khaybar, Tafi and Fadak (Macdonald 1997: 334). The fact that Nabonidus visited Khaybar and Fadak in his conquest of the Hijaz some centuries later suggests that this route had some economic importance. From Tayma, the caravan would have proceeded to Dumat al-Jandal, likely skirting the western edge of the Nafud desert or maybe attempting to cross it directly. A major bifurcation point existed at Dumat al-Jandal. Either the caravan could travel to the northwest via the Wadi Sirhan and onto the King's Highway, or it could head straight north, possibly via Badana, which Macdonald argues might be identified with the Badana noted as bringing tribute to Tiglath-Piliser III following his defeat of Shamsi, queen of the Arabs (Macdonald 1997: 335). The former route, via the King's Highway, seems unlikely for a number of reasons. It is difficult to envisage what economic benefit could have been gained by dromedary caravans engaging with the small polities that existed along this route, and there are few resources in that area that were in such critical demand in Arabia. Such a route would only have increased exposure to raiding and taxation. In contrast, a route straight through the north Arabian desert would have brought them quickly into contact with polities that were engaged with both Assyria and the Mediterranean coast. Following this route was quicker than going through the southern Levant: from Tayma to Dumat al-Jandal and then to Hindanu is about 800 kilometers. If we accept Avanzini's (1997) suggestion of a daily dromedary caravan distance of 40 kilometers, a dromedary caravan would have completed a return trip to Tayma in less than six weeks. In contrast, the distance from Tayma to the Negev and then up the King's Highways to Damascus and the east to Hindanu is approximately 1,300 kilometers, that is, a return trip of nine weeks.

I would argue, therefore, that dromedary caravans chose to avoid too much interaction with settlements and rather kept their trading interactions brief and informal. The goods they acquired, such as iron and decorated garments, were unavailable within the Peninsula and likely played an important role in the expanding economy of the early first millennium BC throughout the Peninsula. Once within Arabia, these precious materials were funnelled through a variety of internal routes. The Sur Jur'eh texts indicate that one of the most important routes linking the Ramlat as-Sabatyn with the Hijaz was already in operation by the eighth century BC. The discovery of southeast Arabian softstone vessels at Ur suggests that north to south routes linked eastern Arabia with the area of southern Mesopotamia in a similar fashion (Reade and Searight 2001). West to east routes were also in operation: the route from Yathrib to southern Mesopotamia has already been noted. The discovery of a three-letter South Arabian inscription from Muweilah (Müller 1999) and incense burners from numerous sites suggests the possibility of trade links between southwestern and southeastern Arabia. These intra-Arabian routes lay above those along which local materials, like food, were transported on an intra-regional level. Although there are more blanks than areas of evidence on these trade routes, it seems fairly certain, then, that by the eighth century BC a dendritic overland system existed within Arabia which permitted the movement of goods across the Peninsula as a whole and the funnelling of exotic goods that were furtively acquired from the edges of the Fertile Crescent and elsewhere.

IMPERIAL RESPONSES TO IRON AGE ARABIA

The Suhu and Hama texts indicate that the traditional methods of state and imperial control were challenged by this new mode of overland trade. That these states saw such trade as a threat is no more clearly indicated than by the response of the largest geopolitical entity of the day, Assyria, and then its successor Babylon. Epigraphic and archaeological evidence suggests that from the middle of the ninth century BC until the middle of the sixth century BC, Neo-Assyrian and Neo-Babylonian intervention in Arabia can be categorized into four main stages, each building upon lessons learned in the preceding one and each increasingly attempting to (re)assert control over trade in this region. Although the latter stages of this intervention extend beyond the chronological framework of this book, they are included here because the shifting and ultimately unsuccessful tactics employed by these Near Eastern states highlight a key theme of this book: the inhabitants of Arabia were organized in a fashion that was fundamentally different from that in Near Eastern states, and interaction between the two was contoured by this asymmetry in economic and political organization.

CONTACT AND INTERVENTION

As we have noted, interaction between Mesopotamia and Arabia stretches back to the Neolithic period. This interaction forms the beginning of a contact episode with various protagonists that plays out over several millennia and has different consequences in each region. However, as I have already discussed, the mechanics of contact had shifted by the ninth century BC and new forms of engagement followed. The first large-scale military contact between a Mesopotamian monarch and the inhabitants of Arabia occurs during the reign of Shalmaneser III (858–824 BC). In his attempts to move west across the Euphrates towards the Syrian coast, he encountered a coalition of forces from the various city-states in the Levant led by the kings of Damascus and Hama (see Byrne 2003). In the Kurkh inscription, we read that Shalmaneser III defeated '1200 chariots, 1200 cavalry, and 20000 troops of Damascus; 700 chariots, 700 cavalry and 10000 troops of Irhuelni, the Hamathite; 2000 chariots and 10000 troops of Ahab, the Israelite; 500 troops of Byblos; 1000 troops of Egypt; 10 chariots of the land Irqanatu; 200 troops of Maniuba'al of the city of Arward'; 200 troops of the Usanatu; 30 chariots and [ ]000 troops of Adon-ba'al of the land of Shiannu; 1000 camels of Gindibu' of Arabi' (Van De Mieroop 2007: 227).

In considering this text, it is important to note that the term 'Arabi' as employed by the Assyrians included a range of peoples, some of whom occupied regions that lay outside the boundaries of this book. Indeed, the term 'Arab' as employed by ancient (as well as some modern) writers refers to different groups of people at different times exploiting different subsistence strategies. However, regardless of where Gindibu lived, he represented a new form of adaptation to the desert that was reliant upon dromedary control. It is very likely that Gindibu's inclusion in the text and, in particular, the mention of his dromedaries are a testament to his 'entrepreneurial prestige' (Byrne 2003: 12), and one could well imagine that he was a tribal leader who was responsible for organizing the furtive trading caravans that we have discussed. Furthermore, in his exhaustive study, Eph'al (1974, 1982) has noted that prior to the late-eighth-century BC epigraphic evidence for the penetration of people with Arab names was very limited in Mesopotamia. Therefore, this battle was the beginning of an engagement between Assyria and these 'Arab' tribes. Even if control over this trade was not the intention of this initial engagement, it is clear from subsequent events that Assyria's attention was increasingly geared towards attempting to control not only north Arabian trade routes but also the means by which these operated, that is, dromedaries.

ENGAGEMENT, EXPLOITATION AND WAR

The next stage of Assyrian intervention in northern Arabia is represented by Tiglath-Pileser III's account of a battle in which we read: 'As for Shamsi, the queen of the Arabs at Mount Saqurri I defeated 9400 of people, 1000 people, 30000 camels, 20000 cattle.... 5000 pouches of all kinds of spices.... thrones of her gods, arms and staffs of her goddess, and her property I seized. And she, in order to save her life, to a desert, an arid place, like an onager, made off' (Tadmor 1994: 141.4: 19–24). The text then continues to describe the bringing of tribute by Shamsi to the Assyrian court, which includes female dromedaries (presumably for breeding) and, as previously noted, the bringing of tribute from the people of Tayma. Already this attempt to systemize Assyrian intervention in northern Arabia, through the bringing of tribute, stands in contrast to the one-off military encounter of Shalmaneser III with Gindibu the Arab. Tiglath-Pileser III's north Arabian intervention is cast in terms of controlling the goods associated with trade, for example, 'pouches of all kinds of spices', but also, significantly, the mechanisms of trade: female dromedaries. This point can hardly be overemphasized: by having a stock of dromedaries the Assyrians could engage in trade itself and also create an effective military force that could conduct forays into the desert.

The attempts by Tiglath-Pileser III to integrate northern Arabia into the yoke of Assur were, however, unsuccessful. In his inscriptions at Dur Shurrakin (Khorsabad) his eventual successor, Sargon II, claims to have defeated tribes in northern Arabia and settled them in Samaria in the southern Levant. There is also a hint that Sargon understood that Arabian society was organized in a different fashion than society in Assyria and the surrounding areas of the Fertile Crescent. The inhabitants of northern Arabia are described as those 'who live far away in the desert and who know neither overseers nor officials' (Hoyland 2001: 8). In this inscription we read a recognition that the forces that had shaped Arabian society for millennia had resulted in a social structure that differed from that in the Fertile Crescent. This recognition on the part of the Assyrian king probably explains his appointment of local tribesmen as 'trade guardians' along the most significant trade routes. It is doubtful that such a title ever existed in north Arabian society, since trade routes were likely guarded and their use facilitated by tribal agreement and convention. This 'invention of tradition' (Hobsbawm and Ranger 1983) by the Assyrians was aimed at controlling the trade routes according to their own conceptualization of power and authority.

In addition, Sargon attempted to establish diplomatic relations with the emerging Sabaean Federation of southwestern Arabia. Around 715 BC, he receives tribute from an It'amra who must be identified with the Sabaean ruler Yita amar Watar bin Yakrubmalik, whose monumental inscription was recently excavated at Sirwah in Yemen (Nebes 2007). This strategy of engaging with the Sabaean Federation reflects exactly the form of state-to-state diplomacy that Assyria practised with other politically hierarchical polities throughout the Near East. If, however, this tactic was aimed at controlling overland trade, then it was based on a false premise: the emerging Sabaean Federation did not control the movements of the north Arabian tribes, nor did it necessarily control the movement of goods from southwestern to northwestern Arabia.

Ultimately, therefore, Sargon's attempts to control north Arabian trade were unsuccessful. Moreover, during the eighth century BC increasing evidence for the presence of people with north Arabian names is found in southern Mesopotamia (Eph'al 1982). Such contact is likely the result of trade and contact between the two regions, but this interaction also brought with it political intrigue: in 703 BC Sennacherib attacks Babylon in retribution and captures the brother of the queen of the Arabs, who had joined the Babylonian revolt. He also destroyed some nearby walled towns, some of which had north Arabian names (Eph'al 1982).

SHOCK AND AWE

As noted by Beaulieu (1989: 180–185), the campaigns of Assurbanipal, nearly a century later, reflect different strategies for dealing with Arabia than those pursued by Sargon. The actions of this Assyrian king represent the culmination of Assyria's frustrated attempts to control overland trade routes. His account of the attack upon Uaite, a king of northern Arabia, is worth quoting in full:

> Uaite son of Haza'el, king of Arabia, threw off the yoke of my rule.… He incited the people of Arabia to revolt, raiding again and again the kings of the west, the subject vassals entrusted to me. Against him I sent my troops who were within his territory, and they defeated him. The people of Arabia, inasmuch as they had rebelled with Uaite, they overcame by force of arms. The steppe-houses, the tents in which they lived, they kindled and set on fire. People of both sexes, donkeys, camels, cattle and flocks without number I brought to Assur. The area of my whole lands, in its entirety, they filled as far as it stretches. Camels like flocks I divided up and shared out to the people of Assur. Within my land one bought a camel at the market gate for a few pence. The alewife obtained for one portion, the brewer for one jar, the gardener for a bundle of cress, camels and people. The rest of Arabia, which had fled before my weapons, Erra the strong [god of plague and famine] overcame them. Famine broke out among them so that they ate the flesh of their children to keep from starving.… The people in Arabia asked one other: 'Why has such a disaster befalled Arabia?' It is because we did not abide by the great oaths of Assur, we sinned against the kindness of Assurbanipal, the king who pleased the heart of Enlil. To Uaite came misfortune so that he fled alone into the land of Nabayoth. (Hoyland 2001: 62)

Setting aside for a moment the hyperbole typical of Assurbanipal, it is clear that Assurbanipal's campaign aimed to destroy the economic livelihood of Uaite's dominion in northern Arabia. The intent of doing so would be to render the region unproductive in terms of long-distance trade. Underlying the text is the theme that diplomacy in this case had failed and devastation was the outcome of the failed co-opting of Uaite as a vassal king.

It is precisely at this time that Assyria begins to re-engage with the Arabian Gulf. Although there is no question that Assyria viewed the Arabian Gulf as distinct and separate from northern Arabia, both Sargon II and Sennacherib boast of how their campaigns resulted in tribute from the king of Dilmun, who took fright at the terrible defeats inflicted upon the enemies of Assyria (Potts 1991a). Although these machinations are quite separate from those that were occurring in northern Arabia at this time, there is little doubt that a desire to ensure control over trade routes and the supply of precious materials motivated this re-engagement with the Gulf. Although outside the purview of the volume, this time frame witnesses a considerable expansion of Bahrain: a palace had been (re)constructed on Qala'at al-Bahrain (Period IV), and a king is mentioned in Assyrian sources (Højlund and Andersen 1994). Assyrian ceramics and cylinder seals have been noted in the graves at al-Hajjar (Rice 1988) and on the east Arabian mainland at the salt mine site (Lombard 1985). Oppenheim (1954: 17) emphasized that Sennacherib's claim of bronze tools brought by the workmen of Dilmun to help demolish Babylon was evidence of a desire to reopen traditional trade routes that had lain dormant for nearly a thousand years. Just a few decades later, the Assyrian king Assurbanipal claims to have received tribute not only from Dilmun but also from a political leader dwelling in the city of Izki, a toponym that is almost certain to be identified with Izke in the Sultanate of Oman, a town whose falaj system is considered to be one of the oldest in Oman and in which Iron Age II remains have been discovered (Potts 1991a). There is no evidence in southeastern Arabia, however, that copper production was geared towards export in the manner that had occurred in the late third millennium BC, and as already noted, the material culture and economy of the region at this time were overridingly local in character.

COLONIZATION

Following the demise of the Assyrian Empire in 612 BC, control of northern Arabia and the Arabian Gulf was still beyond the grasp of Mesopotamian powers. Their attempts at coercion, military devastation and resurrection of the previous maritime systems of exchange had failed. It would be left to Assyria's imperial successors, the Neo-Babylonians and in particular their king, Nabonidus, to engage the ultimate mechanism to control northern Arabia: colonization.

In Near Eastern scholarship, the establishment of Nabonidus's court at the distant centre of Tayma highlights the quixotic and almost impulsive nature of Near Eastern regimes. Ever since Dougherty (1930) established beyond doubt that the Tayma of the Babylonian Chronicle was one and the same as the city in northern Arabia, scholars have been puzzled by Nabonidus's motives. Initially following Dougherty's identification, some scholars entertained the notion that Nabonidus was motivated by the desire to economically control the north Arabian trade. The publication of Nabonidus's inscriptions from Harran changed this view considerably (Gadd 1958). To Gadd, Nabonidus's ten-year excursion to a place as 'obscure and remote' (Gadd 1958: 79) as Tayma had been hitherto inexplicable. The Harran inscriptions finally provided a reason for Nabonidus's behavior: his desire to worship the moon god Sin and his increasing conflict with the priesthood in Babylon led him to seek refuge in an area that was distant from Babylon's control but that also had a predilection for solar and lunar worship. Trade or commercial interest 'played no part at all' in Nabonidus's decision, according to Gadd (1958: 89).

An approach that takes into account the longue durée of Mesopotamian relations with northern Arabia and a closer reading of the texts suggests that Gadd's interpretation cannot be supported. Several aspects of Nabonidus's

actions suggest a systematic and well-thought-out policy that built upon earlier failures of the Assyrian kings to co-opt, threaten and militarily control
north Arabian trade. The route of Nabonidus's expedition to Tayma has been
much debated. If the rock relief from Sela in Jordan depicts Nabonidus, then it
appears he travelled a circuitous route through the Fertile Crescent and down
through Jordan (Byrne 2003: 19; Dalley and Goguel 1997: 143). Regardless of
how he travelled there, when he arrived in the Hijaz, Nabonidus did not simply take over the city of Tayma. According to the Harran inscriptions, he first
travelled to Dedan (modern al-Ula) and then to Padakku, which Gad identifies
with Fadak; Hibra, which is probably modern Khaybar; Iadihu, which Gadd
suggests is modern Yadi, a district between Fadak and Khaybar where in the
recent past there are wells of Banfu Fazara and Banfi Murra; and to Yathrib,
modern Medina. This route involved occupying or at the least receiving alle-
giance from the most important north Arabian oasis towns. Dedan we have
noted in reference to Assyrian campaigns against the region. While we know
little of it in this period, it is likely that it too was an important oasis that was
later to play such an important role in trade. Fadak is insufficiently explored
to warrant comment on its antiquity, but its commercial importance can be
assumed if it can be identified with the Futuk noted by al-Hamdani as an
important trade station on the way to Riyadh (de Maigret 1998: 222).

Very recent epigraphic discoveries provide important information on
the composition and tactics of Nabonidus's expedition. Inscriptions in both
Taymanitic and Aramaic that mention both Nabonidus by name (NBND) and
a king of Babylon have been found in the region around Tayma (Hayajneh
2001). They also mention individuals such as MRDN, who came 'as a servant
of Nabonidus in the attack/invasion [or: "in the emigration"; "for inspection/
supervision"] behind the desert' (Hayajneh 2001: 82). It is significant that several of the personal names mentioned in these inscriptions are not known in
north Arabian onamastica. To Hayajneh, this indicates that they 'were ethni-
cally Arabs who have non-Arabic names and were resident in the Babylonian
Kingdom' (Hayajneh 2001: 90). Nabonidus's employment of first-generation
(Arab) Babylonians hints at his motivation in moving to the Hijaz. Those who
left their names on rocks around Tayma were knowledgeable about the languages and cultures of both Babylonian and north Arabian culture; they would
have played a critical role in negotiating between the colonisers and the local
merchants and traders. In other words, instead of sitting in Tayma and worship-
ping the moon god, as some argue was Nabonidus's purpose in travelling to
Arabia, it is probable that he was there to engage with the north Arabian community with a view to controlling the trade that remained so elusive to previous Mesopotamian rulers who had engaged in the area.

The current excavations at Tayma will undoubtedly throw light on what
happened during these ten years. However, Nabonidus's decision to leave
Tayma with no known agreement or alliance with its ruler suggests that the

economic motivation for moving there had not come to fruition. By the time he returned to Babylon, the politics of that city and the geopolitics of the region as a whole had shifted and a new power was emerging in the east. Soon, the last vestiges of a Mesopotamian-based empire were to give way to an Iranian power whose control stretched from the Indus to Libya and which engaged afresh with Arabia. The decision of these new Achaemenid rulers to form alliances with the inhabitants of northern Arabia rather than attempt to conquer them is perhaps the clearest indication of the failure of previous attempts to control this region.

CONCLUSIONS

The utilization of the domesticated dromedary for overland trade fundamentally altered the economic landscape of Arabia. Several different scales of economic integration were now possible, from the local level, in which staple products moved across deserts, to a regional level and inter-regional level, in which the tribes and polities of Arabia engaged with their neighbours in the Fertile Crescent. Further research is needed to more fully explore how these trade systems operated, particularly in the centuries before writing becomes increasingly common in western Arabia. It is clear, however, on the basis of existing archaeological evidence and Assyrian texts that, by the eighth century BC, the inhabitants of Arabia were exploiting the unique ability made possible by the dromedary to acquire and transport a range of materials that were unavailable within Arabia. At the same time, the movement of goods itself became a commodity, as the inhabitants of northern Arabia were able to bypass and undermine traditional methods of state control over trade routes. This revolution was not an opportunistic development focused upon transporting incense to the Levant, as some have argued, but rather evolved from a unique configuration of the environmental and social forces that shaped Arabian society over millennia.

CHAPTER 10

ADAPTATION AND SOCIAL FORMATION IN ANCIENT ARABIA

The inhabitants of ancient Arabia forged a unique relationship with their environment from the Neolithic onwards. They adapted their subsistence practices to a climate regime that underwent several major changes, each of which affected the variegated ecology of the Arabian Peninsula in different ways. The first and most important change occurred during the Arabian Neolithic. During the millennia in which the Indian Ocean monsoon brought summer rainfall to most of the Peninsula, a landscape of opportunity arose that was perfectly suited to a hybridity of sheep, goat and cattle nomadic pastoralism, the hunting of abundant wild animals and the exploitation of the rich marine biota of the coast. The evidence from Jebel Buhais indicates that this subsistence strategy brought dietary stability and comparatively healthy lifeways. The inhabitants of Arabia engaged with each other across most of the Peninsula, which provided an opportunity for ideological alignment that relied upon and reinforced social mechanisms that ensured access to resources. This in turn resulted in the rejection of the social disharmony that increasingly characterized adjacent societies throughout the Near East. It is this social ideology, based upon cohesion rather than division, which I believe is a precursor to the concept of assabiya that Ibn Khaldun wrote of in his *muqaddimah* of 1377 and which he considered characteristic of desert societies. Ibn Khaldun considered that assabiya was lost through a cyclical development of urban growth and eventual decay, and while we have not deployed this component of his ideas in this book, it is clear that also within the context of ancient Arabia this social ideology was never static and was subsequently negotiated and, for the most part, maintained during times of inter-regional contact and exchange with those cultures that lay across the Arabian Gulf and Red Sea. It continued to distinguish prehistoric Arabian society from its neighbours in the ancient Near East. Since it is manifested in the archaeological record by a lack of monumental buildings, such as palaces and temples, it paradoxically resulted in a marginalization of the study of ancient Arabia throughout the nineteenth and early twentieth centuries and the creation of a dominant narrative that viewed the drive towards state-level complexity as the defining feature of change in the ancient Near East.

The cessation of the Holocene Moist Phase brought new challenges to the stable existence that had characterized the Arabian Neolithic. As pasturelands decreased in the inland plains and desert lakes dried, new subsistence strategies were employed that relied upon intensification of existing niche resources. This included intensive exploitation of the coast, an increased reliance on hunting in the desert interiors and the first experimentation with agriculture. Recent evidence from Shi'b Kheshiya and Akab reveals mechanisms that were geared towards the maintenance of shared access to resources through feasting and ritual commensality during these challenging millennia. In the following centuries, stone-constructed tombs placed on high visible landmarks were increasingly relied upon to demarcate, and perhaps mediate, a developing sense of place amongst mobile groups.

By the middle of the third millennium BC, the Umm an-Nar culture of the Arabian southeast, the Bronze Age cultures in western Arabia and intensified hunting in central Arabia mark the beginning of divergent settlement trajectories throughout the Peninsula. These are characterized by material culture production that remained regionalized for the next two millennia. Engagement with states in Africa, Egypt and the rest of the Near East increased during this period. In southeastern Arabia, this engagement took the form of the requisition of large amounts of copper that fuelled the machinations of the Akkadian Empire and Ur III state. Attempts by these powers to render the social fabric of southeastern Arabia into a recognizable form, possibly to induce an 'invention of tradition' that would further facilitate exploitation, were wholly rejected when such demands led to increasing social tension and the potential fraying of social cohesion. The exception to this pattern was the emergence of a state on Bahrain, ancient Dilmun, which was marked by monumental palaces and temples. In this book, I have suggested that this trajectory owes much to the sustained engagement between this region and the hierarchical states of southern Mesopotamia from the fifth millennium BC onwards. However, even on Bahrain the archaeological record suggests a persistent societal ideology, gleaned from the excavations at Saar, that embodies practices that at the least resist, if not reject, the imported trappings of a materialist hierarchy rendered in monumental constructions and unequal access to resources.

Continual adaptation to a post–Holocene Moist Phase climate characterizes much of Arabia during the subsequent centuries. Experimentation with agriculture occurred in southwestern and southeastern Arabia and, judging from the evidence revealed by ongoing excavations at Tayma, probably in northwestern Arabia as well. The record from each of these areas is still unclear on the extent to which agriculture became the main subsistence strategy during the third and second millennia BC. It is clear, however, that an increased reliance on hunting, especially dromedary hunting, also occurred. As the number of wild dromedaries decreased, the inhabitants of prehistoric Arabia undertook an adaptive strategy that was to fundamentally alter their existence.

The domestication of the dromedary sometime towards the end of the second millennium BC marks the single most important transition in the human occupation of Arabia. First and foremost, it provided a ready source of meat and milk from an ecological niche that had become increasingly ill-suited to pastoralism. Second, it provided the means to move goods and people across the landscape in a manner that had not been possible since the Neolithic. These developments coincided with the perfection of irrigation systems in the southwest and southeast that permitted dense settlement on the edge of the desert and resulted in increased agricultural production across the landscape. The combination of these adaptations resulted in settlement intensification to an extent hitherto unknown in Arabia and rarely matched until the modern era. Approached from this perspective, the rise of the Sabaean Federation in the early first millennium BC, an event that has long been Arabia's entry point into the broader framework of Near Eastern archaeology, should be understood as a culmination of millennia of human–environmental relations rooted in Arabian prehistory.

The incomplete archaeological record from large parts of Arabia makes it difficult to examine subsequent developments in every part of the Peninsula. For the Arabian southwest, we are well informed by inscriptions of the shifting centres of political control from Marib to Ma'in that characterize most of the first millennium BC, but archaeological research which focuses upon the human ecology in this landscape is still in its infancy. For the Arabian north, epigraphic sources and archaeological evidence also paint a picture of strong oasis centres and nomadic groups based upon existing tribal structures, but scientific excavations have only recently commenced and much more has to be done before we can fully understand the development of irrigation systems and the impact of engagement with Mesopotamia and the Levant. For the Arabian southeast, our picture is drawn from extensive archaeological data. In this region, the widespread settlement intensification that characterizes the Iron Age II period does not continue past c. 600 BC for reasons that are not yet understood. What is clear, however, is that in the following centuries a culture emerges throughout much of Arabia that is marked by similarities in language, religion and craft traditions. There can be little doubt that this process owed as much to the use of the dromedary for trade and engagement as it did to the shared social ideologies that had characterized the inhabitants of this region from the Neolithic and which permitted a subsequent ideological alignment.

Viewing these developments through 8,000 years across a land mass that is greater than that of the other countries of the Middle East (Chapter 1) combined with Greece, Italy and Cyprus, leaves little doubt that prehistoric Arabia was a unique society built upon continual and innovative adaptation to its environment. This adaptation resulted in social and economic behaviours that differed considerably from those that prevailed in the rest of the Near East. The similarities in these developments are persistent enough through time and space that we can begin to conceptualize an 'Arabian archaeology'. This book is only the first stage in that process; vast swaths of Arabia remain unexamined, and more detailed work is required even in those areas that have already been the focus of intensive fieldwork since the 1960s. In particular, archaeological fieldwork is desperately needed in western and northern Arabia, where our understanding of the interplay between environmental adaptation and relationships with Egypt and the Levant has for too long been dominated by narratives constructed on the archaeological record outside Arabia.

I wrote in the introduction that I hoped this book would have an emancipatory as well an explanatory function. Ultimately, however, the epistemological frameworks with which we practice our study of the past rarely yield to change from within. It is more likely that geopolitical and economic forces, rather than the desire for a more nuanced understanding of the ancient world, will guide future research. In Chapter 1, I described how the practice and aims of European colonialism in the nineteenth and early twentieth centuries did much to contour and solidify the practice of Near Eastern archaeology. The creation of European mandates in Palestine, Syria and Iraq after World War I was a key moment in this process. Since I started writing this book, vast changes in the political situation of the Middle East have occurred. In just the past year, dictators who for years ruled with oppression have been swept away. The landscape for archaeological research throughout the region has shifted dramatically, and it will be interesting to see where large Western academic projects are able to obtain permission and support for fieldwork in the future.

In any case, I hope that for those readers whose focus remains on the well-studied areas of the ancient Near East, this book will serve as a reminder that the ancient Middle East was a vast region which encompassed a wide variety of social practices and ideologies from the Palaeolithic period onwards.

REFERENCES

al-Abri, A. et al. 2012: Pleistocene-Holocene boundary in southern Arabia from the perspective of human mtDNA variation, *American Journal of Physical Anthropology* 149: 291–298.

Abu Duruk, H. I. 1989: A preliminary report on the industrial site excavation at Tayma, first season, *Atlal* 12: 7–9.

Abu Duruk, H. I. 1990: Preliminary report on industrial site excavation at Tayma second season, *Atlal* 13: 9–20.

Abu Duruk, H. I. 1996: Preliminary report on the industrial site excavation at Tayma. Third season, *Atlal* 14: 11–24.

Abu el-Haj, N. 2001: *Facts on the ground, archaeological practice and territorial self-fashioning in Israeli society*, Chicago.

Abu Laban, A. 2010: New studies in Dilmun stamp seals from Failaka, Kuwait, Paper presented at the Seminar for Arabian Studies, London, July.

Achrati, A. 2006: The story of the Arabian rock art: A 'Thamudic' informant, *Rock Art Research* 23: 153–164.

Algaze, G. 2001: Initial social complexity in southwestern Asia, *Current Anthropology* 42: 199–233.

Algaze, G. 2005: The Sumerian takeoff, *Structure and Dynamics* 1 online.

Almazroui, M. 2011: Calibration of TRMM rainfall climatology over Saudi Arabia during 1998–2009, *Atmospheric Research* 99: 400–414.

Alt, K. W. et al. 1995: Familienanalyse in kupferzeitlichen Kollektivgräbern aus Umm an-Nar, Abu Dhabi, *Arabian Archaeology and Epigraphy* 6: 65–80.

Amiet, P. 1986: *L'Âge des échanges inter-Iraniens*, Paris.

Anati, E. 1968a: *Rock art in central Arabia*, vol. 1: *The oval headed people of Arabia*, Louvain.

Anati, E. 1968b: *Rock art in central Arabia*, vol. 2: *Fat-tailed sheep in Arabia*, Louvain.

Anati, E. 1972: *Rock art in central Arabia*, vol. 3: *Corpus of the rock engravings*, Pts. I, II, Louvain.

Anati, E. 1974: *Rock art in central Arabia*, vol. 4: *Corpus of the rock engravings*, Pt III, Louvain.

Andersen, H. H. 1986: The Barbar temple: Stratigraphy, architecture and interpretation. In: H. A. al Khalifa and M. Rice (Eds.), *Bahrain through the ages: The archaeology*, London: 165–177.

Andersen, H. H. and Højlund, F. 2003: *The Barbar Temples*, vols. 1 and 2, Aarhus.

André-Salvini, B. and Lombard, P. 1997: La découverte épigraphique de 1995 à Qal'at al-Bahrein: Un jalon pour la chronologie de la phase Dilmoun Moyen dans le Golfe arabe, *Proceedings of the Seminar for Arabian Studies* 27: 165–170.

al-Ansary, A. R. 2002: *al-Bid: History and archaeology by al-Ansary*, Riyadh.

Archi, A. 1987: gín DILMUN "sicle pesé, standard", *Reallexikon der Assyriologie* 81: 186–187.

Armitage, S. J. et al. 2011: The southern route, "Out of Africa": Evidence for an early expansion of modern humans into Arabia, *Science* 331: 453–456.

Artzy, M. 1994: Incense, camels and collared rim jars: Desert trade routes and maritime outlets in the second millennium, *Oxford Journal of Archaeology* 13: 121–47.

Arz, H. W. et al. 2003: Mediterranean moisture source for an early-Holocene humid period in the northern Red Sea, *Science* 300: 118–121.

Ascalone, E. and Peyronel, L. 1999: Typological and quantitative approach to the ancient weight systems: Susa, Persian Gulf and Indus Valley from the end of the III mill. to the beginning of the II mill. BC, *Altorientalische Forschungen* 26: 352–76.

Asouti, E. and Fuller, D. 2011: From foraging to farming in the southern Levant: The development of Epipalaeolithic and Pre-pottery Neolithic plant management strategies, *Vegetation History and Archaeobotany* 21: 149–162.

Avanzini, A. 1996: Saba and the beginning of epigraphic documentation in the Jawf, *Arabian Archaeology and Epigraphy* 7: 63–68.

Avanzini, A. 1997: The frankincense road from Najran to Ma'an: A hypothetical itinerary. In: A. Avanzini (Ed.), *Profumi d'Arabia*, Pisa: 315–331.

Avanzini, A. 2005: Some thoughts on ibex on plinths in early South Arabian art, *Arabian Archaeology and Epigraphy* 16: 144–153.

Avanzini, A. 2008: *Khor Rori Report: A port in Arabia between Rome and the Indian Ocean*, Rome.

Avanzini, A. 2010: Two Inscriptions from Nashshan: New data on the history of the town. In: S. Graziani (Ed.), *Studi sul Vicino Oriente antico dedicati alla memoria di Luigi Cagni*, Rome: 1231–1247.

Avanzini, A. and Phillips, C. 2010: An outline of recent discoveries at Salut in the Sultanate of Oman. In: A. Avanzini (Ed.), *Eastern Arabia in the first millennium BC*, Rome: 93–108.

Baadsgaard, A. et al. 2011: Human sacrifice and intentional corpse preservation in the Royal Cemetery of Ur, *Antiquity* 85: 27–42.

Badre, L. 1991: Le sondage stratigraphique de Shabwa, 1976–1981, *Syria* 68: 229–314.

Bahrani, B. 1998: Conjuring Mesopotamia: Imaginative geography and a world past. In: L. Meskell (Ed.), *Archaeology under fire: Nationalism, politics and heritage in the eastern Mediterranean and Middle East*, London: 159–174.

al-Bahrany, A. M. 2002: Chemical composition and fatty acid analysis of Saudi Hassawi rice *Oryza sativa* L., *Pakistan Journal of Biological Sciences* 5: 212–214.

Bailey, G. et al. 2007: Coastal prehistory in the southern Red Sea basin, underwater archaeology and the Farasan Islands, *Proceedings of the Seminar for Arabian Studies* 37: 1–16.

Bakiewicz, W. et al. 1982: Hydrogeology of the Umm Er Radhuma aquifer, Saudi Arabia with reference to fossil gradients, *Quarterly Journal of Engineering Geology and Hydrogeology* 15: 105–126.

Bandy, M. 2004: Trade and social power in the southern Titicaca Basin Formative, *Archeological Papers of the American Anthropological Association* 14: 91–111.

Barca, D. et al. 2012: The provenance of obsidian artifacts from the Wadi ath-Thayyilah 3 Neolithic site (eastern Yemen plateau) by LA-ICP-MS, *Archaeometry* 54: 603–622.

Barker, D. 2002: Wadi Suq and Iron Age ceramics from Sharm, Fujairah (U.A.E.), *Arabian Archaeology and Epigraphy* 13: 1–94.

Barker, E. B. B. 1876: *Syria and Egypt under the last five Sultans of Turkey: Being experiences, during fifty years of Mr. Consul-General Barker*, London.

Barker, G. 2006: *The agricultural revolution in prehistory: Why did foragers become farmers?* Oxford.

Bar-Oz, G. et al. 2011: Role of mass-kill hunting strategies in the extirpation of Persian gazelle (*Gazella subgutturosa*) in the northern Levant, *Proceedings of the National Academy of Science* 108: 7345–7350.

Barraud, C. 1990: A turtle turned on the sand in the Kei islands: Society's shares and values, *Bijdragen tot de Taal-, Land- en Volkenkunde* 146: 35–55.

Barta, P. et al. 2008: Al-Khidr on Failaka island: Preliminary results of the fieldworks at a Dilmun culture settlement in Kuwait, *TÜBA-AR, Turkish Academy of Sciences Journal of Archaeology* 11: 121–134.

Bauer, A. 1998: Cities of the sea: Maritime trade and the origin of Philistine settlement in the Early Bronze Age southern Levant, *Oxford Journal of Archaeology* 17: 149–168.

Bauer, J. et al. 1998: *Mesopotamien. Späturuk-Zeit und Frühdynastische Zeit*, Freiburg.

Baustian, K. M. 2010: *Health status of infants and children from the Bronze Age tomb at Tell Abraq, United Arab Emirates*, Unpublished master's thesis, University of Nevada.

Bawden, G. 1992: Continuity and disruption in the ancient Hejaz: An assessment of current archaeological strategies, *Arabian Archaeology and Epigraphy* 3: 1–22.

Beaulieu, P.-A. 1989: *The reign of Nabonidus, King of Babylon, 556–539 B.C.*, New Haven, CT.

Becker, C. 2008: Die Tierknochenfunde aus Tall Šēh Hamad/Dūr Katlimmu. Eine zoo-geographisch-haustierkundliche Studie. In: H. Kühne (Ed.), *Umwelt und Subsistenz der Assyrischen Stadt Dūr-Katlimmu am unteren Habur*, Wiesbaden: 61–132.

Bednarik, R. G. and Khan, M. 2005: Scientific studies of Saudi Arabian rock art, *Rock Art Research* 22: 49–81.

Beech, M. and Elders, J. 1999: An 'Ubaid-related settlement on Dalma Island, United Arab Emirates, *Bulletin of the Society for Arabian Studies* 4: 17–21.

Beech, M. and Shepherd, E. 2001: Archaeobotanical evidence for early date consumption on Dalma Island, United Arab Emirates, *Antiquity* 75: 83–89.

Beech, M. et al. 2005: New evidence for the Neolithic settlement of Marawah island, Abu Dhabi, United Arab Emirates, *Proceedings of the Seminar for Arabian Studies* 35: 37–56.

Beech, M. et al. 2009: Prehistoric camels in south-eastern Arabia: The discovery of a new site in Abu Dhabi's Western Region, United Arab Emirates, *Proceedings of the Seminar for Arabian Studies* 39: 17–30.

Beeston, A. F. L. 1972: Kingship in ancient South Arabia, *Journal of the Economic and Social History of the Orient* 15: 256–258.

Begemann, F. et al. 2010: Lead isotope and chemical signature of copper from Oman and its occurrence in Mesopotamia and sites on the Arabian Gulf coast, *Arabian Archaeology and Epigraphy* 21: 135–169.

Beja-Pereira, A. et al. 2004: African origins of the domestic donkey, *Science* 304: 1781.

Bellini, C. et al. 2011: Interpretative scenarios emerging from plant micro- and macrore-mains in the Iron Age site of Salut, Sultanate of Oman, *Journal of Archaeological Science* 38: 2775–2789.

Ben-Yosef, E. et al. 2012: A new chronological framework for Iron Age copper production at Timna (Israel), *Bulletin of the American Schools of Oriental Research* 367: 31–71.

Benoist, A. 2007: An Iron Age II snake cult in the Oman peninsula: Evidence from Bithnah (Emirate of Fujairah), *Arabian Archaeology and Epigraphy* 18: 34–54.

Benoist, A. 2010: Authority and religion in south-east Arabia during the Iron Age. In: A. Avanzini (Ed.), *Eastern Arabia in the first millennium BC*, Rome: 109–141.

Benoist, A. and Ali Hassan, S. 2010: An inventory of the objects in a collective burial at Dadna. In: L. Weeks (Ed.), *Death and burial in Arabia and beyond: Multidisciplinary perspectives*, London: 85–100.

Benoist, A. and Méry, S. 2012: Initial results from the programme of petrographic analysis of Iron Age pottery from the United Arab Emirates, *Arabian Archaeology and Epigraphy* 23: 70–91.

Bent, J.T. 1890: The Bahrein Islands, in the Persian Gulf, *Proceedings of the Royal Geographical Society and Monthly Record of Geography* 12: 1–19.

Bergstrom, R. E. and Eten, R. E. 1965: Natural recharge and localization of fresh ground water in Kuwait, *Journal of Hydrology* 2: 213–231.

Bernbeck, R. 2009: Class conflict in ancient Mesopotamia: Between knowledge of history and historicising knowledge, *Anthropology of the Middle East* 4: 33–64.

Betts, A.V. G. 1987: The hunter's perspective: 7th millennium BC rock carvings from eastern Jordan, *World Archaeology* 19: 214–225.

Beyer, D. 1986: Les Sceaux. In: Y. Calvet and J. F. Salles (Eds.), *Failaka: Fouilles françaises, 1984–1985*, Lyon: 89–103.

Bibby, T. G. 1969: *Looking for Dilmun*, New York.

Bibby, T. G. 1973: *Preliminary survey in east Arabia 1968*, Copenhagen.

Bienkowski, P. and Van der Steen, E. 2001: Tribes, trade, and towns: A new framework for the late Iron Age in southern Jordan and the Negev, *Bulletin of the American Schools of Oriental Research* 323: 21–47.

Blackman, M. J. et al. 1989: Production and exchange of ceramics on the Oman peninsula from the perspective of Hili, *Journal of Field Archaeology* 16: 61–77.

Blakely, J.A. 1985: The stratigraphic probe at Hajar at-Tamrah. In: J. A. Blakely et al. (Eds.), *The Wadi al-Jubah Archaeological Project*, vol. 2: *Site reconnaissance in North Yemen, 1983*, Washington, DC: 55–145.

Blakely, J. A. 1996: Introduction. In: M. J. Grolier et al. (Eds.), *The Wadi al-Jubah Archaeological Project*, vol. 5: *Environmental research in support of archaeological investigations in the Yemen Arab Republic, 1982–1987*, Washington, DC: 1–5.

Blau, S. 1999: The people at Sharm: An analysis of the archaeological human skeletal remains, *Arabian Archeology and Epigraphy* 10: 190–204.

Blau, S. and Beech, M. 1999: One woman and her dog: An Umm an-Nar example from the United Arab Emirates, *Arabian Archaeology and Epigraphy* 10: 32–42.

Boivin, F. and Fuller, D. 2009: Shell middens, ships and seeds: Exploring coastal subsistence, maritime trade and the dispersal of domesticates in and around the ancient Arabian peninsula, *Journal of World Prehistory* 22: 113–180.

Bökönyi, S. 1991: The earliest occurrence of domestic asses in Italy. In: R. H. Meadow and H.-P. Uerpmann (Eds.), *Equids in the ancient world*, vol. 2, Weisbaden: 178–216.

Bondioli, L. et al. 1998: From the coast to the oasis in prehistoric Arabia: What the skeletal remains tell us about the transition from a foraging to the exchange economy – Evidence from Ra's al-Hamra (Oman) and Hili North (UAE). In: M. Tosi (Ed.), *Proceedings of the XIII Congress, 8–14 September 1996, International Union of Prehistoric and Protohistoric Sciences*, vol. 5, Forli: 229–234.

Borowski, O. 1999: *Every living thing: Daily use of animals in ancient Israel*, Los Angeles.

Boucharlat, R. 1992: Note on an Iron Age hill settlement in the Jebel Buhais. In R. Boucharlat (Ed.), *Archaeological surveys and excavations in the Sharjah emirate, 1990 and 1992: A sixth interim report*, Lyon: 19.

Boucharlat, R. 1997: Excavations at al-Thuqaibah site, al-Madam plain by the Department of Archaeology, Sharjah: A short note on the results, *Sharjah Archaeology* 4: 33–43.

Boucharlat, R. and Lombard, P. 1985: The oasis of al-Ain in the Iron Age – Excavations at Rumeilah, 1981–1983: Survey at Hili 14, *Archaeology in the United Arab Emirates* 4: 44–73.

Bouchaud, C. et al. 2011: Cotton cultivation and textile production in the Arabian peninsula during antiquity: The evidence from Mada'in Salih (Saudi Arabia) and Qal'at al-Bahrain (Bahrain), *Vegetation History and Archaeobotany* 20: 405–417.

Bourdieu, P. 1977: *Outline of a theory of practice*, R. Nice (Trans.), Cambridge.

Braemer, F. et al. 2001: Le Bronze ancien du Ramlat as Sabatayn (Yémen): Deux nécropoles de la première moitié du IIIe millénaire à la bordure du désert Jebel Jidran et Jebel Ruwaiq, *Paléorient* 27: 21–44.

Bray, H. E. and Stokes, S. 2003: Chronologies for Late Quaternary barchan dune reactivation in the southeastern Arabian Peninsula, *Quaternary Science Reviews* 22: 1027–1033.

Bray, H. E. and Stokes, S. 2004: Temporal patterns of arid–humid transitions in the south-eastern Arabian Peninsula based on optical dating, *Geomorphology* 59: 271–280.

Breton, J.-F. 1991: L'épigraphie de l'Arabie avant l'Islam: Intérêt et limites, *Revue du Monde Musulman et de la Méditerranée* 61: 13–24.

Breton, J.-F. 1994: Hajar Yahirr, capital de Awsan? *Raydan* 6: 41–47.

Breton, J.-F 1996: Quelques dates pour l'archeologie sudarabique. In: C. Robin (Ed.), *Arabia Antiqua: Early origins of south Arabian states*, Rome: 87–110.

Breton, J.-F. 2000: *Arabia Felix: From the time of the Queen of Sheba – Eighth century BC to first century A.D.*, Notre Dame, IN.

Bron, F. 2010: Quelques nouvelles inscriptions du Jawf, *Arabian Archaeology and Epigraphy* 21: 41–45.

Brunner, U. 1983: *Die Erforschung der antiken Oase von Marib mit Hilfe geomorphologischer Untersuchungsmethoden. ABADY II*, Mainz am Rhein.

Brunner, U. 1997: Geography and human settlements in ancient southern Arabia, *Arabian Archaeology and Epigraphy* 8: 190–202.

Brunswig, R. H. 1989: Culture, history, environment and economy as seen from an Umm an-Nar settlement: Evidence from test excavations at Bat, Oman, 1977/78, *Journal of Oman Studies* 10: 9–50.

Bulliet, R. W. 2011: *Cotton, climate and camels in early Islamic Iran: A moment in world history*, New York.

Burkholder, G. 1971: Steatite carvings from Saudi Arabia, *Artibus Asiae* 33: 306–322.

Burkholder, G. 1984: *An Arabian collection: Artifacts from the Eastern Province*, Boulder City, NV.

Burns, S. J. et al. 2001: Speleothem evidence from Oman for continental pluvial events during interglacial periods, *Geology* 29: 623–626.

Byrne, R. 2003: Early Assyrian contacts with Arabs and the impact of Levantine vassal tribute, *Bulletin of the American Schools of Oriental Research* 331: 11–25.

Calvet, Y. and Gachet, J. (Eds.) 1990: *Failaka: Fouilles françaises, 1986–1988*, Lyon.

Calvet, Y. and Salles, J.-F. (Eds.) 1986: *Failaka: Fouilles françaises, 1984–1985*, Lyon.

Carruthers, D. 1910: A journey in north-western Arabia, *Geographical Journal* 35: 225–245.

Carter, R. 1997: The Wadi Suq period in south-east Arabia: A reappraisal in the light of excavations at Kalba, UAE, *Proceedings of the Seminar for Arabian Studies* 27: 87–98.

Carter, R. 2001: Saar and its external relations: New evidence for interaction between Bahrain and Gujarat during the early second millennium BC, *Arabian Archaeology and Epigraphy* 12: 183–201.

Carter, R. 2003: Tracing Bronze Age trade in the Arabian Gulf: Evidence for way-stations of the merchants of Dilmun between Bahrain and the Northern Emirates. In: D. T. Potts et al. (Eds.), *Archaeology of the United Arab Emirates: Proceedings of the First International Conference on the Archaeology of the U.A.E.*, London: 123–131.

Carter, R. 2005a: The history and prehistory of pearling in the Persian Gulf, *Journal of the Economic and Social History of the Orient* 48: 139–209.

Carter, R. 2005b: Pottery analysis: Typological analysis. In: R. Killick and J. Moon (Eds.), *The early Dilmun settlement at Saar*, London: 235–277.

Carter, R. 2006: Boat remains and maritime trade in the Persian Gulf during the sixth and fifth millennia BC, *Antiquity* 80: 52–63.

Carter, R. 2010: The social and environmental context of Neolithic seafaring in the Persian Gulf. In: A. Andersen et al. (Eds.), *The global origins and development of seafaring*, Cambridge: 191–202.

Carter, R. and Crawford, H. (Eds.) 2010: *Maritime interactions in the Arabian Neolithic*, Leiden.

Carter, R. et al. 1999: The Kuwait-British archaeological expedition to As-Sabiyah: Report on the first season's work, *Iraq* 61: 43–58.

Caubet, A. 2009: The historical context of the Sumerian discoveries, *Museum International* 61: 74–80.

Cavigneaux, A. and Ismail, B. K. 1990: Die Statthalter von Subu und Mari im 8. Jh. v. Chr. anhand neuer Texte aus den irakischen Grabungen im Staugebiet des Qadissiya-Damms, *Baghdader Mitteilungen* 21: 321–456.

Charbonnier, J. 2008: L'agriculture en Arabie du Sud avant l'Islam, *Chroniques Yéménites* 15: 1–28.

Charpentier, V. 2001: Les industries lithiques de Ra's al-Hadd, *Proceedings of the Seminar for Arabian Studies* 31: 31–45.

Charpentier, V. 2004: Trihedral points: A new facet to the "Arabian Bifacial Tradition", *Proceedings of the Seminar for Arabian Studies* 34: 53–66.

Charpentier, V. 2008: Hunter-gatherers of the "empty quarter of the early Holocene" to the last Neolithic societies: Chronology of the late prehistory of south-eastern Arabia (8000–3100 BC), *Proceedings of the Seminar for Arabian Studies* 38: 93–116.

Charpentier, V. et. al. 2003: La nécropole et les derniers horizons V^e millénaire du site de Gorbat al-Mahar (Suwayh, SWY- 1, Sultanat d'Oman): Premiers résultats, *Proceedings of the Seminar for Arabian Studies* 33: 11–19.

Charpentier, V. et al. 2012: Pearl fishing in the ancient world: 7500 BP, *Arabian Archaeology and Epigraphy* 23: 1–6.

Chaudhary, S. A. 1983: Vegetation of the Great Nafud, *Saudi Arabian Natural History Society* 3: 32–37.

Ciuk, C. and Keall, E. 1996: *Zabid Pottery Project manual, 1995: Pre-Islamic and Islamic ceramics from the Zabid area, North Yemen*, Oxford.

Cleuziou, S. 1979: The second and third season of excavations at Hili 8, *Archaeology in the United Arab Emirates* 2/3: 30–69.

Cleuziou, S. 1981: Oman Peninsula in the early second millennium B.C. In: H. Hartel (Ed.), *South Asian Archaeology, 1979*, Berlin: 279–293.

Cleuziou, S. 1982: Hili and the beginnings of oasis life in Eastern Arabia, *Proceedings of the Seminar for Arabian Studies* 12: 15–22.

Cleuziou, S. 1989a: Excavations at Hili 8: A preliminary report on the 4th to 7th campaigns, *Archaeology in the United Arab Emirates* 5: 61–87.

Cleuziou, S. 1989b: The chronology of protohistoric Oman as seen from Hili. In: P. M. Costa and M. Tosi (Eds.), *Oman Studies*, Rome: 47–78.

Cleuziou, S. 1992: The Oman peninsula and the Indus civilization: A reassessment, *Man and Environment* 17: 93–103.

Cleuziou, S. 1997: Construire et protéger son terroir: Les oasis d'Oman à l'Age du bronze. In: J. Burnouf (Ed.), *La dynamique des paysages protohistoriques, antiques, médiévaux et modernes*, Antibe: 389–412.

Cleuziou, S. 2002: The early Bronze Age of the Oman peninsula: From chronology to the dialectics of tribe and state formation. In S. Cleuziou et al. (Eds.), *Essays on the late prehistory of the Arabian peninsula*, Rome: 191–236.

Cleuziou, S. 2009: Extracting wealth from a land of starvation by creating social complexity: A dialogue between archaeology and climate? *Comptes Rendus Geosciences* 341: 726–738.

Cleuziou, S. and Costantini, L. 1980: Premiers elements sur l'agriculture protohistorique de l'Arabie orientale, *Paléorient* 6: 245–251.

Cleuziou, S. and Tosi, M. 1989: The southeastern frontier of the ancient Near East. In: K. Frifelt and P. Sorensen (Eds.), *South Asian Archaeology 1985*, London: 15–48.

Cleuziou, S. and Tosi, M. 2000: Ra's al-Jinz and the prehistoric coastal cultures of the Ja'alan, *Journal of Oman Studies* 11: 19–74.

Cleuziou, S. and Tosi, M. 2007: *In the shadow of the ancestors: The prehistoric foundations of the early Arabian civilization in Oman*, Muscat.

Clutton-Brock, J. 1992: *Horse power: A history of the horse and the donkey in human societies*, Cambridge, MA.

Cole, S. W. 1996: *The early Neo-Babylonian governor's archive from Nippur. Nippur IV*, Chicago.

Cope, J. M. et al. 2005: Robusticity and osteoarthritis at the trapeziometacarpal joint in a Bronze Age population from Tell Abraq, United Arab Emirates, *American Journal of Physical Anthropology* 126: 391–400.

Coppa, A. et al. 1985: The prehistoric graveyard of Ra's al-Hamra CRH5: A short preliminary report on the 1981–83 excavations, *Journal of Oman Studies* 8: 97–102.

Corboud, P. et al. 1994: *Archaeological survey of Fujairah 3 (1993)*, Geneva.

Córdoba, J. M. 2003: Villages of shepherds in the Iron Age. In D. T. Potts et al. (Eds.), *Proceedings of the First International Conference on the Archaeology of the UAE*, London: 173–180.

Córdoba, J. M. 2010: L'architecture domestique de l'Age du Fer (1300–300 A.C.) dans la péninsule d'Oman. In: A. Avanzini (Ed.), *Eastern Arabia in the first millennium BC*, Rome: 143–158.

Costa, P. M. and Wilkinson, T. J. 1987: *The hinterland of Sohar: Archaeological surveys and excavations within the region of an Omani seafaring city* (= *Journal of Oman Studies* 9), Muscat.

Costantini, L. 1990: Ecology and farming of the protohistoric communities in the central Yemeni highlands. In A. De Maigret (Ed.), *The Bronze Age culture of Hawlan al Tiyal and al-Hada*, Rome: 187–204.

Crassard, R. 2009: Modalities and characteristics of human occupations in Yemen during the Early/Mid-Holocene, *Comptes Rendus Geosciences* 341: 713–725.

Crassard, R. et al. 2006: Manayzah: Early to mid-Holocene occupations in Wâdî Sanâ (Hadramawt, Yemen), *Proceedings of the Seminar for Arabian Studies* 36 : 151–173.

Crassard, R. et al. 2013: Beyond the Levant: First evidence of a Pre-Pottery Neolithic incursion into the Nefud desert, Saudi Arabia, *PloS ONE* 8(7): e68061.

Crawford, H. 1973: Mesopotamia's invisible exports in the third millennium B.C., *World Archaeology* 5:232–241.

Crawford, H. 1998: *Dilmun and its Gulf neighbours*, Cambridge.

Crawford, H. 2001: *Early Dilmun seals from Saar: Art and commerce in Bronze Age Bahrain*, Ludlow.

Crawford, H. 2005: Mesopotamia and the Gulf: The history of a relationship, *Iraq* 67: 41–46.

Crawford, H. et al. 1997: *The Dilmun temple at Saar*, London.

Crombé, P. 2000: A Neolithic site at Bida Al Mitawaa in western Abu Dhabi (U.A.E.), *Arabian Archaeology and Epigraphy* 11: 9–14.

Culcasi, K. 2000: Constructing and naturalizing the Middle East, *Geographical Review* 100: 583–597.

Cuttler, R. et al. 2007: Pastoral nomad communities of the Holocene climatic optimum: Excavation and research at Kharimat Khor al-Manahil and Khor al-Manahil in the Rub al-Khali, Abu Dhabi, *Proceedings of the Seminar for Arabian Studies* 37: 61–78.

Dalley, S. 2013: Gods from north-eastern and north-western Arabia in cuneiform texts from the First Sealand Dynasty, and a cuneiform inscription from Tell en-Nasbeh, c. 1500 BC, *Arabian Archaeology and Epigraphy* 25: 177–185.

Dalley, S., and Goguel, A. 1997: The Sela sculpture: A Neo-Babylonian rock relief in southern Jordan, *Annual of the Department of Antiquities of Jordan* 41: 169–76.

David, H. 1996: Soft stone vessels during the Bronze Age in the Oman Peninsula, *Proceedings of the Seminar for Arabian Studies* 26: 31–46.

David, H. 2002. Softstone vessels from Umm an-Nar tombs at Hili (UAE): A comparison, *Proceedings of the Seminar for Arabian Studies* 32: 175–185.

al-Dayel, K. A. and al-Shadukhi, 1986: Excavation at Dumat al-Jandal, 1405/1985, *Atlal* 10: 64–80.

Deadman, W. M. 2012: Defining the early Bronze Age landscape: A remote sensing-based analysis of Hafit tomb distribution in Wadi Andam, Sultanate of Oman, *Arabian Archaeology and Epigraphy* 23: 26–34.

de Beauclair, R. 2010: Ornamental objects as a source of information on Neolithic burial practices at al-Buhais 18, UAE and neighbouring sites. In: L. Weeks (Ed.), *Death and burial in Arabia and beyond: Multidisciplinary perspectives*, London: 1–10.

de Beauclair, R. et al. 2006: New results on the Neolithic jewellery from al-Buhais 18, UAE, *Proceedings of the Seminar for Arabian Studies* 36: 175–188.

de Cardi, B. 1988: The grave goods from Shimal Tomb 6 in Ras al-Khaimah, U.A.E. In: D. T. Potts (Ed.), *Araby the Blest: Studies in Arabian archaeology*, Copenhagen: 44–71.

de Cardi, B. et al. 1976: Excavations and survey in Oman, 1974–1975, *Journal of Oman Studies* 2: 101–187.

de Cardi, B. et al. 1979: Excavations at Tawi Siliam and Tawi Sa'id in the Sharqiya, 1978, *Journal of Oman Studies* 5: 61–94.

de Cardi, B. et al. 1994: Five thousand years of settlement at Khatt, UAE, *Proceedings of the Seminar for Arabian Studies* 24: 35–95.

de Cardi, B. et al. 1997: Third-millennium and later pottery from Abu Dhabi airport, *Arabian Archaeology and Epigraphy* 8: 161–173.

de Maigret, A. 1984a: A Bronze Age for southern Arabia, *East and West* 34: 75–106.

de Maigret, A. 1984b: Archaeological activities in the Yemen Arab Republic, 1984, *East and West* 34: 423–454.

de Maigret, A. 1985: Archaeological activities in the Yemen Arab Republic, *East and West* 35: 337–395.

de Maigret, A. (Ed.) 1988: *The new Sabaean archaeological complex in the Wādī Yalā (Eastern Hawlān at-Tiyāl, Yemen Arab Republic): A preliminary report*, Rome.

de Maigret, A. 1990: *The Bronze Age culture of Hawlan al Tiyal and al-Hada*, Rome.

de Maigret, A. 1998: The Arabic nomadic people and the cultural interface between the 'Fertile Crescent' and 'Arabia Felix', *Arabian Archaeology and Epigraphy* 10: 220–224.

de Maigret, A. 2002: *Arabia Felix: An exploration of the archaeological history of Yemen*, London.

de Maigret A. 2005: *The Italian archaeological mission: An appraisal of 25 years of research (1980–2004)*, Sanaa.

de Maigret, A. and Robin, C. 1989: Les fouilles italiennes de Yalā (Yémen du Nord): Nouvelles données sur la chronologie de l'Arabie du Sud préislamique, *Académie des Inscriptions & Belles-lettres, Comptes Rendus* 1989: 255–291.

Demarchi, B. et al. 2011: Amino acid racemization dating of marine shells: A mound of possibilities, *Quaternary International* 239: 114–124.

Démare-Lafont, S. 2011: Judicial decision making: Judges and arbitrators. In: K. Radner and E. Robson (Eds.), *The Oxford handbook of cuneiform culture*, Oxford: 335–357.

de Miroschedji P. 1973: Vases et objets en steatite susiens de Musée du Louvre, *DAFI* 3: 9–79.

Denton, B. 1994: Pottery, cylinder seals, and stone vessels from the cemeteries of al-Hajjar, al-Maqsha and Hamad Town on Bahrain, *Arabian Archaeology and Epigraphy* 5: 121–151.

Denton, B. 1999: More pottery, seals and a 'face-pendant' from cemeteries on Bahrain, *Arabian Archaeology and Epigraphy* 10: 134–160.

De Waele, A. and Haerinck, E. 2006: Etched (carnelian) beads from northeast and southeast Arabia, *Arabian Archaeology and Epigraphy* 17: 31–40.

Dietler, M. 2010: *Archaeologies of colonialism: Consumption, entanglement, and violence in ancient Mediterranean France*, Berkeley, CA.

Dietrich, M. and Loretz, O. 1988: *Die Keilalphabete: Die phönizisch-kanaanäischen und altarabischen Alphabete in Ugarit*, Münster.

Destrées, M. 1874: Note sur l'arrondissement d'El Haça, *Bulletin de la Société de Géographie de Paris* 8: 314.

Donkin, R. A. 1998: *Beyond price: Pearls and pearl-fishing – origins to the Age of Discoveries*, Philadelphia.

Doughty, C. M. 1888: *Travels in Arabia Desert*, London.

Doughtery, R. P. 1930: A Babylonian city in Arabia, *American Journal of Archaeology* 34: 296–312.

Drechsler, P. 2007: Spreading the Neolithic over the Arabian peninsula, *Proceedings of the Seminar for Arabian Studies* 37: 93–109.

Drechsler, P. 2008: Environmental conditions and environmental changes in the Jebel Buhais area: The history of an archaeological landscape. In: H.-P. Uerpmann et al. (Eds.), *The natural environment of Jebel Buhais, past and present*, Tübingen: 17–42.

Drechsler, P. in press: Places of contact, spheres of interaction: The 'Ubaid phenomenon in the Central Gulf area as seen from a first season of re-investigations at Dosariyah, Eastern Province, Saudi Arabia, *Proceedings of the Seminar for Arabian Studies* 41.

Dunham, S. 2007: Ancient Near Eastern architecture. In: D.C. Snell (Ed.) *A companion to the ancient Near East*, London: 266–280.

Durand, E. L. 1880: Capt. extracts from report on the islands and antiquities of Bahrein, *Journal of the Royal Asiatic Society and Ireland* 12: 189–201.

During Caspers, E. C. L. 1971: New archaeological evidence for maritime trade in the Persian Gulf during the late Protoliterate period, *East and West* 21: 21–44.

During Caspers, E. C. L. 1989: Some remarks on Oman, *Proceedings of the Seminar for Arabian Studies* 19: 13–31.

Dutton, R. W. and Bray, D. (Eds.) 1988: The scientific results of the Royal Geographical Society's Oman Wahiba Sands Project, 1985–1987, *Journal of Oman Studies*, Special Report No. 3.

Ebert, C. H.V. 1965: Water resources and land use in the Qatif oasis of Saudi Arabia, *Geographical Review* 55: 496–509.

Edens, C. 1982: Towards a definition of the Rub al Khali "neolithic", *Atlal* 6: 109–124.

Edens, C. 1988: The Rub al-Khali "neolithic" revisited: The view from Nadqan. In: D. T. Potts (Ed.), *Araby the Blest: Studies in Arabian archaeology*, Copenhagen: 15–43.

Edens, C. 1992: Dynamics of trade in the ancient Mesopotamian "World System", *American Anthropologist* 94: 118–139.

Edens, C. 1999a: Khor Ile-Sud, Qatar: The archaeology of Late Bronze Age purple-dye production in the Arabian Gulf, *Iraq* 61: 71–88.

Edens, C. 1999b: The Bronze Age of highland Yemen: Chronological and spatial variability of pottery and settlement, *Paléorient* 25: 105–28.

Edens, C. 2002: Before Sheba. In: Simpson St. John (Ed.), *Queen of Sheba: Treasures from ancient Yemen*, London: 80–85.

Edens, C. 2005: Exploring early agriculture in the highlands of Yemen. In: A. M. Sholan et al. (Eds.), *Sabaean studies: Archaeological, epigraphical, and historical studies*, Sanaa.

Edens, C. and Bawden, G. 1989: History of Tayma and Hejazi trade during the first millennium B. C., *Journal of the Economic and Social History of the Orient* 32: 48–103.

Edens, C. and Wilkinson, T. J. 1998: Southwest Arabia during the Holocene: Recent archaeological developments, *Journal of World Prehistory* 12: 55–119.

Edens, C. et al. 2000: Hammat al-Qa and the roots of urbanism in southwest Arabia, *Antiquity* 74: 854–862.

Eichmann, R. et al. 2006a: Archaeology and epigraphy at Tayma, Saudi Arabia, *Arabian Archaeology and Epigraphy* 17: 163–176.

Eichmann, R. et al. 2006b: Tayma – Spring 2004: Report on the Joint Saudi-Arabian–German Archaeological Project, *Atlal* 19: 91–115.

Eichmann, R. and Sperveslage, G. 2011: Egyptian cultural impact on north-west Arabia in the 2nd and 1st millennium BC, Abstract presented to the *Seminar for Arabian Studies*, London.

Eidem, J. 1997: Cuneiform inscriptions. In: F. Højlund and H. H. Hellmuth-Andersen (Eds.), *Qala'at al-Bahrain,* vol. 2: *The central monumental buildings*, Aarhus: 76–80.

Eidem, J. and Højlund, F. 1993: Trade or diplomacy? Assyria and Dilmun in the eighteenth century BC, *World Archaeology* 24: 441–448.

Ekstrom, H. and Edens, C. 2003: Prehistoric agriculture in highland Yemen: New results from Dhamar, *Bulletin of the American Institute of Yemeni Studies* 45: 23–35.

Elath, E. 1958: The Bedouin of the Negev, *Journal of the Central Asian Society* 45: 123–140.

ElMahi, A. T. 2001: The traditional pastoral groups of Dhofar, Oman: A parallel for ancient cultural ecology, *Proceedings of the Seminar for Arabian Studies* 31:131–43.

ElMahi, A. T. and Ibrahim, M. 2003: Two seasons of investigations at Manāl site in the Wādi Samāyil area, Sultanate of Oman, *Proceedings of the Seminar for Arabian Studies* 33: 77–98.

Engel, M. et al. 2011: The early Holocene humid period in NW Saudi Arabia: Sediments, microfossils and palaeo-hydrological modeling, *Quaternary International* 266: 131–141.

Englund, R. 1991: Hard work: Where will it get you? Labor management in Ur III Mesopotamia, *Journal of Near Eastern Studies* 50: 255–280.

Englund, R. 2009: The smell of the cage, *Cuneiform Digital Library Journal* 4 online.

Eph'al, I. 1974: "Arabs" in Babylonia in the 8th century B.C., *Journal of the American Oriental Society* 94: 108–115.

Eph'al, I. 1982: *The ancient Arabs: Nomads on the borders of the Fertile Crescent, 9th to 5th centuries BC.*, Leiden.

Faris, N. A. 1957: Derivation and orthography of al-Rub al-Khali, *Journal of the Royal Central Asian Society* 44: 28–30.

Fattovich, R. 1985: Elementi per la preistoria del Sudan orientale e dell'Etiopia settentrionale. In: M. Liverani et al. (Eds.), *Studi di paletnologia in Onore di Salvatore M. Puglisi*, Rome: 451–463.

Fattovich, R. 1997: The Near East and eastern Africa. In J. O. Vogel (Ed.), *Encyclopedia of precolonial Africa: Archaeology, history, languages, cultures and environments*, Walnut Creek, CA: 484–489.

Fedele, F. 1985: Archaeological activities in the Yemen Arab Republic, 1985: Research on Neolithic and Holocene paleoecology in the Yemeni highlands, *East and West* 35: 369–373.

Fedele, F. 1986: Archaeological activities in the Yemen Arab Republic, 1986: Neolithic and protohistoric cultures, excavations and researches in the eastern highlands, *East and West* 36: 396–400.

Fedele, F. 2009: Early Holocene in the highlands: Data on the peopling of the eastern Yemen plateau, with a note on the Pleistocene evidence. In: M. D. Petraglia and J. I. Rose (Eds.), *The evolution of human populations in Arabia: Paleoenvironments, prehistory and genetics*, New York: 215–236.

Fedele, F. in press: New data on domestic and wild camels (*Camelus dromedarius* and *Camelus* sp.) in Sabaean and Minaean Yemen.

Ferguson, B. R. and Whitehead, N. L. (Eds.) 1992: *War in the tribal zone: Expanding states and indigenous warfare*, Santa Fe, NM.

Field, H. 1958: Stone implements from the Rub' al Khali, Saudi Arabia, *Man* 58: 93–94.

Field, H. 1960: Stone implements from the Rub' al Khali, *Man* 60: 25–26.

Field, H. 1971: *Contributions to the anthropology of Saudi Arabia*, Miami.

Finkelstein, I. 1984: The Iron Age "fortresses" of the Negev Highlands: Sedentarization of the nomads, *Tel Aviv* 11: 189–209.

Finkelstein, I. 1988: Arabian trade and socio-political conditions in the Negev in the twelfth-eleventh centuries B.C.E., *Journal of Near Eastern Studies* 47: 241–252.

Finkelstein, I. 1995: *Living on the fringe: The archeology and history of the Negev, Sinai, and neighboring regions in Bronze and Iron Ages*, Sheffield.

Finkelstein, I. 2002: The campaign of Shoshenq I to Palestine: A guide to the 10th century BCE polity, *Zeitschrift des Deutschen Palästina-Vereins* 118: 109–135.

Finkelstein, I. and Perevolotsky, A. 1990: Processes of sedentarization and nomadization in the history of Sinai and the Negev, *Bulletin of the American Schools of Oriental Research* 279: 67–88.

Finster, B. and Schmidt, J. 2005: The origin of 'desert castles': Qasr Bani Muqatil, near Karbala, Iraq, *Antiquity* 304: 339–349.

Fleitmann, D. and Matter, A. 2009: The speleothem record of climate variability in Southern Arabia. *Comptes Rendus Geoscience* 341: 633–642.

Fleitmann, D. et al. 2003: Holocene forcing of the Indian monsoon recorded in a stalagmite from southern Oman, *Science* 300: 1737–1739.

Foley, D. 2007: Leadership: The quandary of Aboriginal societies in crises, 1788–1830, and 1966. In: *Transgression: Critical Australian indigenous histories*, Canberra: 177–192.

Fouache, E. et al. 2012: When was irrigation first used in Bat (Wadi Sharsah, northwestern Oman)? Paper presented at the EGU general assembly, April 2010. Viewed online at adsabs.harvard.edu/abs/2012EGUGA..14..104F on 20 June 2012.

Frachetti, M. D. 2012: Multiregional emergence of mobile pastoralism and non-uniform institutional complexity across Eurasia, *Current Anthropology* 53: 2–38.

Francaviglia, V. 1985: In search of ancient Arabian obsidian sources, *East and West* 35: 373.

Francaviglia, V. 1990: Obsidian sources in ancient Yemen. In A. de Maigret (Ed.), *The Bronze Age culture of Hawlan al Tiyal and al-Hada*, Rome: 129–136.

Francaviglia, V. 2000: Dating the ancient dam of Marib (Yemen), *Journal of Archaeological Science* 27: 645–653.

Frangipane, M. 2007: Different types of egalitarian societies and the development of inequality in early Mesopotamia, *World Archaeology* 39: 151–176.

Frifelt, K. 1975: On prehistoric settlement and chronology of the Oman Peninsula, *East and West* 25: 359–424.

Frifelt, K. 1976: Evidence of a third millennium BC town in Oman, *Journal of Oman Studies* 2: 57–73.

Frifelt, K. 1979: Oman during the third millennium BC: Urban development or fishing/farming communities? In: M. Taddei (Ed.), *South Asian archaeology, 1977*, Naples: 567–588.

Frifelt, K. 1980: Jemdet Nasr graves on the Oman peninsula. In: B. Alster (Ed.), *Death in Mesopotamia*, Copenhagen: 273–279.

Frifelt, K. 1985: Further evidence of the third millennium BC town at Bat in Oman, *Journal of Oman Studies* 7: 89–104.

Frifelt, K. 1990: A third millennium kiln from the Oman Peninsula, *Arabian Archaeology and Epigraphy* 1: 4–15.

Frifelt, K. 1995: *The island of Umm an-Nar: The third millennium settlement*, Aarhus.

Fritz, C. 2007: *Iron Age settlement patterns in the United Arab Emirates*, Unpublished PhD dissertation, Bryn Mawr College.

Fritz, C. 2010: Collective burials and status differentiation in Iron Age II southeastern Arabia. In: L. Weeks (Ed.), *Death and burial in Arabia and beyond: Multidisciplinary perspectives* London: 101–107.

Fritz, V. 1981: The Israelite "Conquest" in the light of recent excavations at Khirbet el-Meshâsh, *Bulletin of the American Schools of Oriental Research* 241: 61–73.

Frohlich, B. and Mughannum, A . 1985: Excavations at Dhahran burial mounds, *Atlal* 9: 9–40.

Fuller, D. Q. 2003: African crops in prehistoric South Asia: A critical review. In K. Neumann et al. (Eds.), *Food, fuel and fields: Progress in African archaeobotany*, Cologne: 239–271.

Gadd, C. J. 1932: Seals of ancient Indian style found at Ur, *Proceedings of the British Academy* 18: 191–210.

Gadd, C. J. 1958: The Harran inscriptions of Nabonidus, *Anatolian Studies* 8: 35–92.

Gage, T. B. and De Witte, S. 2009: What do we know about the agricultural demographic transition? *Current Anthropology* 50: 649–655.

Garcia, M. and Rachad, M. 1989: *Mission de relève d'art rupestre en République Arabe du Yémen, rapport de mission à Sana'a et Sadah*, Paris.

Garcia, M. and Rachad, M. 1990: *Rapport de mission à Saada, relèves d'art rupestre et décapages*, Paris.

Garcia, M. and Rachad, M. 1997: *L'Art des origins au Yémen*, Paris.

Garfinkle, S. J. 2002: Turam-ili and the community of merchants in the UR III period, *Journal of Cuneiform Studies* 54: 29–48.

Garrard, A. N. and Harvey, C. P. D. 1981: Environment and settlement during the Upper Pleistocene and Holocene at Jubba in the Great Nefud, Northern Arabia *Atlal*, 5: 137–148.

Gates, W. E. 1967: The spread of Ibn Khaldun's ideas on climate and culture, *Journal of the History of Ideas* 28: 415–422.

Gelb, I. J. and Kienast, B. 1990: *Die altakkadischen Koniginschriften des Dritten Jahrtausends v. Chr.* Stuttgart.

Genge, H. 1979: *Nordsyrisch-südanatolische Reliefs: Eine archaologisch-historische Untersuchung, Datierung und Bestimmung*, Copenhagen.

Gentelle, E. 1981: Les irrigations antique a Shabwa, *Syria* 68: 5–54.

Gerig, M. 1982: Beiträge zur erforschung der antiken un mittelalterlichen Oase von Marib, *Archäologische Berichte aus dem Yemen* 1: 33–55.

Ghaleb, A. O. 1990: *Agricultural practices in ancient Radman and Wadi al-Jubah (Yemen)*, Unpublished PhD dissertation, University of Pennsylvania.

al-Ghazzi, A. S. 1990: *A comparative study of pottery from a site in the al-Kharj valley, Central Arabia*. Unpublished PhD dissertation, Institute of Archaeology, University College London.

al-Ghazzi A. S. 2000: Dating and ascertaining the origins of the painted al-Ula pottery, *Atlal* 15: 179–190.

Gibson, M. 2010: The dead hand of Deimel. In: R. A. Carter and G. Philip (Eds.), *Beyond the Ubaid: Transformation and integration in the late prehistoric societies of the Middle East*, Chicago: 85–92.

Gilmore, M. et al. 1982: Preliminary report on the northwestern and northern region survey, 1981 (1401), *Atlal* 6: 9–23.

Ginau, A. et al. 2012: Holocene chemical precipitates in the continental sabkha of Tayma (NW Saudi Arabia), *Journal of Arid Environments* 84: 26–37.

Giraud, J. 2009: The evolution of settlement patterns in the eastern Oman from the Neolithic to the Early Bronze Age (6000–2000 BC), *Comptes Rendus Geosciences* 8/9: 739–749.

Giumlia-Mair, A. et al. 2002: Investigation of a copper-based hoard from the megalithic site of al-Midamman, Yemen: An interdisciplinary approach, *Journal of Archaeological Science* 29: 195–209.

Glanzman, W. D. 1987: Conclusions. In: W. D. Glanzman and A. O. Ghaleb (Eds.), *The Wadi al-Jubah Archaeological Project*, vol. 3: *Site reconnaissance in the Yemen Arab Republic, 1984: The stratigraphic probe at Hajar ar-Rayhani*, Washington, DC: 207–208.

Glanzman, W. D. 1994: *Toward a classification and chronology of pottery from HR3 (Hajar ar-Rayhani), Wadi al-Jubah, Republic of Yemen*, Unpublished PhD dissertation, University of Pennsylvania.

Glanzman, W. D. 2004: Beyond their borders: A common potting tradition and ceramic horizon within South Arabia during the later first millennium BC through the early first millennium AD, *Proceedings of the Seminar for Arabian Studies* 34: 121–38.

Glanzman, W. D. 2005: "Is your cup half empty, or half full?" The function and significance of the Wavy Rim Bowl in pre-Islamic South Arabia, *Bulletin of the Society for Arabian Studies* 10: 9–15.

Glanzman, W. and Ghaleb, A. O. (Eds.) 1987: *The Wadi al-Jubah Archaeological Project*, vol. 3: *Site reconnaissance in the Yemen Arab Republic, 1984: The stratigraphic probe at Hajar ar-Rayhani*, Washington, DC.

Glassner, J. J. 1984: Inscriptions cuneiforms de Failaka. In: J. F. Salled (Ed.), *Failaka: Fouilles françaises, 1983*, Lyon: 31–50.

Glassner, J. J. 1999: Dilmun et Magan: La place de l'écriture. In: K. van Lerberghe and G. Voet (Eds.), *Languages and cultures in contact: At the crossroads of civilizations in the Syro-Mesopotamian realm, Proceedings of the 42nd RAI*, Louvain: 133–144.

Glennie, K. W. 1995: *The geology of the Oman Mountains: An outline of their origin*, Beaconsfield.

Glob, P.V. 1959: Arkæologiske undersøgelser i fire arabiske stater, *Kuml* 1959: 238.

Glob, P. V. 1960: Danish archaeologists in the Persian Gulf, *Kuml* 1960: 208–213.

Glover, E. 1991: The molluscan fauna from Shimal, Ras alKhaimah, United Arab Emirates. In: K. Schippmann et al. (Eds.), *Golf archaologie Mesopotamien, Iran, Kuwait, Bahrain, Vereinigte Arabische Emiraten und Oman*, Göttingen: 205–220.

Glover, E. 1998: Mangroves, molluscs and man: Archaeological evidence for biogeographical changes in mangrove around the Arabian Peninsula. In: C. Phillips et al. (Eds.), *Arabia and her neighbours: Essays on prehistorical and historical developments presented in honour of Beatrice de Cardi*, Turnhout: 63–78.

Goblot, H. 1979: *Les Qanats: Une technique d'acquisition de l'eau*, Paris.

Goetze, A. 1952: The texts Ni. 615 and 641 of the Istanbul Museum, *Journal of Cuneiform Studies* 6: 142–145.

Goez, W. 1958: *Translatio Imperii*, Tübingen.

Gregoricka, L. 2011: *Mobility, exchange, and tomb membership in Bronze Age Arabia: A biogeochemical investigation*, Unpublished PhD dissertation, Ohio State University.

Grigson, C. 2012: Camels, copper and donkeys in the Early Iron Age of the southern Levant: Timna revisited, *Levant* 44: 82–100.

Grupe, G. and Schutkowski, H. 1989: Dietary shift during the second millennium BC in prehistoric Shimal, Oman peninsula, *Paléorient* 15: 77–84.

Gunneweg, J. et al. 1991: 'Edomite', 'Negbite' and 'Midianite' pottery from the Negev desert and Jordan, *Archaeometry* 33: 239–253.

Haines, S. B. 1845: Memoir of the south and east coasts of Arabia, Part II, *Journal of the Royal Geographical Society of London* 15: 104–160.

al-Hajri, M. 2006: Brief preliminary report on the excavations at the industrial site in Tayma, *Atlal* 19: 21–26.

al-Hajri, M. et al 2005: Archaeological excavations at the site of Rajoom Sa'sa – Tayma, *Atlal* 18: 23–29.

Hall, S. 2000: Burial and sequence in the later Stone Age of the Eastern Cape Province, South Africa, *South African Archaeological Bulletin* 55: 137–146.

Hallo, W. W. and Buchanan, B. 1965: A 'Persian Gulf' seal on an Old Babylonian mercantile agreement. In: H. G. Güterbock and T. Jacobsen (Eds.), *Studies in honor of Benno Landsberger on his seventy-fifth birthday, April 21, 1963*, Chicago: 199–209.

Hamann, M. et al. 2008: Wasserwirthschaftliche Anlagen in der historischen Oasenstadt Tayma, Saudi-Arabien. In: C. Ohlig (Ed.), *Cura Aquarum in Jordanien* 12: 155–175.

Härke, H. 1997: Early Anglo-Saxon military organisation: An archaeological perspective. In: A.N. Jorgensen and B. L. Clausen (Eds.), *Military aspects of Scandinavian society in a European perspective, AD 2–1300*, Copenhagen: 93–101.

Harris, A. 1998: A Late Stone Age site south of the Liwa Oasis, *Tribulus (Journal of the Emirates Natural History Group)* 47: 1011–1021.

Harrower, H. 2006: *Environmental versus social parameters, landscape and the origins of irrigation in southwest Arabia (Yemen)*, Unpublished PhD dissertation, Ohio State University.

Harrower, M. 2008: Hydrology, ideology, and the origins of irrigation in ancient Southwest Arabia, *Current Anthropology* 49: 497–510.

Hashim, S. A. 2007: *Pre-Islamic ceramics in Saudi Arabia*, Riyadh.

Hauptmann, A. 1985: 5000 jahre kupfer in Oman, Band 1: Die Entwicklung der Kupfermetallurgie vom 3. Jahrtausend bis zur Neuzeit. In *Der Anschnitt, Zeitschrift für Kunst und Kultur im Bergbau*, suppl. vol. 4, Bochum.

Hausleiter, A. 2010: The oasis of Tayma, In: A. I. al-Ghabban et al. (Eds.), *Roads of Arabia: Archaeology and history of the Kingdom of Saudi Arabia*, Paris: 219–261.

Hayajneh, H. 2001: First evidence of Nabonidus in the ancient North Arabian inscriptions from the region of Tayma, *Proceedings of the Seminar for Arabian Studies* 31 : 81–95.

Healey, J. F. 1991: Ugarit and Arabia: A balance sheet, *Proceedings of the Seminar for Arabian Studies* 21: 69–78.

Heck, G. W. 2003: "Arabia without Spices": An alternate hypothesis – The issue of "Makkan Trade and the Rise of Islam", *Journal of the American Oriental Society* 123: 547–576.

Hehmeyer, I. 1989: Irrigation farming in the ancient oasis of Marib, *Proceedings of the Seminar for Arabian Studies* 19: 33–44.

Hehmeyer, I. and Schmidt, J. 1991: Der Bewässerungslandbau auf der antiken Oase von Marib, *Archäologische Berichte aus dem Yemen* 5: 9–112.

Heide, M. 2011: The domestication of the camel: Biological, archaeological and inscriptional evidence from Mesopotamia, Egypt, Israel and Arabia, and literary evidence from the Hebrew Bible, *Ugarit Forschungen* 42: 331–382.

Heimpel, W. 1980: Kamel, *Reallexikon der Assyriologie* 5: 330–332.

Heimpel, W. 1982: A first step in the diorite question, *Revue d'Assyriologie* 76: 65–67.

Hellyer, P. 1988: *Filling in the blanks: Recent archaeological discoveries in Abu Dhabi*, Dubai.

Hellyer, P. 1992: Islands survey, *Tribulus* 2: 37

Hellyer, P. and Beech, M. 2001: C14 dating of Iron Age hearths on the island of Rufayq, Abu Dhabi, *Tribulus* 11: 21–23.

Helms, S. and Betts, A. V. G. 1987: The desert "kites" of the Badiyat Esh-Sham and North Arabia, *Paléorient* 13: 41–67.

Hilprecht, H. V. 1903: *Explorations in Bible Lands during the 19th century*, Philadelphia.

Hirsch, H. 1963: Die Inschriften der Könige von Agade, *Archiv für Orientforschung* 20: 1–82.

Hirth, K. G. 1978: Interregional trade and the formation of prehistoric gateway communities, *American Antiquity* 43: 35–45.

Hobsbawm, E. J. and Ranger, T. O. 1983: *The invention of tradition*, Cambridge.

Hoch, E. 1979: Reflections on Prehistoric life at Umm an-Nar (Trucial Oman) based on faunal remains from the third millennium BC. In: M. Taddei (Ed.), *South Asian archaeology, 1977: Papers from the Fourth International Conference of the Association of South Asian Archaeologists in Western Europe, Held in the Istituto Universitario Orientale, Naples*, Naples: 589–638.

Hoch, E. 1995: Animal bones from the Umm an-Nar settlement. In: K. Frifelt (Ed.), *The island of Umm an-Nar 2: The third millennium settlement*, Aarhus: 249–256.

Hogarth, D. G. et al. 1914: *Carchemish: Report on the excavations at Djerabis on behalf of the British Museum*, vol. III, London.

Højgaard, K. 1980: Dentition on Umm al-Nar (Trucial Oman), 2500 B.C., *Scandinavian Journal of Dental Research* 88: 355–364.

Højlund, F. 1987: *Failaka/Dilmun: The second millennium settlements – The Bronze Age pottery*, Aarhus.

Højlund, F. 1990: Date honey production in Dilmun in the mid-2nd millennium B.C.: Steps in the technological evolution of the Madbasa, *Paléorient* 16: 77–86.

Højlund, F. 1993: The ethnic composition of the population of Dilmun, *Proceedings of the Seminar for Arabian Studies* 23: 1–8.

Højlund, F. 2000: Dilmun stamp seals and the royal cap, *Arabian Archaeology and Epigraphy* 11: 15–21.

Højlund, F. 2008: *Burial mounds of Bahrain: Social complexity in early Dilmun*, Aarhus.

Højlund, F. 2010: Between the temple and the palace in Tell F6, Failaka, Kuwait: Two seasons of excavation by the Kuwait-Danish Mission, 2008–2009, Paper presented at the Seminar for Arabian Studies, London.

Højlund, F. and Andersen, H. (Eds.) 1994: *Qala'at al-Bahrain 1: The northern city wall and the Islamic fortress*, Aarhus.

Højlund, F. and Andersen, H. (Eds.) 1997: *Qala'at al-Bahrain 2: The central monumental buildings*, Aarhus.

Holzer, A. et al. 2010: Desert kites in the Negev desert and northeast Sinai, *Journal of Arid Environments* 74: 806–817.

Hommel, F. 1903: Explorations in Arabia. In: H.V. Hilprecht (Ed.), *Explorations in Bible Lands during the 19th century*, Philadelpia: 693–752.

Horsfield, G. et al. 1933: Prehistoric rock drawings in TransJordan, *American Journal of Archaeology* 37: 381–386.

Horwitz, L. K and Rosen, B. 2005: A review of camel milking in the southern Levant. In: J. Mulville and A. K. Outram (Eds.), *The zooarchaeology of fats, oils, milk and dairying*, London: 121–131.

Hourani, A. 1992: *History of the Arab Peoples*, London.

Howard-Carter, T. 1987: Dilmun: At sea or not at sea? *Journal of Cuneiform Studies* 39: 57–117.

Hoyland, R. 2001: *Arabia and the Arabs from the Bronze Age to the coming of Islam*, London.

Humphries, J. 1974: Harvard Archaeology Survey in Oman, II: Some later prehistoric sites in the Sultanate of Oman, *Proceedings of the Seminar for Arabian Studies*, 4: 49–77.

Ibn Khaldun, A. [1377] 1967: *The muqaddimah*, F. Rosenthal (Trans.), Princeton. NJ.

Ingraham, M. L. et al. 1981: Preliminary report on a reconnaissance survey of the northwestern province (with a note on a brief survey of the northern province), *Atlal* 5: 59–84.

Inizan, M. L. and Rachad, M. 2007: *Art rupestre et peuplements préhistoriques au Yémen*, Sanaa.

Intilia, A. 2010: Area C. In: R. Eichmann et al. (Eds.), Tayma – Autumn 2004 and Spring 2005, 2nd Report on the Joint Saudi-Arabian–German Archaeological Project, *Atlal* 20: 101–147.

Jacobsen, T. 1960: The waters of Ur, *Iraq* 22: 174–185.

al-Jahwari, N. 2009: The agricultural basis of Umm an-Nar society in the northern Oman peninsula (2500–2000 BC), *Arabian Archaeology and Epigraphy* 20: 122–133.

al-Jahwari, N. and Kennet, D. 2008: A field methodology for the quantification of ancient settlement in an Arabian context, *Proceedings of the Seminar for Arabian Studies* 38: 203–214.

Janzen, J. 1986: *Nomads in the sultanate of Oman: Tradition and development in Dhofar*, Boulder, CO.

Jasim, S. A. 2012: *The necropolis of Jebel Buhais: Prehistoric discoveries in the Emirate of Sharjah United Arab Emirates*, Sharjah.

Al-Jassir, M. S. et al. 1995: Studies on samh seeds *Mesembryanthemum forsskalei* growing in Saudi Arabia, 1: Anatomy of Samh seed, *Plant Foods for Human Nutrition* 47: 327–331.

Jennings, R. P. et al. 2013: Rock art landscapes beside the Jubbah palaeolake, Saudi Arabia, *Antiquity* 87: 666–683.

Jorgensen, D. G and al-Tikriti, W. Y. 2002: A hydrologic and archeological study of climate change in Al Ain, United Arab Emirates, *Global and Planetary Change* 35: 37–49.

Kabawi, A. et al. 1989: Comprehensive report on the fourth season of comprehensive rock art and epigraphic survey of northern Saudi Arabia, *Atlal* 11: 41–52.

Kabawi, A. et al. 1990: Preliminary report on the fifth season of comprehensive rock art and epigraphic survey of the kingdom of Saudi Arabia, *Atlal* 13: 35–40.

Kabawi, A. et al. 1996: Comprehensive rock art and epigraphic survey, Southern Region, Wadi Dawasir, *Atlal* 14: 55–72.

Kallweit, H. 2001: Remarks on the Late Stone Age in the UAE. In: D. T. Potts et al. (Eds.), *Proceedings of the First International Conference on Archaeology of the U.A.E.*, London: 55–63.

Kantner, J. and Vaughn, K. J. 2012: Pilgrimage as costly signal: Religiously motivated cooperation in Chaco and Nasca, *Journal of Anthropological Archaeology* 31: 66–82.

Karsgaard, P. 2010: The Halaf–Ubaid transition: A transformation without a center? In: R. A. Carter and G. Philip (Eds.), *Beyond the Ubaid: Transformation and integration in the late prehistoric societies of the Middle East*, Chicago: 51–68.

Keall, E. J. 1998: Encountering megaliths on the Tihamah coastal plain of Yemen, *Proceedings of the Seminar for Arabian Studies* 28: 139–47.

Keall, E. J. 2004: Possible connections in antiquity between the Red Sea coast of Yemen and the Horn of Africa. In: P. Lunde and A. Porter (Eds.), *Trade and travel in the Red Sea region: Proceedings of the Red Sea Project*, Oxford: 43–56.

Keall, E. J. 2005: Placing al-Midamman in time: The work of the Canadian archaeological mission on the Tihama Coast, from the Neolithic to the Bronze Age, *Archaologische Berichte aus dem Yemen* 10: 87–100.

Kennedy, D. L. and Al-Saeed, A. 2009: Desktop archaeology, *Saudi Aramco World*, July/August: 2–9.

Kennedy, D. L. and Bishop, M. C. 2011: Google Earth and the archaeology of Saudi Arabia: A case study from the Jeddah area, *Journal of Archaeological Science* 38: 1284–1293.

Kennet, D. and Velde, C. 1995: Third and early second millennium occupation at Nud Ziba, Khatt (U.A.E), *Arabian Archaeology and Epigraphy* 6: 233–244.

Kervran, M. et al. 1987: The occupational enigma of Bahrain between the 13th and the 8th century BC, *Paléorient* 13: 77–93.

Khalidi, L. 2005. The prehistoric and early historic settlement patterns on the Tihamah coastal plain (Yemen): Preliminary findings of the Tihamah coastal survey 2003, *Proceedings of the Seminar for Arabian Studies* 35: 115–127.

Khalidi, L. 2009: Holocene obsidian exchange in the Red Sea region. In: M. D. Petraglia and J. I. Rose (Eds.), *The evolution of human populations in Arabia: Paleoenvironments, prehistory and genetics*, New York: 279–291.

Khalidi, L. 2011: New perspectives on regional and interregional obsidian circulation in prehistoric and early historic Arabia, Paper presented at the Seminar for Arabian Studies, London, July.

Khalidi, L. et al. 2010: Obsidian sources in highland Yemen and their relevance to archaeological research in the Red Sea region, *Journal of Archaeological Science* 37: 2332–2345.

Khan, M. 2008: Symbolism in the rock art of Saudi Arabia: Hand and footprints, *Rock Art Research* 25: 13–22.

Kiesewetter, H. 2006: Analyses of the human remains from the Neolithic cemetery at al-Buhais 18 (Excavations, 1996–2000). In: H.-P. Uerpmann et al. (Eds.), *Funeral monuments and human remains from Jebel al-Buhais*, Tübingen: 103–266.

Killick, R. and Moon, J. (Eds.) 2005: *The early Dilmun settlement at Saar*, London.

Kimura, B. et al. 2010: Ancient DNA from Nubian and Somali wild ass provides insights into donkey ancestry and domestication, *Proceedings of the Royal Society B* 278: 50–57.

Kirkbride, D. 1974: Umm Dabaghiyah: A trading outpost? *Iraq* 36: 85–92.

Kirkbride, D. 1975: Umm Dabaghiyah, 1974: A fourth preliminary report, *Iraq* 37: 3–10.

Kitchen, K. A. 2002: Egypt, Middle Nile, Red Sea and Arabia. In: S. Cleuziou et al. (Eds.), *Essays*

on the late prehistory of the Arabian Peninsula, Rome: 383–401.

Kjærum, P. 1980: Seals of the 'Dilmun type' from Failaka, Kuwait, *Proceedings of the Seminar for Arabian Studies* 10: 45–54.

Kjærum, P. 1983: The stamp and cylinder seals: Plates and catalogue descriptions. In: *Failaka/Dilmun: The second millennium settlements*, Aarhus.

Kjærum, P. 1994. Stamp-seals, seal impressions and seal blanks. In F. Højlund and H. Andersen (Eds.), *Qala'at al-Bahrain*, vol. 1: *The Northern City Wall and the Islamic Fortress*, Aarhus: 319–350.

Kjærum, P. 2003: Stamp seals and seal impressions. In: H. Andersen and F. Højlund (Eds.), *The Barbar Temples*, vol. 1, Aarhus: 289–305.

Klasen, N. et al. 2011: Optically stimulated luminescence dating of the city wall system of ancient Tayma (NW Saudi Arabia), *Journal of Archaeological Science* 38: 1818–1826.

Kmoskó, M. 1917: Beiträge zur Erklärung der Inschriften Gudeas, *Zeitschrift für Assyriologie und Vorderasiatische Archäologie* 31: 58–90.

Knauf, E. A. 1989: The migration of the script, and the formation of the state in south Arabia, *Proceedings of the Seminar for Arabian Studies* 19: 79–91.

Kohl, P. 1978: The balance of trade in southwestern Asia in the mid-third millennium B.C. *Current Anthropology* 19: 463–492.

Köhler-Rollefson, I. 1992: A model for the development of nomadic pastoralism on the Transjordanian plateau. In: O. Bar-Yosef and A. Khazanov (Eds.), *Pastoralism in the Levant*, Madison, WI: 11–18.

Korotayev, A. 1994: Internal structure of the Middle Sabaean Bayt, *Arabian Archaeology and Epigraphy* 5: 174–183.

Kunter, M. 1981: Bronze- und eisenzeitliche Skelettfunde aus Oman: Bemerkungen zur Bevölkerungsgeschichte Ostarabiens, *Homo* 32: 197–210.

Kunter, M. 1983: Chronologische und regionale Unterschiede bei pathologischen Zahnbefunden auf der arabischen Halbinsel, *Archäologisches Korrespondenzblatt* 13: 339–343.

Kuper, R. and Kröpelin S. 2006: Climate-controlled Holocene occupation in the Sahara: Motor of Africa's evolution, *Science* 313: 803–807.

Kupper, J.-R. 1957: *Les nomads en Mésopotamie au temps des rois de Mari*, Liege.

Kutterer, A. 2010: Remarks on Neolithic burial customs in south-east Arabia. In: L.Weeks (Ed.), *Death and burial and beyond: Multidisciplinary perspectives*. London: 1–19.

Kutterer, J. et al. 2012: Remarks on the Bronze Age mining and smelting site HLO 1 in Wadi Hilou (Sharjah, UAE), Paper presented at the Seminar for Arabian Studies, London, July.

Kuzucuoğlu, C. and Marro, C. 2007: *Sociétés humaines et changement climatique à la fin du troisième millénaire: Une crise a-t-elle eu lieu en haute Mésopotamie? Actes du Colloque de Lyon, 5–8 décembre 2005*, Istanbul.

Kveiborg, J. 2007: Animal bones from the Aali, Saar and Dar Kulayb mound cemeteries. In: F. Højlund (Ed.), *The burial mounds of Bahrain*, Aarhus: 149–153.

Kwartend, Y. et al. 2000: Formation of fresh ground-water lenses in northern Kuwait, *Journal of Arid Environments* 46: 137–155.

Laessøe, J. 1971: The irrigation system at Ulhu, 8th century BC, *Journal of Cuneiform Studies* 5: 21–32.

Lamberg-Karlovsky, C. C. 1982: Dilmun: Gateway to immortality, *Journal of Near Eastern Studies* 41: 45–50.

Lambert, W. G. 1960: The domesticated camel in the second millennium: Evidence from Alalakh and Ugarit, *Bulletin of the American Schools of Oriental Research* 160: 42–43.

Lancaster, W. and Lancaster, F. 1990: Desert devices: The pastoral system of the Rwala Bedu. In: J. G. Galaty and D. L. Johnson (Eds.), *The world of pastoralism*, New York: 177–194.

Landsberger, B. 1974: *Three essays on the Sumerians*, Los Angeles.

Larsen, C. E. 1983: *Life and land use on the Bahrain islands: The geoarchaeology of an ancient society*, Chicago.

Larsen, C. S. 1995: Biological changes in human populations with agriculture, *Current Anthropology* 24: 185–213.

Laursen, S. 2008: Early Dilmun and its rulers: New evidence of the burial mounds of the elite and the development of social complexity, c. 2200–1750 BC, *Arabian Archaeology and Epigraphy* 19: 156–167.

Laursen, S. 2009: The decline of Magan and the rise of Dilmun: Umm an-Nar ceramics from the burial mounds of Bahrain, c. 2250–2000 BC, *Arabian Archaeology and Epigraphy* 20: 134–155.

Laursen, S. 2010: The westward transmission of Indus Valley sealing technology: Origin and development of the 'Gulf Type' seal and other administrative technologies in early Dilmun, c. 2100–2000 BC, *Arabian Archaeology and Epigraphy* 21: 96–134.

Leemans, W. F. 1960: *Foreign trade in the Old Babylonian period – as revealed by the texts from Southern Mesopotamia*, Leiden.

Legge, A. J. and Rowley-Conwy, P. 1987: Gazelle killing in Stone Age Syria, *Scientific American* 257: 76–83.

Lemée, M. et al. 2013: Jabal al-Aluya: An inland Neolithic settlement of the late fifth millennium BC in the Adam area, Sultanate of Oman, *Proceedings of the Seminar for Arabian Studies* 43: 197–212.

Lézine, A.-M. 2009: Timing of vegetation changes at the end of the Holocene Humid Period in desert areas at the northern edge of the Atlantic and Indian monsoon systems, *Comptes Rendus Geosciences* 341: 750–759.

Lézine, A.-M. et al. 1998: Holocene lakes from Ramlat-as Sab'atayn (Yemen) illustrate the impact of monsoon activity in Southern Arabia, *Quaternary Research* 50: 290–299.

Lézine, A.-M. et al. 2002. Mangroves of Oman during the late Holocene: Climatic implications and impact on human settlements, *Vegetation History and Archaeobotany* 11: 221–232.

Lézine, A.-M. et al. 2010: Climate change and human occupation in the southern Arabian lowlands during the last deglaciation and the Holocene, *Global and Planetary Change* 72: 412–428.

Lightfoot, D. 2000: The origin and diffusion of qanats in Arabia: New Evidence from the northern and southern peninsula, *Geographical Journal* 166: 215–226.

Liverani, M. 1992: Early caravan trade between South-Arabia and Mesopotamia, *Yemen* 1: 111–115.

Liverani, M. (Ed.) 1993: *Akkad, the first world empire: Structure, ideology, traditions*, Padova.

Liverani, M. 2005: Imperialism. In: S. Pollock and R. Bernbeck (Eds.), *Archaeologies of the Middle East: Critical perspectives*, Oxford: 223–243.

Livingstone, A. 1999: Taima: A nexus for historical contact and cultural interchange within the desert borders. In: K. Van Lerberghe and G. Voet (Eds.), *Languages and cultures in contact: At the crossroads of civilisations in the Syro-Mesopotamian realm – Proceedings of the 42nd RAI*, Leuven: 233–236.

Llewellyn O. A. et al. 2011: Important plant areas in the Arabian peninsula 4. Jabal Aja, *Edinburgh Journal of Botany* 68: 199–224.

Lloyd, S. and Safar, F. 1943: Tell Uqair, *Journal of Near Eastern Studies* 2: 131–158.

Lombard, P. 1985: *L'Arabie Orientale à l'Age du Fer*, Unpublished PhD dissertation, University of Paris.

Loreto, R. 2012: The Saudi-Italian-French archaeology mission at Dumat al-Jandal (ancient Adumatu): A first relative chronological sequence for Dumat al-Jandal – architecture and pottery, *Proceedings of the Seminar for Arabian Studies* 42: 165–182.

Lückge, A. et al. 2001: Monsoonal variability in the northeastern Arabian Sea during the past 5000 years: Geochemical evidence from laminated sediments, *Palaeogeography, Palaeoclimatology, Palaeoecology*, 167: 273–286.

MacAdam, H. I. 1990: Dilmun revisited, *Arabian Archaeology and Epigraphy* 1: 49–87.

Macchiarelli, R. 1989: Prehistoric "fish-eaters" along the eastern Arabian Coasts: Dental variation, morphology, and oral health in the Ra's al-Hamra community (Qualm, Sultanate of Oman, 5th–4th Millennia BC), *American Journal of Physical Anthropology* 78: 575–594.

Macdonald, M. C. A. 1997: Trade routes and trade goods at the northern end of the 'Incense Road' in the first millennium B.C. In: A. Avanzini (Ed.), *Profumi d'Arabia*, Pisa: 333–349.

Macdonald, M. C. A. 2000: Reflections on the linguistic map of pre-Islamic Arabia, *Arabian Archaeology and Epigraphy* 11: 28–79.

Magee, P. 1996a: Excavations at Muweilah: Preliminary report on the first two seasons, *Arabian Archaeology and Epigraphy* 7: 195–213.

Magee, P. 1996b: The chronology of the southeast Arabian Iron Age, *Arabian Archaeology and Epigraphy* 7: 240–252.

Magee, P. 1998: The chronology and regional context of late prehistoric incised arrowheads in southeastern Arabia, *Arabian Archaeology and Epigraphy* 9: 1–12.

Magee, P. 1999: A proposed function for late prehistoric incised arrowheads in Southeastern Arabia, *ISIMU* 2: 353–363.

Magee, P. 2002: Settlement complexity in the southeast Arabian Iron Age, Paper presented at the International conference on the Archaeology of the Ancient Near East, Paris, April.

Magee, P. 2003: New chronometric data defining the Iron Age II period in south-eastern Arabia, *Proceedings of the Seminar for Arabian Studies* 33: 1–10.

Magee, P. 2004: *Excavations at Tepe Yahya, Iran, 1967–1975: The Iron Age settlement*, Cambridge, MA.

Magee, P. 2007: Beyond the Desert and the Sown: Settlement intensification in late prehistoric southeastern Arabia, *Bulletin of the American Schools of Oriental Research* 347: 83–105.

Magee, P. 2011: Ceramic production and exchange and the impact of domesticated *Camelus dromedarius* in southeastern Arabia. In: N. J. Conard et al. (Eds.), *Between sand and sea: The archaeology and human ecology of southwestern Asia – Festschrift in honor of Hans-Peter Uerpmann*, Tübingen: 213–227.

Magee, P. 2012: The foundations of antiquities departments. In: D. T. Potts (Ed.), *A companion to the archaeology of the ancient Near East*, London: 70–87.

Magee, P. and Carter, R. 1999: Agglomeration and regionalism: Southeastern Arabia between 1400 and 1100 BC, *Arabian Archaeology and Epigraphy* 10: 161–179.

Magee, P. et al. 2002: Further evidence of desert settlement complexity: Report on the 2001 excavations at the Iron Age site of Muweilah, Emirate of Sharjah, United Arab Emirates, *Arabian Archaeology and Epigraphy* 13: 133–156.

Magee, P. et al. 2009: Multi-disciplinary research on the past human ecology of the east Arabian coast: Excavations at Hamriya and Tell Abraq (Emirate of Sharjah, United Arab Emirates), *Arabian Archaeology and Epigraphy* 20: 18–29.

Maktari, A. 1971: *Water rights and irrigation practice in Lahj*, Cambridge.

Mallory-Greenough, L. et al. 2000: Iron Age gold mining: A preliminary report on camps in the al-Maraziq region, Yemen, *Arabian Archaeology and Epigraphy* 11: 223–236.

Mallowan, M. E. L. 1972: Carchemish: Reflections on the chronology of the sculpture, *Anatolian Studies* 22: 63–85.

Mandaville, J. P. 2011: *Bedouin ethnobotany: Plant concepts and uses in a desert pastoral world*, Tucson, AZ.

Martin, L. 1999: Mammal remains from the eastern Jordanian Neolithic, and the nature of caprine herding in the steppe, *Paléorient* 25: 87–104.

Masry, A. H. 1974: *Prehistory in northeastern Arabia: The problem of interregional interaction*, Coconut Grove, FL.

Matthews, R. 2002: Zebu: Harbingers of doom in Bronze Age western Asia? *Antiquity* 76: 438–446.

McClure, H. A. 1976: Radiocarbon chronology of late Quaternary lakes in the Arabian Desert, *Nature* 263: 755–756.

McCorriston, J. 2000: Early settlement in Hadramawt: Preliminary report on prehistoric occupation at Shi'b Munayder, *Arabian Archaeology and Epigraphy* 11: 129–153.

McCorriston, J. 2011: *Pilgrimage and household in the ancient Near East*, Cambridge.

McCorriston, J. et al. 2005: Foraging economies and population in the middle Holocene Highlands of southern Yemen, *Proceedings of the Seminar for Arabian Studies* 35: 143–154.

McCorriston, J. and Martin, L. 2009: Southern Arabia's early pastoral population history: Some recent evidence, In: M. D. Petraglia and I. J. Rose (Eds.), *The evolution of human populations in Arabia: Paleoenvironments, prehistory and genetics*, New York: 237–250.

McNiven, I. J. 2003: Saltwater people: Spiritscapes, maritime rituals and the archaeology of Australian indigenous seascapes, *World Archaeology* 35: 329–349.

McSweeney, K. S. et al. 2008: Rewriting the end of the Early Bronze Age in the United Arab Emirates through the anthropological and artefactual evaluation of two collective Umm an-Nar graves at Hili (eastern region of Abu Dhabi), *Arabian Archaeology and Epigraphy* 19:1–14.

Méry, S. 1991: Origine et production des récipients de terre cuite dans la péninsule d'Oman à l'Âge du Bronze, *Paléorient* 17: 51–78.

Méry, S. 1997: A funerary assemblage from the Umm an-Nar period: The ceramics from Hili North tomb A, UAE. *Proceedings of the Seminar for Arabian Studies* 27: 171–191.

Méry. S. 2000: *Les Ceramiques d'Oman et l'Asie Moyenne*, Paris.

Méry, S. 2007: Indus pottery. In: S. Cleuziou and M. Tosi (Eds.), *In the shadow of the ancestors: The prehistoric foundations of the early Arabian civilization in Oman*, Muscat: 200–202.

Méry, S. and Schneider G. 1996: Mesopotamian pottery wares in eastern Arabia from the 5th to the 2nd millennium BC: A contribution of archaeometry to the economic history, *Proceedings of the Seminar for Arabian Studies* 26: 79–96.

Méry, S. et al. 2009: A dugong bone mound: The Neolithic ritual site on Akab in Umm al-Quwain, United Arab Emirates, *Antiquity*: 83: 696–708.

Michalowski, P. 1986: Mental maps and ideology: Observations on Subartu. In: H. Weiss (Ed.), *The origins of cities in dry-farming Syria and Mesopotamia in the third millennium BC*, Guilford: 129–156.

Michalowski, P. 1990: The shekel and the vizier, *Zeitschrift für Assyrologie und Vorderasiatische Archäologie* 80: 1–8.

Michalowski, P. 1999: Sumer dreams of Subartu: Politics and the geographical imagination. In: K. Van Lerberghe and G. Voet (Eds.), *Languages and cultures in contact at the crossroads of civilizations in the Syro-Mesopotamian realm*, Leuven: 305–316.

Midant-Reynes, B. and Braunstein-Silvestre, F. 1977: Le chameau en Egypte, *Orientalia* 46: 337–362.

Millard, A. R. 1973: Cypriot copper in Babylonia, c. 1745 BC, *Journal of Cuneiform Studies* 25: 211–214.

Mitchell, T. C. 2000: Camels in the Assyrian bas-reliefs, *Iraq* 62: 187–194.

Molleson, T. 1994: The eloquent bones of Abu Hureya, *Scientific American* 271: 70–75.

Monchablon, C. et al. 2003: Excavations at Ras al-Jinz RJ-1: Stratigraphy without tells, *Proceedings of the Seminar for Arabian Studies* 33: 31–47.

Mortensen, P. 1986: The Barbar Temple: Its chronology and foreign relations reconsidered. H. A. Al Khalifa and M. Rice (Eds.), *Bahrain through the ages: The archaeology*, London: 178–185.

Mouton, M. et al. 2011: Makaynun and its territory: The formation of an urban centre during the south Arabian period in the Hadramawt, *Arabian Archaeology and Epigraphy* 22: 155–165.

Müller, W. 1999: Zur Inschrift auf einem Krugfragment aus Muweilah, *Arabian Archaeology and Epigraphy* 10: 51–53.

Murad, A. A. 2010: An overview of conventional and non-conventional water resources in an arid region: Assessment and constraints of the United Arab Emirates (UAE), *Journal of Water Resource and Protection* 2: 181–190.

Murray, M. A. 2000: Fruits, vegetables, pulses and condiments. In: P. Nicholson and I. Shaw

(Eds.), *Ancient Egyptian materials and technology*, Cambridge: 609–655.

Na'aman, N. 2007: The contribution of the Suhu inscriptions to the historical research of the Kingdoms of Israel and Judah, *Journal of Near Eastern Studies* 66: 107–122.

al-Najam, H. 2000: Irrigation systems and the ancient water sources in Tayma area, *Atlal* 15: 191–200.

Nashef, K. 2010: Saruq al-Hadid: An industrial complex of the Iron Age II period. In: A. Avanzini (Ed.), *Eastern Arabia in the first millennium BC* (= Arabia Antiqua 6), Rome: 213–226.

al-Nasif, A. 1980: Qanats at al-'Ula', *Proceedings of the Seminar for Arabian Studies* 10: 75–80.

al-Nasif, A. 1981: Al-'Ula (Saudi Arabia): A report on a historical and archaeological survey, *British Society for Middle Eastern Studies* 8: 30–32.

Nebes, N. 2007: Ita'amar der Sabaer: Zur Datierung der Monumentalinschift der Yi amar aus Sirwah, *Arabian Archaeology and Epigraphy* 18: 25–33.

Nehmé, L. et al. 2006: Mission archéologique de Madain Salih (Arabie Saoudite): Recherches menées de 2001 à 2003 dans l'ancienne Hijrsa des Nabatéens, *Arabian Archaeology and Epigraphy* 17: 41–124.

Nesbitt, M. 1993: Archaeobotanical evidence for early Dilmun diet at Saar, Bahrain, *Arabian Archaeology and Epigraphy* 4: 20–47.

Neumann, H. 1999: Ur-Dumuzida and Ur-Dun: Reflections on the relationship between state-initiated foreign trade and private economic activity in Mesopotamia towards the end of the third millennium BC. In: J. G. Dercksen (Ed.), *Trade and finance in Ancient Mesopotamia*, Leiden: 43–53.

Newton, L. S. and Zarins, J. 2000: Aspects of Bronze Age art of southern Arabia: The pictorial landscape and its relation to economic and socio-political status, *Arabian Archaeology and Epigraphy* 11: 154–179.

Nigro, L. 1998: The two steles of Sargon: Iconology and visual propaganda at the beginning of royal Akkadian relief, *Iraq* 60: 85–102.

Nyberg, H. S. 1960: The new corpus inscriptionum Iranicarum, *Bulletin of the School of Oriental and African Studies* 1960: 40–46.

Oates, J. 1976: Prehistory in northeastern Arabia, *Antiquity* 50: 20–31.

Oates, J. et al. 1977: Seafaring merchants of Ur? *Antiquity* 51: 221–34.

Olijdam, E. 1997a: Nippur and Dilmun in the second half of the fourteenth century BC: A re-evaluation of the Ilī-ippašra letters, *Proceedings of the Seminar for Arabian Studies* 27: 199–203.

Olijdam, E. 1997b: Babylonian quest for lapis lazuli and Dilmun during the City III period, *South Asian archaeology* 1995: 119–126.

Olijdam, E. 2000: Towards a more balanced assessment of land use on Bahrain during the City II period, *Proceedings of the Seminar for Arabian Studies* 30: 157–163.

Olijdam, E. in press: Sealings from Middle Dilmun levels at Qal'at al-Bahrain (1995–1996) and preliminary observations on function, seal-styles and chronology. In: *Proceedings of the Conference "Twenty Years of Bahrain Archaeology (1986–2006)."*

Oppenheim, A. L. 1954: The seafaring merchants of Ur, *Journal of the American Oriental Society* 74: 6–17.

Oppert, J. 1880: Le siege primitive des Assyriens et des Phéniciens, *Journal Asiatique* 12: 90–92.

Orchard, J. and Stanger, G. 1994: Third millennium oasis towns and environmental constraints on settlement in the al-Hajar Region, *Iraq* 56: 63–100.

Orchard, J. and Stanger, G. 1999: Al-Hajar oasis towns again! *Iraq* 61: 89–119.

Paribeni, R. 1907: Ricerche nel Luogo dell'Antica Adulis (Colonia Eritrea), *Monumenti Antichi* 18: 445–451.

Parker, A. et al. 2006: A record of Holocene climate change from lake geochemical analyses in southeastern Arabia, *Quaternary Research* 66: 465–476.

Parpola, S. 1990: A letter from Marduk-apla-usur of Anah to Rudamu/Urtamis, King of Hamath. In: P. J. Riis and M.-L. Buhl (Eds.), *HAMA: Fouilles et recherches de la Fondation Carlsberg, II 2: Les objets de la période dite Syro-Hittite*, Copenhagen: 257–265.

Parpola, S. et al. 1977: The Meluhha villages: Evidence of acculturation of Harappan traders in late third millennium Mesopotamia? *Journal of the Economic and Social History of the Orient* 20: 129–165.

Parr, P. 1988: Pottery of the late second millennium B.C. from North West Arabia and its historical implications. In: D. T. Potts (Ed.),

Araby the Blest: Studies in Arabian Archaeology, Copenhagen: 73–89.

Parr, P. 1993: The early history of the Hejaz: A response to Garth Bawden, *Arabian Archeology and Epigraphy* 4: 48–58.

Parr, P. 1996: Further reflections on late second millennium settlement in North West Arabia. In: J. Seger (Ed.), *Retrieving the past: Essays on archaeological research and methodology in Honor of Gus W. van Beek*, Winona Lake, IN: 213–217.

Parr, P. et al. 1970: Preliminary survey in n.w. Arabia, 1968, *Institute of Archaeology Bulletin* 8/9: 193–242.

Parr, P. et al. 1978: Preliminary report on the second phase of the Northern Province Survey, 1387–1977, *Atlal* 2: 29–50.

Pauketat, T. 2007: *Chiefdoms and other archaeological delusions*, Lanham, MD.

Perkins, M. 1998: Timeless cultures: The 'Dreamtime' as colonial discourse, *Time & Society* 7: 335–351.

Peterson, J. 2010: Domesticating gender: Neolithic patterns from the southern Levant, *Journal of Anthropological Archaeology* 29: 249–264.

Petrie, C. 1998: The Iron Age fortification of Husn Awhala (Fujairah, UAE), *Arabian Archaeology and Epigraphy* 9: 246–260.

Peyronel, L. 2000: Some remarks on Mesopotamian metrology during the Old Babylonian period: The evidence from graves LG/23 and LG/45 at Ur, *Iraq* 62: 177–186.

Phillips, C. S. 1987: *Wadi al Qawr, Fashgha-1: The excavation of a prehistoric burial structure, ras al Khaimah, U.A.E., 1986*, Edinburgh.

Phillips, C. S. 1997. The pattern of settlement in the Wadi al Qawr, *Proceedings of the Seminar for Arabian Studies* 27: 205–218.

Phillips, C. S. 2002: Prehistoric shell middens and a cemetery from the southern Arabian Gulf. In: S. Cleuziou et al. (Eds.), *Essays on the late prehistory of the Arabian Peninsula*, Rome: 169–186.

Phillips, C. S. 2007: The third-millennium tombs and settlement at Mowaihat in the Emirate of Ajman, U.A.E., *Arabian Archaeology and Epigraphy* 18: 1–7.

Phillips, W. 1955: *Qataban and Sheba*, London.

Pietsch, D and Kühn, P. 2012: Early Holocene paleosols at the southwestern Ramlat as-Sabatyn desert margin: New climate proxies for Southern Arabia, *Palaeogeography, Palaeoclimatology, Palaeoecology* 365–366: 154–165.

Podany, A. 2010: *Brotherhood of kings: How international relations shaped the ancient Near East*, Oxford.

Pollock, S. 2007: The royal cemetery of Ur: Ritual, tradition, and the creation of subjects. In: M. Heinz and H. Feldman (Eds.), *Representations of political power: Case histories from times of changes and dissolving order in the ancient Near East*, Winona Lake, IN: 89–110.

Postgate, N. 1975: Hindanu, *Reallexikon der Assyriologie und vorderasiatischen Archäologie*, 415–416.

Postgate, N. 1992: *Early Mesopotamia: Society and economy at the dawn of history*, London.

Potts, D. T. 1981: Towards an integrated history of culture change in the Arabian Gulf area: Problems of Dilmun, Makkan and the economy of ancient Sumer, *Journal of Oman Studies* 4: 29–52.

Potts, D. T. 1983: Dilmun's further relations: The Syro-Anatolian evidence from the third and second millennia BC. In: H. A. Al Khalifa and M. Rice (Eds.), *Bahrain through the ages: The archaeology*, London: 389–391.

Potts, D.T. 1986: Booty of Magan, *Oriens Antiquus* 25: 271–285.

Potts, D. T. 1990: *A prehistoric mound in the Emirate of Umm al-Qaiwain, UAE: Excavations at Tell Abraq in 1989*, Copenhagen.

Potts, D. T. 1991a: *The Arabian Gulf in Antiquity*, Oxford.

Potts, D. T. 1991b: *Further Excavations at Tell Abraq*, Copenhagen.

Potts, D.T. 1991c: Tayma and the Assyrian Empire, *Arabian Archaeology and Epigraphy* 2: 10–23.

Potts, D. T. 1993a: The late prehistoric, proto-historic, and early historic periods in Eastern Arabia (ca. 5000–1200 B.C.), *Journal of World Prehistory* 7: 163–212.

Potts, D. T. 1993b: A new Bactrian find from southeastern Arabia, *Antiquity* 67: 591–596.

Potts, D. T. 1993c: Rethinking some aspects of trade in the Arabian Gulf, *World Archaeology* 24: 423–440.

Potts, D. T. 1994a: Contributions to the agrarian history of Eastern Arabia II: The cultivars, *Arabian Archaeology and Epigraphy* 5: 236–275.

Potts, D. T. 1994b: South and Central Asian elements at Tell Abraq (Emirate of Umm al-Qaiwain, United Arab Emirates), c. 2200 BC–300 AD. In: A. Parpola and P. Koskikallio (Eds.),

South Asian archaeology, 1993, vol. II, Helsinki: 615–628.

Potts, D. T. 1997: Rewriting the late prehistory of south-eastern Arabia: A reply to Jocelyn Orchard, *Iraq* 59: 63–71.

Potts, D. T. 1998: Some issues in the study of the pre-Islamic weaponry of southeastern Arabia, *Arabian Archaeology and Epigraphy* 9: 182–208.

Potts, D. T. 2000: *Ancient Magan: The secrets of Tell Abraq*, London.

Potts, D. T. 2001: Before the Emirates: An archaeological and historical account of developments in the region ca. 5000 BC to 676 AD. In: P. al-Abed and P. Hellyer (Eds.) *United Arab Emirates: A new perspective*, London: 28–69.

Potts, D. T. 2003: The mukarrib and his beads: Karib'il Watar's Assyrian diplomacy in the early 7th century BC, *Isimu* 6: 197–206.

Potts, D. T. 2004: Camel hybridization and the role of *Camelus bactrianus* in the Ancient Near East, *Journal of the Economic and Social History of the Orient* 47: 143–165.

Potts, D. T. 2005: In the beginning: Marhashi and the origins of Magan's ceramic industry in the third millennium BC, *Arabian Archaeology and Epigraphy* 16: 67–78.

Potts, D. T. 2006: Elamites and Kassites in the Persian Gulf, *Journal of Near Eastern Studies* 65: 111–119.

Potts, D. T. 2007: Revisiting the snake burials of the late Dilmun building complex on Bahrain, *Arabian Archaeology and Epigraphy* 18: 55–74.

Potts, D. T. 2009: Urartian and Assyrian echoes at Saruq al-Hadid (Emirate of Dubai), *Liwa* 2: 3–9.

Potts, D. T. 2010: Cylinder seals and their use in the Arabian Peninsula, *Arabian Archaeology and Epigraphy* 21: 20–40.

Potts, D. T. and Reade, W. 1993: New evidence for late third millennium linen from Tell Abraq, Umm al-Qaiwain, UAE, *Paléorient* 19: 99–106.

Potts, D. T. et al. 1978: Preliminary report on the second phase of the Eastern Province Survey, *Atlal* 2: 7–28.

Potts D. T. et al. 1996: Husn Awhala: A late prehistoric settlement in southern Fujairah, *Arabian Archaeology and Epigraphy* 7: 214–239.

Prange, M. 2001: 5000 Jahre Kupfer im Oman, Band 2: Vergleichende Untersuchungen zur Charakterisierung des omanischen Kupfers mittels chemischer und isotopischer Analysenmethoden, *Metalla* 8: 1–126.

Price, B. 1978: Secondary state formation: An exploratory model. In: R. Cohen and E. R. Service (Eds.), *Origins of the state: The anthropology of political evolution*, Philadelphia: 161–224.

Pullar, J. 1985: A selection of aceramic sites in the Sultanate of Oman, *Journal of Oman Studies* 7: 49–87.

Pullar, J. and Jäckli, B. 1978: Some aceramic sites in Oman, *Journal of Oman Studies* 1: 53–74.

Radies, D. et al. 2005: Paleoclimatic significance of Early Holocene faunal assemblages in wet interdune deposits of the Wahiba Sand Sea, Sultanate of Oman, *Journal of Arid Environments* 62: 109–125.

ur-Rahman, S. 1979: Report on the Hili 2 settlement excavations, 1976–1979, *Archaeology in the United Arab Emirates* 2/3: 8–18.

Rathbun, T. A. 1982: Morphological affinities and demography of metal-age southwest Asian populations, *American Journal of Physical Anthropology* 59: 47–60.

Ratnagar, S. 1981: *Encounters: The westerly trade of the Harappan civilization*, Oxford.

Rawlinson, H. 1880: Notes on Capt. Durand's report upon the island of Bahrein, *Journal of the Royal Asiatic Society of Great Britain and Ireland* 12: 201–227.

Reade, J. 1983: Commerce or conquest: Variations in the Mesopotamia-Dilmun relationship, In H. A. Al Khalifa. and M. Rice (Eds.), *Bahrain through the ages: The archaeology*, London: 332–333.

Reade, J. 2008: The Indus-Mesopotamian relationship reconsidered. In: E. Olijdam and R. H. Spoor (Eds.), *Intercultural relations between South and Southwest Asia: Studies in commemoration of E. C. L. During Caspers (1934–1996)*, Oxford: 12–18.

Reade, J. and Searight, A. 2001: Arabian softstone vessels from Iraq in the British Museum, *Arabian Archaeology and Epigraphy* 12: 156–172.

Redard, R. 1964: Camelina: Notes de dialectologie iranienne, II. In: *Indo-Iranica: Mélanges présentés à Georg Morgenstierne à l'occasion de so soixante-dixiéme anniversaire*, Wesibaden: 155–162.

Rice, P. M. 1981: Evolution of specialized pottery production: A trial model, *Current Anthropology* 22: 219–240.

Rice, M. 1988: al-Hajjar revisited: The grave complex at al-Hajjar, Bahrain, *Proceedings of the Seminar for Arabian Studies* 18: 79–94.

Ripinsky, M. 1975: The camel in ancient Arabia, *Antiquity* 49: 295–298.

Ripinsky, M. 1985: The camel in Dynastic Egypt, *Journal of Egyptian Archaeology* 71: 134–141.

Roaf, M. 1982: Weights on the Dilmun standard, *Iraq* 44: 137–141.

Roaf, M. and Galbraith, J. 1994: Pottery and p-values: 'Seafaring merchants of Ur?' re-examined, *Antiquity* 68: 770–783.

Robin, C. 1991: Quelques épisodes marquants de l'histoire sudarabique, *Revue du Monde Musulman et de la Méditerranée* 61: 55–70.

Robin, C. 1996: Sheba, II: Dans les inscriptions d'Arabie du Sud. In: *Supplement au Dictionnaire de la Bible*, Paris: 1047–1254.

Rose, J. I. 2004: The question of Upper Pleistocene connections between East Africa and South Arabia, *Current Anthropology* 45: 551–555.

Rosen, L. 2005: Theorizing from within: Ibn Khaldun and his political culture, *Contemporary Sociology* 34: 596–599.

Rothenberg, B. 1972. *Timna: Valley of the biblical copper mines*, London.

Rothenberg, B. and Glass, J. 1983: The Midianite pottery. In: J. F. A. Sawyer and D. J. A. Clines (Eds.), *Midian, Moab and Edom: The history and archaeology of Late Bronze and Iron Age Jordan and North-West Arabia*, Sheffield: 65–124.

Rouse, L. M. and Weeks, L. 2011: Specialization and social inequality in Bronze Age SE Arabia: Analyzing the development of production strategies and economic networks using agent-based modeling, *Journal of Archaeological Science* 38: 1583–1590.

Rowley-Conwy, P. 1988: The camel in the Nile Valley: New radiocarbon accelerator (AMS) dates from Qasr Ibrim, *Journal of Egyptian Archaeology* 74: 245–248.

Rowley-Conwy, P. et al. 1997: Ancient DNA from archaeological sorghum (*Sorghum bicolor*) from Qasr Ibrim, Nubia: Implications for domestication and evolution and a review of the archaeological evidence, *Sahara* 9: 23–34.

Rutter, E. 1930: The habitability of the Arabian desert, *Geographical Journey* 76: 512–515.

Ryckmans, J. 2001: Origin and evolution of South Arabian minuscule writing on wood, *Arabian Archaeology and Epigraphy* 12: 223–235.

Safar, F. et al. 1981: *Eridu*, Baghdad.

Said, E. 1978: *Orientalism*, London.

Al-Said, S. F. 2010: Dedan (al-Ula). In: A. I. al-Ghabban et al. (Eds.), *Roads of Arabia: Archaeology and history of the Kingdom of Saudi Arabia*, Paris: 262–269.

Saitta, D. J. 2005: Marxism, tribal society and the dual nature of archaeology, *Rethinking Marxism* 17: 385–397.

Sallaberger, W. and Westenholz, A. 1999: *Mesopotamien: Akkade-Zeit und Ur III-Zeit*, Freiburg.

Salles, J.-F. (Ed.) 1983: *Failaka: Fouilles françaises, 1983*, Lyon.

Salvatori, S. 1996: Death and ritual in a population of food foragers in Oman. In G. Afanas'ev et al. (Eds.), *The prehistory of Asia and Oceania*, Forli: 205–222.

Salvatori, S. 2007: The prehistoric graveyard at Ra's al-Hamra RH-5. In S. Cleuziou and M. Tosi (Eds.), *In the shadow of the ancestors: The prehistoric foundations of the early Arabian civilization in Oman*, Muscat: 98–102.

Salvini, M. 2001: Pas de qanats en Urartu! In: Irrigation et drainage dans l'antiquité: Qanats et canalisations souterraines en Iran, en Égypte et en Grèce, séminaire tenu au Collège de France sous la direction de Pierre Briant, *Persika* 2: 143–155.

as-Samiya, M. H. 2006: *Mantaqa rajoom Sasa bi Tayma*, Riyadh (in Arabic).

Sanlaville, P. 1992: Changements climatiques dans la péninsule arabique durant le Pléistocène supérieur et l'Holocène, *Paléorient* 18: 5–26.

Sass, B. 1991: *Studia alphabetica: On the origin and early history of the Northwest Semitic, South Semitic and Greek Alphabets*, Freiburg.

Sayce, A. H. 1889: Ancient Arabia, *Science* 14: 406–408.

Scagliarini, F. 2002: The origin of the qanat system in the al-Ula area and the Gabal Ikma inscriptions, *ARAM* 13/14: 569–579.

Schachner, A. 2007: *Bilder eines Weltreichs. Kunst- und kulturgeschichtliche Untersuchungen zu den Verzierungen eines Tores aus Balawat (Imgur-Enlil) aus der Zeit von Salmanassar III., König von Assyrien*, Turnhout.

Schaloske, M. 1995: *Untersuchungen der Sabäischen Bewässerungsanlagen in Marib*, Archaologische Berichte aus dem Yemen 7, Mainz.

Schiettecatte, J. 2007: Urbanization and settlement patterns in ancient Hadramawt (1st millen. BC), *Bulletin of Archaeology of the Kanazawa University* 28: 11–28.

Schiettecatte, J. et al. 2013: The oasis of al-Kharj through time: First results of archaeological fieldwork in the province of Riyadh (Saudi Arabia), *Proceedings of the Seminar for Arabian Studies* 43: 285–308.

Schreiber, J. 2010: The Iron I period in south-eastern Arabia: A view from central Oman. In: A. Avanzini (Ed.), *Eastern Arabia in the first millennium BC*, Rome: 81–90.

Schultz, E. and Whitney, J. W. 1986: Upper Pleistocene and Holocene lakes in the An Nafud, Saudi Arabia, *Hydrobiologia* 143: 175–190.

Scigliuzzo, E. 2003: A South Arabian ivory vessel from Hama reconsidered, *Ugarit- Forschungen* 35: 629–647.

Sedov, A. V. 1996: On the origin of the agricultural settlements in Hadramawt. In C. Robin (Ed.), *Arabia antiqua: Early origins of south Arabian states*, Rome: 67–86.

Semsar Yazdi, A. A. and Labbaf Khaneiki, M. 2010: Veins of desert: A review of the technique of Qanat/Falaj/ Karez, UNESCO & International Centre on Qanats and Historic Hydraulic Structures, Iran Water Resources Management Organization, Tehran.

al-Shanfari, A. B. and Weisgerber, G. 1989: A Late Bronze Age warrior burial from Nizwa, Oman. In: P. Costa and M. Tosi (Eds.), *Oman studies: Papers on the archaeology and history of Oman*, Rome: 17–30.

Sherif, M. et al. 2012: Modeling groundwater flow and seawater intrusion in the coastal aquifer of Wadi Ham, UAE, *Water Resource Management* 26: 751–774.

Simpson, St. John. 1994: Gazelle-hunters and salt-collectors: A further note on the Solubba, *Bulletin of the American Schools of Oriental Research* 293: 79–81.

Singer-Avitz, L. 1999: Beersheba: A gateway community in southern Arabian long-distance trade in the eighth century B.C.E., *Tel Aviv:* 26: 3–74.

Smith, B. 2001: Low level food production, *Journal of Archaeological Research* 9: 1–43.

Smith, G. 1976: New neolithic sites in Oman, *Journal of Oman Studies* 2: 189–198.

Smith, G. 1977: New prehistoric sites in Oman, *Journal of Oman Studies* 3: 71–81.

Sollberger, E. and Kupper, J.-R. 1971: *Inscriptions royales sumériennes et akkadiennes*, Paris.

Staubwasser, M. et al. 2002: South Asian monsoon climate change and radiocarbon in the Arabian Sea during the early and mid Holocene, *Paleoceanography* 17: 1–12.

Steimer-Herbet, T. 2007: Un sanctuaire ouvert du IVe millénaire avant l'ère chrétienne (Wadi 'Idim, Hadramawt), *Chroniques Yéménites* 14: 15–22.

Steimer-Herbet, T. 2010: Three funerary stelae from the 4th millennium BC. In: A. I. al-Ghabban et al. (Eds.), *Roads of Arabia: Archaeology and history of the Kingdom of Saudi Arabia*, Paris: 166–169.

Stein, A. 1934: Archaeological reconnaissances in southern Persia, *Geographic Journal* 83(2): 119–134.

Stein, G. 1994: Economy, ritual and power in Ubaid Mesopotamia. In: G. Stein and M. Rothman (Eds.), *Chiefdoms and early states in the Near East: The organizational dynamics of complexity*, Sheffield: 35–46.

Stein, G. et al. 2006: A tale of two Oikumenai: Variation in the expansionary dynamics of Ubaid and Uruk Mesopotamia. In: E. C. Stone (Ed.), *Settlement and society: Ecology, urbanism, trade and technology in Mesopotamia and beyond (Robert McC. Adams Festschrift)*, Santa Fe, NM: 356–370.

Steinkeller, P. 1982: The question of Marhasi: A contribution to the historical geography of Iran in the third millennium BC, *Zeitschrift für Assyriologie und Vorderasiatische Archäologie* 72: 237–265.

Steinkeller, P. 1989: *Sale documents of the Ur III period*, Stuttgart.

Steinkeller, P. 1995: Sheep and goat terminology in Ur III sources from Drehem, *Bulletin of Sumerian Agriculture* 8: 49–56.

Steinkeller, P. 2004: Toward a definition of private economic activity in third millennium Babylonia. In: R. Rollinger and U. Christoph (Eds.), *Commerce and monetary systems in the ancient world: Means of transmission and cultural interaction*, Stuttgart: 91–111.

Stephan, E. 1995: Preliminary report on the faunal remains of the first two seasons of Tell Abraq / Umm al-Quwain / United Arab Emirates. In: H. Buitenhuis and H.-P. Uerpmann (Eds.), *Archaeozoology of the Near East II*, Leiden: 53–63.

Stevens, J. H. 1978: Post-Pluvial changes in the soils of the Arabian peninsula. In: W.C. Brice (Ed.), *Environmental history of the Near and Middle East since the last ice age*, London: 263–274.

Stewart, R. 1987: Appendix 4: Botanical remains. In: W. Glanzman and A. O. Ghaleb (Eds.), *The Wadi al-Jubah Archaeological Project,* vol. 3: *Site reconnaissance in the Yemen Arab Republic, 1984: Stratigraphic probe at Hajar ar-Rayhani*, Washington, DC: 162–163.

Stewart, R. 1996: Summarized species list for the botanical remains excavated in 1987 at Hajar ar-Rayhani, Yemen Arab Republic. In: W. Overstreet and J. Blakely (Eds.), *Environmental research in support of archaeological investigations in the Yemen Arab Republic, 1982–1987*, Washington, DC: 299.

Stronach, D. 2003: Early Achaemenid Iran: New considerations. In: W. G. Dever and S. Gitin (Eds.), *Symbiosis, symbolism, and the power of the past: Canaan, ancient Israel, and their neighbors from the Late Bronze Age through Roman Palaestina*, Jerusalem: 133–144.

al-Suad, A. S. et al. 2005: Report on the rock art survey of Jubbah, *Atlal* 18: 39–42.

Tadmor, H. 1994: *The inscriptions of Tiglath-pileser III, King of Assyria*, Jerusalem.

Taha, M. 1983: The archaeology of the Arabian Gulf during the first millennium B.C., *Al Rafidan* 3–4: 75–87.

Tebes, J. M. 2007: Pottery makers and premodern exchange in the fringes of Egypt: An approximation to the distribution of Iron Age Midianite pottery, *Buried History* 43: 11–26.

Tengberg, M. 1998: *Paléoenvironnements et économie végétale en milieu aride: Recherches archéobotaniques dans la région du Golfe arabo-persique et dans le Makran pakistanais (4ème millénaire av. notre ère – 1er millénaire de notre ère)*, Unpublished PhD dissertation, University of Montpellier II.

Tengberg, M. in press: Beginnings and early history of date palm cultivation in the Middle East, *Journal of Arid Environments*.

Thesiger, W. 2008: *Arabian Sands*, London.

al-Tikriti, W. Y. 1985: The archaeological investigations on Ghanadha island, 1982–1984: Further evidence for the coastal Umm an-Nar culture, *Archaeology in the United Arab Emirates* 4: 9–19.

al-Tikriti, W. Y. 1989a: The excavations at Bidiyah, Fujairah: The 3rd and 2nd millennia BC culture, *Archaeology in the United Arab Emirates* 5: 101–114.

al-Tikriti, W. Y. 1989b: Umm an-Nar culture in the northern Emirates: Third millennium BC tombs at Ajman, *Archaeology in the United Arab Emirates* 5: 89–99.

al-Tikriti, W. Y. 2002: The south-east Arabian origin of the falaj system, *Proceedings of the Seminar for Arabian Studies* 32: 117–138.

al-Tikriti, W. Y. 2010: Heading north: An ancient caravan route and the impact of the falaj system on the Iron Age culture. In: A. Avanzini (Ed.), *Eastern Arabia in the first millennium BC*, Rome: 227–247.

al-Tikriti, W. Y. 2011: *Rock art in Abu Dhabi Emirate*, Abu Dhabi.

al-Tikriti, W. Y. et al. 2004: New approaches to a collective grave from the Umm an-Nar period at Hili (UAE), *Paléorient* 30: 163–178.

Tixier, J. 1986: The prehistory of the Gulf, recent finds. In: H. A. Al Khalifa and M. Rice (Eds.), *Bahrain through the ages: The archaeology*, London: 76–78.

Tosi, M. 1986a: Archaeological activities in the Yemen Arab Republic, 1986: Survey and excavations on the coastal plain (Tihamah), *East and West* 36: 400–415.

Tosi, M. 1986b: The emerging picture of prehistoric Arabia, *Annual Review of Anthropology* 15: 461–490.

Troy, J. 1993: *King plates: A history of Aboriginal gorgets*, Canberra.

al-Turki T. A. and al-Olayan, H. A. 2003: Contribution to the flora of Saudi Arabia: Hail Region, *Saudi Journal of Biological Science* 10: 190–222.

Twitchell, K. S. 1944: Water resources of Saudi Arabia, *Geographical Review* 34: 365–386.

Uerpmann H.-P. 1991: *Equus africanus* in Arabia. In R. H. Meadow and H.-P. Uerpmann (Eds.), *Equids in the ancient world*, vol. 2, Weisbaden: 12–33.

Uerpmann, H.-P. and Uerpmann, M. 2002: The appearance of the domestic camel in SE-Arabia, *Journal of Oman Studies* 12: 235–260.

Uerpmann, H.-P. et al. (Eds.) 2006: *Funeral monuments and human remains from Jebel al-Buhais*, Tübingen.

Uerpmann, H-P. et al. 2008: *The natural environment of Jebel Buhais, past and present*, Tübingen.

Uerpmann, H-P. et al. 2009: The Holocene (re-)occupation of eastern Arabia. In: M. D. Petraglia and J. I. Rose (Eds.), *The evolution of human populations in Arabia: Paleoenvironments, prehistory and genetics*, New York: 205–214.

Uerpmann, M. 1992: Structuring the Late Stone Age of southeastern Arabia, *Arabian Archaeology and Epigraphy* 3: 65–109.

Uerpmann, M. 2003: The dark millennium: Remarks on the final stone age in the Emirates and Oman. In: D. T. Potts et al. (Eds.), *Proceedings of the First International Conference on the Archaeology of the UAE*, Abu Dhabi: 73–84.

Uerpmann, M. and Uerpmann, H.-P. 1997: Animal bones. In F. Højlund and H. Andersen (Eds.), *Qala'at al-Bahrain 2: The central monumental buildings*, Aarhus: 235–259.

Uerpmann, M. and Uerpmann, H.-P. 2005a: Fish exploitation at Bronze Age harbour sites in the Arabian Gulf area, *Paléorient* 31: 108–115.

Uerpmann, M. and Uerpmann, H.-P. 2005b: Animal bone finds and their relevance to the ecology and economy of Saar. In: R. Killick and J. Moon (Eds.), *The early Dilmun settlement at Saar*, London: 293–308.

Uerpmann, M. and Uerpmann, H.-P. 2007: Animal economy in an early oasis settlement. In: S. Cleuziou and M. Tosi (Eds.), *In the shadow of the ancestors: The prehistoric foundations of the early Arabian civilization in Oman*, Muscat: 158–159.

Uerpmann, M. and Uerpmann, H.-P. 2008a: Neolithic faunal remains from al-Buhais 18 (Sharjah, UAE). In: H.-P. Uerpmann et al. (Eds.), *The natural environment of Jebel Buhais, past and present*, Tübingen: 97–132.

Uerpmann, M. and Uerpmann, H.-P. 2008b: Animal economy during the Early Bronze Age in South-East Arabia. In: E. Vila et al. (Eds.), *Archaeozoology of the Near East VIII: TMO 49*, Lyon: 465–485.

Uerpmann, M. and Uerpmann, H.-P. in press: Archaeozoology of camels in South-Eastern Arabia.

Van Beek, G. 1969: *Hajar Bin Humeid: Investigations at a pre-Islamic site in South Arabia*, Baltimore.

Van Beek, G. 1997: 'Hajar Bin Humeid'. In: E. M. Meyers (Ed.), *The Oxford encyclopedia of archaeology in the Near East*, vol. 2, Oxford: 457–458.

Van Berg, P.-L. et al. 2004: Desert kites of the Hemma Plateau, *Paléorient* 30:89–99.

Van De Mieroop, M. 1992: Old Babylonian Ur: Portrait of an ancient Mesopotamian city, *Journal of the Ancient Near Eastern Society* 21: 119–130.

Van De Mieroop, M. 2007: *A history of the ancient Near East*, London.

Varisco, D. M. 1983: Sayl and Ghayl: The ecology of water allocation in Yemen, *Human Ecology* 11: 365–383.

Velde, C. 1991: Preliminary remarks on the settlement pottery in Shimal. In: K. Schippmann et al. (Eds.), *Golf-Archaologie*, Leidorf: 265–288.

Velde, C. 2003: Wadi Suq and Late Bronze Age in the Oman Peninsula. In: D. T. Potts et al. (Eds.), *Proceedings of the First International Conference on the Archaeology of the UAE*, Abu Dhabi: 102–149.

Veldhuis, N. 2000: Kassite exercises: Literary and lexical texts, *Journal of Cuneiform Studies* 52: 67–94.

Vermaak, P. S. 2008. Guabba, the Meluhhan village in Mesopotamia, *Journal for Semitics* 17: 553–570.

Vilos, J. D. 2011: *The bioarchaeology of compassion: Exploring extreme cases of pathology in a Bronze Age skeletal population from Tell Abraq, UAE*, Unpublished master's thesis, University of Nevada.

Vincent, P. 2008: *Saudi Arabia: An environmental overview*, London.

Vogt, B. 1985: *Zur Chronologie und Entwicklung der Gräber des späten 4.-2. Jtsd. V Chr. auf der Halbinsel Oman*, Unpublished PhD dissertation, University of Göttingen.

Vogt, B. 1994: *Asimah: An account of a two months rescue excavation in the mountains of Ra's al-Khaimah, United Arab Emirates*, Dubai.

Vogt, B. 1996: Bronze Age maritime trade in the Indian Ocean: Harappan traits on the Oman peninsula. In: J. Reade (Ed.), *The Indian Ocean in antiquity*, London: 107–132.

Vogt, B. and Franke-Vogt, U. 1987: *Shimal, 1985/1986: Excavations of the German Mission in Ras al-Khaimah, U.A.E., – A preliminary report*, Berlin.

Vogt, B. and Sedov, A. 1998: The Sabir culture and coastal Yemen during the second millennium BC: The present state of the discussion, *Proceedings of the Seminar for Arabian Studies* 28:261–70.

Vogt, B. et al. 2002: Ma 'layba and the Bronze Age irrigation in coastal Yemen, *Archäologische Berichte aus dem Yemen* 9: 15–26.

von den Driesch, A. et al. 2008: The hunt for wild dromedaries at the United Arab Emirates coast during the 3rd and 2nd millennia BC: Camel bones from the excavations at Al Sufouh 2, Dubai, UAE. In: E. Vila et al. (Eds.), *Archaeozoology of the Near East VIII*, Lyon: 487–498.

Waetzoldt, H. 1972: *Untersuchungen zur neosumerischen Textileindustrie*, Rome.

Waetzoldt, H. 1983: Leinen (Flachs), *Reallexikon der Assyriologie* 6: 583–594.

Waltham, T. 2008: Salt terrains of Iran, *Geology Today* 24: 188–194.

Wapnish, P. 1981: Camel caravans and camel pastoralists at Tell Jemmeh, *Journal of Near Eastern Studies* 13: 101–121.

Wapnish, P. 1984: The dromedary and Bactrian camel in Levantine historical settings: The evidence from Tell Jemmeh. In: J. Clutton-Brock and C. Grigson (Eds.), *Animals and archaeology 3: Early herders and their flocks*, Oxford: 171–200.

Watkins, T. 2010: New light on Neolithic revolution in south-west Asia, *Antiquity* 84: 621–634.

Weeks, L. R. 1999: Lead isotope analyses from Tell Abraq, United Arab Emirates: New data regarding the 'tin problem' in western Asia, *Antiquity*, 73/279: 49–64.

Weeks, L. R. 2003: *Early metallurgy of the Persian Gulf: Technology, trade, and the Bronze Age world*, Cambridge, MA.

Weeks, L. R. et al. 2009: Lead isotope analyses of Bronze Age copper-base artefacts from al-Midamman, Yemen: Towards the identification of an indigenous metal production and exchange system in the southern Red Sea, *Archaeometry* 51: 576–597.

Weisgerber, G. 1980: '... und Kupfer in Oman' – Das Oman-Projekt des Deutschen Bergbau-Museums, *Der Anschnitt* 32(2/3): 62–110.

Weisgerber, G. 1981: Mehr als Kupfer in Oman: Ergebnisse der Expedition 1981, *Der Anschnitt* 33(5/6): 174–263.

Weisgerber, G. 1991: Die Suche nach dem alt-sumerischen Kupferland Makan, *Das Altertum* 37: 76–90.

Weisgerber, G. 2007. Copper production as seen from al-Moyassar-1. In: S. Cleuziou and M. Tosi (Eds.) 2007: *In the shadow of the ancestors: The prehistoric foundations of the early Arabian civilization in Oman*, Muscat: 251–254.

Weisgerber, G. and Yule, P. 1999: Preliminary report on the 1996 season of excavation in the Sultanate of Oman. In: P. Yule (Ed.), *Studies in the archaeology of the Sultanate of Oman*, Rahden: 97–118.

Weiss, H. et al. 1993: The genesis and collapse of third millennium north Mesopotamian civilization, *Science* 261: 995–1004.

Wellbrock, K. and Grottker, M. 2010: Reconstruction of mid-Holocene climate conditions for north-western Arabian oasis Tayma. In: *Proceedings of the 4th International Conference on Water Resources and Arid Environments*, Riyadh: 694–703.

Wellsted, J. R. 1838: *Travels in Arabia*, London.

Wilkinson, J. C. 1997: *Water and tribal settlement in Oman*, Oxford.

Wilkinson, T. J. 2003: *Archaeological landscapes of the Near East*, Tucson, AZ.

Wilkinson, T. J. 2009: Environment and long-term population trends in southwest Arabia. In: M. D. Petraglia and J. I. Rose (Eds.), *The evolution of human populations in Arabia: Paleoenvironments, prehistory and genetics*, New York: 51–66.

Wilkinson, T. J. and Edens, C. 1999: Survey and excavation in the central highlands of Yemen: Results of the Dhamar Survey Project, 1996 and 1998, *Arabian Archaeology and Epigraphy* 10: 1–33.

Wilkinson, T. J. et al. 1997: The archaeology of the Yemen high plains: A preliminary chronology, *Arabian Archaeology and Epigraphy* 8: 99–142.

Wilkinson, T. J. et al. 2012: From human niche construction to imperial power: Long term trends in ancient Iranian water systems, *Water History* 4: 155–176.

Willcox, G. et al. 2012: From collecting to cultivation: Transitions to a production economy in the Near East, *Vegetation History and Archaeobotany* 21: 81–83.

Winter, I. J. 1983: Carchemish sa kisad puratti, *Anatolian Studies* 33: 177–197.

Yesner, D. R. 1980: Maritime hunter-gatherers: Ecology and prehistory, *Current Anthropology* 26: 727–750.

Yoffee, N. 2005: *The myth of the archaic state*, Cambridge.

Zaccagnini, C. 1986: The Dilmun standard and its relationship with Indus and Near Eastern weight systems, *Iraq* 48: 19–23.

Zarins, J. 1978: Steatite vessels in the Riyadh Museum, *Atlal* 2: 65–93.

Zarins, J. 1979: Rajajil: A unique Arabian site from the fourth millennium B.C., *Atlal* 3: 73–77.

Zarins, J. 1989a: Ancient Egypt and the Red Sea trade: The case for obsidian in the Predynastic and Archaic periods. In: A. Leonard, Jr. and B. B. William (Eds.), *Essays in ancient civilization presented to Helene J. Kantor*, London: 339–368.

Zarins, J. 1989b: Eastern Saudi Arabia and external relations: Selected ceramic, steatite and textual evidence, 3500–1900 B.C. In: K. Frifelt and P. Sorensen (Eds.), *South Asian archaeology, 1985*, London: 74–103.

Zarins, J. 1990: Obsidian and the Red Sea Trade: prehistoric aspects. In: M. Taddei and P. Callieri (Eds.), *South Asian archaeology, 1987*, Rome: 507–541.

Zarins, J. 1992. Pastoral nomadism in Arabia: Ethnoarchaeology and the archaeological record: A case study. In: O. Bar-Yosef and A. Khazanov (Eds.), *Pastoralism in the Levant*, Madison, WI: 219–240.

Zarins, J. and Badr, H. 1986: Archaeological investigations in the Tihama plain I, 1405/1985, *Atlal* 10: 36–57.

Zarins, J. and Zahrani, A. 1985: Recent archaeological investigations in the southern Tihama plain, 1404/1984, *Atlal* 9: 65–107.

Zarins, J. et al. 1979: Preliminary report on the survey of the central province, 1978, *Atlal* 1: 9–42.

Zarins, J. et al. 1980: Preliminary report on the Central and Southwestern provinces survey, *Atlal* 4: 9–36.

Zarins, J. et al. 1981: The second preliminary report on the Southwestern Province, *Atlal* 5: 9–42.

Zarins, J. et al. 1982: Preliminary report on the archaeological survey of the Riyadh area, *Atlal* 6: 25–38.

Zarins, J. et al. 1984: Excavations at Dhahran South: The Tumuli Field (208–92), 1403

A.H./1983: A preliminary report, *Atlal* 8: 25–54.

Zeder, M. 1991: *Feeding cities: Specialized animal economy in the ancient Near East*, Washington, DC.

Zeder, M. 1994: After the revolution: Post-Neolithic subsistence in northern Mesopotamia, *American Anthropologist* 96: 97–126.

Zeder, M. 2006a: Archaeozoology in southwest Asia: A status report based on the 8th meeting of the ASWA working group, 2005, *Paléorient* 32: 137–147.

Zeder, M. 2006b: Documenting domestication: The intersection of genetics and archaeology, *Trends in Genetics* 22: 139–155.

Zeder, M. 2011: The origins of agriculture in the Near East, *Current Anthropology* 52: 221–235.

Zeder, M. and Hesse, B. 2000: The initial domestication of goats (*Capra hircus*) in the Zagros mountains 10,000 years ago, *Science* 287: 2254–2257.

INDEX

Aali, 87–8, 163–7, 177
Abu Khamis, 68, 71–3
ad-Durayb Yala, 205, 245–9
ahlamu, 180–1
Ain-Ghazal, 49
Ain-Qannas, 68, 73
Akab, 72, 79–81
Amlah, 100
Ancient South Arabian (language), 244–5
Aquifers
    Saudi Arabia, 32–3
    UAE and Oman, 25–6
Asimah, 100, 238
Asir, 29, 36, 41, 56, 150
Ass domestication and appearance in Arabia.
        See donkey
Assabiya (social cohesion), 11–12, 62,
        251, 275–6
Assurbanipal, 271
    battles in northern Arabia, 271–2
Assur-bel-kala, 207
Assyrian empire
    and the Arabian Gulf, 271–2
    and northern Arabia, 268–72
Azraq 31, 50

Babylon, 1, 3, 178–9, 195, 270, 272–4, 281
Bahrain
    Bronze Age. *See* Dilmun
Barbar, 163
Barbar temple, 158–61, 164, 177
Barqa el-Hetiye, 262
Bat, 98, 100–1, 225, 282
Batinah coast, 23
Baynunah, 199

Belghalem, 234
Bell, Gertrude, 4
Beth Shemesh, 244
Bida al-Mutawa, 57
Bida Bint Saud, 216, 219–20, 236–7
Bidya, 100
Bisyah, 98, 100
Bithna, 238
Burqu, 27, 50

Carchemish, 208, 210, 257, 264, 266
Childe, V. G., 46
Climate (ancient), 42–5
Climate (today)
    Dhofar, 27
    Saudi Arabia, 29–31
    UAE and Oman, 25
    Yemen, 28–9

Dadna, 189
Dalma, 57–8, 71–2
Dar Kulaib, 163
date palm
    early domestication, 58
Dhahran, 89, 173, 178, 254
Dhahret al-Hasa, 216, 219–20
Dhamar
    Bronze Age, 128
    early agriculture, 126–8
Dhofar, 26–7, 38, 42, 55, 78, 97, 137
Dilmun
    Bronze Age burials, 163–5
    Bronze Age seals, 166–70
    decline of Bronze Age state, 176–7
    discovery, 87–8

Dilmun (*cont.*)
    emergence in the late third millennium
        BC, 152–4
    Iron Age occupation, 271–2
    Kassite control, 177–9
    nature of Bronze Age state, 173–6
    use of the term before 2500 BC, 90–3
donkey (ass)
    domestication and appearance in
        Arabia, 105–6
Dosariyah, 57, 68, 70–2
Dromedary camel
    evidence for domesticated dromedary in
        southeastern Arabia, 205, 210–12
    evidence for domesticated dromedary in
        southwestern Arabia, 205–6
    evidence for domesticated dromedary in
        Syria, 207–10
    hunting of wild, 201
    markers of domestication, 203–4
    textual sources, 203
    and trade to Syria, 264–8
    and trade to the southern Levant, 263
Dumat al-Jandal (ancient Adummatu),
    256–7, 267

Ea-naṣir, 166, 168, 173–5

Fadak, 267, 273
Failaka, 109, 164, 169–70, 178, 181
    Bronze Age, 170–2
    Kassite control, 180
Falaj system, 215–21
Fasad points, 48
Frankincense, 38–9

Guabba, 167

Hadabah, al-, 127
Hafit culture
    burials, 93–4, 96–7
    settlements, 94–6
Hajar bin Humeid, 245, 249
Hajar Yahirr, 242
Hajjar mountains, 15
    geological history, 15–18
Hama, 264, 266
Hammat al-Qa, 128, 132, 286
Hamriya, 190, 227
Harrat Khaybar, 148
Hasa, 32
Hawa, al-, 48
Hayt al-Suad, 78, 126, 131

Haza'el, king of northern Arabia, 271
Highlands, 37
    Bronze Age, 126–32
    rainfall, 37–8
Hijaz
    Bronze Age, 144–5
    Egyptian imperialism and settlement
        growth, 258
    Iron Age, 252–8
Hili
    Umm an-Nar burials, 122–4
Hili 1, 100
Hili 14, 215, 236
Hili 15, 215, 219, 236–7
Hili 17, 215, 220, 227
Hili 2, 219–20
Hili 3, 186
Hili 8, 94–5, 98, 102–5, 107, 186, 199, 218, 283
Hilprecht, Hermann, 4
Hindanu, 265, 267
Hodeidah, 138
Hofuf, 33–4, 57, 90, 93
Hommel. Fritz, 4, 7
Hoota Cave, 42–3, 74
Husn Awhala, 225
Husn Madhab, 225, 236

Ibn Khaldun, 11–12, 275
Indian Ocean monsoon, 14, 25, 28, 35, 40, 42,
    44, 61, 74, 76, 275
Iron Age in northwestern Arabia, 252–8
Iron Age in southeastern Arabia
    Iron Age I period, 189–95
    Iron Age II bronze production, 225
    Iron Age II burials, 240
    Iron Age II ceramic production, 222
    Iron Age II pilgrimage, 239
    Iron Age II settlement patterns, 214–35
Iron Age in southwestern Arabia
    evidence for agriculture, 249–50
    Hadramawt culture, 250–1
    'Sayhadic tradition', 249–50
Izki, 272

Janub al-Mutabthat, 56
Jebeeb, 216, 219
Jebel Arrayig al-Yusri, 59
Jebel Buhais, 189
Jebel Buhais (Iron Age building), 236
Jebel Buhais (Wadi Suq period burials),
    189
Jebel Buhais 18, 62–7, 198
Jebel Faya, 47–8

Jebel Hafit, 93
Jebel Jidran, 136
Jebel Qara, 200
Jebel Ruwaiq
    Bronze Age burials, 136
Jiladah, 56
Jiroft, 107
Jubabat al-Juruf, 78, 126, 131

Kalba, 100, 186–7, 190, 196
Karib'il Watar, 242–3, 248
Kashwaba, 138
Kawr al-Jaramah, 44, 74
Khalwan
    Bronze Age, 131–2
Kharayb, 133
Kharimat Khor al-Manahil, 57
Khaybar, 267, 273
Khirbet el-Meshash, 261
Khor al-Manahil, 57
Khor al-Milkh, 72
Khor-ile Sud, 178
Kilwa, 58
Kites. *See* mass-kill traps

Lagash, 90, 116, 167
Lake Awafi, 187
Late Bronze Age in southeastern Arabia, 189–95
Lawrence of Arabia (movie), 14, 31
Lizq, 236
Lothal, 169
Lu-Enlilla (Ur III period merchant), 116–17, 119, 173–4

Ma'layba, 138
Magan
    discovery of ancient name, 99–100
Makaynun, 250
Manayzah, 51–2, 55–6
Manishtushu, 116, 118
Marawah, 49, 52, 57–8
Marhashi, 92
Mari, 176
Marib, 242, 258
Markh, al-, 69
Masafi, 237–8
Masirah, 184
mass kill traps, 147–50
Massanah, al- site 1, 131
Maysar, 100–1, 103–5, 114–15, 199, 220
Midamman, al-, 138, 141–3
Midianites, 244

Midianites and Midianite pottery, 261–2
Mowaihat, 100, 106, 120, 297
Moyassar, al-, 114
Mundigak, 109
Muweilah, 24, 204, 210, 216, 218, 227–31, 234, 237–8, 245, 267

Nabonidus, 267
    sojourn in Tayma, 272–4
Nafud, 7, 30, 36
    vegetation, 32
Naram-Sin, 116, 118
Nashshan, 242
Neolithic period
    climate, 49
    economy, 50–1
    obsidian use, 54–5
    origins, 49
    rock art, 60–1
    trade with Ubaid Mesopotamia, 68–74
Niebuhr, Carsten, 4–7, 9, 39
Ninurta-kudurri-usur, 266
Nippur, 177
Nisaba, 93
Nizwa, 190, 192
Nud Ziba, 186

Oasis North Arabian (language), 256
Obsidian trade in the Neolithic period.
    See Neolithic period obsidian use
Oryx, Arabian, 32, 34

Palaeolithic period, 47
Palmyra, 266
Punt, 143
Puzur-Inshushinak, 167

Qala'at al-Bahrain, 154, 156, 177, 182
    period III, 177
    period IV, 271
    periods I and II, 152–4
Qanat. *See* Falaj system
Qataban, 243
Qattara, 190
Queen of Sheba, 7, 282, 286
Qunf Cave, 42–3, 74
Qurayyah, 255, 262
Qurayyah ware, 253, 255
Qusais, al-, 190, 234, 237–8
Qutran, 54

Rajajil, 84
Ramesses III, 145

Ramlat as-Sabatyn, 28–9, 38, 136, 243, 267
Ras Aburuk, 69
Ras al-Hadd 6, 96
Ras al-Hamra 5, 75–8
Ras al-Jinz 1, 96, 186–7
Ras al-Jinz 2, 101, 105, 111–12, 117
Ras Ghanadha, 100
Rawk, 83–4
Raybun, 137, 245, 250
Rayhani, 206, 245, 248–9
Rock art
    Bronze Age, 146–7, 200
    Neolithic, 59–61
Rub al-Khali, 18, 27, 42, 56, 233
    vegetation, 56
    in western imagination, 18–21
Rufayq, 227
Rumeilah, 216, 219, 238

Saar, 114, 154–7, 164, 175, 177, 182
Sabaean Federation, 240–4, 251
    and relations with Assyrian empire, 270
Sabir (archaeological site), 138–40
Sabir (culture). *See* Tihama, Bronze Age
Sabiyah, as-, 68–9, 71–2
Sabkha Hammam, 90
Safouh, al-, 120, 199
Salut, 216, 220, 238
Sargon II, 87, 217, 270
    battles in northern Arabia, 270
Sarouq al-Hadid, 227, 232, 237–8
Sayl irrigation, 138, 143
Sedd adh-Dhraa, 127
Sela, 273
Sennacherib, 272
Shabwa, 136–7, 245, 288
Shahr-i Sokhta, 109
Shalmaneser III, 210, 265, 268
    battles in Syria and capture of dromedary
        camels, 268–9
Shamshi-Adad, 165, 176
Shamsi, Queen of the Arabs, 269
Sharm, 192
Sharorah, 56
Shi'b Kheshiya, 79
Shi'b Munaydir, 250
Shimal, 106, 114, 120, 187, 189–90, 194
Shulgi, 116, 118–19
Shuwaymas, 60, 200
Sibakhan stone tools, 47
Sibal, al-, 128, 132
Sirwah, 242, 270
Solubba (nomads of northern Arabia), 149

Suhu, 265
Sumhuyafa, 242
Sur Ju'reh, 264–5
Susa, 114, 169
Suwayh 1, 74

Tarut, 90–1, 109, 173
Tawilan, 262
Tayma, 150, 205, 256–7, 264, 267
    Bronze Age, 144–5
    Iron Age, 210, 252–5
    and Nabonidus, 272–4
Tell Abraq, 100–1, 103–6, 109, 117, 120–1, 182,
        186–7, 190, 193, 199–200, 204, 218,
        226–7, 238
Tell el-Oueli, 58
Tell Halaf, 3, 208–10, 255, 264, 266
Tell Ischali, 169
Tell Jemmeh, 201
Tell Masos, 262
Tell Nami, 201
Tell Sheikh Hamad, 207
Tepe Gaz Tavila, 58
Tepe Yahya, 90–1, 109, 157
Thayyilan, 54
Thesiger, Wilfred, 9, 14, 18, 301
Thumamah, 52
Thuqaibah, al-, 216, 220
Tiglath-Pileser III
    battles in northern Arabia, 269–70
Tihama, 29, 36, 53–4, 138, 141, 243, 291, 304
    Bronze Age, 138–44
Timna, 205, 261–2
Tukulti-Ninurta II, 265

Uaite, king of northern Arabia, 271
Ubaid pottery, 68–9
Ubaid trade with Arabia. *See* Neolithic
        period trade with Ubaid Mesopotamia
Ugarit, 203, 244
Ula, al- (ancient Dedan), 84, 255–6, 273
Umm al-Quwain (Neolithic burial site), 58
Umm an-Nar island, 89, 101, 103–4, 106,
        119–20, 199
Umm an-Nar period
    burials, 120–3
    ceramics production, 107–8
    copper trade, 114–17
    discovery, 88–9
    settlements, 101
    softstone production, 108–9
    subsistence, 102–7
Umm an-Nussi, 90

Umm Dabaghiyah, 149
Umm Jidr, 163
Umm Sanman, 60
Ur, 111, 116, 166, 169, 173, 267
Ur-Namma, 167
Ur-Nanshe, 90
Uruk, 3, 9, 72, 87, 89–90, 116, 170, 300

Wadi Akhdar, 59
Wadi al-Ayaay, 216
Wadi al-Qawr, 225
Wadi al-Tayyilah, 51
Wadi Azlam, 59
Wadi Hadramawt, 28–9, 38, 40, 51, 55, 137
Wadi Hilou, 184, 186
Wadi Jilat, 13, 25, 50
Wadi Sana, 55, 78–9, 136
Wadi Sirhan, 148
Wadi Sunaysal, 189

Wadi Suq period
    bronzework, 183–4
    burials, 188–9
    ceramic production, 184–6
    chronology, 182
    settlements, 186–7
    subsistence, 187–8
Wadi Wutayya, 48
Wadi Yana'im, 132
Wahiba Sands, 23, 286
Wasit, al-, 190, 192
Weights and weight systems
    Dilmun, 168–9
    Indus Valley, 113–14
Woolley, Sir Leonard, 4

Yathrib, 267, 273
Yaw Sahhab, 57

Zubaidah, 52